"The genre of New Testament introduction has been remarkably stable for some time and, because of the influence of traditional historical criticism, often focuses on the historical origins of the text—a kind of textual archaeology. While Campbell and Pennington are well aware of the value of introducing the origins of the New Testament texts, their work intentionally focuses on *reading* the New Testament as *Christian Scripture*. That is, they introduce modern readers to the subject matter to which the New Testament testifies—namely, the ultimate revelation of God in Jesus Christ. Campbell and Pennington address student-disciples on their journey of transformation by means of the canonical text of the New Testament. Student-disciples and professor-pastors should take up this introduction with confidence, because it not only gives instruction on what the New Testament is, but more, it illuminates what God does in and through the witness of the New Testament in the lives of faithful readers. Highly recommended."

—**Darian Lockett**, Talbot School of Theology, Biola University

"Campbell and Pennington have gifted both the church and the academy with a text that deftly combines the literary, canonical, and theological sensibilities required to understand the New Testament's message both in its own context and in our world today. I cannot wait to introduce this valuable resource to students."

—**Brandon D. Smith**, Cedarville University

"Eminently navigable and aesthetically pleasing, *Reading the New Testament as Christian Scripture* draws students into the central truths of the Christian faith. Campbell and Pennington come from a particular perspective on debatable topics, and so teachers will want to supplement to provide their students the full range of Christian perspectives, but in every instance the authors discuss such topics with clarity and grace. Therefore, I would be thrilled to offer this text to my New Testament students, both to include perspectives different from my own and, even more importantly, to show the even greater unity among scholars who consider the New Testament as Scripture."

—**Amy Peeler**, Wheaton College

"The challenges facing anyone seeking to introduce the literature and message of the New Testament to this generation are many. Constantine Campbell and Jonathan Pennington have successfully responded to them with this remarkably useful and effective survey, rooted in their exhortation to read the biblical revelation as disciples expecting transformation. Color-coded sidebars punctuate each section, inviting students to consider intriguing insights, questions, and observations. Each chapter ends with 'Christian Reading Questions' that summon further reflection, often in relation to other portions of Scripture or pieces of art inspired by Christian theology. The book is littered with full-color maps, diagrams, tables, and photographs and concludes with a glossary of key terms highlighted throughout."

—**Jonathan Lunde**, Biola University

"For far too long students have been introduced to thoughtful engagement with the Bible through what is essentially an introduction to the discipline of biblical studies. I find that these introductions do a better job of training people to be professional biblical scholars than they do of helping them attend to the subject at hand—namely, God. This book is a welcome change. The book also helpfully attends to the fact that technology has radically changed the way students engage with the Bible (and all texts for that matter)—it is a thing to be searched with a search engine, mined for 'answers,' but not to be read in the purest sense of that word (as a transformative act). The introductory chapter alone is worth the purchase!"

—**Kelly D. Liebengood**, LeTourneau University

"The authors' focus on the New Testament books as Christian Scripture shines through on page after page, expressed in their engaging and lucid writing. The 'Implementation' section and discussion questions for each New Testament book are excellent features, helping Christian readers reflect on how they engage with Scripture today. The sidebars on more detailed points are a mine of useful information, and the chapters are well illustrated with maps, art, and architecture."

—**Steve Walton**, Trinity College, Bristol

READING *the* NEW TESTAMENT *as* CHRISTIAN SCRIPTURE

• READING •
CHRISTIAN
SCRIPTURE

VOLUMES AVAILABLE

———

Reading the New Testament as Christian Scripture
Constantine R. Campbell and Jonathan T. Pennington

———

READING *the* NEW TESTAMENT *as* CHRISTIAN SCRIPTURE

A LITERARY, CANONICAL, AND THEOLOGICAL SURVEY

CONSTANTINE R. CAMPBELL
AND JONATHAN T. PENNINGTON

Baker Academic
a division of Baker Publishing Group
Grand Rapids, Michigan

Published by Baker Academic
a division of Baker Publishing Group
PO Box 6287, Grand Rapids, MI 49516-6287
www.bakeracademic.com

Printed in the United States of America

Library of Congress Cataloging-in-Publication Data
Names: Campbell, Constantine R., author. | Pennington, Jonathan T.,
    author.
Title: Reading the New Testament as Christian scripture : a literary,
    canonical, and theological survey / Constantine R. Campbell and
    Jonathan T. Pennington.
Description: Grand Rapids, Michigan : Baker Academic, a division of Baker
    Publishing Group, 2020. | Series: Reading Christian scripture | Includes
    index.
Identifiers: LCCN 2020007055 | ISBN 9780801097928 (cloth)
Subjects: LCSH: Bible. New Testament—Textbooks.
Classification: LCC BS2535.3 .C36 2020 | DDC 225—dc23
LC record available at https://lccn.loc.gov/2020007055

20   21   22   23   24   25   26   7   6   5   4   3   2   1

Interior design by Brian Brunsting

Contents

Acknowledgments

In the preface to his commentary on Romans, the twelfth-century Benedictine monk William of Saint-Thierry acknowledged his great debt to Augustine, Ambrose, Origen, and others who went before him. He then refers to Horace's fable to describe his own meager contribution to studying Scripture in light of all the greater thinkers who influenced him: "We have festively clothed our little bird in plumes and colors of other birds, so that if these should come and each one carry off what he recognizes as his own, our little crow would be naked or even nonexistent."

So too with this New Testament survey in front of you. This book is the result of us laboring for six years to write a hopefully helpful introduction to the New Testament as Christian Scripture. But it is really the result of two thousand years of thinkers and teachers who have gone before us and whose ideas, articulations, insights can be found on every page. If they were to come and take back what was originally theirs, we would have little left! To change the metaphor, we are able to offer our thoughts on the New Testament because we are happily standing on the shoulders of giants—countless scholars and writers who have gone before us in the great and joyful task of understanding Holy Scripture.

Beyond the unnamable many, we are also glad to acknowledge several named and known friends who have helped bring this six-year project to its completion. First, thanks to Jim Kinney and James Ernest, who approached us and asked if we'd be willing to work together to write Baker's next-generation textbook—to which the answer was an eager yes! This was followed by recurrent gatherings of a group of delightful and bright people from the Baker editorial team (including Bryan Dyer and Dave Nelson) as well as our Old Testament counterparts, Mark Gignilliat and Heath

Thomas. Over several years we wrestled and wrangled our way to conceiving a genre-bending project that would seek to introduce students to a reading of the Old and New Testaments as Scripture, not just as historical and literary documents.

After the many years of writing, others came alongside and served the (nearly) thankless tasks of reading, editing, indexing, and glossary production. In addition to the always-exceptional Baker editorial and production teams, this included Anna Poole Mondal, Ben Hussung, and Billy Wilhelm. We also offer thanks to professorial friends near and far who read portions of the manuscript and gave us valuable feedback, including David Croteau, Jeff Dryden, J. Scott Duvall, Douglas Huffman, Jeffrey Lamp, Darian Lockett, Greg MaGee, and Amy Peeler.

Visit www.bakeracademic.com/professors
to access study aids
and instructor materials for this textbook.

Abbreviations

Old Testament

Gen.	Genesis	Eccles.	Ecclesiastes
Exod.	Exodus	Song	Song of Songs
Lev.	Leviticus	Isa.	Isaiah
Num.	Numbers	Jer.	Jeremiah
Deut.	Deuteronomy	Lam.	Lamentations
Josh.	Joshua	Ezek.	Ezekiel
Judg.	Judges	Dan.	Daniel
Ruth	Ruth	Hosea	Hosea
1 Sam.	1 Samuel	Joel	Joel
2 Sam.	2 Samuel	Amos	Amos
1 Kings	1 Kings	Obad.	Obadiah
2 Kings	2 Kings	Jon.	Jonah
1 Chron.	1 Chronicles	Mic.	Micah
2 Chron.	2 Chronicles	Nah.	Nahum
Ezra	Ezra	Hab.	Habakkuk
Neh.	Nehemiah	Zeph.	Zephaniah
Esther	Esther	Hag.	Haggai
Job	Job	Zech.	Zechariah
Ps(s).	Psalm(s)	Mal.	Malachi
Prov.	Proverbs		

New Testament

Matt.	Matthew	Acts	Acts
Mark	Mark	Rom.	Romans
Luke	Luke	1 Cor.	1 Corinthians
John	John	2 Cor.	2 Corinthians

Gal.	Galatians	Heb.	Hebrews
Eph.	Ephesians	James	James
Phil.	Philippians	1 Pet.	1 Peter
Col.	Colossians	2 Pet.	2 Peter
1 Thess.	1 Thessalonians	1 John	1 John
2 Thess.	2 Thessalonians	2 John	2 John
1 Tim.	1 Timothy	3 John	3 John
2 Tim.	2 Timothy	Jude	Jude
Titus	Titus	Rev.	Revelation
Philem.	Philemon		

General

AT	authors' translation
ca.	circa
ESV	English Standard Version
LXX	Septuagint
NIV	New International Version

CHAPTER ONE

The New Testament as Christian Scripture

What's in a Title?

Titles matter because the title of a book gives a frame of reference, creates expectations, and sets the tone for readers' experience. Indeed, many things have already happened in your mind (and body) between when you first started reading the title of this book and the sentence that is ending right now. Our title, *Reading the New Testament as Christian Scripture: A Literary, Canonical, and Theological Survey*, has already animated various notions and set your expectations in a way that is mostly subconscious.

We hope that these are positive expectations, but we are aware that they may not be! Our chosen title may or may not register much reaction at all and may even cause some confusion. We have carefully chosen this title to stimulate questions and guide your encounter with our book and, more importantly, with the **New Testament** itself. In this opening chapter we will unpack the title to discuss the frame, goal, and vision for this book.

Why Emphasize Reading Today?

"Nothing easy is worthwhile, and nothing worthwhile is easy." "You can rake all day long and get only leaves. But if you take the time to dig, you may find gold." These proverbial statements are pithy and memorable but, more importantly, wise and true. Every generation and culture have obstacles to thoughtful living, but it seems that our culture today has the potential and technology to be more distracted than any other. Screens, notifications, and connection to a global wealth of information in our pockets provide us with dopamine-inspired quick bursts of pleasure that leave us hungering for another fix while dissipating our mental and emotional energy.

This makes reading hard. This makes reading old, foreign, religious documents especially hard. Maybe you don't want to read this book and are being forced to for a grade. We understand. But we want to invite you into the profound pleasure that comes from learning to be attentive and present to yourself and others through reading. Imagine how wonderful it is when you have the opportunity to sit with an engaging and wise friend at a coffee shop discussing the complexities of life and deep thoughts about the soul and relationships. Remember what it's like to be so absorbed that you are undistracted, wholly present to the reality and importance of the discussion.

The beauty and power of books is that they enable us to enter into such life-changing conversations with a world of people that we would never have the opportunity to meet in person. This includes the Bible, wherein we can sit with God himself, learning and reflecting. But this does require some work: the commitment to read and to read thoughtfully. This book will guide you through a reading of the New Testament texts. When we begin a new section with a heading like this—■ READ MARK 1:16–2:12 ■—we are inviting you to pause and devote your energy to listening to these ancient texts. You can browse social media all day and get some leaves, but if you dig into **Scripture** you will find gold.

Why Call This a "Christian" Reading?

What is the significance of adding the descriptor "Christian"? Why are we being invited to read the New Testament as *Christian* Scripture?

Figure 1.1. *Saint Francis Reading* by Christian Wilhelm Ernst Dietrich

In the first instance, this means that we embrace the biblical **canon** as twofold, Old and New Testaments together. As we will discuss below, both parts of the Christian canon mutually inform each other. At the same time, the New Testament claims to provide the ultimate revelation of God himself in **Christ**. This *Logos*, the Son, who is ever with the Father and has been incarnated at a time in history in Jesus, together with the indwelling Spirit, witnesses to the mystery of the **Trinity**. This is no small matter. This means that because of the fullness of

Figure 1.2. *The Supper at Emmaus* by Velázquez

revelation now given in the new **covenant**, *all* of the Bible should be read with the knowledge of the Triune God at hand, even though the **Hebrew Scriptures** do not explicitly speak in this way. This reading backward of the whole Bible is an important element in what it means to read Christianly. One does not *have* to read the Bible in this way, but one must do so in order to read it as *Christian* Scripture.

There is also another vital facet of reading the New Testament as Christian Scripture: reading it as a **disciple**. To read the New Testament (and the whole Bible) as Christian Scripture is to read it "with the grain," in line with its clear intention, which is to make disciples of Jesus Christ. The foreignness of the Bible to modern readers inclines us to think that we need to make a pilgrimage into the world of the Bible and then take its meaning back out and transform it into something relatable to us today. Rather, as one biblical scholar observes, "'Pilgrimage' is more appropriately a description of the character of our lives in this world, with our status as strangers in the world attributable to our making our home in the world of Scripture. In this hermeneutical scenario, it is not the message of the Bible that requires transformation; it is we who require transformation."[1] That is, we are not taking a pilgrimage into the Bible and back; the Bible is transforming the journey of our lives.

The ideal reader of the New Testament, then, is one who is reading in order to be formed according to God's vision for humanity. Our goal in reading is not merely to garner *information* but also to experience *transformation*: not to be smarter people but to become a different kind of people. The reason for listening to the teaching of Jesus and of the **apostles** is to come to trust in Jesus as the revelation of God and, from this, to entrust our lives to his ways. The New Testament has a radical and beautiful goal of deconstructing our values and re-forming them in line with God's nature and coming kingdom. Therefore, to read the New Testament as Christian Scripture is to read it so as to become conformed to the image of Christ himself, imitating the apostles, who themselves were imitating/following Jesus (John 13:12–15; 1 Cor. 11:1; 1 Pet. 2:21). Anything less than this transformative pilgrimage is less than a *Christian* reading of the New Testament. ⓘ

What's New about the New Testament?

We encounter the word "new" most frequently today through the world of advertising. Whether it is the new iPhone, a new plan from politicians, or a new dishwashing detergent, we are trained to spot and covet the "new and improved." This is not necessarily bad, of course, as "new" can and does often mean an improvement. Rarely do people want the "old and inferior," unless it signals some retro technology or sports a throwback look. Even then, the old is desirable because there is some perceived greater value or quality, not simply because it is old.

But what does the "new" in New Testament communicate? Why did early Christians describe the writings of the apostles as a "new testament"? First, we must understand that this word "testament" comes to us through Latin and basically means the same thing as "covenant." In fact, the title for the New Testament in Greek is *Hē Kainē Diathēkē*, which translates as "the new covenant," wording that comes from Jeremiah 31:31; Luke 22:20; 1 Corinthians 11:25; Hebrews 8:8; and elsewhere. What is a covenant? A covenant is a relationship between two parties (like a marriage or a mortgage) that has spelled-out expectations. So when we call a piece of writing a covenant or testimony, we are referring to the instructions and explanations that relate to a specific relationship. In this case, for both the **Old Testament** and the New Testament, we are learning about the relationship of God with humanity.

This collection of writings titled "New Covenant/Testament" implies that there was something before, an "Old Covenant/Testament." The earliest

Christians did not use this phrase explicitly, but they understood Jesus as the Promised One, who ushered in the era of a new covenant. By the early third century of the Christian era this "Old/New Testament" description comes into usage, and it continues to this day.

However, this language of "new" does not necessarily mean that the preceding was bad or is now completely irrelevant, as would be the case with a consumer product today (who wants an iPhone 3 anymore?). Rather, "renewed and completed" might be a better sense of how the New Testament is linked to what came before it.

Matthew 5:17–20 is one of the most important biblical passages for understanding the relationship of the two parts of the Christian Bible, even if its exact meaning is still being debated two thousand years later. In his first teaching in the First Gospel Jesus addresses the issue head-on: "Do not think that I have come to abolish the Law or the Prophets. I have not come to abolish them but to fulfill them" (Matt. 5:17 AT). Jesus is not dismissing or disregarding God's earlier revelation. He is not deeming the past as irrelevant. The New Testament does not *abolish* the Old Testament but rather *fulfills* it. In the Bible "fulfill" primarily focuses not on prediction or replacement but on renewal, consummation, and fullness. This means that when we think about the relationship of the Old Testament to the New Testament, there is both continuity and discontinuity, a shared foundation with positive change toward its goal.

Thus we can recognize some real sense in which the new (Jesus) covenant *is* superior to the old (Mosaic) covenant. The apostle Paul and the author of Hebrews particularly make this clear: the old covenant was not able to give life in the same way (Rom. 8:2–4), or provide a perfect, conscience-cleansing **sacrifice** (Heb. 8:6–13), or be fully internalized and transformative from the inside (Jer. 31:33; Ezek. 36:26; Heb. 10:16). To be a Christian means to believe precisely in this distinction, that Jesus has come and brought a new covenant in his blood (Matt. 26:28; Luke 22:20), bringing us to a mountain greater than Sinai, to Zion (Heb. 12:18–24).

However, this fulfillment should not be misunderstood as a negating or dismissing of the Hebrew Scriptures. The story of Israel is not old news, or "inferior" like an early, buggy version of hardware or software. The same Paul who speaks boldly about the transforming shift from the Mosaic covenant to the **law of Christ** (1 Cor. 9:21; Gal. 6:2) also emphasizes that God still cares for the Jewish people, that they have some understanding of God that the world does not naturally have, and that **gentiles** should not think of themselves as somehow superior (Rom. 3:1–2; 9:1–11:36).

To think about this relationship, we need a metaphor other than that of mere superiority. From a Christian perspective, "fulfillment" is the best way to frame the matter. God's good plans for humanity come to their completion and consummation in Jesus. This means that going back to the Mosaic covenant would be foolish and even deadly because of what it is unable to do for humanity—provide true and lasting life. However, it does not mean that the **Jewish Scriptures** themselves are flawed or irrelevant to the Christian life. At the end of Luke's Gospel, in the story he tells about Jesus on the road to Emmaus, Luke highlights this same fact, that Jesus is understood properly by going back and rereading the whole Old Testament in light of what Jesus has now said and done (Luke 24:13–49). ⓘ

What Does the New Testament Have to Do with the Old Testament?

Following directly from this idea of the New Testament's fulfillment of the Old Testament, we then can ask more specifically: What does the New Testament have to do with the Old Testament? We have already noted that we must not think of the Old in a flat-footed way of being replaced with the relevant and instructive New.

Nor should we think of the relationship of the Old Testament and the New Testament as unidirectional only. There is a very old and venerable Christian tradition of reading the Old Testament in light of the New. We might describe this as a front-wheel-drive arrangement. The New Testament drives the whole Bible and pulls the Old Testament along where it is going. Some have suggested instead a rear-wheel-drive understanding, where a plain-sense reading of the Old Testament pushes along and we understand the New Testament in light of what the Old Testament is already doing.[3]

In contrast to either a front-wheel-drive-only or rear-wheel-drive-only analogy, we propose a four-wheel-drive model where both the Old Testament and the New Testament alternate in taking the lead. We should think of the Testaments as two parts in a *two-testament Christian canon.* Together the Hebrew Scriptures (Old Testament) and the writings of the apostles (New Testament) form something new and authoritative (see below on "canon"). By being read together (and, very early on, being physically bound together), the two parts of the Christian Bible inform each other in a bidirectional way. The Old Testament sets the foundation, reveals God's character and actions in the world, and points toward the restoration of humanity under his good reign. The New Testament completes this story, enabling a more thorough and particularly trinitarian and Christ-centered rereading of the whole Bible. You can read the Old Testament without the

Figure 1.3. Design for a cupola with Old and New Testament figures by Pietro de Angelis

New Testament and understand a lot about God, though to be part of the people of God now requires embracing the **Messiah** he has finally sent. You can read the New Testament without the Old Testament, but it will be a thin and decontextualized reading of the whole story.

Why Is the New Testament Called "Scripture"?

So far, we have explored the newness of the New Testament and how to think about the relationship of the Old to the New. We may now ask, What is the significance of calling the Old and New Testaments "Scripture"? After all, we are focusing on documents written between two thousand and three thousand years ago by people in cultures very different from our own. Are these documents really relevant today for individuals and for society?

Even if understood as a collection of merely human documents, the Bible still has abiding antiquarian and historical interest. But the perspective operative in this book, in line with the ancient Jewish and Christian conviction, is that the Bible is not only a record of religious understanding but is also more: *it is Holy Scripture*. This means that in addition to providing human wisdom and lessons from human history, the Old Testament and the New Testament are witnesses to God's self-disclosure, a *revelation* of who God is—his character, his name, his identity, his actions, his ways. To understand the Bible as Scripture, then, is to approach it with a posture of humility, teachability, and submission, not because the Bible itself is magical or glows in the dark, but because it faithfully does what no other speech or writing in the world does fully: it reveals the Triune God of the universe. It is the revelation of God himself in verbal form. And this calls for a response. Erich Auerbach writes, "The world of the Scripture stories is not satisfied with claiming to be a historically true reality—it insists that it is the only real world, is destined for autocracy. . . . The Scripture stories . . . seek to subject us, and if we refuse to be subjected we are rebels."[4]

This is why we refer to the Bible as a "canon," meaning that the books that make up the Bible together are separate and distinct and worthy of heeding closely. The books of the Bible have a unique authority because they are part of the canon, or rule. There is plenty of wisdom and truth all throughout the world, but to identify some writings as canonical is to set them apart, to recognize and honor their authoritative contribution. So to read the New Testament as Scripture is to recognize its revelatory nature.

We may also think of the Bible as "Scripture" in another way, as providing the "script" for our lives. Not only does Scripture show us truth and falsehood, but also it guides how we are to live in the world. This sense of "script(ure)" is analogous to that of a play. The script guides the direction of the story, but a good actor will always make the performance his or her own. Performing is more than reading lines on a script with monotone obedience; it is understanding and being present to the voice and power of the script, interpreting and emphasizing with wholehearted presence, and even ad-libbing and expanding as the need arises. Of course, this analogy breaks down eventually, but the point is that to read the New Testament as Scripture is to be in a lively and humble dialogue with the voice of the text, seeking to understand and live according to its direction as we encounter obstacles, tensions, and other people.

What Can You Expect from This Book?

This leads us to the final question for this opening chapter: What can you expect from this book? This is a textbook, and, more specifically, it can be classified in the genre of a New Testament survey or introduction. This kind of book developed relatively late in the reading of the Bible, only a couple of hundred years ago, as a product of modern scholarship. Various New Testament surveys or introductions emphasize different aspects, depending on the interests and perspectives of various writers. Our introduction to the New Testament is no exception, reflecting a particular vision. We hope that our readers will discover some modes and means of reading the New Testament that have largely been lost in the modern era and therefore are not found in other New Testament surveys. These include reading the New Testament texts in dialogue with each other, with the Old Testament, with other interpreters throughout history, and with Christian creeds and theological statements.

Our conviction is that direct engagement with the biblical texts themselves is more important than anything we can say about them. As a result, the major goal of this New Testament survey is to offer a guide for students to thoughtfully read the texts of Scripture themselves, with helps supplied by those who are a bit

Figure 1.4. *Reading the Scriptures* by Thomas Waterman Wood

further along on the journey. These helps include the use of **bold** type to indicate that a term appears in the glossary at the end of the book. Don't forget to look there when you have a question! Each chapter also ends with some study questions to help you reflect and deepen your understanding. As we trek through each book, we encourage you to read the biblical texts before you read our interpretive guide.

In addition to this main interpretive guide, each chapter contains a series of sidebars organized into five different categories: Historical Matters, Literary Notes, Theological Issues, Canonical Connections, and Reception History. This unique approach comes from the conviction that the kinds of questions we ask of texts determine the kinds of answers we get from them. If we ask historical questions, we get historical answers; theological questions yield theological answers; moral and practical questions produce moral and practical answers; and so on. (The introductory chapters also include some general sidebars that contain information that helps prepare us to read the text well.) Icons corresponding to the various types of sidebars are placed within the main text to prompt readers to pause and read the relevant sidebar(s).

Scripture is not afraid of questions; we believe that these five query categories are valuable for a truly Christian reading of the whole Bible.

HISTORICAL MATTERS

Historical Matters boxes provide information about issues going on behind the text of Scripture. This includes information about authorship, date, and historical setting of the biblical books. This also includes cultural information that sheds light on certain customs and practices mentioned in the biblical texts.

LITERARY NOTES

Literary Notes boxes focus on the structure and form of the scriptural writings. What are the ways the New Testament author has structured the argument or story, and what can we learn from this? For example, recognizing that Matthew has collected Jesus's teachings into five major blocks helps us to interpret them as collections and to note their particular literary structure.

THEOLOGICAL ISSUES

Theological Issues boxes build bridges between Scripture and categories of systematic and constructive theology. While the Bible and theology can and do overlap, they often use different categories and language to describe the truth. Theological Issues boxes help to make connections between particular biblical texts and the categories that are used to organize the biblical witness into theological categories.

CANONICAL CONNECTIONS

Canonical Connections boxes show some of the myriad ways in which the whole Bible can be read as one story. The canon is beautifully diverse, but as a canon it also has a unity and singularity of voice in witnessing to the Triune God. Canonical Connections boxes highlight how a particular biblical text can be read in fruitful dialogue with other passages in the Old Testament and the New Testament.

RECEPTION HISTORY

Reception History boxes give examples of ways in which a portion of the Scriptures has been received and applied throughout the history of the church. This reception may be in the form of visual art, music, or application to particular social situations. Reception History boxes can help us to see the biblical texts with fresh eyes.

Christian Reading Questions

1. What makes a *Christian* reading of Scripture different from another way of reading the Bible?
2. What traits mark the life of the ideal disciple reader?
3. How does the New Testament relate to the Old Testament? How is this understanding different from or similar to the way you thought about the two Testaments before reading this chapter?
4. Why is it important that we call the Old Testament and the New Testament "Scripture"? How does this influence the way we read them?

CHAPTER TWO

The New Testament as a Book

At the heart of both Judaism and Christianity is the belief that God's truth is found in a book—sacred writings that are honored, studied, and obeyed (or not) and that outlast every generation of their believers. "All humanity is grass. . . . The grass withers, . . . but the word of our God remains forever" (Isa. 40:6–8). In the previous chapter we discussed what it means to call the New Testament "Scripture." In this chapter we will address key issues concerning the New Testament as a book: the reliability of the ancient **manuscripts**, differences among translations and editions, and the impact of binding together the apostles' writings into one volume.

From Speaking to Manuscripts to a Book

As with the Old Testament, the New Testament did not begin as writing. Both Testaments began with historical events, memories about these events, and then people discussing the meaning and interpretation of these events. Some of these memories and oral interpretations came from authoritative leaders, inspired by God through the Holy Spirit to record in writing what happened and how to understand the significance. These writings included both generic and detailed accounts of historical events as well as poems, songs, prophecies, sermons, letters, and proverbs. Sometimes these were written down by an authoritative **prophet**, king, priest, or apostle, and sometimes by their disciples.

For the New Testament, this progression from oral traditions to written records materialized very quickly—within twenty to seventy-five years and within the lifetime of the first generation of people who experienced Jesus. In the case of the Gospels particularly, influential disciples gathered the memories and traditions about what Jesus said and did, and they produced theological interpretations of these in the form of four biographies (see chap. 5). One of these disciples, Luke, also wrote a companion volume, the book of Acts, that explains the birth of the church and the events of its first decades (see chap. 10). Several of the leading, authoritative disciples (called apostles) traveled widely, preaching the **gospel** and establishing Christian churches. As they did so, they often wrote letters explaining theological ideas, exhorting people to godliness and faithfulness, and addressing moral and doctrinal problems that arose. Some of these letters ("epistles") are very personal (e.g., Galatians, Philemon), while others are more generalized and were intended for circulation among a larger number of people and churches (e.g., James, Revelation). ⓘ

The New Testament's Table of Contents

Each document in the New Testament started as an individual text, but eventually they were collected into what became a standard grouping and ordering. The New Testament consists of twenty-seven different documents, organized not chronologically but according to **genre** and author. There is also an intentional pattern: four biographies about Jesus followed by the continuing story in Acts, followed by Paul's nine letters to seven different churches, Paul's four letters to individuals, the Letter to the Hebrews, seven general letters, and the book of Revelation, which is addressed to seven churches.

The four Gospels—The largest section of the New Testament contains four overlapping stories that describe Jesus's life and teaching. The authors traditionally are understood to be two of Jesus's original disciples (Matthew and John) and two students of the apostles Peter (Mark) and Paul (Luke).

The book of Acts—Also written by the Gospel author Luke, this book continues the story of some of Jesus's disciples after his **resurrection**, recounting how the church grew and spread throughout the Roman world, with particular emphasis on Peter and then Paul.

The apostle Paul's letters to churches—The early Christian missionary Paul started churches all over the Roman world. He subsequently wrote letters to these people to encourage and teach them. We have nine of these letters, each bearing the name of the city or area of the church's location, organized by length from lon-

gest to shortest: Romans, 1 Corinthians, 2 Corinthians, Galatians, Ephesians, Philippians, Colossians, 1 Thessalonians, and 2 Thessalonians.

The apostle Paul's letters to individuals—Paul also wrote letters to individual disciples, offering instructions and encouragement. We have four of these personal letters, again organized according to length: 1 Timothy, 2 Timothy, Titus, and Philemon.

The Letter to the Hebrews—Some people link this letter to Paul, but we don't know for certain who wrote it. This highly structured piece gives a Greek and Christian reinterpretation of key aspects of the Hebrew Scriptures, hence its name.

The General or Catholic Letters—This group consists of seven letters that are named according to their authors. They are no less important than the letters written by Paul, but they are called "general" or "catholic" (meaning "universal") because they seem to be intended for a wider readership and application. These letters are James, 1 Peter, 2 Peter, 1 John, 2 John, 3 John, and Jude.

The book of Revelation—The New Testament collection ends with a very different kind of document, one that combines the letter form with another type of ancient writing, the **apocalypse**. An apocalypse uses poetic and **allegorical** images to describe the world from a heavenly perspective, revealing to God's faithful people what is happening now and in the future under God's control.

In every case the written form of these biographies, teachings, and letters was recorded as a manuscript—that is, a handwritten document on some type of paper (**papyrus**) or, a more expensive option, a kind of leather (**vellum**). These manuscripts were then courier-borne to other places, where they were copied by hand so that they could be preserved and read aloud in the churches. As a result, these texts that eventually became the New Testament spread like wildfire as Christians traveled throughout the Greco-Roman Empire, calling people to believe in the risen Christ.

As Christianity continued to grow, and as the apostles' generation began to die (often as **martyrs**), the need arose to preserve and clarify which manuscripts were really from apostles—meaning that they were authoritative and worthy of maintaining in the church. Several false teachers and errors had arisen in the church (Matt. 7:15; Rom. 16:17–18; Gal. 1:7–8), and these people and their disciples wrote letters and treatises as well. Therefore, an authoritative list of which documents were trustworthy and beneficial was needed. This kind of list is called a canon. ⓘ

Texts were canonized not just through putting their titles on a list but also through binding and publishing an authorized group of documents together. By putting several texts together with the stamp of approval from recognized authorities, the collection verified these documents as official and authoritative. A canon book gave people a reliable, authoritative collection of texts to study.

The physical mechanics of creating such a clearly demarcated collection, however, proved very difficult with **scrolls**. Rolled pieces of parchment (scrolls) can easily get separated from one another, and one can lose track of which texts were supposed to be included, not to mention the hassle of trying to find a section to read by unrolling a long document. In the first couple of centuries AD, however, a newer technology was on the rise: the technique of slicing manuscripts into pieces and then sewing or gluing them together in a stack. This produced something called a **codex**, and it is the earliest form of what today we would call a book. (If you look closely at the binding on a modern book, you will see that the technique is still very much the same.)

INTRODUCTORY MATTERS

Canon Lists

A "canon list" is a list of books that an author or a council has determined are authoritative because they make up what should be in the Bible. For the Christian Bible (both Old and New Testaments together), many canon lists were made throughout the first several centuries of the church. This included lists by Greek authors such as Melito of Sardis, Eusebius, and Athanasius, and Latin leaders including Hilary, Jerome, Augustine, and Pope Innocent I.

These lists are not always identical, but they do show a growing consensus about which books were regarded as biblical. The canonical books were not the only books that were read by Christians, however. Other works, such as Wisdom of Solomon and the Shepherd of Hermas, were still seen as beneficial and worth reading, even if they were not always considered part of the canon.

Even though the canon lists became more standard in the Middle Ages, distinct branches of the church (Roman Catholic and Eastern Orthodox) had some differences. With the Reformation in the sixteenth century, canon lists became a hot issue again, with Protestants often arguing for the exclusion of some books that the Roman Catholic tradition included in its canon.[1]

Christians were some of the earliest adopters of this new binding and publishing technique, and the significance was great. Selected manuscripts could be collected, organized, titled, and distributed in one piece. This happened with the Gospels, which soon began circulating as the Fourfold Gospel Book (see chap. 5). This happened with the letters by Paul, which were collected—maybe by Paul himself—and given various titles and an order. The other parts of the New Testament canon took shape as well, as we can see in some early and large whole-Bible codices. Very significantly, the codex enabled Christians to bind together not only the authoritative New Testament books themselves but also the New Testament canon with the Jewish Scriptures (later called the Old Testament). This created a two-fold canon that honored the Old Testament as authoritative, while also setting the New Testament documents on the same level of authority and inspiration. ⓘ

The Whole-Bible Codices

While we have many individual manuscripts of the New Testament writings from the first few centuries AD, some of the most important witnesses we have to the New Testament come from the large whole-Bible codices (bound books) from the third and fourth centuries. These are called **majuscules**, because they are written entirely in capital Greek letters with no spaces between the words. They were written on vellum by professional scribes. These include:

- *Codex Vaticanus*—ca. AD 325; oldest of the majuscules; preserved in the Vatican Library
- *Codex Sinaiticus*—ca. AD 350; discovered at St. Catherine's Monastery at Mount Sinai
- *Codex Alexandrinus*—ca. AD 425; named for its earlier location in Alexandria, Egypt
- *Codex Ephraemi*—ca. AD 450; so named because it was discovered on manuscripts under the writings of the theologian Ephrem of Syria

These beautiful, expensive, handcrafted books show how Christians thought about their Holy Scriptures—the Old Testament and New Testament together, preserved with great care.

The recent digitization project on Codex Sinaiticus has produced high-quality interactive images of this important book (http://www.codexsinaiticus.org).

The British Library [Add MS 43725, f.244.v].

Figure 2.1. Codex Sinaiticus (AD 350)

Are These Old Texts Reliable? The Art and Science of Textual Criticism

Before the printing press was invented in the fifteenth century, all textual reproductions were created by hand, one copy at a time. Even with modern printing technologies it is easy for errors and derivations from the original to creep in. The same thing was true in the ancient world with the hand copying of manuscripts. The process of canonization highlights which books, letters, and biographies are authoritative and worthy of preservation and study. The study of **textual criticism** seeks to establish the most reliable version of the content and wording of each of these books. "Criticism" here does not mean a posture of judgment or an assumption of inaccuracy, but instead the scholarly practices and techniques used to make reasonable decisions about the accuracy of the manuscripts.

Are the Greek texts that we now call the New Testament accurate compared to what was originally written and distributed? In short, the answer is a confident yes. This can be argued for several reasons. First, Christianity, rooted in Jewish heritage, shares with Judaism the religious and cultural values to preserve sacred texts and to care very much about the particular wording. As this was true for the Jews, so it was naturally true from the beginning for Christianity.

Second, Christianity spread rapidly and deeply throughout the ancient world, resulting in multiple copies of the New Testament texts being made and distributed, thus providing us with many manuscripts to compare and evaluate. The long-term impact of Christianity on the Mediterranean basin and throughout Europe meant that the lengthy time between Jesus and the printing press was filled with thousands of people and institutions that dedicated themselves to the preservation and accurate reproduction of the biblical texts.

Third, stemming from the second point, at the sheer material level the fact is that we have many and varied manuscript witnesses to the ancient New Testament texts. This mass of manuscripts (numbering nearly six thousand and dating back to the second century AD) consists of papyri, majuscules, **minuscules**, **lectionaries**, and translations into other languages, including Latin, Coptic, and Syriac. Beyond this, the extant writings of the church's prominent theologians and preachers of the first centuries (often called the **church fathers**) constantly quote the biblical texts, giving us another point of comparison to what the original documents likely said.

Fourth, based on this large body of manuscript witnesses, scholars have developed sophisticated procedures by which they are classified and compared and their relationships to one another analyzed. This work has been done since ancient times and by a wide variety of scholars all over the world, resulting in many **critical editions** of the Greek New Testament that provide reconstructed Greek texts that are recognized as reliable. ⓘ

The fact that we have so many different manuscripts means that every page of our modern critical editions of the Greek New Testament has a wide variety of alternative readings (variants). It has been estimated that about 12 percent of all the words of the New Testament have some alternative reading. This may sound surprising, and some scholars have used this statistic in a misleading way. But the reality is that there are so many variants precisely because we have such a wealth of manuscripts; this is a positive effect, not a negative one. More importantly, only about 1.5 percent of the New Testament could be classified as having significant variants, meaning that some thought is required to determine which is the best reading. The vast majority of variants are obvious and insignificant differences such as misspellings, alternate spellings, or the accidental repeating of a word or line—all common errors that occur in manuscript reproduction. Only about one out of every one thousand words in the New Testament provides substantial difficulties to determine which wording is original, and very few of these have any significant effect on the

Types of Ancient Manuscripts

Many different types of manuscripts developed before the age of the printing press:

Papyri—Manuscripts written on an early form of paper (papyrus) made from a reed plant. Some of the earliest portions of the New Testament are on papyrus, some as early as the second century AD.

Majuscules—Manuscripts written in a style of all capital letters. These date especially from the fourth to eighth century.

Minuscules—Manuscripts, usually on parchment, written in a small cursive style of Greek letters. We have thousands of minuscules, most dating from the eleventh to thirteenth century.

Lectionaries—Books of biblical readings to be used in worship services. These were written in many different styles and languages, and most date from the eleventh to thirteenth century.

The British Library [Papyrus 2484, f.1v].

Figure 2.2. Papyrus with parts of John 16 (third century)

A critical edition of the Greek New Testament is a reconstructed text that scholars put together based on these ancient manuscripts, providing a text that a committee has decided is most likely original. Critical editions also include examples of variants, wording that is different in some manuscripts but that has been decided to be not original. These editions frequently include notes that indicate how confident the scholars are on different variants and their reasoning for the decisions they have made in creating their text.

The Metropolitan Museum of Art. Purchase, Mary and Michael Jaharis Gift and Lila Acheson Wallace Gift, 2007.

Figure 2.3. Jaharis Byzantine Lectionary (ca. 1100)

meaning. Such difficult variants usually consist of complications in determining which of similar words like "your" and "our" was original. Of the difficult variants, not one affects any major Christian doctrine or understanding. Thus, we can have more than reasonable confidence in the faithfulness of our critical editions. ⓘ

Of course, as with any field of study, there are deeper levels of nuance and complexity than this overview can provide. The scholarly discipline of textual criticism and related fields is always undergoing revisions and improvements, even today. More manuscripts are regularly discovered and cataloged, and scholars debate fine details of different approaches. All of this is good and inspires confidence in the reliability of our New Testament texts.

The Myriad of Translations and Editions of the New Testament

We have mentioned already that because of the rapid and geographically expansive spread of Christianity, combined with Christianity's valuing of sacred writings, very quickly there appeared many manuscript copies of the New Testament writings. Some New Testament writers even give directions for their letters to be copied and sent on to other cities to spread the message and teachings (Col. 4:16; 1 Thess. 5:27). This meant that the New Testament writings were soon translated into other languages as part of the church's missionary efforts. This follows the model of Judaism in the **Second Temple period** (see chap. 3), which also made translations of the Hebrew Scriptures (into Aramaic, Greek, etc.) so that believers could read them in their native tongues. (This is very different from Islam, which does not allow the Qur'an to be officially translated into any other language.)

This copying and translation of the two-part Christian Scriptures has continued mostly unabated throughout the centuries. Today the entire

New Testament has been translated into over 1,500 languages, and portions of the Bible into another thousand-plus languages. Large organizations such as Wycliffe Bible Translators are dedicated to the difficult and demanding work of translating the Bible into every one of the approximately 7,100 living languages. The English language is particularly rich in Bible translations (estimated at around 900 versions since Tyndale's first English translation in 1526), each with its own goals, philosophy of translation, and pros and cons.

Starting in the ancient world, copies of New Testament texts began to contain little headings that describe the contents of each section of the text, such as "Jesus Stills the Storm" right before the text of Mark 4:35–41. These types of headings or titles are found in almost every version of the New Testament today, guiding readers in identifying and interpreting each section. By the Middle Ages, manuscripts also began to demarcate larger sections within New Testament books, and when Bibles were first printed in mass, a system of chapter and verse notation became increasingly standardized. Today, every New Testament book can be referenced by a name and numbering system that may seem odd at first, but this standard format makes it easy for everyone to locate specific sayings within the texts and to discuss them. Each New Testament book is divided into chapters, and then each chapter into verses. Thus we can say, "Matthew 5:48," meaning the Gospel of Matthew, chapter 5, verse 48. ⓘ

There are many versions of the Bible and the New Testament that serve different purposes. There are diglot versions that provide two languages that can be compared. There are study Bibles, which provide the biblical text along with notes written by scholars (usually from a certain theological perspective) to guide readers in their interpretation. Red-letter editions of the New Testament, in which Jesus's words are printed red to make them stand out from the black print, first appeared in 1899. Children's Bibles range from

"Minority Report" New Testament Versions

Although almost all printed New Testaments today follow a traditional ordering of the books, use standardized chapter and verse divisions, and provide descriptive titles for separate sections of the stories or letters, there are some versions that seek to offer an alternative and fresh approach to guide readers.

Some publishers have produced "manuscript Bibles" that remove all chapter and verse notations and instead present the New Testament texts in a singular flow. This makes the stories and letters look and feel more like a modern book. In recent years some have also attempted to rearrange the books of the New Testament (and the whole Bible) according to a structure other than the traditional canonical form, often based on the perceived chronological order of the writings.

Because the standard chapter and verse divisions are sometimes misleading and distracting, the "manuscript Bibles" can provide a fresh and more engaging experience of reading, though they are not practical for referencing. The attempts at reordering the New Testament books can likewise provide an interesting and fresh reading experience, especially for those who are long accustomed to the New Testament.

While there are some helpful aspects to these minority-report editions of the New Testament, readers (and publishers) shouldn't begin to see these editions as superior to the traditional canonical forms. There are good reasons that the New Testament canon has been ordered and read the way it has, and alternative orderings of the books are no less an interpretation than the traditional approach.

easier-to-read translations of the whole Bible to retellings of select stories, complete with illustrations.

The New Testament as a Library

This chapter is titled "The New Testament as a Book" because this is how readers experience these New Testament writings collected from eight or nine different authors: they are gathered together into one volume. This "book," however, is not like most books we see. The New Testament is more like a little library dedicated to one topic, with appropriate and helpful diversity within it. It's somewhat like a music library within a university, with a diversity of volumes collected around a field of study. This New Testament library includes different genres of literature: biographies, stories, wisdom teachings, letters designed to correct and train, personal correspondence, and fantastical visions to inspire hope.

Yet there is unity in this New Testament library. This unity within diversity can be seen historically, literarily, and theologically. Historically, the New Testament documents come from a short period of time, sharing the culture and geography of Hellenistic Judaism in the first-century Greco-Roman world. Literarily, the New Testament texts share the common Greek language of the day (with some authors obviously more skilled and educated than others) and use conventional genres and styles. Theologically, the New Testament library is intensely focused on the person and work of Jesus Christ, shaped and shepherded by the apostles' teachings.

To change the image: the New Testament is like a choir singing in many parts, interlacing harmony, rhythm, and melody—but singing together as one, directed by one conductor, God himself. These complementary images of the New Testament as a unified choir and a topical library are important to remember as we step, as readers, into the world of the New Testament.

Christian Reading Questions

1. Consider the earliest period of the church, when memories and oral interpretations preceded many of the New Testament writings. How do you think that life as a Christian then differed from a current Christian life?

2. Discuss the diverse genres of writing in the New Testament. Why do you think this diversity adds value to the New Testament?

3. How has textual criticism increased our confidence in the accuracy of the New Testament that we read today?

4. What translation and type of Bible do you read from? What are some of its advantages and disadvantages?

CHAPTER THREE

The World around the New Testament

I n the previous chapters we discussed what it means for the New Testament to be called Scripture and how this influences our reading of it. We have also talked about the idea of the New Testament as a book, or a library of assorted letters and biographies with its own history that has been arranged, copied, and preserved for two thousand years. Before diving into the content of the New Testament books, we must explore one more aspect of reading the New Testament as Christian Scripture: the world around the New Testament.

Why Should We Study the World around the New Testament?

The New Testament is more than a historical record; it aims to teach eternal truth and transform its hearers. But the New Testament comes from and to real people living in a real world. Unlike many other mystical religions claiming supernatural insight, Christianity is rooted in real history and sees this history as valuable. The Bible doesn't avoid historical realities and act like it is disconnected from them. Therefore, understanding some things about this world enables a rich and thoughtful reading of the New Testament.

Of course, it is possible to read the New Testament without knowledge of the ancient world, and much of its message will still be very clear. However, some parts of the New Testament won't make much sense, and many aspects will be easily misunderstood. Our reading will always be enhanced through understanding the culture, history, people, and society that the New Testament came from and first addressed.

Cultures in every time and place have their own values, expectations, symbols, ideas, and influences. But some moments in history are particularly complicated. Some periods of history involve major upheaval and the clashing and meshing of varied people groups. In times like these, the stakes are high, and many cultural values are highlighted and challenged. The world of the first-century Mediterranean basin, a corner of which contained the ancient land of Israel, was particularly complex because it was embroiled in a lengthy conflict of different empires, religions, and philosophies.

Early Christianity was born at the crucial juncture of two intersecting cultures: the Jewish and Greco-Roman worlds. Christianity subsequently created a new society that would soon transform Western civilization.

Our task in this chapter is to explore the **symbolic world** of the New Testament. We are interested not just in facts and figures—influential kings or revolutionary movements—but in the cultural world of the New Testament. This is because cultures have elaborate systems of meaning that provide a framework for how people understand their lives individually and corporately. We call this the "symbolic world"—the system of values, habits, and beliefs that operate at a conscious and subconscious level. Historical facts are insufficient, and the typical modern "historical-critical" approach to the New Testament is too shallow to enable a meaningful reading.

Rather, we need a method of reading the New Testament that is sensitive to historical facts but, most importantly, understands that individuals live within cultures, not just historical events. To read the New Testament well, then, we need to understand something about the complex, conflicted symbolic world in which early Christianity found itself. In this chapter, after offering a historical overview of this period, we will discuss the symbolic worlds of Judaism, Greco-Roman society, and early Christianity. For each of these overlapping worlds we will explore the same series of topics: literature, beliefs, people, and culture. ⓘ

The History of the Second Temple Period

The history of the Jewish world in the first century AD goes all the way back to Genesis 1:1. The Hebrew people have always understood their identity as rooted in God's creation of the world and particularly the story that starts with Abraham (Gen. 12). This story includes the twists and turns of the accounts of the **patriarchs** (Abraham, Isaac, and Jacob) and the subsequent history of Israel, from their slavery in Egypt to their sojourn to the promised land, to the rise of King David and the precipitous fall of the kingdom into disarray and eventual destruction and exile to a foreign land. ⓘ

The Judaism that birthed Jesus and other first-century Jews is called Second Temple Judaism. In 586 BC, only remnants of the once-great kingdom of Israel were left: the two southern tribes of Benjamin and Judah, centered in Jerusalem. But Babylonia (roughly modern-day Iraq), the world power of the day, attacked and easily conquered Jerusalem, desecrating the glorious temple, killing and enslaving the Hebrews, and taking into exile any whom they thought useful. This Babylonian exile is recorded in the biblical accounts, predicted by several prophets as God's judgment on unfaithful Israel (Jer. 25; Ezek. 12–24), and gives us stories such as those of Daniel and his friends (Shadrach, Meshach, and Abednego, renowned because of the fiery furnace), Ezra, Esther, and Nehemiah.

After seventy years, some faithful Hebrews desired to return and reestablish Jerusalem and the temple, which they did with great difficulty (see the books of Ezra and Nehemiah). The cleansing and rebuilding of the temple and Jerusalem that began in earnest in 515 BC gives us the name for the subsequent period that we call Second Temple Judaism. This era goes from 515 BC until the devastating destruction of the

INTRODUCTORY MATTERS

The Term "Second Temple Period"

Scholarship in the last few centuries spoke of the time preceding the New Testament as the "intertestamental period" and referred to first-century Judaism as "Late Judaism" (because it was about to be "replaced" by Christianity). Today we recognize that both expressions are flawed. Instead, we refer to the period 515 BC– AD 70 (or AD 135) as the Second Temple period, with the "second" referring to the rebuilding of the first Jerusalem temple after the Hebrew people returned from exile in Babylon. The problem with "intertestamental" is that it creates the impression that Hebrew history and writings, and God's activity, ceased between the latest books of the canonical Old Testament and the time of Jesus. This is clearly not the case: God was still at work in the world. Hebrew people experienced many important events and wrote influential history and theology books. It is better to treat the period from the Hebrews' return from exile (515 BC) to the destruction of the temple (AD 70) as one period in Jewish history. "Late Judaism" is problematic in that it assumes that Judaism was at the end of its life and ceased to exist with the birth of Christianity—something obviously untrue and arrogant in its framing.

temple by the Romans in AD 70. It is this period that provides the complex background to Jesus and early Christianity.

The events of Second Temple Judaism and the New Testament occurred in the corner of a much larger world stage. In the centuries that followed the rebuilding of Jerusalem and the temple, power began to shift from the Middle East to Europe, particularly Greece. In the fifth century BC the powerful Persians had reached from the Middle East all the way to Athens, attacking the city and desecrating the temple of Athena, only to be defeated in an important sea battle in 480 BC. This set the stage for the Greek states to organize, eventually unified by military victories under the Greek king Philip II of Macedon (382–336 BC). His son Alexander received training in the thriving military and intellectual world of ancient Greece, including tutoring from the great philosopher Aristotle. Building on his father's success and armed with a vision for a Panhellenic people, Alexander the Great (as he came to be known) concentrated power around his new kingdom.

Alexander set out on a campaign to spread the superiority of Greek language and culture. He departed Greece in 334 BC and headed east to capture and transform all the lands of the once-great Middle Eastern empires, taking along with him not only an army but also a retinue of philosophers, artists, and historians. Alexander's project is called **Hellenization**—the spread of Greek culture. Though his mission of Hellenization was very successful, Alexander never returned to his homeland; he died in Babylon in 323 BC.

Upon Alexander's death, a power struggle ensued among his various generals who controlled different parts of the vast empire he had created. This was an empire that ran from Greece in the west all the way to India and the Himalayas in the east, from the Black and Caspian Seas in the north to Egypt and the Arabian Sea in the south, with **Palestine** as a crossroads. Over the next century various post-Alexander kingdoms were established, while constant fighting triggered ever-shifting borders and alliances. By the beginning of the second century BC there were two great kingdoms throughout this area, the Seleucid and the Ptolemaic, with the Seleucid ruler Antiochus III rising to power and taking over more territories, including Palestine.

INTRODUCTORY MATTERS

BC and AD

Throughout history different societies have tracked time in a variety of ways, often based on the beginning and end of dynasties, cities, or creation itself. While some countries continue to have their own systems (e.g., the Chinese maintain their own year-numbering system connected to zodiac animal signs, currently in the 4700s), the international standard is based on developments in Christian western Europe in the Middle Ages. The Gregorian calendar was established in the sixteenth century, solidifying the language of "AD" (Latin, *anno domini*, "in the year of the Lord"), based on a calculation that Jesus was born in AD 1 (though Jesus was born probably in what would be 4–6 BC in this calendar). In English "BC" (before Christ) came to refer to the time before AD 1. "AD" is placed before the year number; "BC" is placed after the year number.

Today, for a standard that is not so explicitly tied to Christianity, many prefer the designations "BCE" (before the common era) and "CE" (common era) instead of BC and AD, respectively. In this book we use the latter, traditional forms.

A number of events occurred at this time that would shape Judaism and thereby Christianity. The next Seleucid ruler, Antiochus IV, who took upon himself the name Epiphanes ("divine manifestation"), aggressively deepened the project of Hellenization. For most of the populace this was not a problem—Hellenization had certain benefits, and the Greek gods could be incorporated into existing practices. But for the Jewish people, certain aspects of Hellenization violated core beliefs and practices, especially when forced on them by a foreign ruler. Antiochus Epiphanes taxed, murdered, and plundered the Jewish people, ultimately breaking into the holy of holies in the temple and sacrificing a pig on the altar there in December 167 BC.

This act—the "abomination of desolation" that Daniel had prophesied (Dan. 9:26–27; 11:31; cf. Matt. 24:15–16)—combined with centuries of oppression, galvanized many of the Jewish people to rise up and throw off the shackles of foreign leaders and their culture and idolatrous religion. The spark that lit the Jewish flame was the resistance of an old priest named Mattathias. When Antiochus tried to force the worship of Zeus on Mattathias and his sons, they rose up and killed the king's agent (1 Maccabees 2:19–26) and then fled to the hills. They joined forces with other pious Jews who were in rebellion against the Seleucids and began a guerrilla war throughout Judea and beyond. One of Mattathias's sons, Judas, became the leader and took the nickname Maccabeus ("the hammer"). Remarkably, the **Maccabees** were successful in defeating their oppressors, and after some key battles in 165–164 BC they recaptured Jerusalem. Almost exactly three years after Epiphanes's sacrilege in the temple, the Maccabees cleansed and rededicated the temple with an eight-day festival that the Jewish people still celebrate today as Hanukkah (the **Feast of Dedication/Lights**). ⓘ

During the years 63–37 BC some of the descendants of the Hasmonean dynasty served as priests and rulers in Jerusalem, but ineffectively and only under the appointment and rule of the

Kingdoms and Empires of the Second Temple Period

Judas Maccabeus continued to fight to expand the area outside Jerusalem where Jews could be free to worship and live according to God's laws. He and his brothers led the reestablished Jewish kingdom in turn, each of them gaining some victories. This became known as the **Hasmonean dynasty** (based on the name of one of Mattathias's ancestors). Wars and politics continued, and the Hasmonean kingdom established relationships with the emerging Roman Empire, largely to help keep the Seleucid powers in check. The high point of this time was the leadership of Mattathias's son Simon (142–134 BC), who established peace, security, and relative prosperity. The Jewish people gave to Simon the position of **high priest**, which would be passed on through his family line. Simon's son John Hyrcanus I was particularly successful as priest and ruler, guiding the Jews for about thirty years (134–104 BC) and spreading the Jewish kingdom to a size almost as large as David and Solomon's kingdom. This was not the case with his sons, however, who ruled ruthlessly and foolishly, especially Alexander Jannaeus. During his twenty-seven-year rule Alexander lost the support of the increasing population of pious Jews (led by the new group, the **Pharisees**) and slaughtered thousands for their opposition. After his death in 76 BC more infighting and rebellion broke out until 63 BC, when the Roman general Pompey arrived. By this time the Roman Empire had established a firm and broad rule over the entire Mediterranean world, and the takeover of the weakened Hasmonean kingdom was simple and complete, thus ending a one-hundred-year period of Jewish independence.

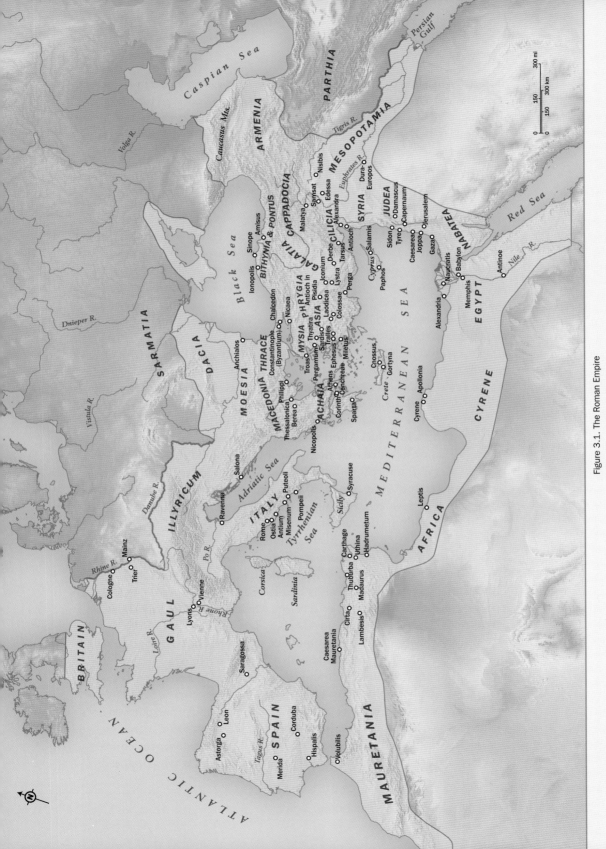

Figure 3.1. The Roman Empire

© Baker Publishing Group

Roman government. It was a tumultuous time that increased and hardened the conflicts within the Jewish community that was fractured into various allegiances. The year 37 BC is significant because it marks the end of the Hasmonean period and the establishment of the **Herodian dynasty**. Rome was experiencing its own civil war with intrigue, assassinations, and wars involving Julius Caesar, Brutus, Antony, and Octavian. This affected Palestine because the Romans awarded rulership of that area to loyal subjects. Herod (the Great) had conquered Jerusalem in 37 BC, and although he was an Idumean (not a Jew), he married into the Hasmonean line to establish his claim to be king. The Romans authorized Herod, who expanded his power with an iron fist, killing any whom he suspected of opposition, including his wife and mother-in-law, and any potential challengers to his throne—like the newborn Jesus (Matt. 2:1–18). His tyrannical rule did, however, provide a kind of stability in Palestine for the Jewish people, including his rebuilding and expansion of the temple, though pious Jews like the Pharisees did not support him.

After Herod the Great's death in 4 BC, the Romans granted three of his sons portions of their father's kingdom to rule, with mixed success. Archelaus was notoriously brutal and feared. His failed leadership resulted in the Romans taking his lands and ruling them directly through a series of Roman governors, including Pontius Pilate (AD 26–36), who ruled during the end of Jesus's life. Another son, Herod Antipas, appears in the Gospels because he ruled over the areas of Galilee and Perea, where Jesus ministered. His immorality was called out by the prophet John the Baptizer, whom Herod Antipas eventually beheaded (Mark 6:17–29), and he was involved in the arrest and trial of Jesus (Luke 23:6–12). One of Herod the Great's grandsons, Herod Agrippa I, also appears in the New Testament (Acts 12:1–4). In AD 37 he was given the title of king by the **Roman emperor** Caligula, and over the following years he gained more and more of the regions of Palestine, eventually controlling almost as much as his grandfather had. His son Herod Agrippa II ruled during the years AD 44–66 and was the ruler whom Paul appeared before when he was imprisoned in Caesarea (Acts 25:13–26:32), around AD 60.

One more historical moment should be mentioned as part of the background to the New Testament and early Christianity. In AD 66, worn down by oppressive Roman rule and the tyranny of the Herodian dynasty, many Jews finally revolted. The strong religious convictions of the Jews led them to seek once again to establish freedom as under the glorious days of the Hasmoneans. But it was not to be. The Jews had some successes, but the loss of life and the destruction were devastating. Over the course of a few years the Romans systematically slaughtered any who opposed them, culminating in the utter destruction of Jerusalem and the temple in AD 70. The city was leveled and its citizens tortured, enslaved, crucified, and killed. This event would forever change both Judaism and Christianity. Judaism no longer controlled the city of David or had control of its holy place, resulting in a temple-less religion, focused instead on the study and practice of **Torah** in **synagogues**. The center of Christianity shifted as well, becoming more widely established throughout the Roman Empire in city churches.

This brief survey of the historical events of the Second Temple period gives some insight into the radical changes that were occurring during this very unstable time. The actions of kings and governments inevitably affect the lives of individuals, but this only scratches the surface of the question of what people believe and why they do what they do. We must move beyond historical events to explore the interrelated symbolic world of people's experience.

The Jewish Symbolic World of the First Century AD

Although we often think of Judaism and Christianity as two distinct world religions, it is important to remember that Christianity was born out of Judaism and shares much of its worldview, holy writings, and history. Christianity has always understood itself as the *fulfillment*, or end goal, of the story of God's work that begins in Genesis, not as something entirely different. For Jesus, the apostles, and all the writers of the

© Baker Publishing Group

Figure 3.2. Administrative regions during the time of Jesus. By Jesus's day several administrative districts existed. On the western side of the Jordan River were Galilee, Samaria, and Judea. On the eastern side of the Jordan River, a collection of smaller districts ruled by Herod's son Philip and the Decapolis were in the north, and to the south was Perea, ruled by Herod Antipas (who also ruled Galilee).

New Testament books, "the Scriptures" refers to the Hebrew Scriptures, what Christians would later call the Old Testament. Therefore, the primary context and world behind the New Testament will always be the Scriptures of Israel (both Hebrew and Greek versions) and the story of Israel.

Literature

Both Judaism and Christianity are faiths rooted in beliefs and practices guided by writings—books understood to be revelations from God himself. For the Hebrew people, the foundation of this collection of holy writings is the **Pentateuch**—the five books of Moses that tell the story from the creation of the world to Israel's liberation from slavery in Egypt and to God's establishing of a special relationship with his people in the promised land. The remaining thirty-nine books of the Hebrew Scriptures consist of a wide variety of genres: the ups and downs of Israel's history, poetry, songs, instructions in wisdom, and the writings of many prophets sent by God to instruct, rebuke, and encourage God's people. All of this was written in the Hebrew language, with the exception of a few small portions written in Aramaic (a related language). Every Hebrew child learned and memorized the stories and songs of the Hebrew Scriptures to shape their understanding of the world.

In addition to these central writings, the Hebrew people produced many other texts, especially during the Second Temple period. These included the **Old Testament Pseudepigrapha**, a collection of stories and prophecies ascribed to famous people from biblical times, such as Enoch, Solomon, and Abraham. We have many such writings in full or partial form, often translated into later languages, and many of these books circulated in their day but are now lost.

Also during this period various subgroups within Judaism produced writings that reflected their own way of interpreting the Scriptures. Over time the role of the **rabbi**, or teacher of the law, became fixed within Judaism, and the sayings and particular interpretations of these rabbis were memorized and eventually written down. This occurred over several hundred years and was codified into two major collections called the Jerusalem Talmud and the Babylonian Talmud. The **Talmuds** consist of the teachings of various rabbis called the **Mishnah**, with later expansions and sayings called the **Gemara**. Even though the final form of these collections dates from the fourth and fifth centuries AD, they contain many sayings and interpretations dating back to the Second Temple period.

This is also the case with a large body of texts called the **Midrash**, which comes from the Hebrew word meaning "to seek answers." Midrash seeks to answer contemporary theological and practical questions by investigating the Scriptures. It consists of two categories: *halakah*, which inquires about laws and religious practices, and *haggadah*, which interprets biblical narratives. Writings from this time also included sectarian works like those found in the **Dead Sea Scrolls**, a wide collection of writings that came from a community of Jews who had separated themselves from the rest of Judaism. This diverse library of some eight hundred writings includes copies of the biblical texts, commentaries on and paraphrases of the Bible, pseudepigraphal writings, devotional material, and instructions about the community's life together.

One of the most important developments during the Second Temple period was the translation of the Hebrew Scriptures into other languages. This was necessary because an increasing number of Jews lived outside Israel and spoke other languages. Even within Palestine, as the generations progressed, the Hebrew language became less well known outside the specific study of Torah. The need for a translation of the Scriptures into contemporary languages was necessary for the continuation of the faith. Translations into Aramaic (the language commonly used in Palestine and probably what Jesus spoke) were called **Targums**. The Targums not only translated the Hebrew Scriptures but also provided paraphrases and various explanations. Even more significant was the massive translation project of the Hebrew Scriptures into Greek, called the Septuagint (often abbreviated as "LXX," the Roman numeral for seventy, because of the story of its original seventy [or seventy-two] translators). This translation began with the Pentateuch probably around 250 BC and was completed in various versions over time. The Septuagint is significant because it enabled Jewish people living throughout the Greco-Roman world, where Greek was the common language, to read and understand the Bible in their own everyday language. This Greek translation also enabled Judaism to interact with the broader world of religious culture, including many gentiles who were attracted to Judaism, called **God-fearers**.

The Septuagint contains all the books of the Hebrew Scriptures plus an additional fourteen or fifteen books (depending on how portions are calculated) in Greek that were produced during the Second Temple period that we now call the **Apocrypha**. The Apocrypha consists of additions to some of the Hebrew books (additional parts of Esther and Daniel); some prayers and psalms; instructions in wise living; enjoyable novellas like Susanna, Tobit, and Judith; and the four large histories of the Maccabean period (1–4 Maccabees). The Septuagint was not only convenient for non-Palestinian Jews; it was also highly influential as the Old Testament of many early Christians (at least half of the New Testament quotations from the Old Testament are from the Septuagint), especially as Christianity evolved from being a Jewish sect to its own increasingly gentile religion throughout the ancient world. The Septuagint continues to serve as the Old Testament for the Eastern Orthodox branch of the church. The Roman Catholic tradition continues to consider the books of the Old Testament Apocrypha as part of the canon, while the Protestant tradition emphasizes the Hebrew texts over the Greek and sees the Apocrypha as informative but not authoritative.

The symbolic world of first-century Jews was rich with many writings and ideas. Jews of this period were very aware of their own history and identity as distinct from others. Ideas and their consequences were not just the purview of an elite group of scholars but were influential for the everyday lives of the Jewish people. ⓘ

Beliefs

As we have noted, Second Temple Jews inherited a world full of texts and ideas. As a result, their symbolic world was driven by many deeply held beliefs, some very ancient (even in their day) and some developing through circumstance and need. We will briefly discuss some of these core ideas, but we must first note that for the Jewish people, "theology" was not a set of abstract propositions that can be ground down like garlic powder from a bulb. Rather, the primary theology of the Old Testament and Judaism is a *story*—the story of God's creation of the world and his activity to care for and rule over his people. That is, while there are core beliefs that we can identify, Judaism is a worldview and practice, a way of seeing and being in the world under submission to God, rooted and explained as a historical story.

Mindful of this, we can identify some core beliefs within that story. Scholars David Wenham and Steve Walton helpfully list "Five Key Marks of Second Temple Judaism":[2]

1. There is one true God.

Foundational to Jewish understanding and daily life is the **Shema**: "Listen, Israel, the LORD our God, the LORD is one" (Deut. 6:4). This radical **monotheism**, belief in only one true and superior God—not just henotheism, the worship of one god among many—means that the gods that other people worship are truly only idols, creations not creators. Jewish monotheism includes the belief that this one true God created all that exists, that this God is still actively involved in the world, and that he makes relationships with his creatures through covenants.

2. God has chosen Israel.

God relates to his creatures through covenants—contractual relationships—and he has chosen one particular people group, the descendants of Abraham, Isaac, and Jacob (who was renamed Israel). This covenant shows God's character and is the means through which he will redeem and restore the world. God loves his creation and will eventually bless all nations, as promised to Abraham. This will come through his chosen people Israel.

3. God has provided a way to live.

The God of Israel is not a distant deity who simply demands sacrifices to appease his anger. He wants his covenant people to flourish, and so he has given them wise instructions on how to worship, to work, and to relate to him and one another. This is Torah (best understood as "covenantal instructions" rather than "law"). The other parts of the Jewish Scriptures reinforce and apply these instructions throughout Israel's difficult history.

4. God has given his people a land, focused on the temple.

Central to the covenant that God established with Abraham and that he renewed at the exodus from Egypt was the promise of a land that Israel would possess and flourish in with God as their king. After God delivered them from slavery in Egypt, they did eventually enter the promised land under the leadership of Joshua. The height of this kingdom realm was under David and Solomon, resulting in the building of Jerusalem and the temple. The subsequent centuries-long decline and the eventual loss of sovereignty over the promised land explain much of the Jews' fervency and devotion to this land, as seen even today in the Middle East.

5. God has given hope for the future.

At the time of Kings David and Solomon, God promised a future when their descendants would reign over God's people in joy. The Old Testament prophets continually reiterated this message throughout the dark decades and generations that followed. This great hope centered on a future Messiah/Christ, one anointed as a king, who would return to restore Israel's glory, to bless all the nations of the world, and to consummate a perfect relationship of peace with God himself (see especially Isa. 40–66). This would create a time and place of for-giveness, purity, joy, and shalom called the **kingdom of God**. During the Second Temple period it seemed that this was happening with the Hasmonean dynasty, but it too ended in corruption and destruction. By the first century AD, under the heavy hand of the Roman Empire, the Jews were desperate for God's kingdom to come through the promised Messiah.

Each of these core beliefs can be found in the Hebrew Scriptures. Dur-ing the Second Temple period some of these beliefs became more or less important based on the changing political and social world the Jews lived in. For example, the vision for Israel to become a blessing to all nations goes back to Abraham's story and was repeated by the prophets. However, the centuries of oppression inflicted on the Jews by countless foreign na-tions meant that few Jews saw their relationship with outsiders as one of priestly grace; rather, they saw outsiders as enemies whom God should de-stroy. Also, certain practices prescribed in the Torah—such as **circumcision**, Sabbath observance, and strict kosher food laws—received even greater emphasis. These became marks of what it meant to be a faithful Jew in the Second Temple era because the worship practices of the temple were either unavailable (when the temple was destroyed or controlled by others) or far-removed for Jews living throughout the world. Additionally, these practices marked devout Jews as distinct from the surrounding dominant culture and even from other Jews who they felt had compromised their faith by accom-modating too much to those around them (see below on Hellenism).

Also during this era additional Jewish beliefs and practices developed from other biblical teachings. Many of these are reflected in the additional writings of this period. For example, the Second Temple period saw the rise of the practice of Jewish people centering their lives on meeting in syna-gogues and the custom of rabbis gathering disciples to teach them how to interpret and live by Torah. During this period Jewish thinking about heaven, hell, demons, and angels became much more detailed.

What is the significance of all of this? Understanding the symbolic world of these Second Temple beliefs, values, and commitments makes sense of much of what we read in the New Testament, which is part of this same world. Specifically, this backdrop of beliefs explains why Jesus said and did the things he did concerning the kingdom of God. It also explains why he encountered so much opposition by the Jewish leadership of his day. On every point Jesus shared these core beliefs but also transformed them through his teaching and actions. This does much to explain how early Christianity is simultaneously rooted in Judaism and also in conflict with it.

People

At the most foundational level, in the Jewish mind there have always been two groups of people in the world—Jews and non-Jews/gentiles. This is rooted in the Jewish self-understanding of their being the **elect** of God. But even within a culture such as Judaism, which is racially and religiously homogenous, there is some diversity of views and practices among the people. In times of upheaval and transition even more variety is found. First-century Judaism was remarkably varied, with many subgroups that often contended with one another. ⓘ

The most well-known subgroup from the pages of the New Testament is the group called the Pharisees. These were the Jewish conservatives of the day who focused on the strict study and practice of God's commandments in the Torah and the rabbinic traditions that developed along those lines. Their name derives from the idea of being "separate" from others, and their focus was on purity or ritual cleanness. Their roots are from the Maccabean period, with its fervor for rediscovering and defending traditional Judaism. As the Hasmonean dynasty became more political and corrupt, this movement of pious people arose, often running into conflict with the Jewish rulers and sometimes earning persecution for their strong stance. Many of the professional class of experts in the law (**scribes** or **lawyers**) were Pharisees, as were many rabbis or teachers of the law who gathered disciples around themselves and achieved high social status. By Jesus's day the Pharisees exercised great influence over the mass of poor, rural, less-educated Jewish people, the *Am ha-Eretz* ("the people of the land"), because they were seen as the reliable authorities in the many details of how to live faithfully as a Jew in relation to complex issues such as Sabbath observance and keeping pure in the midst of a world of non-Jewish people.

On the other end of the spectrum are Jewish people who were part of the religio-political establishment in Jerusalem. Chief among them was the group called the **Sadducees**, who typically were from the families that controlled the priesthood and political power going back to the later generations of the Hasmonean dynasty. Members of this group usually were wealthy, controlling taxes and temple activities, and in political relationship with the Roman government. They were followers of Moses and honored the Torah as binding, but not other writings such as those of the prophets, or other beliefs that had developed in the Second Temple period, such as the bodily resurrection and angels. As those in control of wealth and power, they had little interest in the hope for a messiah to come and overthrow the government to establish a new kingdom. Similar in sentiment was a smaller group called the **Herodians** (Matt. 22:16; Mark 3:6; 12:13), who supported the Herodian dynasty and were therefore part of the Roman imperial establishment.

Other Jewish people found their identity in their opposition to the corruption they perceived around them, both religious and political. One such group that was even stricter than the Pharisees was the **Essenes**, a priestly group that focused on **asceticism** (typically including celibacy) and the rejection of the current priesthood as fraudulent. Some Essenes apparently lived in villages and others in a portion of Jerusalem, while yet others isolated themselves completely, living in communes in the wilderness. The community at Qumran, which produced and maintained the library that we call the Dead Sea Scrolls, may have been Essene, following their own strict laws and a separate holy calendar and having their own "Teacher of Righteousness." Another group, the **Zealots**, focused on Jewish political independence from their Roman oppressors, often engineering assassinations, kidnappings, and Robin Hood–like attacks and thefts on Roman caravans. In Roman eyes, these revolutionaries were terrorists best beaten down by torture and crucifixion.

Another group from this period, who also appears several times in the New Testament, is the **Samaritans**. Samaria, the area north of Judea and south of Galilee in ancient Israel, was destroyed by the Assyrians in 722 BC. There were centuries of conflict and hatred between the Samaritans, who considered themselves Jews, and the other Jewish people of the surrounding areas. The Samaritans had their own version of the Pentateuch, along with their own temple on Mount Gerizim. By Jesus's time the Jews avoided the Samaritans completely (cf. John 4:9), even traveling a long distance to avoid going through the Samaritan region.

Finally, we should mention a couple individual Jews from this period who are known to us because of their large and influential writings. The first is **Josephus** (AD 37–100), a Jewish general who surrendered to the Romans in AD 70 and ended up living in Rome, where he wrote several important works, including the lengthy *History of the Jewish War*, and from whom much of our information about Second Temple Judaism comes. The other is **Philo** (20 BC–AD 50), a highly educated Jewish philosopher in Alexandria, Egypt—the intellectual capital of the world at that time. Philo integrated the Greek philosophical system and methods of interpreting texts with Jewish thought and study of the Old Testament. His extensive writings were influential not only for Jews but also for many early Christian theologians.

Culture

Philo of Alexandria provides a good segue to a discussion of the culture of Second Temple Judaism, because he is a prime example of the cultural effect of Hellenization on Jewish thought and life. As mentioned above, "Hellenization" refers to Alexander the Great's project of spreading Greek culture throughout the lands he conquered. Unlike many other conquering rulers, Alexander did not seek to destroy the cultures he subjugated. Instead, he encouraged a transformation of the occupied societies with what he understood to be the superior language, architecture, military, and form of government—Greek.

This resulted in a pervasive and lasting impact of Greek culture because it was integrated into existing societies, like leaven spreading through a lump of dough. Greek architecture, sports, temples, public baths, schools, hairstyles, philosophies, and statues popped up all over Asia Minor, Palestine, the Middle East, North Africa, and India. And most notably, an amalgamated form of the Greek language became the lingua franca, or universal language, that enabled a wide variety of people to communicate with one another, like Latin in later Europe and English throughout the world today.

The significance of Hellenization on the Judaism of this period cannot be overstated. Hellenization affected Judaism (and thus Christianity) at a level deeper than politics or ideas, at the layer of the symbolic world itself—the way people think and interact with the world. Of course, the roots of Judaism are God's revelation and the story of Israel, but from the time of Alexander through the rise of Christianity, the history of Judaism is the story of Judaism's interaction with Hellenism. This interaction varied radically—from full adoption of Greek culture to utter rejection—but in every case it is Hellenism that defines the issues and shapes the debates and practices.

In fact, it is largely the various reactions to Hellenism that created the diversity of groups within Second Temple Judaism. Many Jews such as Philo deeply integrated Jewish theology with Greek philosophy.

Figure 3.3. Buddha statue in Greco-Roman clothing (first to mid-second century) from Pakistan. One striking example of the pervasive influence of Hellenism is the thousand-year tradition of Greco-Buddhist art. When Alexander and his entourage established a Greek presence in modern-day Afghanistan, Pakistan, and the Indian subcontinent, they generally had a favorable relationship with Buddhism. Very quickly the architecture, coins, carvings, and statues within Buddhism reflected Greek themes, hairstyles, clothing, and gods. The result was that even the mainstream depictions of the Buddha that became standard down to today show the influence of Greek culture infused into their tradition.

Countless Jews learned to read their Bibles only in Greek (the Septuagint), and Hasmonean Jewish rulers gave their children obviously Greek names such as Alexander and Aristobulus. On the other side, it was the extreme promotion of Hellenism over Jewish practices (Antiochus Epiphanes) that caused the Maccabean revolution and resulted in a renewed emphasis on Jewish piety over against foreign influence (the Pharisees), with some Jews withdrawing from society altogether (the Essenes). At the level of ideas, we see in the Septuagint ways of speaking and concepts that reflect interaction with Hellenism. The fact that it is a translation into Greek is the starting point, but Greek education also affects the development of the wisdom and apocalyptic traditions as well as the modes of interpreting texts; even the rabbis' principles of interpretation are easily traceable back to Greek principles coming from Alexandria, Egypt.

During the Second Temple period most Jews lived in rural-agricultural or village economies, often poor and on the precipice of disaster. In Palestine some Greek-style cities were developing, along with trade and industries such as fish oil and fish pastes. For all Jewish people the culture was rooted in the local family and clan and more broadly in their ethnic and religious identity as distinct from the world, chosen and set apart by God. They maintained this identity across generations by a careful and diligent observance of holidays that rehearsed the history of Israel—the Sabbath, **Passover**, the **Feast of Booths**, Hanukkah, and others. Thus, Jewish culture during this period can be understood as founded deeply on their religious story, worked out differently by varying groups in the complex new world of Hellenism.

The Greco-Roman Symbolic World of the First Century AD

So far we have explored the Jewish world during the Second Temple period to understand the historical backdrop of Jesus and early Christianity. We have seen that while Jewish identity was primarily rooted in the history of Israel, the intersection of this story with Greek culture had a major impact.

When we talk about the first century, typically we add another bit to the description of the culture of the day: it is not just Greek but Greco-Roman. This is because, as we saw in the history above, the mighty Greek empire went through an inevitable decline and eventually was taken over by the next world superpower, Rome. The Roman Empire came to control the vast area that Alexander had carved out and expanded its reign in every direction. By the first century AD it is the Romans, not the Greeks, who are taxing, governing, and oppressing the Jewish people. Despite this political change from Greece to Rome, Hellenistic culture persisted. In fact, much of Roman culture was born of an adoption and mild transformation of Greek life: the Greek gods got new names (e.g., Zeus became Jupiter), the Roman philosophers were translating Aristotle, and Latin poets were Romanizing the stories, plays, and songs of Athens. Eventually, the Romans' own language, Latin, became the dominant mode of speech (at least in the West), but in the first century Greek was still the main way people communicated (hence, the New Testament was written in Greek). Thus, when talking about the first century, it is best to describe this symbolic world as Greco-Roman.

Literature

The literature of the Greco-Roman world was diverse and sophisticated. Works of philosophy, histories, politics, plays, songs, epic poems, education, religion, and moral teachings were ubiquitous. Much of this literature is still foundational to Western thought and forms the base of classical education. Examples include the poetry of Homer such as *The Iliad* and *The Odyssey*, philosophical works such as Aristotle's *Nicomachean Ethics*, which is designed to teach people to live virtuously, and Plato's *Republic*, which casts a vision for how to structure society so that people can experience human flourishing. Greek playwrights wrote works that are still performed today, such as Sophocles's *Oedipus the King* and *Antigone*. Historians such as Herodotus (considered the father of history writing) and Thucydides produced detailed accounts of wars and journeys and great figures. Building on the Greek heritage, the Latin author Virgil produced the epic national poem for the Romans, *The Aeneid*, while Ovid mastered love and mythological themes in works such as his influential *Metamorphoses*. The Romans also continued the Greek tradition of moral philosophy, as can be seen in the prolific and influential works of Seneca, who continued the ideas of **Stoicism** through hundreds of letters and philosophical works.

We've only scratched the surface of the rich literary heritage of the Greco-Roman world and its abiding influence on Western civilization. More directly, we can see the influence of this literature on the New Testament. The New Testament documents are written within and to people living in the Greco-Roman world. The New Testament consists of types of literature that are adopted from this literary sphere, such as the biography of a great leader (the Gospels), the history of a movement (Acts), wisdom exhortation (James, the Sermon on the Mount), and letters written to influence people's lives (the Letters).

Beliefs

Even though it was not monotheistic, the Greco-Roman world was just as religious and interested in big ideas as Judaism was. Both Greeks and Romans cared about questions concerning the meaning of life, how to live and die well, and how to be truly happy. The Greco-Roman tradition of philosophy provided a sophisticated number of ways of answering these questions. Nearly every philosophical system focused on learning to live intentionally with certain virtues such as courage, justice, and temperance, so that one could experience a good and beautiful life. Beyond this there were different schools of thought, such as **Epicureanism**, Stoicism, and **Cynicism**. ⓘ

The Greeks and the Romans also had a rich religious culture. Going back deep in their history are the stories of the gods still known to us today from Greek and Roman mythology, such as Zeus/Jupiter, Aphrodite/Venus, Artemis/Diana, and Apollo. There were temples to many such gods, and multitudes in the first century believed in them and participated in rituals related to them. Others saw these ancient gods more as symbols of ideas but still participated as part of the societal structure. Over time, the Roman emperors were divinized and came to be honored and worshiped, with statues that devotees bowed to in allegiance. Many people also participated in what are known as mystery religions—secret societies with rituals surrounding food and sex and furtive actions. In the second century AD a related set of beliefs and practices called **Gnosticism** developed, which often syncretized with Judaism, Christianity, and other religions.

People throughout the ancient Mediterranean world were deeply spiritual. They believed in spiritual beings, in divine oracles and prophecies, and in the importance of interpreting dreams. These varied religious and philosophical beliefs are part of

ⓘ INTRODUCTORY MATTERS

Varied Philosophical Systems in the Greco-Roman World

Platonism—Plato's influential philosophy emphasized that the world as we know it is an imperfect copy of invisible, universal Ideal Forms, the highest of which is the Good.

Skepticism—This school of philosophy avoided making any absolute truth claims, emphasizing that nothing can be known certainly or communicated clearly enough for us to have confidence.

Cynicism—This was a radical philosophy whose followers rejected wealth, power, and fame, seeing virtue as living a life of shameless austerity.

Stoicism—This highly influential way of life saw true happiness as achievable by learning self-control, to not be controlled by emotions and circumstances.

Epicureanism—Founded by Epicurus, this philosophy taught that happiness comes through living a life of modest pleasures, seeking tranquility, freedom from fear and bodily pain.

the world of Second Temple Judaism and early Christianity, sharing some beliefs but also offering elements against which the Judeo-Christian worldview distinguished itself.

People

We have already mentioned a smattering of the many important philosophers, historians, and poets who populated the Greco-Roman world of the first century. More directly intersecting with the New Testament, there are several notable groups and individuals. In the realm of government, the Roman Empire provided many characters who make appearances in the New Testament, including the emperors of Rome (Luke 2:1; 3:1; Acts 11:28; 18:2; 25:11) and various levels of appointed officials such as governors/vice-regents, such as Herod the Great and his sons (Matt. 2:1; 14:1–12), **proconsuls** such as Pontius Pilate (Matt. 27:11; Luke 23:1), Sergius Paulus (Acts 13:7), Gallio (Acts 18:12), and Felix (Acts 23:26), and tribunes/judges such as Claudius Lysias (Acts 23:26). Several Roman soldiers also appear in the pages of the New Testament, including some **centurions**, a class designation for an important captain of one hundred soldiers (Luke 3:14; 7:1–10; Acts 10:1; 27:1).

From the perspective of the Jews, all of these people fell into the primary designation of "non-Jew" and therefore were seen as outsiders at best and enemies at worst. An important subgroup of these non-Jews was the God-fearers (Acts 13:16, 26; 17:4, 17; 18:7)—gentiles who revered the God of the Jews, often attaching themselves to synagogues as secondary citizens. These God-fearers sometimes followed the commands of Moses and donated financially to Jewish communities (Luke 7:4–5; Acts 10:2), though they were not proselytes (full converts to Judaism). Many of the early converts to Christianity likely came from this group who heard the preaching of the gospel in the synagogues by Paul and others and learned of Jesus's own welcoming of gentiles (Acts 10:1–48). The benefactor Theophilus, to whom the Gospel of Luke and the book of Acts are dedicated, may have been a God-fearer (Luke 1:3; Acts 1:1).

Culture

The culture of the Greco-Roman world shared many values with the Jewish people and myriad other subcultures in the Mediterranean basin. There were distinctives among the groups—maybe especially with the Jews and their radical monotheism

Figure 3.4. Head of the Greek god Zeus (AD 69–96)

and long heritage—but there were many cultural aspects that inclined these people groups to see and experience the world in certain ways. This can be compared to the unity and diversity within American culture today: there are many differences and subcultural values, yet commitments such as freedom of speech, the possibility for financial advancement, and legal rights are valued by every American.

Many of the cultural elements that are shared by both Jews and non-Jews in the Greco-Roman world stem from the pervasive influence of Hellenism on everyone in the first century, as discussed above. Beyond this we can identify several key cultural values:

1. **Honor and shame**

   Sociologists and anthropologists have long recognized that, unlike most modern Western cultures, many societies in the ancient world functioned with the central social categories of honor and shame. "Honor refers to the public acknowledgment of a person's worth, granted on the basis of how fully that individual embodies qualities and behaviors valued by the group."[3] That is, honor is like a currency that gives people status in society (much like money does in modern Western societies). Honor is granted according to what the society values. Conversely, one receives shame by not conforming to the established standards of good and bad. Shame is not the same thing as personal guilt, but is a recognizable social value that determines one's success in society. **Honor-shame cultures** use a lot of language concepts such as reputation, glory, name, boasting, and "face." Honor-shame cultures tend to be more cohesive and collective than individualistic; group identity is dominant, with honor and shame as the primary means of social behavioral control. Understanding these dynamics deepens our understanding of much of the language and many of the ideas in the New Testament, especially the ways in which Jesus challenges what his culture deems as honorable versus shameful: the first become last (Matt. 19:30), the persecuted and ridiculed are honored (Matt. 5:10–12), the lame and blind and poor are welcomed and lifted up (Luke 14:15–24).

2. **Patron-client relationships**

   Overlapping with the honor-shame dynamic, the ancient Jewish and Greco-Roman world was structured economically very differently from Western societies today. A small percentage of the population—determined almost entirely by birth—owned nearly all the wealth and resources, and typically these persons served as rulers. Nearly everyone else in these ancient societies lived very meager lives, always potentially on the precipice of disaster, with little safety net except their family relationships. This was not a period with a large middle class, free-market economies, government welfare, and the possibility of social and financial upward mobility.

Instead, the social structures and economy worked together in a strongly hierarchical system of patrons and clients, or benefactors and dependents. Everyone had a clearly defined place in society. Most were dependent on those above them, because the majority of resources were controlled by a few people. Patrons might provide money, grain, employment, land, or social advancement. In exchange, the client was obligated to express gratitude to publicize the favor of the patron and thereby contribute to his reputation. Naturally, giving thanks and showing honor became one of the highest virtues, while ingratitude was a great vice. Thus, the honor-shame culture contributed to and perpetuated the **patron-client relationship**, with goods and resources flowing down the ladder and with honor flowing up in response.

This deep-seated cultural reality is manifested in the New Testament in many of the stories that reflect this kind of socioeconomic system, often in the form of agricultural and financial **parables**. There is a very real sense in which God himself can be considered the good and perfect patron, providing for his dependent creatures all that they need, with their proper response being honor and gratitude (Rom. 1:18–25). At the same time, we can see through Jesus's teachings and actions that he often challenged certain aspects of this patron-client structure, emphasizing God's exorbitant giving while also encouraging those with power to become lowly, his own sacrificial death being the prime example (Phil. 2:5–11).

3. Family and kin

Many aspects of family life are universal across all cultures—and many are not. Societies have varying customs about marriage, parenting, children, siblings, and extended families. The Jewish and the Greco-Roman worlds overlapped significantly in how families functioned in their societies. These were often more similar to each other than to how families function in the modern era. Biblical teachings and the Greco-Roman moral philosophers said much the same things about life together as family.

Much more so than in the modern West, a person's family of origin and ancestry formed one's primary identity. To be the "son of" someone—either positively or as a vulgar criticism—was the starting point for one's place in the world. Individuals were first a part of an extended family or kin group before they were individuals; one's reputation and standing in society were primarily determined by one's ancestry, unless one greatly shamed or distinguished oneself. Ancient households typically consisted of extended relations, all of whom worked together in some trade or industry, sharing their resources and their reputation, and seeking to protect and promote their own kin before anyone else. One difference in marriage practices was that Jewish people tended to marry within their extended kin group to preserve inheritances and lineage, whereas Romans often sought to marry outside their kin for strategic and economic reasons.

The Christian Symbolic World of the First Century AD

To everyone's surprise (except Jesus's), the tiny group of "Nazarenes" or "Christians" that started as a persecuted sect within Judaism would expand and transform both Jewish and Greco-Roman societies. Rooted in the intersecting point of Jewish and Greco-Roman cultures, Christianity created its own symbolic world that eventually would affect world history. Early Christianity inevitably overlapped with both symbolic worlds, but it is also original and makes its own contribution to a new symbolic world centered on the man Jesus, the Christ.

Literature

At its beginning Christianity had no holy writings beyond the Jewish Scriptures. When the New Testament quotes the "Scriptures," it refers to the Hebrew Bible or the Septuagint. The same set of additional Second Temple texts (Septuagintal Apocrypha and other writings) was also part of the early Christians' conceptual world. The big change for Christianity came in oral and then written traditions about Jesus's teaching and actions. These **Jesus traditions** were transmitted through storytelling and preaching during Jesus's day and served as the foundation of early Christian understanding. Eventually they were written down in the form of biographies called the Gospels. Key to this process was the testimony of eyewitnesses to the events, especially from Jesus's disciples who became apostles, with Peter as their leader.

The apostles' teaching (Acts 2:42) then became the authoritative way to understand and transmit the stories about Jesus and, importantly, the way to interpret Jewish Scriptures anew in light of Jesus's coming. Apostolic teaching and preaching consisted of a combination of rereading the Jewish Scriptures Christianly and applying Jesus's own teachings. Eventually these apostles began to write letters to explain the orthodox way of reading the Scriptures and understanding Jesus and to combat moral and theological problems. These texts were circulated throughout the fledgling early Christian communities and, based on their apostolic source, were recognized as authoritative. Eventually the combination of Jewish Scriptures with apostolic teaching formed a two-part Christian canon of Scripture that we now call the Old and New Testaments.

As within Second Temple Judaism, early Christianity also produced many other texts that were circulated and became influential, and were representative of the ideas of the time, even if not having the same universal authority as the apostolic teachings. This body of literature included many other Jesus sayings and stories, additional accounts of what various apostles did beyond the book of Acts, letters to instruct the churches, and apocalyptic visions (see chap. 2 above). The following generation of the disciples of the apostles continued the tradition of teaching, preaching, and writing, from which we have many texts, often gathered together under the group known as the **Apostolic Fathers**. ⓘ

Beliefs

As with the theology of Judaism, Christianity's belief system is primarily a story, composed of historical events in which God revealed himself and acted to change the world. Based on this story, certain ideas can be articulated in the form of doctrines (especially when wrong understanding and applications appear), but doctrines can never be divorced from the larger narrative framework from which they derive their meaning. For Christians, this narrative framework is the story of Israel coming to its end goal through the **incarnation**, life, death, resurrection, and **ascension** of Jesus. A number of these narratively

Figure 3.5. Byzantine tile with Ignatius of Antioch (tenth century)

Walters Art Museum. Partial museum purchase with funds provided by the S. & A.P. Fund, 1956, and partial gift of Mr. Robert E. Hecht Jr., 1957.

embedded beliefs became central to Christianity's symbolic world and can be articulated in the form of worldview statements:

1. **The God of the Jews is three in one, with Jesus as the incarnate Son of God.**

   Central to Jewish understanding, there is only one God. Christianity affirms this fully but must also account for the fact that Jesus claimed to be divine, performed actions that only God could do (such as forgiving **sin** directly and controlling nature), and was vindicated as righteous through his resurrection and ascension. Additionally, God's own Spirit is at work in and through Jesus and his disciples. Rather than dismissing the Old Testament's revelation, Christianity holds to this radical monotheism, explaining that this one God has always existed in three persons—Father, Son, Spirit—and has now been revealed in a clearer way than ever before through the incarnation of the Son, Jesus (Heb. 1:1–2). The New Testament and early Christianity are full of such trinitarian language (e.g., Matt. 28:19; 2 Cor. 13:13), though it took several centuries, and a number of missteps, for orthodox Christianity to find the best ways to articulate this complex reality.

2. Jesus fulfilled all of God's promises and work in the world.

   Starting with the first book of the New Testament canon (Matthew), Christianity understands Jesus to be the *fulfillment* of all that God has been doing with his creation since Genesis 1. Jesus's own teaching, and the apostolic teaching that follows, focuses on understanding the whole of God's revelation in light of Jesus's actions. Every promise that God made concerning the future restoration of humanity, and his reign on the earth through the Davidic Messiah, has now been set into motion through Jesus (2 Cor. 1:20). The promise of a new and perfect covenant between God and humanity—with forgiveness of sins and the transformation of people into godlikeness and through which people from every nation become God's children—is central to Christianity's self-understanding. Jesus is the authoritative teacher and Lord, and his life, death, resurrection, and ascension become the epicenter of history itself. In other words, Christianity's understanding of who Jesus is requires a total commitment to Jesus only; Jesus cannot be simply added on to other beliefs or practices.

3. The Lord Jesus was raised from the dead, now reigns with God, and will return to consummate God's reign on the earth.

The claims about the history-changing reality of Jesus are founded on his miracles and power, but ultimately they are rooted in the fact that Jesus was resurrected by God after his death, honored and glorified with a new physical-spiritual body, and then taken up into heaven to reign with God over all the world. Countless other people have taught with authority, gathered followers, and even performed miracles. But Christianity stands or falls based on the historical claims of Jesus's bodily resurrection and ascension, which vindicates that Jesus was speaking the truth and was both human and divine in nature. Jesus's resurrection inaugurates the new messianic/kingdom era, serving as a foretaste of humanity's resurrection and transformation. This is a cosmic event that initiates the **redemption** of all of creation. Jesus's current ascended place at the right hand of the Father means that he plays the ongoing role of priest, standing in the place of humanity, having borne the penalty for our sins. Jesus's position as king, or as the ruling Son of God, means that he reigns and controls the world from heaven. Christianity then becomes forward leaning, anticipating the time when Jesus as prophet, priest, and king consummates his reign with a wedding feast, bringing justice, peace, blessings, and shalom from heaven to earth, for all who submit to his kingship. The church is his bride, awaiting this future time.

4. The Holy Spirit sent by God is at work in the world, especially through the church, which is the **body of Christ** in the world.

The Spirit of the three-in-one God was at work in the world from the creation (Gen. 1:2) and was manifested powerfully through Jesus's ministry. After Jesus's ascension, God sent the Spirit to be his witness in the world, filling and empowering all Christians to be agents of the kingdom. It is only through the Spirit that people can follow and see Jesus for who he is. Jesus's Spirit-filled authority is transferred to his disciples, the church, the body of Christ. The Spirit-filled church individually and corporately is the primary means by which God continues Jesus's work in the world as his followers await the return of the king.

5. Jesus is the Full Human who teaches the true philosophy of the world.

   In addition to all the other claims about Jesus as divine and his priesthood and kingship, the New Testament makes clear that Jesus also completes God's creative project with humanity itself. Jesus is the second and perfect Adam who not only succeeds where Adam and Eve failed but also brings humanity to its intended *telos*, or end goal. Jesus embodies and models what true human flourishing looks like, and he teaches others to follow his way of being in the world so that they too might enter this fullness of life. Jesus teaches not just doctrines and morals but rather a whole way of seeing and being in the world—what people in his time meant by the term "philosophy." The New Testament and early Christianity claimed that Jesus was the True Philosopher of the world and that Christianity should be understood as the true philosophy for all humans, individually and corporately.

People

The first Christians were not created out of thin air but were real people living in the Second Temple period, complete with their own hopes, personalities, and worldviews. Obviously, most of Jesus's first disciples were Jewish people, as Jesus, the Jewish Messiah, traveled around Palestine teaching and preaching in synagogues, quoting and explaining the Jewish Scriptures. The early church continued this pattern, centered in Jerusalem at first and then, as it spread beyond Judea, within synagogues and Jewish communities (Acts 1:8). Yet from the beginning some gentiles sought out Jesus (Matt. 8:5–13; 15:21–28; Mark 7:24–30) and found healing and grace—Roman centurions, Samaritans, and Syrophoenicians. Many of these likely were God-fearers, as discussed above—gentiles who had some knowledge and interest in Judaism but not full knowledge. Judaism and Jerusalem continued to be the epicenter of Christianity until around AD 70, with James, the biological half brother of Jesus, as leader. But the apostles and disciples scattered far and wide so that the Christian church was soon composed of both Jews and gentiles together (Eph. 2:11–22), was more urban than rural, and was larger outside Palestine than within.

The New Testament speaks of many different people and roles within early Christianity. First are the apostles. The original apostles were the twelve that Jesus called out of the multitudes of disciples following him (Matt. 10:2; Luke 6:13), with Peter as the head. After Jesus's resurrection and ascension, the apostles appointed Matthias to replace the traitor Judas

Iscariot (Acts 1:26). These twelve apostles are described as the foundation of the church, of which Jesus is the cornerstone (Eph. 2:20; Rev. 21:14), and are said to be "first" in the church (1 Cor. 12:28), though this "firstness" means primarily the most persecuted and suffering, even unto death (1 Cor. 4:9). At the same time, some other leaders are also called apostles, most notably Paul (Rom. 1:1; Eph. 1:1), but also James (Gal. 1:19), Barnabas (Acts 14:14), Andronicus and Junia (Rom. 16:7), and others.

A second group of people in the church is prophets. Prophets were people filled with the Spirit who spoke words of direction and encouragement (Acts 15:32; 21:10; 1 Cor. 14:29–32; Eph. 3:5). There were prophets in the Old Testament whose writings became part of the canon. Prophets in the New Testament play an important role (1 Cor. 12:28; Eph. 4:11), though it seems that the role of Old Testament prophet is more comparable to New Testament apostles. The apostle Paul also mentions the role of **teachers** in the church (1 Cor. 12:28; Eph. 4:11; cf. James 3:1)—those who are skilled in explaining the Scriptures, like Apollos (Acts 18:24–28). Those who are responsible for overseeing the church in general, including the preaching of the word, are called **elders, pastors,** or **shepherds** (Acts 11:30; 15:2; 20:28; Eph. 4:11; Titus 1:5; James 5:14; 1 Pet. 5:1; 2 John 1). Helping with the practical service needs of the church were **deacons/deaconesses** (Acts 6:1–6; Rom. 16:1; 1 Tim. 3:8–13). One of the most striking things about early Christianity is that within its congregations was a wide mix of men, women, and children from all strata of society—the wealthy, slaves, Jews, Romans, Greeks, barbarians, soldiers, widows, orphans, the educated, the lowly, and the powerful—all welcome and all of equal rank and worth (Gal. 3:25–29). Together they are called the body of Christ, with different gifts and abilities but all united as one people (1 Cor. 12:12–31; Eph. 4:1–16). This body must be vigilant, because the potential for false apostles, false prophets, and false teachers is always present (Matt. 7:15–20; 24:24; Acts 20:28–30; 2 Cor. 11:13; 1 John 4:1–6; Rev. 2:2).

Culture

Because early Christianity was rooted in Judaism and existed in the Hellenized Jewish and Greco-Roman worlds, we should not be surprised to learn that its cultural habits overlapped with both worlds. Yet there was a newness within the Christian community, a transformation of many cultural values, that created a new kind of society. Indeed, Christianity's culture can be helpfully understood by how it stands in contrast with much of the society around it, both Jewish and Greco-Roman. For example, the experience of honor and shame was still central to the Christian worldview (as it was for both Jews and Romans), but it had been turned upside down. Christians honor and worship a man who was lowly, shamed, and crucified, and who by any worldly standard was unworthy. As a result, Christians embraced this same posture for themselves, not seeking their own glory and honor but boasting in Christ crucified (Gal. 6:14), being willing to be considered foolish and lowly in society—"The last will be first, and the first last" (Matt. 20:16). Additionally, the lowly and "lessers" of society (both Jewish and Roman)—such as orphans, widows, the poor, the sick, women, slaves, children—were valued, and even exalted, as equal members of society (Eph. 5:22–6:9; Col. 3:18–4:1; James 2:1–13).

Christian culture also took a different view of family and wealth. Early Christians, following Jesus's model, began to call one another "brother" and "sister," which reflected a radical new view of family and kinship. For Christians, one's biological family became of secondary importance compared to their new identity with one another in Christ (Matt. 12:46–50; 19:29; Luke 14:25–27). Regardless of ethnic origin, social status, or moral background, anyone following Christ became part of a family, the family of God. Similarly, the patron-client cultural-economic system was transformed by the Christian vision: God himself is seen as the great benefactor who gives abundantly, with his creatures as the recipients who in turn should help those in need by sharing wealth (Acts 2:44–46; 1 Tim. 6:17–19; James 1:27; 1 John 3:17).

Early Christianity adopted the Greco-Roman vision of *paideia*—educating people intellectually and morally for individual flourishing and to build a society of peace, with Jesus as the Philosopher or Pedagogue—but many of the values were transfigured. Instead of justice as the greatest virtue, or rhetorical ability as the greatest skill, Christians taught the highest virtue of love and compassion toward others, while rhetorical skill was supplanted by empowerment from the Holy Spirit. The **fruit of the Spirit**—love, joy, peace, patience, kindness, generosity, faithfulness, gentleness, self-control (Gal. 5:22–23)—became the measure of what it means to be a Christian.

All of this means that New Testament Christianity comes from and sits within the Jewish and Greco-Roman worlds but creates its own society and culture centered on the revelation of Jesus the Christ. Early Christians eventually talked about themselves as a third race, a new humanity, not because of their own

ⓘ **INTRODUCTORY MATTERS**

Rescuing Infants in the Roman Empire

In the first-century Roman Empire male children generally were considered more important than female, and the practice of infanticide—done by leaving infants outside, exposed to the elements to die—was not uncommon. Christians valued the life of all creatures and began to rescue such infants—sometimes only to give them a proper burial (as many funeral inscriptions show), or, if they lived, to adopt, raise, and educate them. Later, monasteries often took on this responsibility of caring for and raising orphans. The result from the early days of the church was that Christianity grew, especially among women, as the faith gained a reputation for compassion and care for those in need.

greatness but because of their identity with Jesus. The writings of the New Testament make much more sense when read with this complex symbolic world as their backdrop. ①

Christian Reading Questions

1. How does understanding the "symbolic world" of the New Testament influence your reading of the New Testament? Give a specific example of a particular passage that opens up when you understand it within its "symbolic world."

2. Read Matthew 2. How does learning about the background of the Herodian dynasty in the Second Temple period help you to understand the situation behind the visit of the magi and Joseph and Mary's flight to Egypt?

3. This chapter mentions many texts written within several hundred years of the Bible (the Old Testament Pseudepigrapha, the Talmuds, the writings of Josephus and Philo, Greek philosophy, etc.). Why do you think it is important to have knowledge of these texts in addition to the Bible?

4. Read the parable of the laborers in the vineyard (Matt. 20:1–16) in light of the cultural values of honor-shame dynamics and patron-client relationships. How does this cultural information inform your reading?

CHAPTER FOUR

Jesus's Life and Teaching

Jesus the Christ—Founder and Focus of Christianity

Whatever else Christianity was or is—in its best versions and at the church's worst moments—there is no Christianity without the person of Jesus. And by the "person of Jesus" we mean two things simultaneously: (1) the historical Jewish man who lived in Palestine for a few decades around 6 BC–AD 30; (2) the incarnate Second Person of the Triune God of Christianity, who is worshiped and obeyed by millions of people throughout the world.

Judaism has had countless rabbis and leaders, some of whom are especially important (Abraham, Moses, David, Isaiah), as has Christianity (Peter, Paul, Augustine, Aquinas, Luther, Calvin, Edwards, Barth). But Judaism can continue apart from any individual leader or teacher because it is codified primarily in a history, a tradition, and books of instructions. Christianity, by contrast, has always been and will forever be focused on a singular person who ultimately defines and incarnates the faith. The book of Christianity, the Bible, is crucial to Christianity's existence, but the essence of Christianity is God revealed to the world through the person of Jesus. Taken as a whole, the New Testament paints a rich and complex picture of how Christianity understands the world. But whatever picture we perceive from our study of the New Testament, it must primarily depict Jesus the person before it outlines a set of doctrines or moral instructions (as important as those are).

This chapter is split into two parts, corresponding to the dual reality of who Jesus is. First, we will examine Jesus's life and activities while he lived (and died) on the earth. Second, we will explore the theological content of his message and the message about him according to the apostles. This harmonized sketch will provide a guiding trajectory to be traced in more detail throughout the rest of the book. ①

Jesus's Life, Death, and New Life

During Jesus's own day, and even throughout the first century AD, few people outside the Christian community wrote anything substantive about Jesus. We have only occasional references from other historians at the time such as Josephus, Tacitus, and Suetonius, as well as some critical remarks in the Jewish literature. This lack of literature is understandable, however, because while Christianity did spread rapidly among a wide variety of people, it was not until the second and third centuries that it had become so extensive and influential that rulers, philosophers, and other literate people had to take notice. Therefore, our primary resource for understanding Jesus's life comes from the New Testament itself.

Jesus's Beginnings

Nearly all modern biographies of famous individuals begin with their background and childhood. This was generally true of biographies in the ancient world as well. Of our four canonical Gospels, two of them provide this kind of background information (Matthew and Luke), while the other two begin Jesus's story with his adult actions (Mark and John). In fact, on the assumption that Mark was written first, it probably was this lack of information about Jesus's origins that in part inspired Matthew and Luke to write their own, fuller Gospel accounts, which include several stories about the events surrounding Jesus's birth.

The first thing to note about Jesus's early life is that, even though it is his birth that would later become the way that Western civilization divides human history into BC and AD, Jesus almost certainly was born in what we would call 6 BC, not AD 1. On the surface this seems like an impossibility (like dry water), that Jesus was born six years "before Christ." The problem is simply that when people in the Middle Ages created the calendar system that we now use, they did not have as much information as we now do about how to calculate these ancient dates. They were close, but we have now been able to discern—based on aspects of Jewish and

---

INTRODUCTORY MATTERS ⓘ

Jesus's Life and Death
(Approximate dates)

6 BC—Jesus is born in Bethlehem

4 BC—**Magi** arrive and offer gifts

AD 6—Jesus as a young man in the temple

AD 26—Jesus's adult ministry begins

AD 30—Jesus dies on a cross and is resurrected

Roman history—that Jesus was born somewhere around 6 BC and died around AD 30. ⓘ

Melding pieces from Matthew and Luke together with general historical information, we can offer a rough sketch of Jesus's birth and childhood. Herod the Great ruled over the Jewish people from Jerusalem as a vassal of the Roman Empire during the years 37–4 BC. Somewhere around 7 BC the angel Gabriel appeared to Zechariah, an old Jewish priest who was performing his duties in the Jerusalem temple (Luke 1:8–12). Gabriel told Zechariah that he and his wife would have a son who would grow up to be a great prophet (Luke 1:13–17). Gabriel then appeared to a young woman named Mary and informed her that, although she was a virgin, she would have a child who would be God's own Son (Luke 1:26–33). Mary was engaged to a good and gracious man named Joseph, and when he found out that Mary was pregnant, and knowing that the child was not his, he planned to end their engagement privately (Matt. 1:18–19). But an angel appeared to Joseph and told him that he should stay with Mary, that this was God's work, and that their son's name would be Jesus (Matt. 1:20–25).

Around 6 BC, when Mary was close to delivering this mysterious son, she and Joseph were forced to travel south to Bethlehem to register for the Roman census (Luke 2:1–5). While there, in this crowded and chaotic time, Mary gave birth to Jesus in a stable (Luke 2:6–7). Angels appeared to some shepherds in the fields and announced this miraculous birth, and the shepherds came in amazement to find the child (Luke 2:8–20). On the same

What Was the Star of Bethlehem?

Christmas carols and cards regularly include the image of the star of Bethlehem—a star shining its light down onto the stable where Jesus was born. We know that something appeared in the sky that prompted the magi to begin their journey from the east to Jerusalem (Matt. 2:2). We also know that when they got to Bethlehem, this same star somehow "led them" and guided them directly to Jesus (Matt. 2:9).

Some have suggested an astronomical phenomenon, such as a supernova, to explain this. It is difficult to understand, however, how a "star" or supernova would lead and guide anyone to a specific house.

The key is to understand that in many ancient texts, both outside Judaism and within, stars were understood as animate beings, typically represented as angels. The biblical accounts share the same understanding, with the "host of heaven" simultaneously referring to stars and angels (Ps. 148:1–4; Rev. 1:20; 9:1). Especially in light of the angelic activity in all the surrounding stories, Matthew's original readers would have understood the star of Bethlehem to be an angel sent by God as part of the revelatory acts surrounding Jesus's birth.

Figure 4.1. View of Bethlehem from the Shepherds' Field

night, some fifteen hundred miles away, some **sages** in Babylon witnessed something in the heavens that made them realize that a king had been born (Matt. 2:2). Seven days later, Joseph and Mary took Jesus to Jerusalem for the required circumcision and other temple rituals, where they met two elderly saints who blessed them and prophesied over the child (Luke 2:21–38).

Some months later, the foreign sages from Babylon arrived in Jerusalem and inquired at Herod's court regarding the king who had been born, assuming from their research that this child would be king of the Jewish people. The paranoid despot Herod was greatly disturbed and sent the sages to find the child, under the pretense that he wanted to honor this newborn king as well (Matt. 2:1–8), though in fact he planned to murder him. Through consulting the Jewish Scriptures and by the reappearance of a star in the heavens (probably an angelic appearance again) the sages found Joseph, Mary, and the young Jesus in their house, and they bowed down in reverence, giving the young family royal gifts. An angel then warned them in a dream not to return to Herod (Matt. 2:9–12). When Herod learned of this, he sent troops to kill all the young boys in Bethlehem to make sure he would destroy any claimant to the throne. On the night before this massacre the angel appeared once again and warned Mary and Joseph to flee. They escaped to Egypt and lived among the Jewish community there (Matt. 2:13–15).

Eventually Mary and Joseph heard that Herod the Great had died (4 BC) and were told by an angel to return to Israel. They decided not to return to Bethlehem, because one of Herod's sons was now reigning in that area. So they went as far away as they could within Palestine—Nazareth in Galilee

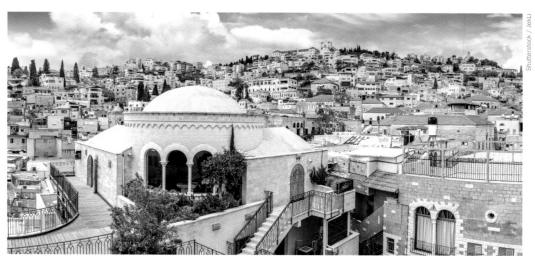
Figure 4.2. View of Nazareth

Other Infancy and Childhood Stories about Jesus

As Jesus's fame grew and the influence of Christianity spread, many Christians were un-satisfied with the relatively few stories about Jesus's infancy and childhood. As a result, some people, probably with good motives, wrote additional stories that filled in more details about Jesus's early life. These accounts are not considered inspired or authoritative by the church, but they were popular enough to be preserved in books and to inspire sacred art. These books include the Infancy Gospel of Thomas and the Protevangelium of James. The Infancy Gospel of Thomas, which is Gnostic in origin, describes many miracles performed by Jesus but depicts him as an ornery and arrogant miracle worker, healing and raising the dead but in constant conflict with people. The Protevangelium of James has a different feel and is more expan-sive, filling in details before and after Jesus's birth, such as the birth of Mary his mother, the birthplace of Jesus being a cave, Mary's perpetual virginity (even after giving birth to Jesus), and the death of Zechariah during Herod's slaughter of the young boys.

Figure 4.3. *The Adoration of the Shepherds* by Bartolo di Fredi

in the north. Therefore, although he was in the line of David and born in Bethlehem near Jerusalem, Jesus grew up as a Galilean (Matt. 2:19–23).

We know little about Jesus's childhood and young adulthood. The only story the Gospels tell us comes from when Jesus was twelve years old, on a trip with his parents to Jerusalem. As their group of travelers began the journey home, Jesus, unbe-known to his parents, stayed behind in Jerusalem, conversing with the rabbis in the temple, proving to be a young man of wisdom and piety beyond his years (Luke 2:41–52).

This brief sketch of Jesus's birth and early years shows him to be something more than a typical human. His conception was a unique miracle ("by the Holy Spirit"), and his birth was foretold as the harbinger of great change in the world. But then there is silence for a long time. We know almost nothing about what happened between these events and Jesus's sudden appearance as a prophet and preacher, at around the age of thirty to thirty-three. ⓘ

Jesus's Ministry

Apart from the brief birth narratives and the one Lukan story about Jesus as a twelve-year-old, the Gospels focus almost all their attention on Jesus's ministry as an adult, starting when he was somewhere around thirty to thirty-three years old. Just as we don't have precise dates for his age, we also don't know the exact length of Jesus's minis-try. But using references to various Jewish festivals in the Gospel of John, we can reasonably calculate that Jesus taught and preached for about three or three and a half years before he was arrested, tried, and crucified in Jerusalem, around AD 30. ⓘ

The basic shape of the adult Jesus's ministry is consistent across all four Gospel accounts. First, we meet a wilderness dweller nicknamed John the Baptizer. John was sent by God as a prophetic herald before Jesus came, calling people to repent in light of the coming kingdom of God (Matt. 3:1–3; John 1:6–8). Amid John's widespread popularity and influence, preaching and baptizing people on the banks of the famous Jordan River, Jesus himself showed up and submitted himself to John's ritual baptism (Matt. 3:13–15). But unlike any other person baptized, when Jesus emerged from the water, a voice from heaven declared his sonship, while a dove descended and alighted on him as a sign of God's favor (Matt. 3:16–17; Luke 3:21–22; John 1:32). These momentous events set the stage for Jesus's own ministry, which would soon eclipse and supersede John's preparatory work. But there was one more important experience that Jesus needed to undergo before he began teaching and preaching: he had to be tested and tried. Led by God's Spirit, Jesus spent forty days and nights in the Judean desert, fasting and praying. At the end of this time God's ancient enemy, Satan, attempted to thwart Jesus's ministry by tempting him to not completely obey God the Father (Matt. 4:1–11; Mark 1:12–13; Luke 4:1–13). Having successfully resisted these temptations, Jesus then began his public ministry of preaching, teaching, healing, and calling people to become his disciples.

It is these central activities—preaching, teaching, healing, and discipling—that mark Jesus's ministry. All of these activities are performed under the banner of "the kingdom of God." Jesus's preaching and teaching explain what the kingdom is; Jesus's healing of multitudes of people foreshadows the restoration and redemption of humanity in God's coming kingdom; and the calling of disciples reshapes people's values, sensibilities, habits, and hearts in ways that accord with the imminent coming of God's reign.

Did Jesus Have Emotions?

Some Christians throughout history have thought of Jesus as emotionless, a stoic figure. But as John Calvin remarked, "Those who imagine that the Son of God was exempt from human passions [emotions], do not truly and seriously acknowledge him to be a man."[1] That is, Jesus's true and full humanity means necessarily that he experienced this crucial aspect of what it means to be human—to have emotions.

The Gospels show that Jesus, as a fully human man, did indeed experience emotions. We know that he had feelings such as hunger, thirst, weariness, and physical pain. Jesus also wept, moaned, wailed, sighed, chided, and rejoiced. The Gospels highlight three of Jesus's emotions particularly:

Compassion—The most frequently mentioned emotion of Jesus is compassion, which in Greek communicates the internal feeling of pity and the external act of kindness to meet others' needs. This compassion includes sighs and sadness at the pain and affliction of others. Regularly in the Gospels, Jesus's compassion is cited as the reason he healed and cared for so many people (Matt. 9:36; 14:14; 15:32; 20:34; Mark 8:2–3; Luke 7:13).

Anger—While there is an ungodly kind of anger that is never attributed to Jesus, there is also an appropriate form of anger that rises in response to moral injustice or deceit. In instances like Mark 3:5 and 10:14 Jesus is rightly indignant at the Jewish leaders' lack of compassion for those in need, and at his own disciples for preventing those in need from accessing him. Jesus's cleansing/cursing of the temple is also an example of his righteous anger (Matt. 21:12–17; Mark 11:15–19; Luke 19:45–47; John 2:14–16).

Joy—Even though Jesus is often depicted as somber and sorrowful in sacred art and in our imaginations, this is not how he is generally described in the Gospels. Rather, he is regularly shown to be announcing "good news" and giving thanks to God, as experiencing joy and desiring his disciples to share in his joy (John 15:11; 17:13). Moreover, most people loved Jesus and wanted to be around him, indicating that he must have been not stern and off-putting but welcoming and joyful.

While calling people such as fishermen, tax collectors, and others to be his followers, Jesus miraculously healed masses of Jews and gentiles. He became known as compassionate and loving, welcoming the broken, the outcasts, and the moral, physical, and economic "lessers" of society. Jesus, empowered by the Holy Spirit, performed other miracles, which were signs of God's favor on him. These included walking on water, calming a storm at sea, multiplying bread and fish, and raising people from the dead (Matt. 14:22–33; Mark 4:35–41; 5:21–43; Luke 7:11–17; John 6:1–15; 11:1–44). These miracles, often performed only in the presence of his closest disciples, were done not to draw large crowds but to meet the needs of people and to testify to Jesus's unique and authoritative role as God's Son on the earth. In the midst of this regular ministry of miraculous healings, Jesus continually taught what the kingdom of God is like. He regularly insisted that his main purpose in coming was not simply to heal people but to call people into a life of **discipleship** based on his teaching about God's soon-to-be-here reign. Thus, his preaching, teaching, healing, and discipling were all rooted in the great reality of the kingdom of God. ⓘ

Jesus's Death and New Life

The preceding description of Jesus's loving and compassionate ministry is very positive, and we would assume it was received happily by everyone. However, from nearly the very beginning of Jesus's public life he was questioned, opposed, maligned, and ultimately entrapped by the Jewish religious leaders of his day. Both the political and theological leaders smelled trouble with this extremely popular Jesus. Not only were crowds flocking to him, following him, and openly turning their confident hopes to a future time when he would become their king, but also Jesus himself stirred up dissent by openly criticizing the Jewish leaders and many of their most cherished traditions. In this, Jesus showed up as more than a wisdom teacher and miraculous healer; he was also a God-sent prophet. And just like the fate of many of the prophets of the Old Testament, Jesus the prophet faced great opposition and resistance from the very people he was sent to help.

This opposition came to a boiling point in the spring of AD 30, around the time of the Feast of Passover. For some weeks Jesus and his disciples had been heading south to Jerusalem to celebrate this important festival. Along the way he repeatedly predicted that this was going to be their last trip to Jerusalem because there he would be betrayed, captured, tried, and killed (Matt. 16:21–23; Mark 8:31–33; cf. John 13:18–30). And so it came to pass.

Jesus arrived in Jerusalem a week before the Passover amid great fanfare and consternation. The fanfare came from the multitudes of Galileans and other disciples who were following Jesus. They believed Jesus to be the long-awaited **Son of David**, who would restore God's reign on the earth. As Jesus approached Jerusalem, the city of David, they were inspired to give him the royal welcome they believed he deserved. This event is still celebrated today as Palm Sunday, because Jesus's disciples ripped down palm fronds and laid them on the road in front of the donkey-riding Jesus as they sang and shouted their celebration. But not all shared their enthusiasm. The Jerusalemites in general, and the Jewish leadership in particular, saw Jesus's entry into Jerusalem as a threat to their stability and likely to bring punishment from the Roman rulers and soldiers. Moreover, they believed Jesus to be an impostor at best and demonically possessed at worst.

What Jesus did next only amplified the opposition, frustration, and anger against him. More than a passive recipient of all this praise, commotion, and hope, Jesus once again donned his prophetic mantle and proceeded to disrupt the everyday temple activities. Shockingly, he turned over money tables and broke open the containers holding the sacrificial animals, all while criticizing the Jewish leaders for their **hypocrisy** and failed leadership of God's people and temple. The leaders would have gladly arrested and killed Jesus on the spot, but his popularity prevented such bold force. The leaders needed to scheme a way to dispose of Jesus quietly. They found it in Judas Iscariot, one of the twelve disciples, who chose to betray Jesus. For the price of thirty pieces of silver Judas arranged for the Jewish leaders and their soldiers to capture Jesus while he was praying at night in an enclosed, private garden called Gethsemane.

Jesus knew that his time was limited, so he gathered his twelve closest disciples for a final celebration of the Jewish Passover meal together. This **Last Supper** night was very important, with Jesus teaching about his impending death and giving instructions for the future of his disciples to be people of love and service to one another.

After their meal was over, Jesus led his disciples to the garden to pray. The Jewish leaders arrived with armed soldiers. After Judas identified Jesus by greeting him with a kiss, the soldiers proceeded to arrest him. Jesus's lead disciple, Peter, attempted to prevent the arrest by employing his sword and cutting off the ear of the high priest's servant. Jesus rebuked Peter and prevented his disciples from trying to stop the events. Jesus was then bound and taken away while all his disciples fled in fear for their lives, abandoning Jesus as he predicted they would (Matt. 26:31–56; Mark 14:50; John 16:32).

After Jesus was betrayed and abandoned, he spent a long night being shuffled among various leaders, all the while being questioned, mocked, and beaten. First he was interrogated by the former high priest Annas, while the Jewish leadership council (the **Sanhedrin**) gathered. The Sanhedrin and the ruling high priest, Caiaphas, questioned him all night until he was handed over to the Roman governor, Pilate, in hope of a treason charge. Pilate assessed him and then sent him to the Jewish governor, Herod, who questioned him and then returned him to Pilate. Pilate somewhat reluctantly presented Jesus to the Jewish masses as a candidate to be released. The crowds, however, at the instigation of the Jewish leaders, demanded Jesus's crucifixion. Pilate ordered Jesus to be whipped—a torture that included Roman soldiers mocking and beating him.

During these painful hours, which continued into the dawn, Jesus's disciples were terrified of being arrested themselves. Judas regretted his betrayal of Jesus and hanged himself, while Peter tried to follow Jesus's movements. But when Peter was identified as a follower of Jesus, he three times denied it, thus failing to be a faithful witness. The rest of the disciples fled, with the exception of several women who stayed nearby.

Jesus was taken outside the city walls to a place called **Golgotha**, where he was nailed to a wooden cross and hung until he suffocated or bled out.

Figure 4.4. The Tower of David in the Old City of Jerusalem

At noon the sky went dark and remained so until about three in the afternoon, when Jesus cried out and died, at which time an earthquake occurred and the temple curtain was torn in two. A soldier pierced Jesus's side with a spear to make sure he was dead, and then Jesus was removed from the cross and buried in a garden tomb provided by Joseph of Arimathea, a wealthy disciple.

Jesus's disciples were shocked and devastated and went into hiding. On the Sunday morning after these events, some of the women disciples went to Jesus's tomb and found it opened and Jesus's body gone. They thought that his body had been stolen, until an angel appeared to them and announced that Jesus had been raised from the dead by God. Jesus himself then appeared to Mary Magdalene and a small group of other women. The women ran back to the eleven disciples to tell them of Jesus's resurrection. The disciples too found the grave empty, but then Jesus appeared to them several times in various places over a forty-day period, proving that he was alive with a resurrected physical body. He proceeded to appear to a variety of disciples, including the instance in which he restored the failed Peter to his place of leadership among the disciples (Luke 24:13–43; John 20:24–29; 21:15–17; 1 Cor. 15:7). Jesus commissioned his disciples to go throughout the world and make disciples in his name, teaching what he had taught them. After this, Jesus ascended to heaven in the sight of the disciples. About a week later the Holy Spirit came upon Jesus's disciples at the **Feast of Pentecost**, beginning the ministry of the church.

Figure 4.5. Golgotha in Jerusalem

Jesus's Message and the Message about Jesus

In the previous section we offered a historical sketch of Jesus's life from the perspective of the Gospels—that is, an outline of Jesus's life, death, resurrection, and ascension, focusing on what Jesus *did* and what happened as a result.

In this section we can now offer another sketch, this time focusing on what Jesus *taught*, along with what the Gospel writers teach about Jesus. Jesus had a message that the Gospel writers have recorded for us. But beyond merely recording what Jesus taught, the Gospel writers also teach readers how to understand what Jesus said and who Jesus was. Thus, we can speak about both Jesus's message and the message about Jesus.

Jesus's Message—The Themes of Jesus's Teaching

Over the course of his three-year ministry Jesus traversed many miles all over Palestine, always teaching and preaching along the way. Often he taught in the Jewish synagogues, and when the crowds and opposition grew too large, he preached from hillsides and harbor boats so that the multitudes could hear him. He also privately taught certain things only to his closest disciples, such as the meaning of his parables and the instructions he gave at their final supper.

The one consistent response to Jesus was amazement at his words, both for their immediately apparent authority and for their shocking content. Additionally, Jesus's teaching was regularly accompanied by miraculous healings, adding to his credibility. Moreover, when the obviously more-learned religious leaders and teachers tried to refute this son of a tradesman, Jesus consistently showed himself to be wise, bold, and steeped in the wisdom of God. All of this meant that people hung on Jesus's every word, memorizing what he said and then eventually writing down his sayings and teachings. From the Gospel records we can discern several main themes.

1. The kingdom of God / kingdom of heaven

Central to Jesus's teaching was the kingdom of God (which Matthew usually calls the **kingdom of heaven**). The kingdom refers to the space and time of God's absolute, just, and good rule over the whole world, where he is present as king, where justice and peace rule, and where evil, pain, and death are vanquished. This biblical description of the kingdom of God makes it immediately apparent that this reality is at the same time true now and not yet fully realized. God does rule over all the world, and at the same time, mysteriously, he has not yet chosen to completely vanquish death and evil; his presence is not fully known in the world. The difference between the now and the yet to come of the kingdom is most easily summarized in the heart of the **Lord's Prayer**, which is central to the Christian's life during this time of waiting.

Jesus's teaching about the kingdom of God consisted of two elements. First, during his earthly ministry Jesus was constantly preaching that this kingdom is "at hand," meaning that it is about to come from heaven to earth through his own actions. The incarnation, life, death, resurrection, and ascension of Jesus brought the kingdom into its "at hand" / "already but not fully yet" state.

Second, Jesus's kingdom teaching continually described what life in God's kingdom should and will look like. Jesus taught many parables and portrayed vivid images of what God will do to heal the world when his kingdom comes (exalt the humble, humble the proud, destroy evil and death) and what the citizens of the kingdom will be like (loving, forgiving, peacemaking, joyful). Thus, Jesus's repeated emphasis on the kingdom of God is central to Christianity's hope for the future and shape of life now. ⓘ

2. Eternal life

Jesus also regularly taught about inheriting, receiving, and entering into eternal life. To modern Christians this may sound like Jesus is talking about an angelic existence in heaven. But "eternal life" in the Bible is simply another way of describing life in the kingdom of God, a flourishing life that never ends ("eternal"). Both the "kingdom" and "eternal life" refer to the new age when God will return to the world to be present and to rule fully. In the Synoptic Gospels (Matthew, Mark, and Luke) Jesus primarily talks about the kingdom, but he does also refer to eternal life. The Gospel of John does the reverse: John refers to the kingdom a few times but prefers instead to talk about eternal life. In both cases the descriptions and point are the same: there is an era coming through Jesus that will permanently change the whole world. Therefore, those who believe and trust in Jesus must align themselves with him, and his way of being in the world, so that they might enter into this everlasting good life in the kingdom when Jesus returns from the Father at the end of this current age.

3. **The true and greater righteousness**

Closely related to Jesus's teachings about the kingdom and eternal life is the theme of true and greater **righteousness**. The true form of godliness or righteousness that Jesus taught is another way of describing the picture of life together in God's kingdom. According to Jesus, the righteous or godly life can be summed up most comprehensively with one word, "love." According to the two greatest commandments from God (Matt. 22:36–40), this love has two necessary directions: vertical toward God and horizontal toward others. Together, love for God and love for others form the summary of all God's will and law in the world. Love for God looks like piety that is honest, authentic, directed toward God as a good Father, and comes from the heart, the whole person, not just being exterior in form. Love for others looks like compassion toward all, mercy for those in need, and forgiveness for those who have wronged and even persecuted you. Jesus constantly called people to this way of eternal kingdom life or true righteousness, not in a mechanistic or legalistic way, but as an invitation for people to experience fullness of life through God, both now and in the age to come.

4. **Salvation coming for all who respond in faith**

One of the most shocking aspects of (the Jewish) Jesus's teaching was that the kingdom, eternal life, and true righteousness are available to *all* people of the world regardless of ethnicity, moral background, gender, education, or status. **Salvation** is for anyone and everyone who has ears to hear Jesus's call and for whoever responds to him in faith and faithfulness. This theme in Jesus's teaching was the cause of much of the conflict and opposition he faced, and it becomes foundational to Christians' self-understanding in distinction from Judaism. The Jewish leadership resented and rejected this idea in Jesus's teaching, both because it made gentiles equal to Jews and because it offered forgiveness to notoriously sinful people who do not meet the Jewish standards of righteousness. The implications of this teaching reverberate throughout the rest of the New Testament and became the focus of a heated debate in the first century: the relationship between Jews (and the Mosaic law) and gentiles in the new covenant.

5. **The call to a life of discipleship**

   Perhaps the most comprehensive way to describe Jesus's teaching is his call to a life of discipleship. This call to discipleship is the invitation to follow Jesus's own ultimate example of humility, righteous suffering, and love. Jesus both teaches and models God's nature and values: favoring the poor over the rich, the meek over the powerful, the humble over the proud, the wholehearted over the superficial. No servant is greater than his or her master (Matt. 10:24–25; John 13:16; 15:20), and thus, as Jesus was obedient to God's will, even amid suffering, so too must his disciples be. Understanding Jesus's teachings means learning a way of seeing the world, and a way of being in the world, that accords with God's nature, will, and coming kingdom, all revealed through Jesus Christ.

The Message about Jesus—The Gospels' Interpretation of Jesus

As we have noted above, there are two levels of teaching detected in the Gospels: the things Jesus himself taught *and* the lessons the Gospel writers are teaching about Jesus. These are not in contradiction with each other, but rather, taken together, they provide multilayered instruction. The Gospels not only record what Jesus said but also provide the church's understanding of who he was and what he accomplished. (See more about the Gospels in chap. 5.)

The primary question that the Gospel writers seek to answer is the biggest one of all—Who is this man Jesus? Their answer to this central question is multiform.

1. **Teacher, sage, philosopher**

   Jesus's primary earthly activity was instruction. Everywhere he went, he was teaching and preaching about God's kingdom. In all his teaching, Jesus's wisdom and authority were evident to everyone, even his enemies. His teaching style also marked him as a sage, a teacher of wisdom: Jesus used many pithy and memorable sayings and taught with mysterious parables, rich in images and stories. In all of this, the Gospel writers show that Jesus could be considered a philosopher of his day—a sage-teacher who showed people how to live, calling people to become disciples of his wisdom. ⓘ

2. Apocalyptic prophet

In addition to being a sage/philosopher, inviting people to a life of wisdom, Jesus was also an apocalyptic prophet—one who announced God's judgment on unfaithfulness and sin (prophet) and one who brought knowledge revealed only by God (apocalyptic). In this, the Gospel writers present Jesus as one sent by God in line with the many prophets of the Old Testament as well as of Second Temple Judaism (see chap. 3). Throughout the history of Israel God regularly sent prophets to call people to repent and to realign their lives with God's will. They often performed symbolic prophetic acts that pictured God's judgment, such as Ezekiel lying on his side next to an image of Jerusalem on a clay tablet or shaving his head and beard with a sword and dividing the hair into three piles (Ezek. 4:1–4; 5:1–2). The Gospel writers likewise recount several things Jesus did that were symbolic, especially his violent cleansing of the temple in judgment (Matt. 21:12–13; Mark 11:15–17; Luke 19:45–46; John 2:13–17).

In the Second Temple period God's prophets often took the form of teachers who invited God's people to lives oriented around his kingdom, based on revealed wisdom about the coming future when God would return. The Gospel writers present Jesus in a way that any first-century Jew would have understood him as such an apocalyptic prophet.

3. Healer and exorcist

Less prominent only than Jesus's teaching and prophetic activities was his work as a healer and exorcist. The Gospel writers report that Jesus regularly healed people of various diseases and delivered them from demonic bondage (exorcism).

Figure 4.6. *Madonna and Child* (possibly 1230s) by Berlinghiero, portraying the child Jesus dressed like a philosopher and holding a scroll

In this, Jesus is regularly described as full of compassion for humanity's brokenness and bondage.

We have general accounts of multitudes coming to Jesus and receiving healing (Matt. 4:23–25). We also have many specific, more detailed stories about instances of healings and exorcisms that the Gospel writers use to teach about Jesus's authority more directly.

Jesus's healings and exorcisms offer testimony to his power and prophetic status, but even more, they are designed as a foretaste of what the kingdom of God will be like when it comes fully upon the earth. The kingdom of God will be the realm in which God will restore his people to health and flourishing, and the dominion of evil and Satan will be destroyed forever. At the height of this real-and-symbolic meaning of Jesus's healings are the instances in which he raised people from the dead (Mark 5:35–43; Luke 7:11–17), with Lazarus being the most striking example (John 11:1–44). The raising of these people from the dead typifies Jesus's work in the world—to bring life where there has been death.

4. Promised messianic king

There are many important titles used of Jesus in the Gospels, one of which is Christ. This is not Jesus's last name but rather a title that refers to his role as the one anointed by the Holy Spirit to be the king of God's kingdom. "Christ" is the English word that comes from the Greek word for "anointed," which itself is the translation for the Hebrew word that we translate as "Messiah." Thus, Christ, Messiah, and Anointed One all communicate the same idea: Jesus is set apart by God to be his good king over his people.

The Gospel writers regularly describe Jesus as the Son of David (beginning with the first verse of the New Testament, Matt. 1:1), which is shorthand for Jesus's role as the Messiah, who has come to fulfill the promises made to Israel—that God would bring a descendant of King David to rule and reign over his people and restore their lives to flourishing and peace. This was the great hope of the Jewish people, especially in the five hundred years leading up to Jesus's day. Jesus's announcement of the kingdom of God taps into this hope. By Jesus's actions and words, the Gospels repeatedly show that he is the promised messianic king who is coming to bring to the whole world (not just Israel) the blessings of God, fulfilling the promise to Abraham that God would bless all nations through him (Gen. 12:1–3).

5. Unique Son of God

From beginning to end the Gospel writers' primary answer to the question of Jesus's identity is that he is the Son of God. This broad description "son of God" could be used in a number of ways: it could refer to a creature of God like Adam (Luke 3:38, based on Gen. 5:1), to a people group like Israel (Exod. 4:22), or to a child of God by faith (Matt. 5:9). But the claims made about Jesus are far higher and more expansive than these senses: Jesus is the unique, beloved Son of God, who is not created but who shares the divine identity, who is the final and true arbiter of God's knowledge and wisdom in the world, the Messiah, who is the fulfillment of all the promises, hopes, and images of God's saving work in the world, and who exists in a unique father-son relationship with the God of Israel.

At the nuclear core of Christianity is this understanding, and the Gospels provide the framework for the church's focus on Jesus. Thus, in the Gospels we find a wide variety of titles used to describe Jesus: Christ, Son of God, **Son of Man**, Son of David, Lord, Emmanuel, the Word. Each of these contributes to the manifold portrait of who Jesus is, but at the core of all the Gospels' witness is Jesus's unique sonship to God the Father.

6. **Sacrificial suffering servant**

The narrative arc of all four Gospels finds its height in Jesus's suffering and death. Each of the Gospel stories slows down considerably and spends a significant percentage of literary space on the last week of Jesus's life and his agonizing death. This highlights a key aspect of Jesus's identity: he came to offer his life in suffering as a sacrifice. Jesus willingly took the role of Isaiah's promised suffering servant, who would come to bear our griefs and carry our sorrows: "He was pierced for our transgressions; he was crushed for our iniquities; upon him was the chastisement that brought us peace, and with his wounds we are healed" (Isa. 53:5 ESV). Jesus and the Gospel writers explicitly understand his ministry through this lens. In his opening chapter Matthew describes Jesus as coming to "save his people from their sins" (Matt. 1:21), and at the crucial moments of the Last Supper Jesus explains that through his body-and-blood sacrifice he is bringing about a new covenant for the forgiveness of sins (Matt. 26:27–29). Thus, central to the Gospel writers' description of Jesus is his role as the sacrificial suffering servant.

7. **Resurrected One**

If the height of the Gospels' narrative arc is Jesus's suffering and death, its resolution is his resurrection from the dead. Jesus's suffering and death serves as a model of righteous endurance and faithfulness to God in the midst of undue suffering. But according to the Gospels, it is more than just a model; it is the beginning of the new age, the kingdom of God. Jesus is not only the Crucified One, but just as importantly, he is the Resurrected One—the first person of the new age to be born again, to be resurrected from the dead as the pioneer who makes resurrection possible for all God's children.

The Gospel writers, along with the rest of the New Testament, make it clear that it is Jesus's resurrection that is central to the Christian understanding, because it is through his resurrection and ascension that new life enters the world. Jesus as the Resurrected One also means that he is present with his people for their mission in the world (Matt. 28:20).

In Sum

Christianity is centered on a person who is understood to be both God and human. Thus, Jesus's life and teachings are central to what Christianity is. Jesus's real, historical life matters to Christianity, as do the things he taught and what the disciples taught about him. This chapter has provided an overview of the historical and theological Jesus, drawn from all four Gospels. But as we will see in the following chapters, a sketch like this is not meant to replace the more important study of each of the four Gospels and the rest of the New Testament for what each of them contributes to our understanding. This overview is but the invitation to a deeper study of the New Testament.

Christian Reading Questions

1. Why does it matter that we understand Jesus's historical life?
2. Read Matthew 9:36; Luke 19:45–47; John 15:11. How do the emotions expressed by Jesus in each of these stories influence the way you understand him?
3. Read the parable of the prodigal son (Luke 15:11–32). How do you think that Jesus's use of this story, rather than moral exhortation (like in the Sermon on the Mount) or another form of teaching, served his goals in teaching people?
4. Many Bibles today delineate the spoken words of Jesus with red letters. Early in the church's life "sayings collections," composed almost exclusively of Jesus's sayings without any narrative scaffolding, began to circulate. Why do you think it is important that the Fourfold Gospel Book that we have received today includes both Jesus's teachings and the narrative describing his life?

CHAPTER FIVE

The Fourfold Gospel Book

What Is a Gospel?

In terms of both influence and literary space, the canonical Gospels (Matthew, Mark, Luke, and John) are the primary documents of the New Testament. Together the four Gospels make up almost 45 percent of the New Testament, and they have long stood at the head of the New Testament's canon of sacred literature. The Gospels have been primary in influence because Christianity is above all else a call to follow a particular person, Jesus of Nazareth, who claimed to be the promised Jewish Messiah and the true king of the whole world. Christianity has always understood itself as a call to believe in, give allegiance to, and worship a certain *person*, not just an invisible god or an intangible and impersonal set of beliefs. Therefore, the Gospel stories about him have played a central role.

This radical belief that Jesus is the incarnation of God means that his actions, teachings, and example are all essential to what Christianity is and what Christians most need to know. Doctrinal teachings about the theological significance of Jesus's death and resurrection are central to Christianity as well, but to be a disciple/follower requires more than theological head knowledge about what Jesus did. Christians need to know Jesus the person. Therefore, early Christians wrote what was needed: biographies that record events and teachings about Jesus in story form and that show, not just tell, who this Jesus is. This is what the canonical Gospels are—theological biographies.

Ancient Christians are not the only ones who have cared about biographies. People throughout all ages, including today, have been fascinated by other people's stories, especially famous and influential figures—athletes, actors, politicians, innovators, religious leaders, artists, and great intellectuals. In the Greek and Roman culture of the first century AD, when Christianity was born and growing into all the world, a very important type of Greek (and Latin) literature was the *bios*, from which we get our word "biography"—the writing (*graphē*) about someone's life (*bios*). The genre of the *bios* was the central means by which important historical figures were represented and remembered, with their ideas and actions recorded so that they could be spread beyond the person's place and time, often with an explicit invitation to imitation. This is what the Gospels of Matthew, Mark, Luke, and John are.

Richard Burridge, one of the leading scholars of ancient biographies, shows how similar the Gospels are to other contemporary *bios* literature.[1] Typical of this genre, the Gospels focus on one person, the subject of a biography, revealing Jesus's teachings and actions. All other characters and events in a biography are directly related to the focal person that the *bios* is about. Hearers of the Greek-language Gospels in the ancient world would have been familiar with this genre and understand its purpose. This is a good example of Christianity contextualizing itself into the surrounding culture, relating the truth of Jesus in a language, genre, and way of thinking that was familiar to the Greco-Roman world.

At the same time, this contextualization of the message about the Jewish Jesus into a Greek *bios* also created its own version of the ancient biography. We may notice that the four Gospels are titled not "The Bios/ Life of Jesus according to . . . " but rather "The Gospel according to . . ." This word "gospel" (Greek, *euangelion*) was how Paul described his own preaching about Jesus (1 Cor. 15:1–2; Gal. 1:6–9) and is first applied to the narratives about Jesus in Mark 1:1: "The beginning of the good news [*euangelion*] about Jesus the Christ, the Son of God" (AT). Then, early on in the church, the four recognized biographies that were compiled by Matthew, Mark, Luke, and John all came to be titled with the superscription "The Gospel according to . . ."

This shift from "life" to "gospel" is very important in tying the story of Jesus into the broader story of Israel, of God's work in the world from the beginning of creation up until Jesus. Specifically, the language of "gospel" comes from the influential writings of the prophet Isaiah. In the Greek translation of Isaiah the verb form of the noun "gospel" (*euangelion*) is used at crucial points to describe the great theme of the book: God is going to return soon to establish his good reign on the earth, forgiving people's sins, vindicating and providing for his faithful people, instituting true peace and flourishing throughout the world (Isa. 40:1–11; 52:7–53:12). This can be described biblically as "the kingdom of God," and it is a forward-looking hope and promise for the future. Thus, our Gospels are Greek biographies, but biographies that set Jesus's teachings and actions into a broader, comprehensive story of the whole world, both human and divine, a story that points forward to its completion.

Why does it matter to understand the Gospels in this way? Simply, the Gospels are not disinterested history but rather have a clear theological goal and a formative purpose. The Gospels are not the mere history that other apostles build on to teach theology in the rest of the New Testament. They *are* historical, and the apostles do reflect on the Jesus traditions for their theological and moral teachings, but the Gospels themselves are also theological documents with the specific goal of inviting people to become disciples of Jesus. The Gospels are kerygmatic—they are preaching, teaching, and calling people to follow Jesus. Additionally, this message is set into the larger story of the world as told in the Old Testament, with a clear past and a promised future. According to Christianity, Jesus's story is the epicenter of God's work in the world. It completes and consummates what began at creation. At the same time, Jesus inaugurates the final age, which is not yet completed. This is what the canonical Gospels are: the central stories about Jesus that tell what happened and why it matters, all with a call to become followers of the Jesus whom they are describing, creating a community around devotion and allegiance to him.[2] ①

How Many Gospels Are There?

To many familiar with the Bible this may seem like a trick question. The obvious answer seems to be "four." This *is* the correct answer to the question of how many Gospels became recognized as canonical and thereby authoritative. But in the early centuries of the church there were actually many accounts of Jesus's life and teaching beyond these four, some of which even took titles such as "Gospel of Peter" or "of Thomas" or "of Mary," and even "Gospel of Judas." Some of these were books that have survived only in partial fragments or in quotations found in other writings. Some accounts probably were only

ⓘ INTRODUCTORY MATTERS

Godspell

The English word "gospel" comes from Old English *gōd* + *spel* and meant the same thing as the Greek *euangelion*, "good news." In 1971 the musician and producer Stephen Schwartz (famous also for his later musical-theater production *Wicked*) wrote a Broadway score for a play based on many of the parables in Matthew. This musical, *Godspell*, became a huge hit and has been performed on and off Broadway ever since, including a film version in 1973. *Godspell* tells a version of the narrative of Jesus contextualized into the hippie culture of the late 1960s. The music and reinterpretation of aspects of Jesus's teaching and story are powerful, though not without controversy, in that Judas apparently is redeemed at the end, and the story concludes without a resurrection.

oral or short notebook-like collections of Jesus's sayings. Luke refers to the fact that "many have undertaken" to produce an account of the events surrounding Jesus and that he himself has researched many before writing his own (Luke 1:1–4).

These other writings all came to be called **apocryphal Gospels** (or non-canonical Gospels), though they vary quite a bit in terms of form, reputation, influence, and value. Sometimes these texts have sayings that are very similar to the canonical Gospels and probably derive from them. Other elements of these apocryphal Gospels are clearly distinct from orthodox Christianity and reflect alternative readings of Jesus, such as Gnosticism, a religion that emphasized levels of secret "knowledge" (Greek, *gnōsis*) that people had to be initiated into. Many of these texts are not really Gospels at all in terms of the *bios* genre. Rather, some of them are merely collections of sayings, such as the Gospel of Thomas, and oddly share the title "Gospel." Others are prequel stories about Jesus's parents, birth, or childhood, such as the Protevangelium of James, or expansions of Jesus's passion, such as the Gospel of Peter.

As centuries passed and Christianity became more widespread and influential, many other supposed Gospels came into being, representing different views and goals. Additionally, an alternative to the four was created by the second-century theologian Tatian (probably under the influence of Justin Martyr), called the Diatessaron ("through four"). This impressive work was a harmony—an attempt to make one story out of the four overlapping but distinct Gospels of Matthew, Mark, Luke, and John. Whether it was meant to supplant or to support the recognized four canonical Gospels is not entirely clear. But we do know that it was influential in some parts of Christianity (especially Syria) but eventually was rejected in the broader church in favor of maintaining the four distinct witnesses.

The four Gospels that the church recognized as canonical rose to the surface because of their close connection to eyewitness testimony and because of their literary and theological clarity. Matthew, Mark, Luke, and John are understood to be given by God and therefore authoritative. They are the canonical Gospels and consequently are set apart from any other writings and sayings about Jesus. Moreover, this canonization of the four creates a new relationship among them. Rather than just having four distinct Gospels, the early church thought and spoke about these writings as *the* singular Gospel *given according to four witnesses*.

Thus, the answer to the question of how many Gospels there are depends on what one means by the question. If one means, "How many people attempted to write down stories and sayings about Jesus?" the answer is "many." If one means, "How many of these accounts are recognized

The Gospel of Thomas

In December 1945 in Nag Hammadi, Egypt, scholars discovered a long-buried cache of manuscripts written in the Coptic language. Among these was a collection of 114 sayings (Greek, *logia*) attributed to Jesus. The introduction announces that these are hidden sayings of Jesus that Didymos Judas Thomas wrote down, thus giving it its modern title, the Gospel of Thomas. While we don't know the date or situation of its composition, the Gospel of Thomas likely was produced by proto-Gnostic Christians. It is not narrative in form like the canonical Gospels but contains a list of Jesus sayings, many of which find parallels in the canonical Gospels. Several of the sayings are familiar, such as logion 20: "The disciples said to Jesus, 'Tell us what the kingdom of heaven is like.' He said to them, 'It is like a mustard seed. It is the smallest of all seeds. But when it falls on tilled soil, it produces a great plant and becomes a shelter for birds of the sky.'" Other sayings clearly come from a worldview very different from canonical Christianity, such as logion 114: "Simon Peter said to him, 'Let Mary leave us, for women are not worthy of life.' Jesus said, 'I myself shall lead her in order to make her male, so that she too may become a living spirit resembling you males. For every woman who will make herself male will enter the kingdom of heaven.'" The Gospel of Thomas contains many early oral sayings associated with Jesus going back to the first century, but in its final form it reflects a later and specific form of Christianity that stands outside the orthodox tradition.

The Book of Four Books

Even though the four canonical Gospels are considered one book in four parts—*the* (singular) Gospel according to Matthew, Mark, Luke, and John—there is also a structure to this unified book. Matthew and John are the lead Gospels, with Matthew introducing the human Messiah, Jesus, in his Jewish context and John picturing the divine Jesus from an eternal viewpoint. This is partially based on the traditional understanding of Matthew and John as disciples offering eyewitness accounts, while Mark and Luke are disciples of apostles, Peter and Paul, respectively. The canonical shape of the Fourfold Gospel Book reflects this understanding and guides the Christian reader's experience of the Gospels, beginning with Matthew and working through to the heights of John.

in the church as canonical and thereby authoritative?" the answer is "four." But if one means, "How did the church talk about these canonical accounts?" the answer is "as one"—they understood that God gave one Gospel in four forms, enabling a quadrophonic hearing.

How Do the Gospels Relate to One Another?

We have just noted that very early on in the church the four canonical Gospels were recognized as authoritative and distinct from other writings. They are seen as one Gospel in four forms. Below we will discuss more fully the significance of this singular Fourfold Gospel Book. Before doing so, however, we must explore another question. It concerns the literary and historical relationships of the four Gospels to one another.

While it is impossible to know the precise details of how Matthew, Mark, Luke, and John came into being, we can piece together a number of plausible ideas. First, we know that Jesus's actions and sayings first spread by word of mouth. Even during Jesus's ministry, word about him spread so far and wide that it became difficult for him even to enter a village without being overwhelmed by crowds (Mark 2:1–2). These oral traditions continued and expanded after Jesus's death and resurrection and the explosive growth of the church at Pentecost and beyond.

Ancient cultures (like many today) valued and maintained complex oral traditions with remarkable artistry and accuracy. In first-century Judaism, and subsequently in early Christianity, scribes memorized, interpreted, recorded, and taught the message of the faith. As time passed, and influential people passed away, many of these memorized sayings and interpretations were codified and written down. In Jewish tradition the record of different rabbis' interpretations of Torah are written down in the Mishnah, a book that helped people to study and live according to God's laws (*halakah*). Stories about things the rabbis did (*haggadah*) and things they said about Torah were remembered and then written down in the Talmud and Midrash. The development of the Gospels as written texts about the rabbi/sage Jesus likely followed the same pattern. Jesus's deeds and words were memorized, organized, interpreted, and then eventually written down by his disciples, particularly those with some scribal education, or dictated to scribes. We can think of the Gospels as *halakah* and *haggadah* from Jesus, written in the style and language of the Greek *bios*.

With the recognition of this oral-to-written progression, the question remains: What is the relationship of the four Gospels to one another? They certainly all drew on the oral (and eventually written down) snippets of Jesus's teachings and deeds. But beyond that it seems apparent that there was also a *literary* relationship between the Gospels, most clearly between the Synoptic Gospels—Matthew, Mark, and Luke. While each of these Gospels contains stories that are unique to it, the vast majority of their accounts overlap significantly. This overlap extends beyond general information about Jesus to the specific ordering of groups of stories, as well as very specific wording at several points. In other words, the Gospel writers apparently happily depended on the other accounts already written (recall Luke 1:1–4). ⓘ

INTRODUCTORY MATTERS

Parallel Sequence of Stories in the Synoptic Gospels

The relationship of the Synoptic Gospels to one another is seen not only in close verbal parallels but also in their sequence of stories. One may initially suppose that this is simply because this sequence was the order in which these events occurred in history. However, this seemingly simple explanation cannot account for why there is also much variation in the sequence of stories. The best understanding is that, within the conventions of ancient history writing, the Gospel writers depended on one another but also varied their material based on their own goals.

Story	Mark	Luke	Matthew
Jesus's teaching in Capernaum	1:21–22	4:31–32	
Jesus's healing of demonized man	1:23–28	4:33–37	
Jesus's healing of Peter's mother-in-law	1:29–31	4:38–39	8:14–15
Jesus healing and exorcizing—summary	1:32–34	4:40–41	8:16–17
Jesus leaves Capernaum	1:35–38	4:42–43	
Jesus preaching in Galilee—summary	1:39	4:44	4:23
Miraculous catch of fish		5:1–11	
Jesus heals a leper	1:40–45	5:12–16	8:1–4
Jesus heals a paralyzed man	2:1–12	5:17–26	9:1–8
Jesus calls Levi to follow him	2:13–17	5:27–32	9:9–13
Question about fasting	2:18–22	5:33–39	9:14–17
Question about plucking grain on the Sabbath	2:23–27	6:1–5	12:1–8
Question about healing on the Sabbath	3:1–6	6:6–11	12:9–14
Healing by the sea—summary	3:7–12	6:17–19	12:15–16
Jesus chooses the Twelve	3:13–19	6:12–16	

Source: Adapted from Robert Stein, *The Synoptic Problem* (Grand Rapids: Baker, 1994), 35.

This insight is not just a modern notion; it was recognized and understood in the ancient church. One of the clearest and most influential explorations of the relationship of the Gospels to one another can be found in Augustine's *Harmony of the Gospels*. Augustine, like most Christians up until the twentieth century, believed that the Gospels depended on and built on one another's writings in the canonical order. Thus, Matthew wrote first; Mark wrote a brief version of Matthew; Luke used both Matthew and Mark in his work; and, finally, John provided a very different but complementary perspective.

Scholarly work in the modern era has led most interpreters of the Gospels to believe that Mark was written first and the others followed. There are differences of opinion about the relationship between Matthew and Luke: some say Matthew used Luke, and others that Luke used Matthew, while yet other scholars believe that both used a common source (called **Q**, from the German word *Quelle*, "source"). Regardless, the point remains the same: the Gospel writers were aware of one another and depended on one another's work, not to supplant those who came before them, but to expand and to complement. The words of the Fourth Gospel's epilogue sum up well the joy the early church found in recognizing the richness of the four interrelated Gospels: "Jesus did many other things as well. If every one of them were written down, I suppose that even the whole world would not have room for the books that would be written" (John 21:25 NIV).

The Metropolitan Museum of Art. Gift of J. Pierpont Morgan, 1917.

Figure 5.1. Plaque with the Lamb of God on a cross between symbols of the Four Evangelists (1000–1050)

What Is the Fourfold Gospel Book and Why Does It Matter?

As noted above, for much of the church's early history the four canonical Gospels were thought of primarily not as individual accounts but rather as a beautifully diverse unity, as one single Gospel given through four inspired witnesses. The word "gospel" (*euangelion*) was used in the singular form as the title to the collection of Matthew, Mark, Luke, and John in one book.

Ancient Christians called this the Tetraeuangelion (Greek) or Tetraevangelium (Latin). We may now call it the Fourfold Gospel Book. The idea that this book was four-in-one was communicated not just through the title and the frequent binding of the four accounts into one manuscript, but also through pictorial images. The Fourfold Gospel Book was represented ubiquitously through what are called the Four Symbols of the Evangelists. The Four Symbols were based on the four winged creatures surrounding God's throne in Ezekiel 1:4–14 and retooled in John's Revelation (Rev. 4:6–8). These creatures—a human, lion, ox, and eagle—are likely meant to stand for the highest representatives of distinct areas of God's creation: humanity, the wild, the domestic beasts, and the birds of the air. Early Christian theologians and artists used these memorable images to describe the diversity within the unity of the Fourfold Gospel Book. Whether it be in marble carvings, paintings, frescoes, altar pieces, architectural forms, or book covers, the Four Symbols appear regularly as figures of Matthew (human), Mark (lion), Luke (ox), and John (eagle), witnessing to Jesus, the Word of God. Less commonly, but closely related, one also finds this relationship depicted through a **tetra-morph**, a combination of the four creatures into one image. These artistic renderings make a strong theological point that church fathers such as Irenaeus, Jerome, and Augustine explained: the four Gospel writers have distinct voices and perspectives, but all are faithfully pointing to the one Jesus.

Beyond the widespread use of the Four Symbols in Christian art, many theologians from ancient times until now have written on how each individual Gospel contributes to the Fourfold Gospel Book. For example, according to Augustine, Matthew provides the human lineage of Jesus, Mark is a mere epitomizer of Matthew, Luke shows us the priestly lineage of Jesus, and John reveals Jesus as the eternal Word of God.[3] The Jesuit scholar Carlo Martini suggested that the four Gospels serve as manuals that correspond to four distinct phases in a disciple's conversion

Figure 5.2. This book-cover plaque with Christ in majesty (eleventh century) shows the Four Symbols of the Evangelists: the eagle (John), the human (Matthew), the ox (Luke), and the lion (Mark).

Figure 5.3. This tetramorph column from the parapet of a pulpit (ca. 1302–10) by Giovanni Pisano portrays a man (Matthew) with a lion (Mark) and ox (Luke) on each leg and an eagle (John) lectern that rested on top (only the wings remain).

and maturation, beginning with Mark, who leads to conversion, followed by Matthew the catechist, then Luke-Acts, and finally John.[4] Frederick Dale Bruner creatively offered several metaphorical ways to think about the relationships of the four Gospels to one another: Mark is for evangelists, Matthew for teachers, Luke for deacons or social workers, and John for elders or spiritual leaders.[5] Francis Watson follows the patristic habit of highlighting how each Gospel account begins and uses this to recognize distinct contributions of each: Matthew highlights that Jesus was a Jew, and it is through this Jewish Jesus that the gospel comes to the world; Mark emphasizes that the way of Christ is one of repentance and baptism; Luke highlights Mary as the ideal reader of the gospel story; high-flying John provides a vision of God through the Word that has become flesh.[6] From a literary and theological viewpoint, Mark Strauss summarizes the unique contribution of each Gospel this way: Matthew presents Jesus as the Jewish Messiah who fulfills Old Testament hopes, Mark portrays Jesus as the suffering Son of God, Luke shows Jesus as the Savior for all people and all nations, while John highlights Jesus as the eternal Son of God.[7]

Other ways of relating the four Gospels to one another could be given beyond these examples, but the point remains the same: throughout the church's history Christians have recognized one Gospel given in four forms, each with distinct perspectives, voices, and contributions while speaking in quadraphonic harmony.

How Did People in the Past Interpret the Gospels?

As we have noted, Christianity is concerned not merely with certain teachings but also especially with a certain person, Jesus the Christ. Therefore, the Fourfold Gospel Book played the central role in the experience of the earliest Christians. The apostles' teachings, including the circulated letters from Paul, Peter, James, John, and others, were very important. But they were seen as supplements to the main focus of Christian gatherings: hearing about Jesus's words and deeds, worshiping the Triune God in song, and sharing meals and goods with one another as each had need. This is precisely how Justin Martyr described early Christian gatherings.[8] These oral and written stories and sayings eventually become codified in the four canonical Gospels and then in the Fourfold Gospel Book. The Gospels became the Magna Carta or Mayflower Compact of the Christian community.

Because of this, by the second century AD there were countless homilies and treatises written about the Gospels, sealing their place of priority in the church. In Greek first, then in Latin and other languages, church leaders and theologians produced massive, learned commentaries that unpacked the teachings of the Gospels. Examples include Origen's Greek commentary on Matthew, much of which has been lost, but enough remains to show the care and skill that went into interpreting the Gospels.

Another way in which we can see evidence of the importance of the Gospels is in the writings of Christianity's opponents. Christianity began as a peasant Jewish sect on the remote eastern end of the Roman Empire, but it quickly became an urban, gentile, and empire-wide faith. As a result, educated Roman elites began to take notice, and, with considerable irritation, they often attacked Christianity as being foolish, deceptive, and self-contradictory. One such writer was Celsus, whom we know about because the Christian scholar-theologian Origen wrote an important work titled *Contra Celsum* (*Against Celsus*), which seeks to answer Celsus's charges against Christianity. The point is that, whether in commentaries and sermons by Christians or in works written by Christianity's opponents, the Gospels were seen to be central because Christianity is rooted in what Jesus said and did, above all else.

Juvencus's Epic Poem on the Gospels

As Christianity continued to spread and to transform the ancient world, people at every level of society became disciples, including some highly educated poets and philosophers. For such people, the highest form of literature was the epic poem, a lengthy poem-story written in poetic meter, telling the story of a great hero. In Roman culture, Virgil's *Aeneid* was the high-water mark of this tradition. A great example of the Gospels' central influence is seen around AD 330, when an educated convert named Juvencus created an elaborate epic Latin poem that retells the Gospel story in the style and feel of Virgil. This provides an important contextualization of the Gospels into this educated slice of the ancient world. Juvencus's harmonized poem of the Gospels (along with similar works by Sedulius and Arator) continued to be copied and appreciated throughout the Middle Ages, but it was translated into English for the first time only in 2016. Here are a few lines from Scott McGill's translation of the portion that recounts the events of Luke 2:[9]

> There is a city, Bethlehem, the home
> of singing David; by law it sought its count.
> Here Joseph, David's scion, listed Mary
> as his betrothed and stated she was pregnant.
> Right by the city walls, a tiny hut
> of a poor farm gave shelter to the pair.
> Her time complete, the Virgin bore her son,
> unparalleled. A cradle's bands wrapped him;
> a manger was prepared as his hard bed.

Celsus's Attacks and Origen's Response

We no longer have any copies of the book *The True Discourse* by the anti-Christian philosopher Celsus, but Origen often quotes him in his massive work *Contra Celsum* (written ca. AD 248), providing a thoughtful Christian response.

Here is an example of Origen's response to Celsus's attack, from *Contra Celsum*, book 6, chapter 78. Celsus compares the Christian God to the story from a Greek comedy when Jupiter wants to rescue humanity from evil but sends his messenger Mercury only to the Athenians and Lacedaemonians. This is obviously laughable to the audience. Celsus makes fun of the Christian idea that in wanting to save the whole world God would send his Son only to the Jews rather than breathing his Spirit on the whole world. Origen responds that sending Jesus only to one corner of the world "was founded on good reasons, since it was necessary that He who was the subject of prophecy should make His appearance among those who had become acquainted with the doctrine of one God, and who perused the writings of His prophets, and who had come to know the announcement of Christ, and that He should come to them at a time when the Word was about to be diffused from one corner over the whole world."[10]

Repeatedly throughout his work Origen responds to Celsus's rejection of Christianity as barbaric and uneducated, showing that it is very possible for an educated and philosophical mind to understand the world through a Christian framework.

In addition to commentaries on the Gospels, another important aspect of Gospel reading in the ancient world was influenced by the Eusebian **canon tables**.[11] In the early AD 300s the Christian scholar Eusebius created a cross-reference system for reading the Gospel stories in dialogue with one another. He numbered the stories throughout the Gospels and then assigned a set of numbers that show which stories have parallels in the other Gospels. These were collated into ten tables, or "canons," that readers could use to make connections between parts of the Gospels within the Fourfold Gospel Book. Eusebius did not collapse the Gospels into one but continued the tradition of maintaining the diversity within the unity of the four Gospels. At the same time, his work encouraged a canonical way of reading the Gospels—not just vertically (reading each Gospel from top to bottom) but also horizontally (reading the Gospels across the pages in dialogue with one another). This tradition has dominated the way the Gospels have been treated in sermons, commentaries, and theological treatises of the church throughout most of its history.

In Europe, the age of the Renaissance (ca. 1300–1700) introduced a new set of scholarly habits that also affected the reading of the Gospels. In this era, philology (the study of words) and the reconstruction of history became more of a focus, sometimes in conflict with long-standing traditions

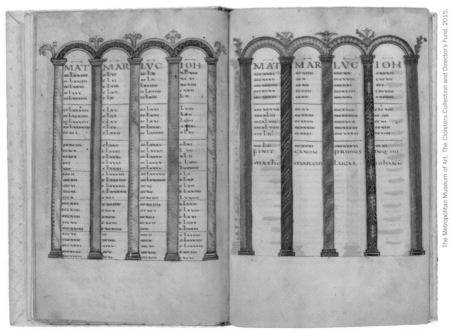

Figure 5.4. These canon tables (folios 1v–2r) from a Carolingian Gospel Book (825–50) compare similar passages from the four Gospels.

in philosophy and theology. One of the greatest minds in the fifteenth and sixteenth centuries was Erasmus (1466–1536), a Dutch Christian scholar who produced, in addition to many other works, one of the first scholarly printed editions of the Greek New Testament. This renewed interest in discovering the original texts affected the reading of the Bible and contributed to the world-shaking events of the Protestant Reformation (1517–1648). Reformers such as Luther, Calvin, and Zwingli renewed interest in preaching from the biblical texts and writing commentaries, including on the Gospels. In this era the Synoptic Gospels typically were treated together in a harmony while the Gospel of John was treated separately. For some of the Reformers the Gospels took a back seat to Paul and his letters because of the sharp theological debates of the day. ⓘ

How Do Modern Scholars Interpret the Gospels?

The past 250 years in Western civilization have seen an explosion of specialized knowledge and scholarship unlike any other time in human history. This is not to say that there wasn't great learning before this time period; there was. In fact, the technology and learning that we experience in the modern era came into being because of developments in the medieval and Renaissance eras and the rise of universities throughout Europe. But in the past 250 years many areas of scholarship have developed increasingly specialized theories and methodologies that have their own ways of reading the Gospels. There are several modern approaches (typically called forms of "criticism"), each of which offers its own perspective on how to interpret the Gospels. We will address here **form criticism, source criticism, redaction criticism, literary criticism,** and **reception history.**

Erasmus's Paraphrases

In addition to his many other theological and biblical works, Erasmus produced a series of paraphrases, which were a unique genre that combined Bible translation and commentary into one, seamless work. In his *Paraphrases* Erasmus wrote flowing, accessible translations of various books of the New Testament, theologically interpreting the texts as he rewrote them so that anyone could read his work and understand what was being said in plain speech. These insightful works are a pleasure to read and were the writings that Erasmus himself was most proud of.

For example, in Matthew 5:20 Jesus says, "For I tell you, unless your righteousness surpasses that of the scribes and Pharisees, you will never get into the kingdom of heaven." Erasmus's paraphrase reads, "To enable you to understand how great a difference there is between Jew and Christian, between a disciple of Moses and one of mine, I say to you unequivocally: if you fulfill whatever the Law prescribes, whatever the Pharisees fulfill (men who are now thought to possess a sort of absolute justice and think so themselves), but you add nothing further of a more perfect kind, so insignificant will you be in this religious profession that in the kingdom of heaven not even the right of admission is to be given."

Figure 5.5. *Desiderius Erasmus* by Hans Holbein the Younger

Form Criticism

The form-critical approach to reading the Gospels started as a method of analysis in Old Testament studies and was then adopted by many Gospels scholars in the early part of the twentieth century. Form criticism seeks to identify the different types ("forms") of literature within the Gospels (parables, wisdom sayings, miracle stories) and speculate on what must have been happening in the church that would lead people to value and retell these stories. For example, Jesus's saying about not putting new wine into old wineskins (Mark 2:22) is interpreted as reflecting a debate in the early church about the role of Judaism and the law in the Christian faith. The advantage of this kind of reading of the Gospels is that it helpfully identifies the fact that there are different genres within the Gospels, often collected together into units, and that these do in part reflect ideas that were important to the early church. The problem with form criticism, and the reason many have abandoned it today, is that its scholars often were overconfident in their assertions that the Gospel writers created the stories about Jesus for the purpose of addressing problems in the church. This approach is not very plausible historically, given that communities of faith cared very much about the eyewitness truthfulness of the stories about Jesus.

Source Criticism

Source criticism deals with the literary relationships of the Gospels to one another: Who wrote first and who used whom as sources? Source criticism is not actually a modern critical method in the same way that the others under discussion here are. As noted above, the question of what order the Gospels were written in, and how they relate to one another literarily, was something that was pondered by the ancient church. The canonical sequence of the Fourfold Gospel Book was considered the order in which the Gospels were written: Matthew, Mark, Luke, and John, one building on the others.

In the modern era, interest was rekindled in the literary relationship of the Gospels to one another, utilizing some new tools, and with differences of opinion about what these relationships are. Most scholars came to believe that Mark, not Matthew, was the first written Gospel. Additionally, scholars began to talk about Q, the supposed source that stood behind the large amount of material shared between Matthew and Luke. Over the decades different scholarly camps have evolved around these issues, with heated debates about whether Q ever existed, what order the Gospels were written in, and what role oral traditions played. ⓘ

Parallel Gospel Stories

This is a sample page from a modern synopsis, in which each story (**pericope**) is numbered and then arranged in parallel across the Gospels so that a comparison can easily be made.

[no. 88, 89]   Matt. 8.16-17, 18-22 – Mark 3.13-19 – Luke 7.11-17 – John 4.46-54   76

88. The Sick Healed at Evening
(cp. no. 38)

Matt. 8.16-17	Mark 1.32-34 *(no. 38, p. 36)*	Luke 4.40-41 *(no. 38, p. 36)*	John
16 That evening they brought to him many who were possessed with demons; and he cast out the spirits with a word, and healed all who were sick. 17 This was to fulfil what was spoken by the prophet Isaiah, "He took our infirmities and bore our diseases."	32 That evening, at sundown, they brought to him all who were sick or possessed with demons. 33 And the whole city was gathered together about the door. 34 And he healed many who were sick with various diseases, and cast out many demons; and he would not permit the demons to speak, because they knew him.	40 Now when the sun was setting, all those who had any that were sick with various diseases brought them to him; and he laid his hands on every one of them and healed them. 41 And demons also came out of many, crying, "You are the Son of God!" But he rebuked them, and would not allow them to speak, because they knew that he was the Christ.	

Matt.: 16 When (And when R) the (– R) even was come, they A R | that were A ; – R | devils A R | his word A ‖ 17 that it might be fulfilled which A R | Esaias (Isiah R) the prophet, saying, Himself took A R | sicknesses A
Mark: 32 And at even, when the sun did set A R | diseased A | and them that were possessed A R | devils A R¹ | divers A R | devils A R¹ | he (– A) suffered not A R | devils A R¹
Luke: 40 any sick A R | divers A R ‖ 41 devils A R¹ | crying out and saying A R | Christ the Son A | And he (– R) rebuking them (+ he R) suffered them not A R | was Christ A

Matt.: 17: Is. 53.4

89. On Following Jesus
(cp. no. 176)

Matt. 8.18-22	Mark 4.35 *(no. 136, p. 122)*	Luke 9.57-62 *(no. 176, p. 164)*	John
18 Now when Jesus saw great crowds around him, he gave orders to go over to the other side. 19 And a scribe came up and said to him, "Teacher, I will follow you wherever you go." 20 And Jesus said to him, "Foxes have holes, and birds of the air have nests; but the Son of man has nowhere to lay his head."	35 On that day, when evening had come, he said to them, "Let us go across to the other side."	57 As they were going along the road, a man said to him, "I will follow you wherever you go." 58 And Jesus said to him, "Foxes have holes, and birds of the air have nests; but the Son of man has nowhere to lay his head." 59 To another	

Matt.: 18 great multitudes about him A R | gave commandment to depart unto the other A R ‖ 19 And there came a scribe and R ; And a certain scribe came and A | Teacher] Master A R¹ | wherever] withersoever A R ‖ 20 him, The foxes A R | and the birds A R | air] heaven R | man hath not where A R
Luke: 57 And (+ it came to pass, that A) as A R | they went in (on R³) the way, a certain man A R | him, Lord, I A | wherever] whithersoever A R ‖ 58 him, The foxes R | and the birds R | air] heaven R | man hath not where A R

Matt.: 18–22: Lk. 8.22

Figure 5.6. Sample Page from Aland, *Synopsis of the Four Gospels*

Redaction Criticism

In the mid-twentieth century Gospels scholars began to pay more attention to the role of the Gospel writers—not just as collectors of stories but as skillful editors (German, *Redaktor*, "editor"). Based on the newly dominant theory that Mark was the first Gospel written, scholars made increasingly sophisticated arguments about Matthew's and Luke's theological points by examining how they had adapted and modified Mark and the other materials they had before them. For example, when comparing Matthew's and Luke's accounts of Jesus's temptation, redaction critics can note that one of the authors changed the order of the temptations from the other to emphasize different theological ideas: bread, temple, worship (Matthew) versus bread, worship, temple (Luke). This way of reading the Gospels—paying attention to the editorial activity of the Gospel writers and extrapolating theological points from this—became the predominant mode of Gospels interpretation throughout the last half of the twentieth century.

Literary Criticism

Beginning in the last twenty-five years of the twentieth century, while redaction-critical approaches dominated Gospels scholarship, other scholars began to focus on the Gospels as literature. This focus on the text of the Gospels as writings, rather than how they came to be written (as in form-, source-, and redaction-critical approaches), was part of a larger trend in the academic study of literature in general. The broad umbrella of literary criticism includes methods of interpreting the Gospels by attending to how they tell their story, including analysis of plot, structure, and character development. Literary-critical studies are conducted with varying degrees of sensitivity to historical context. For some scholars, the Gospels are studied only as pieces of literature. For others, the historical and sometimes the canonical context are factored into literary analysis, and

Peter as a Character in the Gospels

One of the insights that a literary approach to the Gospels can provide is how characters function and develop in a story. Some characters in the Gospels are **flat characters**; that is, they do not develop but rather serve as types or stock figures who play a set role. Examples include the enemies of Jesus (Pharisees, Sadducees), or unnamed characters who express great faith and are healed (Canaanite woman, lepers, centurion). Other characters, especially the disciples, are **round characters**, meaning that they are multifaceted and their character develops during the course of the story. The lead disciple, Peter, is the roundest character in the Gospels (besides Jesus himself). The Gospel writers depict Peter's development from his initial calling to be a follower of Jesus, through his many successes and failures, to become the leader of the disciples and subsequently of the early church. Peter is one of the Twelve and also one of the Three (along with James and John), who are the closest followers of Jesus and share unique experiences with him such as the **transfiguration** and the garden of Gethsemane. Peter shows himself to be a wholehearted leader, being the first to confess that Jesus is the Christ (Matt. 16:16), the one who has the faith to attempt to walk on the water with Jesus (Matt. 14:28–30), and yet he is also one who falls asleep when he is supposed to be praying (Matt. 26:36–46), who starts thinking like Satan (Matt. 16:22–23), and who denies being Jesus's disciple under peer pressure and fear (Matt. 26:69–75). Paying attention to Peter's development as a literary character over the course of the Gospels gives access to a kind of reading and application that mere historical accounts cannot.

these approaches are sometimes referred to as composition criticism or as a form of biblical theology. ⓘ

Reception History

In recent years scholars have begun paying more attention to how the Gospels were read in the past, especially before the modern era. Good scholarship has always been aware of other interpreters' views, but the recent focus on reception history is an exercise in rediscovering voices and perspectives that have long been lost or overlooked. This approach is rooted in a greater awareness of each interpreter's situatedness in his or her own culture. Countless commentaries and homilies on the Gospels have never been translated from Greek or Latin into modern languages. Many scholars are now producing translations of such texts and study how the interpretations by earlier readers of the Gospels offer insights into their own culture and time as well as ours. For example, reception-history study of the **Great Commission** (Matt. 28:16–20) reveals that most interpreters throughout the church's history did not think that this command applied to anyone but the original apostles. Only much later, with people like William Carey, did missionaries regularly use these verses to motivate their international missions.

All these modes of modern inquiry into the Gospels (as well as others we have not discussed) have something to offer. These various ways of reading the Gospels provide certain vantage points by asking different questions of the text, some focusing on how the Gospels came into being, some on how they function as literature, and some on how people have read them over the centuries. None of these methods stands alone or gives a comprehensive reading of the Gospels. Rather, each should be utilized for what it can offer without exclusion of others.

How Do We Read the Gospels as Christian Scripture?

In addition to the assorted ways that scholars have read the Gospels we can and should ask whether there is a distinctly Christian way of reading the Gospels—whether by scholars or not. Is there a mode of reading the Gospels as Christian Scripture?

Yes. There is a mode of reading the Gospels as Christian Scripture that accords with why and how the Gospels were written. This kind of reading is not opposed to a scholarly reading. Indeed, the best reading of any text, including the Gospels, will gain insights from any number of scholarly methodologies. But a Christian reading of the Gospels will pursue specific goals and manifest certain sensibilities. We can summarize this way of reading the Gospels under three categories.

Reading the Gospels to Understand the History of Jesus

Because Christianity is based on a person more than on certain ideas, a Christian reading of the Gospels starts with a focus on who the real Jesus was, in actions and words. The Gospel writers desired to faithfully record the things that Jesus said and did so that people's faith in him would be based on the truth (Luke 1:1–4; John 20:30–31). Central to this faithful witness is the end of the story—Jesus's last week, his suffering, death, and resurrection—that each Gospel highlights through literary space and details. The opposite of this kind of Christian reading would be a mode of interpretation that is skeptical of the faithfulness of the witness or that reads the Gospels as mere symbols or universal ideas divorced from real history.

Reading the Gospels within the Context of the Rest of Holy Scripture

A Christian reading of the Gospels also interprets them as part of the canon of Holy Scripture. First, the Gospels are understood as part of the larger story of the Jewish Scriptures, beginning with creation and focusing on the history and hopes of Israel. Each of the Gospels in its own way indicates that they are to be read as the consummation of the story to which the Old Testament points. Second, reading the Gospels well means interpreting them both as individual books and as part of the Fourfold Gospel Book. Matthew, Mark, Luke, and John should be read individually as theological biographies, but their placement in the Christian canon means that they simultaneously have a dialogical relationship with one another, enabling comparison and harmonization. Third, a Christian reading of the Gospels regards them in conjunction with the rest of the apostolic writings in the New Testament. While the New Testament Letters often address different issues and use different vocabulary, a Christian reading understands the deep unity within this harmonious diversity. The opposite of this kind of reading would interpret the Gospels in isolation from the rest of the canon and would fail to see a fundamental unity of thought and vision.

Reading the Gospels to Become a More Faithful Disciple

Ultimately, the most important aspect of a Christian reading of the Gospels is to read them with the purpose of becoming a more faithful disciple. The Gospels were written as theological biographies, not just to teach history and theological truths but also to provide models for emulation and avoidance. This is why narratives are written—so that readers may reflect on their own lives through observing the lives of others. The stories of Peter's denial and restoration, or of the Canaanite woman's faith, or of Judas's betrayal and regret are far more powerful than the nuggets of doctrinal truth that we may summarize them with. The biography subtype of narrative literature focuses primarily on one person as a model for emulation, but other characters in the story often serve this purpose as well. The Gospel biographies particularly invite readers into a life of discipleship that is rooted in Jesus's teaching. Disciples learn to be in the world by having their thoughts shaped by teaching while their habits are shaped by models. All of this is founded on the core idea of biblical ethics: godliness means learning to imitate God himself (Lev. 19–20; Matt. 5:48; 1 Cor. 11:1; 1 Thess. 1:6).

Throughout the Gospels Jesus is engaged in a project of resocialization of humanity's values and sensibilities. For example, the poor and lowly are valued, treating others with mercy and compassion is exalted, and love is the ultimate mark of what it means to be a Christian. This resocialization often is counterintuitive but is taught powerfully through the stories of the Gospels. The goal of this is to make and shape disciples. Thus, the most faithful reading of the Gospels is a personal one that submits to Jesus's call. One can read the Gospels as literature, as pieces of first-century history,

The Metropolitan Museum of Art. Gift of Herman and Lila Shickman, and Purchase, Lila Acheson Wallace Gift, 1997.

Figure 5.7. *The Denial of Saint Peter* by Caravaggio

as a contribution to comparative-religion studies, or any number of other ways. While these modes of reading are not wrong or useless, they are not ultimately in accord with the purpose of the Gospels or the life of Christian discipleship. The Gospels are kerygmatic in nature, meaning that they are constantly calling for a faith response on the part of readers. "Let anyone who has ears to hear listen" (Mark 4:9).

Christian Reading Questions

1. Why do you think it is important to understand the genre of the Gospels?
2. Compare and contrast the four types of criticism discussed in this chapter (form, source, redaction, literary). What do you think are the pros and cons of each?
3. Off the top of your head, make a list of ten characters from the Gospels. Draw a spectrum between "flat" and "round" (based on the descriptions of different types of characters from this chapter). Now plot each character on this spectrum. Why did you place each character where you did?
4. What goes into a Christian reading of the Gospels? Read John 2–3 and reflect on understanding this particular passage under each of the three categories of a Christian reading of the Gospels.

CHAPTER SIX

The Gospel according to Matthew

Orientation

When the rapid-fire notes of John Williams's *Star Wars* theme song come forth from our speakers, they are immediately recognizable. Leonardo da Vinci's *Mona Lisa*, even if it is modified with a milk mustache or a punk hairdo, is also instantly familiar. Why? It is because these two works of art, one musical and the other visual, are masterpieces. They are widely known and appreciated, spanning hundreds of years and thousands of miles of different eras and cultures. It is always a mystery of history as to why some equally well-crafted pieces of art become universally famous (classics) and others do not. But what all masterpieces have in common is acknowledged beauty and excellence that make them attractive and memorable.

The Gospel according to Matthew is one such masterpiece. Since the earliest days of the church the First Gospel has been recognized as a theological and churchly masterpiece. In

Figure 6.1. *The Inspiration of Saint Matthew* by Caravaggio

89

The Historical Origins of Matthew

Author: There is good evidence to associate this writing with Matthew the apostle (Matt. 9:9; 10:3; "Levi" in Mark 2:14; Luke 5:27).

Date: Likely AD 65–85

Location: Caesarea Maritima or Syrian Antioch

Sources: Matthew originally was written in Greek, dependent on a variety of sources, including some version of Mark and possibly Luke as well, in addition to oral sources and memories. Up until the late modern era Matthew was believed to be the first Gospel written.

Setting: Certain aspects of Matthew's teaching indicate that he was writing during a time of ongoing tension between Jewish Christians and non-Christian Jews, particularly the scribes and Pharisees. The scribes and Pharisees are singled out as Jesus's main enemies.

Matthew and the Didache

Matthew's Gospel was widely influential from the earliest days of the church. For example, we can see the heavy influence of Matthew on another important early Christian document, the Didache. The Didache, or Teaching of the Twelve Apostles, is the oldest surviving Christian **catechism**, dealing with Christian ethics and church practice. The themes and specific wording of the Didache show strong influence of Matthew, such as the form of the Lord's Prayer (Matt. 6:7–15; Didache 8) and the motif of the two ways to live (Matt. 7:13–27; Didache 1–6).

recent decades scholars have come to realize what a literary work of art it is as well.

As a result of its power and beauty, the Gospel of Matthew has always stood at the head of the Fourfold Gospel Book and the whole New Testament. Because of its great influence, much of the church's theological emphases, ways of speaking, and liturgical practices can be traced back to Matthew's Gospel. As one scholar has noted, "Early Christianity was primarily *Matthean* Christianity."[1]

One day many years ago I (Jonathan) asked my young daughter if she knew where to the find the Gospel of Matthew in the Bible. She responded, "Yes, Daddy, it's where the Old and New Testaments meet." From the mouths of babes! This is an accurate way to describe the Gospel according to Matthew. Not only does Matthew physically sit in our Bibles at the place where the Old Testament and the New meet, it also serves this role theologically. As we will see, Matthew is a *profound theological biography* that is written to give us the ability to understand how the whole Bible is put together and how it makes sense. The answer to this, according to Matthew, comes through understanding who Jesus is, what he taught, and what he did through his incarnation, suffering, death, resurrection, and ascension.

The Gospel according to Matthew is a story. It is a particular kind of story—a biography. As a result, the basic outline of Matthew's Gospel account is set out for him before he even starts writing: a biographer needs to tell who the person (the "biographee") is, what they did and said, how they lived and died, usually followed by some discussion of the impact this person had and why he or she is worthy of a biography. In this way all four of the Gospels basically have the same kind of outline that a biography written today of Albert Einstein or John Adams would have. There is always some variation available to the writer, such as how much to tell about the subject's childhood, whether to use flashbacks, which parts of the person's life to emphasize more, and so on. We see these variations play out in the four canonical Gospels (as well as in the noncanonical Gospels).

Matthew's Gospel biography is fairly straightforward. The first two chapters tell about Jesus's ancestral people, his parents, and his early childhood. Then we skip ahead to his adult life, which spans chapters 3–20. Maybe surprising to us as modern readers, Matthew then gives us seven chapters (chaps. 21–27) about Jesus's last week of life and his death. This is important because of the great theological weight that Christianity puts on Jesus's death. Finally, the First Gospel ends with a chapter (chap. 28) that talks about Jesus's resurrection and the sending of his disciples to continue his work. 📖

This chronological or biographical outline is, as we have noted, common to all four of the Gospels, and it likely stems from Mark's original story. In fact, Matthew's story basically follows the plotline of Mark, minus the childhood section. But this is where Matthew adds something highly significant and why his Gospel becomes the first and most prominent of the four in the early church.

In addition to this chronological outline, Matthew adds five major blocks of thematic teaching, weaving them skillfully into his narrative. Each of these blocks or **discourses** has a theme within it, providing a sort of "one-stop shop" for what Jesus taught on these five major topics. Going beyond this, all five discourses also share the overarching theme of revelation and separation. Taken together, the blocks communicate a major Matthean point: God is revealing himself finally in Jesus, and the result of this will be a separating of people into two groups. These two groups are no longer determined by ethnicity, religiosity, gender, social class, educational level, or financial success. Rather, there is a new people of God being formed based solely on one's reception of Jesus, and this includes both Jews and gentiles. 📖

The Holy Family's Flight to Egypt

The story of Joseph, Mary, and Jesus's flight to Egypt (Matt. 2:13–15) has inspired much creative output over the centuries. For example, many paintings depict this event, and there arose an additional legendary aspect of the story that was wedded deeply to the Christian imagination through the apocryphal books Pseudo-Matthew and the Protevangelium of James. In the many retellings of the flight to Egypt through painting and poetry we hear of a time when the Holy Family rested under a palm tree and Mary requested some dates to eat. In some versions Joseph was rather snippy and replied that whoever impregnated Mary should get her some. Then the child Jesus (sometimes in utero) made the tree bend down and provided the dates, causing Joseph to repent. In the medieval English tradition of the Coventry Plays the palm tree is replaced with a cherry tree, which eventually makes its way into the traditional English Christmas carol "The Cherry Tree Carol."

Matthew's Five Major Teaching Blocks

One of the most famous and important things about Matthew's Gospel is that, in addition to telling the story of Jesus's life, Matthew provides five large blocks of Jesus's teaching that he has collected together by theme:

Chapter(s)	Title	Theme
5–7	Sermon on the Mount	Greater righteousness and the right way of being in the world
10	Mission and Witness	Power and persecution of Jesus's witnesses
13	Parables	Separation of all people through the revelation of divine mysteries
18	Ecclesiological	The church as the new people of God
23–25	Judgment	The present and future judgment coming upon all peoples

The Structure of Matthew

In addition to providing a chronological outline, Matthew skillfully interweaves the five discourses with narrative portions. As a result, the overall structure of Matthew looks something like this:

1. Origins and beginnings (1:1–4:22)
   a. Introduction (1:1–4:16)
   b. Bridge (4:17–22)
2. Revelation and separation: in word and deed (4:23–9:38)
   a. First discourse (4:23–7:29)
   b. First narrative (8:1–9:38)
3. Revelation and separation: as master, so disciples (10:1–12:50)
   a. Second discourse (10:1–11:1)
   b. Second narrative (11:2–12:50)
4. Revelation and separation: a new, set-apart people of God (13:1–17:27)
   a. Third discourse (13:1–53)
   b. Third narrative (13:54–17:27)
5. Revelation and separation: inside and outside the new community (18:1–20:34)
   a. Fourth discourse (18:1–19:1)
   b. Fourth narrative (19:2–20:34)
6. Revelation and separation: judgment now and in the future (21:1–25:46)
   a. Fifth narrative (21:1–22:46)
   b. Fifth discourse (23:1–25:46)
7. Endings and beginnings (26:1–28:20)
   a. Bridge (26:1–16)
   b. Conclusion (26:17–28:20)

Figure 6.2. Plaque with the massacre of the innocents

Exploration—Reading Matthew

The Beginning of the Fulfillment

■ READ MATTHEW 1:1–2:23 ■

In chapters 1–2 we see what one would expect from a biography: basic information on who this biography is written about. These chapters answer two basic questions in this regard: Who is Jesus, and where does he come from? The first question is answered with a genealogy. This may seem boring and irrelevant to us, but in fact it strikes a chord that sets the key, tone, and tempo of the whole New Testament: Jesus is the Son of David and is therefore a king, and Jesus is the son of Abraham and is therefore the leader of all nations and peoples. This dual identity of Jesus will work its way out throughout Matthew and the rest of the New Testament. The second question is answered with the geographical information about his birth in Bethlehem, his urgent escape to Egypt, and his final settling in Nazareth in the north.

Across both of these questions and chapters there is one theme woven through like a golden thread. It makes an appearance somewhere in each of the five stories that follow the genealogy and forms a pattern there. It will also appear throughout the rest of Matthew's story in various places. It is the idea of *fulfillment*. By fulfillment Matthew means that what happened with Jesus is *connected to* and is really the *completion of* all the other things God had said and done before. This serves as a lesson in hermeneutics for the whole Bible. It teaches believers how to interpret everything that Jesus said and did as the ultimate completion and goal of God's work in the world. Simultaneously it teaches the disciples of Jesus to read the rest of the Bible as centered on and completed in Jesus. 📜

The Ministry Begins

■ READ MATTHEW 3:1–4:22 ■

In these chapters we fast-forward about thirty years to when Jesus is an adult and ready to begin his public ministry and fulfill his calling. First we meet a wild man dwelling in the wilderness, a linch-pin character who simultaneously serves as the last great Old Testament prophet (see Matt. 11:7–15) and the forerunner to Jesus: John the Baptizer. Just like an Old Testament prophet, he preaches a fiery message calling God's people back to repentance because God is promising to show up and set the world to rights. Just as in the Old Testament, some people respond positively and others do not.

As Jesus's forerunner, he is called to do something that makes even him uncomfortable: baptize Jesus. Matthew returns to his central theme and explains that this event is more than symbolic: it is a *fulfillment of all righteousness* (3:15), meaning that Jesus is once again bringing to completion all that God desires of his people. The result of this event is the declaration that brings us back to 1:1: Jesus is God's beloved *Son*. 📖

This unique sonship may not have been clear to the bystanders that day, but it was easily understood by God's ancient enemy, the devil (who is known by other names as well: Satan, the tempter, the serpent). In a last-ditch attempt to thwart God's inbreaking into the world through his Son, Satan seeks to redirect and derail Jesus's mission. He does so through a series of temptations designed to lure Jesus into using his prerogative as the Son of God to operate outside God's will—in effect, to be a disobedient son like the first Adam. The climactic third temptation asks Jesus to align himself with the prince of this world, Satan, and in exchange he will receive "all the kingdoms of the world and their

CANONICAL CONNECTIONS

The Fulfillment of God's Word in Jesus: Matthew and Hebrews

Matthew argues that all the events of Jesus's earliest days are the *fulfillment* of God's past work. Even though the Letter to the Hebrews and the Gospel of Matthew are different types of literature and have their own purposes, there is significant overlap between them on this point. Hebrews states the same idea this way: "Long ago God spoke to the fathers of the prophets at different times and in different ways. In these last days, he has spoken to us by his Son. God has appointed him heir of all things and made the universe through him" (Heb. 1:1–2). It is now in the final age, inaugurated by Jesus, that God's final and ultimate revelation of himself has come, fulfilling all that God has promised.

LITERARY NOTES

The Gospel of the Kingdom of Heaven

Matthew uses two important phrases that are unique to his Gospel:

The gospel of the kingdom means the message of the good news that God is returning to reign through Jesus. This is unpacked in 4:23–25 and 9:35–38 as having three elements: teaching about how to enter into and live within God's kingdom; healing and restoration of people; and calling of disciples to continue the kingdom work. Often in the church today "gospel" and "kingdom" are thought of as separate notions, but Matthew weaves them together.

The kingdom of heaven is Matthew's unique phrase that means the same thing as "the kingdom of God" in terms of its referent—God's now and future reign—but is different in terms of connotations. Matthew likes to describe God's reign as "of heaven" because this evokes the idea of the strong contrast between the kingdoms of this world and God's heavenly kingdom yet to come.

Figure 6.3. The temptation of Christ from the Book of Kells, a ninth-century book containing the four Gospels, shows Jesus at the pinnacle of the temple as Satan tempts him to jump off.

LITERARY NOTES

The Sermon on the Mount

The highly influential and beautiful Sermon on the Mount shares some material with Luke's Sermon on the Plain (Luke 6:17–49) but is most famous in its Matthean form. It consists of three main parts: the introduction (5:1–16), the body (5:17–7:12), and the conclusion (7:13–8:1). The introduction focuses on the Beatitudes, which paint a picture of what the truly flourishing life looks like according to Jesus. Surprisingly, it is described as a life of suffering while being salt and light in the world. The body of the sermon emphasizes that there is a greater righteousness necessary to enter the kingdom of heaven (5:17–20). This righteousness is not just external but is based on the inner person or the heart. Disciples must be *whole* people (the best translation of 5:48), not hypocrites who have only external righteousness. The conclusion uses three metaphors to exhort people to wisely build their lives on Jesus's teaching, not foolishly on the wisdom of the world.

splendor" (4:8). Jesus successfully resists this temptation and is then fully qualified to offer something greater: the kingdom of heaven (4:17).

This introductory unit ends appropriately with Jesus fully ready to begin his world-changing ministry. He has no plans to do this alone, apart from disciples, the first of which he calls to leave their regular lives in the world and to follow him into the mission that he is about to begin.

Jesus the Teacher of God's Way

■ READ MATTHEW 4:23–7:29 ■

Matthew 4:23–25 is an important summary statement that serves as an introduction to the larger section of 4:23–9:38, indicating that Matthew wants his readers to see this part of his story as having one big point (notice that 4:23–25 and 9:35–38 are nearly identical in wording). This big point is a description of what Jesus's ministry was all about, consisting of three elements: teaching and preaching the "gospel of the kingdom"; healing the sick and afflicted; and calling people to follow him. These three elements will be unpacked in subsequent chapters. 📖

The first part—the teaching and preaching about the gospel of the kingdom—is found in Matthew 5–7. This is called the Sermon on the Mount and is one of the most famous portions of the Bible. The sermon is a well-crafted collection of Jesus's teachings about what the kingdom of heaven looks like and especially the "greater righteousness" that is necessary to enter into the kingdom (5:17–20). This "greater righteousness" is a call to inward purity and to a *wholeness* (5:48) between outer behavior and the heart. This is Jesus's great critique of the religious leaders of his day: they had external behavioral righteousness, but their hearts were not connected to God. This is what Jesus calls hypocrisy. Jesus is painting a picture of the way of being in the world that is required to be his disciples: not being perfect but being authentically whole on the inside and outside, while looking in faith to God and his coming kingdom.

The Gospel of the Kingdom in Deed

■ READ MATTHEW 8:1–9:38 ■

As noted above, this section is the narrative part of the larger unit of 4:23–9:38. The stories collected together here are illustrations of the second and third elements of Jesus's ministry: healing people and calling disciples (along with the first, proclaiming the kingdom). Jesus's healing of all sorts of

LITERARY NOTES

The Lord's Prayer

Central to the church's **liturgy** and Christians' practice of prayer is the "Lord's Prayer" or the "Our Father" (6:9–13). This prayer is found in a shorter version in Luke 11:2–4 (as well as Didache 8.2), but it is Matthew's skillful poetic form that is best known. The Lord's Prayer is found in the structural center of the Sermon on the Mount, highlighting its importance.

The Lord's Prayer is broken into two parts, much like the Ten Commandments. The first set of petitions concerns God's name, fame, and glory being upheld (6:9–10). The second set of petitions relates to the daily life of the believer: God's provision of daily needs, receiving God's forgiveness and extending it to others, and being spared from trials that will test us to the point of tempting God (6:11–13). These petitions are not the only prayers that Christians can make, but they provide an anchoring model, orienting the believer in how to relate to our Father and others in the daily life of faith.

THEOLOGICAL ISSUES

Whole-Person Righteousness and Doing the Will of God

A major theme in Matthew is righteousness, which is defined as doing the will of God. Jesus teaches that one must have a righteousness greater than that of the scribes and Pharisees in order to enter the kingdom (5:17–20). The Sermon on the Mount unpacks this shocking statement by showing what this righteousness looks like. This righteousness is not about performing extra pious acts but is being a *whole* person, righteous not just in external behavior but in the heart or inner person (see 5:21–48; 6:1–21).

Another way of saying the same thing is Jesus's emphasis that one must "do the will of God" to enter life (7:21, 24; 12:50; 21:28–32; see also 6:10; 7:12; 18:14; 26:39, 42). Jesus is presented as the righteous one who does the will of God, and so must his disciples.

Matthew presents his readers with a call toward one of two ways. Those who enter the kingdom of heaven / eternal life are those who exercise this whole-person righteousness and do the will of God versus those who don't.

CANONICAL CONNECTIONS

Matthew in Dialogue with Paul

Paul's salvation-historical argument in Galatians 3–4 serves as an important dialogue partner with Matthew's teaching on the law in the Sermon on the Mount. Paul's argument is that Christians are not bound by the prescriptions of the Mosaic law because it is part of a covenant that was only temporary and whose purpose has been completed. The Mosaic law reflected God's will truly, but it was a temporary addition to something

deeper and eternal: the promise to Abraham that *all* people would be blessed (Gal. 3:15–25). This is informed by Jesus's foundational teaching in Matthew 5:17–20, when he says that he did not come to abolish the law but to *fulfill* it. Paul's fuller explanation helps the Christian reader put this together: later in Galatians Paul speaks in this same way, that Christians can *fulfill* the whole law by loving one another (Gal. 6:2).

Figure 6.4. *The Sermon on the Mount* by Jan Brueghel the Elder depicts Jesus, with a halo over his head, almost lost amid a crowd of socializing onlookers.

diseases and afflictions comes from his heart of compassion (9:36) and at the same time is a picture of God's coming kingdom, when God will bring peace, healing, justice, and wholeness to all of his people. The stories here are all illustrations of the coming time of God's reign as foreseen and promised in Isaiah. The calling of assorted disciples is an important part of this preaching and healing ministry, because Jesus's disciples will continue and even expand this work after his death, resurrection, and ascension. Therefore, Jesus ends this section with a prayer for God to raise up many laborers to work for the gospel as they await the return of the kingdom. 📖

Opposition to Jesus and His Disciples

■ READ MATTHEW 10:1–12:50 ■

Continuing the flow of the story, Matthew now gives Jesus's second major block of teaching (10:1–42), this one concerning what it means to be a called disciple who engages in Jesus's work in the world. The short answer is that it means both power and persecution. The power is that God is present with Jesus's disciples and that they truly stand as his witnesses—whoever receives them receives Jesus (10:40–42). Persecution is to be expected because just as Jesus was opposed by the world, so his disciples should expect to be. "A disciple is not above his teacher, or a slave above his master" (10:24).

This teaching block is followed by two chapters of stories illustrating precisely this, increasing opposition to Jesus. The breaking point is 12:14,

THEOLOGICAL ISSUES

God as the Father in Heaven and Jesus as the Son

Though not unique to Christianity, since the earliest days of the faith Christians have referred to God as their heavenly Father. Matthew especially emphasizes God as Father (44x), particularly the "Father in heaven" (13x) and "heavenly Father" (7x). In the ancient world the idea of fatherhood communicated both intimacy and awe, the security of being part of the family, accompanied by reverent respect. The idea of God as the Father in heaven combines these notions beautifully. He is both high and exalted and yet relational and present.

Even before the details of the interrelationships of the three persons of the Trinity were spelled out fully in the creeds, Christians began referring to God as Father as distinct from Jesus the Son. Jesus's divine sonship was always understood within the context of monotheism. The great question for the early Christians was not whether there was more than one God (the Hebrew Shema made very clear that there is only one God), but rather was how to speak of Jesus as the Son who shares the divine nature yet is distinct from the Father.

where, after two open conflicts with the Pharisees over the true meaning of the Sabbath (12:1–13), they decide once and for all to kill Jesus as soon as they get an opportunity. After they have resolved to do this, they even go so far as to accuse Jesus of being demon-possessed (12:24)! Jesus calls this the unforgivable sin (12:31–32).

Forming the New People of God

■ READ MATTHEW 13:1–17:27 ■

Matthew's third major teaching block (13:1–58) consists of a collection of several of Jesus's famous parables about the kingdom of heaven. Contrary to what we might expect, Jesus's parables are not given as quaint sermon illustrations, but instead we are told that Jesus changes his teaching style from direct authoritative instruction (recall the end of the Sermon on the Mount, 7:28–29) to parables *so that those on the outside would not understand* (13:10–17). This is the epicenter of the dual theme of revelation and separation that is woven throughout Matthew's five teaching blocks (see also 11:25–30). God is revealing himself through Jesus, and this will result in some people believing and others opposing him. This collection of concealing-and-revealing parables fits perfectly here in Matthew's story as Jesus's response to the Pharisees' dead-set opposition to him in chapter 12.

Following this teaching block (which sits right in the middle of Matthew's story), chapters 14–17 present several stories that hinge on this idea of separating people and forming a new people of God out of the deconstruction. Jesus performs a set of actions that are intentionally evocative of the greatest story of Israel—the exodus. Matthew skillfully presents a pair of miraculous wilderness feedings and water crossings, one for Jewish people (14:13–33) and the other for gentiles (15:29–39), which together communicate that God is forming a new people of God out of both Jew and Greek (see

The New People of God and the Church

Through his life, death, and resurrection Jesus has created the new people of God, the church, made up of all Jews and gentiles who follow Christ. In the Old Testament the people of God often were referred to as the assembly (in the Greek Old Testament, the *ekklēsia*, around 75x). Significantly, this is precisely the term that Matthew chooses to describe the newly formed group of Jesus's disciples (16:18; 18:17), or what we call now the church.

Even as Jesus is the fulfillment of Israel, so too his disciples are the fulfillment of the sons of Israel. John the Baptizer sends the warning shot at the beginning that God can and will raise up children for Abraham, from stones if need be; being an ethnic Jew is no guarantee (3:9). Jesus then repeatedly speaks of his disciples as the true people of God, the ones who understand Jesus's sonship (3:17; 11:25–27; 16:17; 17:5). Jesus's disciples are given heaven-sanctioned authority on earth (16:18–19; 18:18–19), akin to Moses's authority, and supplanting the Sanhedrin and temple. The kingdom is being transferred from disobedient sons to the followers of Jesus (8:11–12; 15:12–13; 21:43). Jesus's disciples will sit with authority on twelve thrones from which they will judge the twelve tribes of Israel (19:28). And Jesus asks, "Who is my family?" and answers, "Whoever does the will of my Father in heaven is my brother and sister and mother" (12:50). If Jesus is the true Son of God then his family is the people of God.

Matthew has redefined the people of God based not on ethnicity but on one's faith response to Jesus, on those who as whole people do the will of God as revealed by Jesus. It is on this basis that this Gospel ends with the command to go and make disciples of *all the peoples of the world* by proclaiming who Jesus is and teaching them to follow what he has taught. This is in no way a rejection of the story of Israel or the Old Testament. Jesus's gospel welcomes all who follow him, Jew or gentile.

also Rom. 10:12; Gal. 3:28; Col. 3:11). Along these same lines, Matthew provides several stories that contrast radically different groups of people, showing once again that God is separating people based on how they respond to Jesus. Note the different responses of the scribes and Pharisees from Jerusalem and the "Canaanite" woman (15:1–28).

Also crucial to this part of the story is Peter's confession of Jesus as the Christ, the Messiah (16:13–20). This answers the question that has been lingering over the narrative: Who is this man Jesus? The answer given is that he is God's anointed king, one who is worthy of and will enter into glory, as the story of the transfiguration shows (17:1–13). But he is also the suffering servant and Son of Man who will come into his glory only after enduring persecution and death (16:21–23; 17:22–23; 20:17–19).

Life Together as Jesus's People

■ READ MATTHEW 18:1–22:46 ■

Matthew's fourth major teaching block concerns the new people of God, the "assembly" or "church" (Greek, *ekklēsia*). It flows naturally after the stories of chapters 14–17, when the people of God has been constituted anew of both Jew and Greek. In this way chapter 18, and beyond into chapters 19–20, serves like the instructions in Exodus after God rescued his people through the Red Sea (Exod. 21–23). In both places we find guidelines about life together in the community. The overall message is that kingdom living together is counterintuitive and based on values that are often the opposite of those of the world: the least are the greatest (18:1–5; 19:13–15); the externally righteous and blessed, who appear to be first in the world, don't necessarily get into the kingdom of heaven (19:16–30); God rewards people justly but not necessarily according to human standards or desires (20:1–16, 20–28); and, maybe most importantly in Matthew, disciples of Jesus fully forgive others even when they have been wronged, mistreated, and sinned against (18:15–35). 📜 🏺

Matthew 21–22 marks a major turning point in the book because Jesus has finally arrived in Jerusalem, the heartbeat of Israel. The rest of the book (chaps. 21–28) will cover just the last week of Jesus's life in and around Jerusalem. The consistent theme throughout these chapters is the increasing tension and open conflict with the Jewish religious leaders. They oppose Jesus being praised by the crowds (21:1–11). He opposes their corruption of God's temple (21:12–22). They challenge his authority and try to trap him with tricky theological questions (21:23–27; 22:15–40). He undercuts their authority and rebukes them with a series of pointed parables (21:28–22:14), concluding by stumping them with a question about himself as the true Son of David (22:41–46).

Judgment Now and in the Future

■ READ MATTHEW 23:1–25:46 ■

In this section we have the fifth and final teaching block. These teachings continue and deepen the theme of revelation and separation with an added emphasis on judgment. Judgment is first announced on the hypocrisy of the scribes and Pharisees through a series of woes (23:1–36). Future judgment is explored in chapters 24–25. Jesus foretells a time when great difficulties and destruction will come on the earth, leading up to the return of Jesus himself. At that time the ultimate and final separation will occur, explained through a series of metaphors: ten virgins, three servants, and two types of animals, sheep and goats. The overall message is an exhortation to vigilance and diligence in discipleship. 🏺 📜

The Messiah Is Killed

■ READ MATTHEW 26:1–27:66 ■

A somber darkness hangs over these two lengthy chapters. The pace of the story continues to get

Matthew in Dialogue with the Old Testament

There are nearly seventy explicit quotations of Old Testament texts in Matthew (often in "fulfillment quotations"), in addition to a myriad of allusions (many estimates put the number at nearly three hundred). Additionally, many of Matthew's stories are "shadow stories" of Old Testament texts, mimicking the events and characters without referring to a specific text.

Matthew's dialogue with the Old Testament Scriptures draws on the whole of the Jewish Scriptures, including Genesis, Deuteronomy, and Psalms. The main well from which Matthew draws scriptural water is the prophets. As New Testament scholar Richard Hays has put it, in the final musical mix of Matthew's recording, he has moved up the volume slider on the prophets track.

Matthew's main prophetic source is the book of Isaiah (around 10x), which the early church called the "Fifth Gospel" because of its intimate connection to the gospel message. Many other prophets make an appearance. Especially important are Jeremiah, Hosea, Zechariah, and Daniel. This dialogue means that the language, concepts, and ways of telling the story of Jesus are marked and shaped by the prophets. Matthew's presentation of the Old Testament can be described as a prophetic way of reading the law, now understood fully through Jesus.

From the Last Supper to the Lord's Supper

The Last Supper (Matt. 26:26–30) was Jesus's special version of the Passover celebration meal that Jews have celebrated for millennia, commemorating God's deliverance of the Israelites from bondage in Egypt. It was a special version of this traditional meal because Jesus celebrated it with his disciples rather than his biological family and because he made the meal ultimately about *his own* delivering of God's people from bondage. Jesus uses the Passover event to speak of his death and resurrection, which will bring forgiveness of sins, the new covenant, and the beginning of the kingdom.

The **Lord's Supper** was celebrated from the earliest days of the church both as a remembrance of what Jesus did on the cross and as a celebration of anticipation of Jesus's return (1 Cor. 11:17–34). The church's practice of the Lord's Supper is not a reenactment of the Jewish Passover but is a Christian reappropriation of the Last Supper, even as the Last Supper was a reappropriation of the Passover.

slower and slower, with this section covering the critical final two days of Jesus's life and his crucifixion. Every event is theologically significant: his anointing for burial; his final Passover supper with his new family of disciples; his betrayal by one disciple (Judas), denial by another (Peter), and abandonment by all; his court trials and beatings; and ultimately his death. Most of this section consists of stories, but there is one part that explicitly teaches important theological truths about all that is happening: Jesus's words at the Passover meal on the night he was betrayed and arrested (26:26–29). He explains that he is giving himself in death to bring about the *new covenant*. He invites his disciples to participate in this covenant by partaking in his body and blood and by receiving the forgiveness being offered. And he looks forward to a future time when the kingdom will fully come.

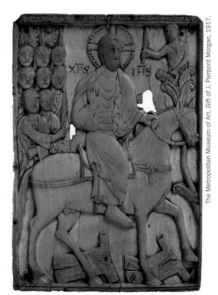

The Metropolitan Museum of Art. Gift of J. Pierpont Morgan, 1917.

Figure 6.5. This plaque from Italy (900–925) shows Jesus entering Jerusalem on a donkey as people place their garments before him.

The New Age Begins

■ READ MATTHEW 28:1–20 ■

If the story ended at chapter 27, it would be a tragedy—an inspiring and admirable portrait of Jesus, but a tragedy still. Jesus preached and taught and healed and changed people's lives, but the bad guys won. They killed him. But chapter 28 turns everything around and transforms Matthew's story into a *eucatastrophe*—a catastrophe or tragedy that is ultimately good and beautiful. Jesus's physical resurrection from the dead is the apex of each of the Gospels because it changes everything. His shameful death is turned into honor, and his defeat by his enemies is turned into victory over death.

Matthew ends his Gospel with a return to Galilee, where everything began. On a mountain in the far northern gentile area of Israel, Jesus forever transforms the world by commissioning his disciples to go throughout the world making more

Johann Sebastian Bach's *St. Matthew Passion*

The greatest master of the Baroque period of music was the devout Protestant Johann Sebastian Bach. One of the most elaborate and sophisticated of Bach's hundreds of pieces of sacred music is his *St. Matthew Passion*, written in the 1720s and performed for the first time on Good Friday, 1727, in Leipzig (in modern-day Germany). This powerful piece of music is nearly three hours long and includes assorted soloists in dialogue with a large chorus and full orchestra. The lyrical text is based on a poetic rendering of the story of Jesus's betrayal, sufferings, crucifixion, death, and burial taken from Matthew's Gospel. (The name "passion" for the last days of Jesus's life comes from the Latin word for "suffering.") Bach's *St. Matthew Passion* provides a theologically thoughtful and emotionally commanding interpretation of these final days of Jesus's earthly life, inviting the listeners into a deep experience of the Gospel story.

Figure 6.6. Portrait of Johann Sebastian Bach by Elias Gottlob Haussmann

The Great Commission?

One of the most famous passages of Matthew is its concluding "Great Commission" (28:18–20), in which Jesus authorizes his disciples to make disciples of all the nations of the world. There is no text more foundational to the modern missions movement. Many will be surprised to learn, however, that throughout much of the church's history this text was read differently: as a command that was given only to the apostles and completed in their lifetimes. With few exceptions, most readers interpreted the text this way up until the time of William Carey in the nineteenth century. The church has always been outward looking, however, and in recent centuries Matthew 28:18–20 has rightly provided a clarity and impetus for this cross-cultural evangelistic impulse.

God with Us

From the beginning of the First Gospel, Matthew emphasizes that Jesus's coming is the dwelling of God with his people; this is why he is ascribed the name Immanuel, which means "God with us" (1:23). This theme continues with Jesus's solemn promise to dwell with his people in the church (18:20). It concludes and is deepened in the final scene of this Gospel, when Jesus promises that he will be with his disciples, even to the end of the age (28:20). This theme not only makes assertions about Jesus's divine nature but also serves the pastoral function of assuring Jesus's disciples of his love, care, and authority while they suffer and await his return. It is also one of the New Testament teachings that leads to the church's robust trinitarian theology and rejection of **Modalism** and **Docetism**.

disciples. The content of this Great Commission focuses on creating followers through baptizing them and teaching them all that Jesus has taught them about what it means to be a disciple awaiting the coming kingdom of heaven. The point of the Gospel according to Matthew finally makes sense now: disciples of disciples of disciples are to use this book to understand, teach, preach, and proclaim who Jesus is and how to respond to the good news of the kingdom.

Implementation—Reading Matthew as Christian Scripture Today

The ideal reader of Matthew is the one who reads, studies, analyzes, and receives this Gospel biography as a Christian disciple, reading it with an openness to its purpose, which is to make and shape disciples through understanding who Jesus is and what he did and taught (28:16–20).

Matthew's call to discipleship has many facets, but one of the most dominant is the call to avoid hypocrisy, the kind of religiosity that is manifested by the scribes and Pharisees. This group of "Extra-Super-Holy People" (as the *Jesus Storybook Bible* calls them) appears very frequently in Matthew and is particularly highlighted as the enemies and opponents of Jesus. This likely reflects Matthew's own social and religious setting—a time of open tension and conflict between Jewish people who have become Christians and those who have not. But for the Christian reader today, the best approach is not to focus just on the historical Pharisees and their problems, but rather to see in the Pharisees a challenge to the individual Christian today as well as to the church. Readers should ask themselves, "Do I approach God and others in this same pharisaical way—focusing on external behavior rather than wholeheartedness toward God and forgiveness and compassion toward others?"

Closely related to this, a Christian reading of Matthew will rightly ask how his emphasis on wholehearted discipleship (the "greater righteousness" that is required according to 5:20) relates to the apostle Paul's repeated theme of **justification** by faith. In light of Paul's teaching that no one can earn standing with God through doing good deeds apart from **union with Christ**, what is the role of obedience, transformation, and following after Christ (discipleship) for entering into the kingdom of heaven? Matthew particularly raises this issue through his strong emphasis on the necessity of doing God's will in order to enter the kingdom. Asking these questions and earnestly seeking their answers is an important part of whole-canon, and spiritually sensitive, Christian reading.

While there is no simplistic way to put all of this intracanonical dialogue together, we can see Matthew and Paul as living in a healthy orthodox dialogue (like Paul and James do as well). They are in ultimate agreement but are putting a necessary emphasis on different aspects of the complexity of salvation and human development. Paul's message about justification by faith primarily addresses the question of whether a sinful human (even a Jewish person) has any inherent rights to stand before God (based on ethnicity or morality), to which his answer is no. Matthew addresses a larger and more comprehensive question of what it means to be a disciple, which he answers by saying that true discipleship looks like whole-person transformation. For both Paul and Matthew, grace and faith are the key ideas, while they address different issues in the complex reality of the Christian life.

The masterpiece that is the Gospel according to Matthew is like a treasure trove that people all over the world keep returning to, and they continue to discover riches old and new (13:52). Like Bach's "Little" Fugue in G Minor for organ or John Steinbeck's novel *East of Eden*, this Gospel is worth revisiting over and over again to learn more and to appreciate more of its depth and artistry.

KEY VERSES IN MATTHEW

- Now all this took place to fulfill what was spoken by the Lord through the prophet: "See, the virgin will become pregnant and give birth to a son, and they will name him Immanuel," which is translated "God is with us." 1:22–23
- Don't think that I came to abolish the Law or the Prophets. I did not come to abolish but to fulfill. . . . For I tell you, unless your righteousness surpasses that of the scribes and Pharisees, you will never get into the kingdom of heaven. 5:17, 20
- Jesus came near and said to them, "All authority has been given to me in heaven and on earth. Go, therefore, and make disciples of all nations, baptizing them in the name of the Father and of the Son and of the Holy Spirit, teaching them to observe everything I have commanded you. And remember, I am with you always, to the end of the age." 28:18–20

Christian Reading Questions

1. Read the Lord's Prayer (Matt. 6:7–15) and answer the following questions: (a) How is this poem structured? What are its different parts and how do they relate to one another? (b) Where else in Matthew do the themes in the Lord's Prayer appear? Where else in the New Testament? (c) If the Lord's Prayer is central to the Christian life, how does this affect how Christians should live and what the church's priorities are?

2. Trace the theme of the new people of God and the church throughout Matthew's whole story. Which texts particularly highlight this theme? How is the new people of God defined, and what does life together as the church look like?

3. Read all the Letter of James, followed by reading the Sermon on the Mount. Make a list of similarities and differences. Why do you think there are so many similarities?

4. Read Revelation 1–4; 21–22. Make a list of similarities of language and theme between Revelation and Matthew. Are there significant differences?

CHAPTER SEVEN

The Gospel according to Mark

Orientation

We need all kinds of stories because life is full of all kinds of people and all kinds of experiences. Different stories reach different people and speak to different experiences. What kind of story is Mark's Gospel? A comic book. A superhero movie. A graphic novel. These are analogies we can use to understand the fury, feel, flow, and flurry of activity that is the Gospel according to Mark. If we think of the four Gospels as four children, Mark is the energetic and wild one, full of action and verve.

Probably the first Gospel written, Mark is the least refined. But it is foundational to this collection of biographies of Jesus and has its own important voice. Mark is the pioneer and provides the basic structure and narrative plot that the more complex Matthew and Luke will build on. What Mark lacks in nuance and polish, he makes up for with a powerful, engaging biography of Jesus. 🖤

Each of the Gospels is a biography, a story centered on one person who serves as a model to follow. But each Gospel also has a particular emphasis, a different flavor and scent. Mark's Gospel focuses on Jesus's actions. Through Jesus's actions readers learn

Figure 7.1. This book cover (eleventh century, Germany) shows Mark writing his Gospel with a lion, his symbol, holding a scroll above him.

The Metropolitan Museum of Art. Gift of J. Pierpont Morgan, 1917.

HISTORICAL MATTERS

The Historical Origins of Mark

Author: There is strong tradition that this Gospel comes from John Mark, who traveled with his cousin Barnabas and the apostle Paul on the first missionary journey (Acts 13:5) and then with Barnabas to Cyprus (Acts 15:36–41). He was also likely with Paul in Rome (Col. 4:10; Philem. 24; 2 Tim. 4:11). The early church also identifies Mark as closely connected with the apostle Peter (1 Pet. 5:13).

Date: Likely mid–AD 50s to late 60s

Location: Rome

Sources: Mark was originally written in Greek and is widely believed to be the first Gospel written, dependent on oral traditions about Jesus and especially influenced by the eyewitness account of the apostle Peter.

Setting: A primary motivation for Mark probably was to preserve the eyewitness account of Peter before his death. Also, Mark emphasizes the Christian life as one of suffering discipleship, which likely relates to the intense persecution that Christians experienced in Rome during this time.

two primary things: who Jesus is and what it means to be his disciples.

These two themes—Jesus's identity and the life of discipleship—are interwoven with mystery and conflict. Mark presents Jesus as the authoritative Messiah, but at the same time Jesus is unpredictable, and his actions and sayings create ambiguity for many. His teaching is mysterious and creates a separation between those who understand and those who don't. Jesus has enemies who don't understand or trust him. This combination of mystery and conflict drives the plot of Mark's Gospel, culminating in Jesus's persecution, suffering, and death. This, then, becomes the ultimate message of discipleship: Jesus suffers on his way to glory, and so too will his followers.

Mark's story is the shortest of the four Gospels. It can be read in its entirety in less than an hour. But its episodes are full of vivid details. We can picture the scenes and feel the action.

Even though his overall story is short, there is a crucial, discernible arc that runs through the whole account. Mark's story of Jesus is based on a three-stage journey narrative: Jesus ministers in and around Galilee in the north in the first stage (1:1–9:50). In the second part he begins the journey south (and higher in altitude) toward Jerusalem (10:1–52). And in the final stage Jesus is in Jerusalem, the place of his death and resurrection (11:1–16:8). We don't know exactly how much time the first two stages took (roughly three years), but we know that the last and most important stage took place within just one week—Jesus's last week of pre-resurrection life. Mark gives a lot of literary real estate to this final stage, leading many readers to observe that he is particularly emphasizing the passion week and its events. 📖

Exploration—Reading Mark

The Beginning of the Gospel

▪ READ MARK 1:1–15 ▪

Mark's introduction begins and ends with references to "the gospel / good news" (1:1, 14–15). Mark proclaims that what we are about to read is the start of something very important. It is great news. He describes this in 1:1 as the good news "of Jesus Christ, the Son of God," in 1:14 as simply "the good news of God," and in 1:15 as the time being "fulfilled" and the "kingdom of God has come near."

The last description makes clear what Mark means by "the gospel." It is the good news that God is now finally returning to reign over the world through his anointed king. The return of God's good and just kingdom was long promised in the Hebrew Scriptures. This is a joyful message that calls for a response: "Repent and believe in the good news!" (1:15). That is to say, turn away from actions that don't align with God's kingdom and put your hope in this coming divine regime change.

Inside this message that bookends the introduction, Mark introduces two people: the forerunner and the One. The forerunner, John the Baptizer, is a wild man with a wild man's clothing and diet (1:4–6). From his mouth comes God's call to repent, symbolized through the physical act of being baptized in the river of the promised land, the Jordan (1:5).

But despite his attractional power, John the Baptizer makes it very clear that he has a specific role to play. There is one far more powerful and important than him, the One who will baptize people with the Holy Spirit (1:7–8), the Messiah himself.

The intersection point between the forerunner and the Messiah is the river. When Jesus comes up from the water of John's baptism, a voice—not from the wilderness but from heaven itself—declares the most important thing: Jesus is the Spirit-anointed Son of God (1:9–11). Jesus, the Son of God, starts in the wilderness, successfully defeating the temptations of the devil (unlike God's son Israel), and then returns to the people of Galilee to proclaim God's kingdom.

The Structure of Mark

While Mark's plot is a three-part journey, his literary structure is clearly built on an introduction and then two main parts. After the introductory setting, which presents John the Baptizer as the forerunner (1:1–15), Mark structured his biography into two halves of almost identical length, like two facing pages of an open book (1:16–8:26 and 8:27–16:8).

> Introduction: The Messiah is coming with his kingdom (1:1–15)
> Part One: The powerful Son of God at work in Galilee (1:16–8:26)
> Part Two: The powerful Son of God must suffer in Jerusalem (8:27–16:8)

The turning point of the book is right at the center of these two parts, with Peter's bold confession of Jesus as the Christ and Jesus's prediction of his own suffering and death that follows (8:27–33). The shocking juxtaposition of two opposite ideas—the clear revelation of Jesus as the Messiah (8:27–30) and the certainty that this Messiah will suffer and die (8:31–33)—exemplifies the paradoxical message of Mark's understanding of Jesus and what it means to follow him, suffering and glory combined.

Jesus the Healer

■ READ MARK 1:16–2:12 ■

We are now in part one of Mark's two-part book. This half highlights the two main themes: Jesus's identity and the call of discipleship. Jesus's identity is filled out more through every story, while the call to discipleship introduces each of the four sections that follow through 8:26. All of this exists under the banner of the introduction, especially its concluding words, which serve as a transition to the main story: "The time is fulfilled, and the kingdom of God has come near. Repent and believe the good news!" (1:15).

The first collection of stories (1:16–2:12) begins with the first disciples and sets the tone that Jesus's ministry is going to be one of gathering people—fishing for them—to follow him (1:16–19). The five stories that follow are aptly summarized with the final words in 2:12: "We have never seen anything like this!"

In these initial stories we learn that Jesus is the Holy One of God (1:24), a new teacher with amazing authority (1:27), a miraculous healer (1:29–34, 40–42; 2:12), a preacher (1:38–39), the "Son of Man" (2:10), and, depending on one's perspective, either a blasphemer or divine forgiver of sins (2:6–10).

Each of these initial stories is positive—or at least awe-inspiring—until we get to the last one. In 2:1–12 we see the first hint of the conflict that will drive the whole story all the way to the point of Jesus's tortured death. The conflict comes from his new enemies, the "scribes"—teachers of the law (2:6). Why? Because Jesus presents himself as more than a miracle worker and teacher. His identity moves into the realm of the divine: he offers forgiveness of sins (2:5) and claims to be the "Son of Man" (2:10).

This understandably provokes controversy. Jesus's enemies are absolutely accurate in their logic but fundamentally fail in their conclusion. They are correct that only God can forgive sins; they are wrong that Jesus is blaspheming. This is because, as Mark wants his readers to understand, Jesus is presented here as God's own Son in the flesh.

Jesus's Mixed Reception

■ READ MARK 2:13–3:12 ■

This portion of Mark once again begins with a story of calling disciples (see above, 1:16–20). But this new disciple is a controversial one. He is a tax collector, from a small segment of Jewish society that worked for the Roman oppressors and was despised for being greedy traitors. Not only does Jesus invite such a sinner to be his disciple, but even worse, Jesus is seen dining in the house with *many* tax collectors. The emotional effect would be comparable to Jesus taking his disciples to a strip club in today's world.

The rest of this section's stories hang together because they are all based on questions. But these are not questions asked simply for the sake of knowledge. They are pointed challenges to Jesus's authority made in an effort to shame and discredit him. In each case Jesus gives a brilliant riposte that deepens our understanding of his identity. When asked why he is eating with notorious sinners, Jesus describes himself as a doctor, one who has come to call sinners to life and health (2:15–17). When asked why Jesus and his disciples are not fasting like the Pharisees and John the Baptizer's disciples, Jesus describes himself as the joyful bridegroom who is with his people, bringing new wine into the world (2:18–22). When asked about eating grain from the fields on the Sabbath (which the Pharisees considered to be forbidden Sabbath work), Jesus analogizes himself to the great king David and mysteriously refers to himself as "the Son of Man" who is "Lord even of the Sabbath" (2:23–28).

These three challenging questions are then turned on their heads when Jesus asks his opponents a question. He is angry that God's own people have no compassion for those who are suffering. So he rebukes them by asking them if it is lawful to do good on the Sabbath, and by physically healing a man right in front of them. They have no answer and plot to kill him (3:1–6), foreshadowing the rising conflict.

The summary paragraph in 3:7–12 shows Jesus's increasing popularity, with masses following him as he healed large numbers of people. Mark shows us that whatever wrong interpretations people may have about Jesus, at least the unclean spirits can't help but cry out, "You are the Son of God!" (3:11).

The Opposition Is Building

▧ READ MARK 3:13–6:6 ▧

The two main themes of Jesus's identity and the call to discipleship are on display once again in this section of Mark's story. But the overall narrative is beginning to darken. The previous section ended with a summary (3:7–12) that was bright and positive, with Jesus healing many and the confession of Jesus as the Son of God. This next section thickens the plot and also ends with a summary (6:1–6), but one that is not so positive. Jesus returns to his hometown and is once again teaching in the synagogue on the

Sabbath, but the response is offense and dishonor and lack of faith. As a result, Jesus heals very few. Conflict is brewing.

What happens between these two very different summaries of Jesus's ministry (3:7–12 and 6:1–6)? The stories that Mark has collected here show Jesus acting in a way that forces one to believe in or reject him. There is no middle ground.

This section is introduced by the full list of the original twelve disciples (3:13–19), following Mark's pattern of starting each story unit with a reference to the disciples (1:16–20; 2:13–17). Immediately the conflict appears with two different groups questioning Jesus's sanity (3:20–35). Jesus's wild popularity and travel make his family think that he has lost his mind. The teachers of the law resort to the desperate argument that Jesus must be demon-possessed. Jesus answers both charges. To the Jewish leaders he observes that it is senseless that Satan would attack his own house. To his Jewish family he makes clear that something greater than biology is operative: "Whoever does the will of God is my brother and sister and mother" (3:35).

Mark 4:1–34 marks a major transition in Jesus's story. Up to this point he has taught in the Jewish synagogues. Now he changes to a different venue (lakeside) and a very different style. Now Jesus teaches in mysterious parables, extended metaphors that are simultaneously engaging and ambiguous. Parables about a seed sower, a lampstand, the growth of grain, and the mustard seed are easy to understand at one level but prove too mysterious to fully comprehend. But Jesus explains that this is precisely the point. As a prophet and teacher of the coming kingdom, his teaching is designed to separate the world into those who understand versus those who do not, between those who will be disciples and those who won't (4:9–12, 33–34).

This emphasis on the disciples' understanding is followed immediately by three shocking stories that reveal Jesus's identity as powerful even beyond what we have seen so far. First, Jesus's power over nature is shown in his stilling of the storm, the result of which is, understandably, fear and wonder (4:35–41). The second story likewise evokes fear and wonder when Jesus heals a wild man full of demons. This time the miracle affects a whole region of people who plead with Jesus to leave—all except the healed man (5:1–20). The third story is a double power-healing narrative, with two amazing miracles woven together. The healing of a long-suffering woman because of her great faith (5:24–34) is embedded within the even more stunning story of a dead girl raised to life (5:21–24, 35–43).

The Prophet Has Come

■ READ MARK 6:7–8:26 ■

As with the preceding sections, this portion begins with a summary paragraph about Jesus's disciples, this time being sent out to continue and expand his own ministry of kingdom preaching and healing (6:7–13).

This section of stories leads up to the midway point of Mark's book, the crucial Caesarea Philippi confession (8:27–30). This unit of vignettes continues the double theme of Jesus's identity and discipleship, but layered onto this is another paired theme: fame and misunderstanding. Throughout these stories we see Jesus's popularity and impact, combined with the fact that people don't truly understand who Jesus is and what this all means, including even his own disciples!

HISTORICAL MATTERS

The Parables of an Apocalyptic Prophet

Parables are not unique to Jesus and are found throughout ancient literature. Parables utilize poetic images and analogies to convey a message. This makes them memorable and powerful but not always clear in meaning. The parables' closest relative in the world of ancient literature is apocalyptic. In apocalyptic literature images and metaphors are used not for the purpose of straightforward teaching but to describe the paradox of God's work in the world, separating hearers into two groups: those who understand and those who do not. Thus, both parables and apocalypses are subversive stories, used by prophets to reinterpret the metanarrative of the world to retool how people live. In this sense, Jesus's extensive use of parables is an important part of his role as an apocalyptic prophet, much like many other prophets throughout Israel's history. This is why Jesus poses such a threat to the religious establishment. He is reinterpreting the story of Israel around himself.

Jesus's fame causes varied reactions: King Herod's guilt-driven paranoia that leads him to kill John the Baptizer (6:14–29); masses passionately following Jesus into the wilderness, where he miraculously feeds them (6:30–44; 8:1–13) and then escapes from them to pray (6:45–56); and gentiles seeking the Jewish Messiah for healing (7:24–37).

Jesus's popularity deepens his conflict with the religious authorities and Jewish conservatives, providing him an opportunity to clearly teach what God cares about: heart-cleanness, the inner person, and not external rituals (7:1–23).

Along with his fame, we see that people misunderstand Jesus's identity and mission. There is a dullness of heart and weakness of faith, even among Jesus's closest disciples. The disciples fail when they are asked by Jesus to provide food for the masses by faith (6:35–37; also 8:3–4), and then they can't fathom his divinity when he walks on water because "their hearts were hardened" (6:52). They also can't understand his teaching about the inner person because they are still "dull" (7:17–18). And when Jesus warns them about "the leaven of the Pharisees and the leaven of Herod," they can't understand that he is not referring to physical bread. Jesus asks why

Apophatic Discipleship

Theologians sometimes distinguish between **cataphatic theology** and **apophatic theology**. The first focuses on affirmations about God and the second on the unknowability of God. Together these two emphases form a balanced paradox: God is simultaneously immanent and transcendent, both knowable and unknowable. Throughout history theologians have tended to emphasize one side of this paradox or the other.

Mark largely emphasizes the apophatic truth. He shows Jesus to be unpredictable and inscrutable, overturning what people thought about God. This emphasis on mystery is found throughout Mark and explains the stress he puts on the people's failure to understand Jesus. Yet it is simplistic to label Mark as only apophatic. Jesus is, after all, the revelation of God in the flesh and the one who calls people to follow him. Mark presents Jesus within the paradox of our relationship to God: we can never fully understand him, but we can follow the one who reveals God to us, Jesus the Son.

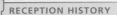

The Syrophoenician Woman

The story of the healing of this gentile woman's daughter has intrigued readers throughout the church's history. Why does Jesus put her off, call her a dog, only then to relent and heal her daughter? For many ancient interpreters, this story is about the progress of salvation from the Jews to the gentiles, with this woman as a model of this salvation-history shift. At the same time, this woman is often commended as a model of humility and tenacious faith. Some preachers, such as John Chrysostom, emphasize the journey of transformation of the soul with Jesus as the pedagogue. Later readings, especially among Protestants, instead explore the relationship of grace and works and questions about human capacity. Others receive this story into their personal prayers, seeing it as a reenactment of their inner lives. Across the interpretive diversity this little story leaves a large impact in its wake.

they still do not understand, why their hearts are hardened, and why they don't remember what he has already shown them (8:14–21).

All of this leads up to the final story before the turning point of the book (8:22–26). Jesus's healing of the blind man at Bethsaida is a two-stage healing in which the man goes from blindness, to seeing partially, to seeing fully. Here at the hinge point of Mark's Gospel, right after the great emphasis on the disciples' lack of understanding, this two-stage healing also serves as a symbol for the disciples' growing into understanding, the healing of their heart-blindness. 🔲 👥

The Revelation of the Suffering Messiah

■ READ MARK 8:27–10:52 ■

We have now reached the second half of Mark's two-part Gospel story. In the first half we see Jesus as the powerful Son of God, preaching about God's coming kingdom and, in accord with this reality, restoring oppressed people. Along the way Jesus gathers followers who understand his message (at least in part) and want to be a part of it.

Driving the story is the burning question of who exactly Jesus is. Various answers have been given: he is the Son of God, the Son of Man, a teacher and healer with amazing authority. Here at the turning point of the book a shocking answer is given. Peter declares that, whatever else people think Jesus to be, he is in fact the Messiah (8:27–30). The Hebrew word "messiah" means "anointed," and it was tied to the hope of the return of a Davidic king to restore God's just reign. Jesus as the Messiah-King is a perfect culminating description after 1:1–8:26.

What no one expected is that this king must be rejected, suffer, die, and rise from the dead. This was inconceivable, and Peter attempts to rebuke Jesus along these lines, only to receive a rebuke himself (8:31–33). As we have seen in Mark's story so far, Jesus's disciples continue to struggle to "see," like the blind man in 8:22–26. They must learn that the glorious Messiah and Son of Man will enter into that glory only through humble suffering. He makes clear that to be a disciple is to follow in the way of cross-bearing (8:34–38). Once again we see the double theme of Jesus's identity and the call to discipleship.

But a new tone will dominate the second half of the story: glory that comes through suffering. This juxtaposition of glory and suffering is exemplified strikingly in the transfiguration story immediately following the turning point of the book (9:1–13). At this high point of Mark's Gospel the disciples see Jesus in full glory, accompanied by the divine voice declaring him to be the beloved Son (9:7). Immediately Jesus reiterates his coming suffering and rejection (9:12; also 8:31–33; 9:30–32; 10:32–34). From this point the story is all downhill, barreling toward the fulfillment of these predictions in Jerusalem.

The hodgepodge of events and declarations (9:14–10:45) between the great confession and the transfiguration (8:27–9:13) and Jesus's entering into Jerusalem for the last week of his life (11:1) can be summed up with the general heading of "life in the coming kingdom." The connective thread through these various teachings on prayer, divorce, and riches is that life in God's kingdom is upside down from that of the world. Children are commended (9:36–37, 42; 10:13–16), being crippled or disfigured is better than having a whole body in hell (9:43–48), riches and success are hindrances to life (10:17–31), and the greatest ones are the servants (10:29–31, 35–45).

Figure 7.2. Exorcism of the Syrophoenician woman's daughter, depicted in *Très Riches Heures du Duc de Berry* (fifteenth century)

THEOLOGICAL ISSUES

The Ransom Theory of the Atonement

In Mark 10:45 Jesus describes himself as the Son of Man who came not to be served but to serve and "to give his life as a ransom for many." The ancient idea of a ransom is basically the same as what that word means today: the price paid to free someone from captivity. Going back at least as far as the third century, many Christians have seen this ransom idea as an important way to describe what happened through Jesus's death. Most would acknowledge that this is not the only way to talk about the complex reality of the **atonement**, but it is one important aspect.

The **ransom theory of the atonement** understands that Jesus's death is a payment that satisfies the debt that humanity owes due to sin, and that Jesus's death frees and breaks the bonds of humanity's enslavement. In addition to Mark 10:45, this idea connects with Paul's language of believers being transferred from the kingdom of darkness to the kingdom of the beloved Son (Col. 1:13), and being "redeemed" or "bought back" (Eph. 1:7; Col. 1:14).

There has been great debate, however, about the ransom theory, because some theologians have objected that Jesus would not pay a debt to Satan; the devil is not that powerful and God does not owe him anything. Instead, many have argued that the ransom that is paid by Jesus's death is paid to God the Father to free humanity from enslavement to our sin.

Jesus is the model of all virtue, but he especially exemplifies this topsy-turvy rule: "For even the Son of Man did not come to be served, but to serve, and to give his life as a ransom for many" (10:45).

This "journey to Jerusalem" section ends with another story of sight restoration (10:46–52) that parallels the previous story (8:22–26). The earlier

THEOLOGICAL ISSUES

Mark's Christological Titles

Mark is not merely a story but is a theological document, and his theology is laser-focused on **Christology**. Who Jesus is is the theological point that Mark cares most about. Mark unpacks this theology through the actions and sayings of Jesus, which are the most important revealers of Mark's Christology. But he also uses several titles that supplement our understanding of who Jesus is.

Son of God—From Mark's heading in 1:1 and throughout the story, this is the primary christological title. God himself identifies Jesus as the Son of God (1:11; 9:7), as do others (15:39), including demons (3:11; 5:7). Jesus identifies himself as the same (14:61).

Messiah—In 1:1 and then six more times, Jesus as the Messiah/Christ is also fundamental. Jesus doesn't publicly declare himself to be the Messiah, though he accepts this designation, including the apex moment of the Caesarea Philippi Confession (8:27–30). But then Jesus immediately bends this Jewish messianic expecta-

tion by saying that the Christ, the Son of Man, will suffer, die, and rise again (8:31).

Lord—Sixteen times Jesus is called Lord in Mark, with a happy ambiguity about how this title is also used to refer to Yahweh of the Old Testament. "Lord" refers to both God and Jesus in Mark.

Teacher—The most frequent appellation of Jesus in Mark is teacher or rabbi, emphasizing that teaching is Jesus's predominant activity.

Son of Man—Jesus alone refers to himself with this somewhat vague title. In light of its background in Daniel 7 and how Jesus uses it, it implies his divine status, power, and transcendent rule.

Son of David—There was a widespread Jewish assumption that the Messiah would be of Davidic descent. This title for Jesus is infrequent in Mark (10:47–48; 12:35), however, possibly because of its politically charged overtones for the Roman government, and because Jesus will redefine this role as nonmilitant, bringing the kingdom through his suffering and death.

RECEPTION HISTORY

The Transfiguration

The story of the transfiguration—Jesus takes Peter, James, and John onto a mountain, becomes radiant, speaks with Moses and Elijah, and is declared the Son of God by a voice out of a cloud—is found in all three Synoptic Gospels. Modern interpreters, including those who believe that this happened and those who don't, typically emphasize the literary and theological connections with the Old Testament and the flow of the Gospel narratives. However, throughout the first thousand years of interpretation the focus was instead on vision and seeing. The transfiguration story is connected to other biblical texts where people saw God, and in this reading Peter is understood to be in an ecstatic, visionary state. This story is read primarily for how it teaches believers about the need to see God and, in doing so, be transformed. Modern interpretations have their own strengths, but the premodern reception of this story adds a deeply spiritual aspect that is rooted in the biblical narratives.

Figure 7.3. Transfiguration mosaic (565–66) from St. Catherine's Monastery, Mount Sinai

healing served as a metaphor for the disciples progressively coming to see and understand Jesus's identity. Now, as Jesus approaches Jerusalem, the same symbolic meaning reappears. Emblematic of what it means to be a disciple, blind Bartimaeus cries out to Jesus, "I want to see" (10:51). Jesus mercifully grants this healing, and the man becomes a follower on the road to the culmination of Jesus's story in Jerusalem (10:52). 📖 👥

Jesus the King Enters Jerusalem

■ READ MARK 11:1–13:37 ■

The Gospel of Mark is broken into two major structural parts. Its plot, however, flows along a threefold journey pattern: Jesus's ministry in Galilee (1:14–9:50), Jesus's journey to Jerusalem (10:1–52), and Jesus's last week in Jerusalem (11:1–16:8). These geographical movements have theological significance. Mark wants his readers to understand that Jesus—though he is Messiah, Son of God, Son of Man—is an outsider. To use the summary words of the Gospel of John, "He came to his own, and his own people did not receive him" (John 1:11). Jesus's ministry is most fruitful the farther he is from Jerusalem, the spiritual and cultural capital of the Jewish people. As Jesus journeys toward Jerusalem, opposition mounts, resulting finally in his imprisonment, ridicule, torture, and death. This communicates something crucial about Jesus and his ministry: he is not continuing the status quo of established religion; he is bringing something new! This is the gospel message, that God is doing something new to establish his reign on the earth.

This newness and the religious establishment's opposition to it explain the heightened tension and intensity of Mark's last sections. The conflict is reaching its climax. So Mark slows the breakneck pace of his story and spends the last section just on Jesus's last week of life. 👥

Chapter 11 begins on an appropriate high note as the true Son of David approaches and enters the city of David, to great acclaim and praise (11:1–11). But quickly we see that before Jesus can bring about the kingdom of God, there is a necessary cleansing that must take place. This cleansing comes in the form of judgment of the religious leadership, both in their worship (11:12–25) and in their authority/teaching (11:27–12:44). Then Jesus takes on the mantle of prophet and

RECEPTION HISTORY

Fig Trees and Leaves

The cursing of the fig tree (Mark 11:12–14; cf. Matt. 21:18–19) has been interpreted in a variety of ways throughout the church's history. Modern commentators tend to note the literary connection with Jesus's cleansing/cursing of the temple (11:15–18), how these two events parallel each other conceptually. Ancient commentators made other interesting connections that are not found in today's writers. For example, Hilary of Poitiers noted how Jesus's physical hunger is part of his identifying with our human poverty. Augustine and Gregory the Great connect the unfruitful tree with the call for Christian lives to bear fruit through love. Cyril of Jerusalem suggests that the last act of Jesus's ministry, the cursing of the fig tree, can be seen as a transformation and reversal of the first human act of sin, which resulted in Adam and Eve's need for fig leaves.[1]

The Sandwich Technique of Storytelling

Although he is not the only Gospel writer to use this technique, Mark frequently utilizes what is called intercalation, a technique that sandwiches two stories together by starting one story (one slice of bread), telling another story inside of it (the meat), and then completing the first story (the other slice of bread). For example, in 11:12–25 Mark recounts Jesus's cursing of a fig tree as he heads toward Jerusalem (11:12–14). In Jerusalem he disrupts the temple court and announces judgment on it (11:15–18). Then Jesus and the disciples leave Jerusalem, and when they return on the next day they see that the cursed fig tree has withered (11:19–25). The intercalating of these stories shows the reader how the events mutually inform each other, deepening the interpretation of both.

The Eschatological Son of Man and Parables of Enoch

The Jewish people produced and read many pieces of literature that are not included in our Bibles but are nonetheless helpful to read as background material in dialogue with our canon. One important example is the collection of writings we call 1 Enoch, especially the portion called the Parables of Enoch. In that section we see an apocalyptic view of the world and read of the "Son of Man," who is coming as the eschatological judge to set the world right. While there is no evidence that Mark directly used 1 Enoch, both documents reflect the expectation of a messiah who will come from heaven to earth and inaugurate the new age. Mark labors to show that this expected Son of Man is in fact Jesus.

pronounces judgment now and in the future on Jerusalem and the temple (13:1–37). Using language full of poetic imagery (like the Old Testament prophets), Jesus speaks of a time coming when God himself will set the world to rights through the return of the Son of Man. The main point of the Olivet Discourse, as it is commonly called, is not to give detailed information about the "end times" but rather to call Jesus's disciples to be on guard, avoiding false teachers and false living. In a word, Jesus's disciples must "Watch!" (13:37), because the new era of the world is beginning.

Jesus Dies and Rises Again

■ READ MARK 14:1–16:8 ■

We now arrive at the high point to which the fast-action story of Mark has been heading. This is where the story finds its focus: Jesus's betrayal, suffering, death, and resurrection. If we imagine a soundtrack accompanying these scenes, it would be dark, somber, and foreboding. Each of these stories contributes to the building sense of doom, all the way to the end of chapter 15, when Jesus cries out in God-centered despair (15:33–37).

Throughout these stories we see characters respond in different, somewhat surprising ways to Jesus at the end of his life. We see an unnamed woman lovingly sacrifice her wealth to anoint Jesus for burial (14:1–9), put into sharp contrast with Judas, one of the original twelve disciples, who betrays Jesus's trust with a kiss of hypocrisy (14:10–11, 43–45). The other disciples don't betray him but prove to be more fearful than faithful. When Jesus is arrested, they all flee (14:50), and worst of all, Peter even denies that he knows Jesus (14:26–31, 66–72). In a stark and surprising contrast, we are told that a Roman centurion, who has just mocked and beaten Jesus (15:16–20), proclaims Jesus to be the Son of God (15:39). Another disciple, Joseph of Arimathea, finds the courage to ask for Jesus's body so that he might bury him respectably (15:42–47).

The Roman and Jewish authorities both play their parts in putting Jesus to death (14:53–65; 15:1–15).

Though Mark's story ends as a cliffhanger (16:8; see the sidebar "Mark in Search of an Ending"), it is not without hope. Jesus does not just die as an example of godly suffering; he rises from the dead and appears to his followers (16:1–8)!

The story that makes sense of this last section of Mark's story is 14:22–26, the record of what Jesus did and said during his last meal with them. In this "Last Supper" he explains two crucial things about his suffering and death: it is both voluntary and world-changing. First, he is giving over his own body and blood, thus making a new covenant with anyone who would follow him (14:22–24). Second, he promises that he will come again, restoring God's reign on the earth; at that time there will be rejoicing and fellowshipping together again (14:25). Together in these two sayings we can understand all these climactic events: Jesus's death and his bodily resurrection. This great Gospel story ends with his disciples believing and awaiting his return to reign.

Figure 7.4. *Jesus Cleansing the Temple* by Bernardo Bellotto

Implementation—Reading Mark as Christian Scripture Today

In C. S. Lewis's famous Chronicles of Narnia series the Christ figure is the lion named Aslan. This is an appropriate biblical way to depict Jesus. As the Son of David, the

CANONICAL CONNECTIONS

The Shema in the New Testament

The message of the Bible is primarily a story—an account of how the world came into being, how it devolved because of disruption with its Creator, and how this God has been engaged in reforming and redeeming the world through making relationships (covenants) with his creatures. The theology of the Bible is mostly a story. The closest thing in the Old Testament to a doctrinal statement is the Shema, the confession from Deuteronomy 6:4 that "the LORD our God is one." This statement is reiterated by Jesus as central. God's unity in himself is the basis for what Jesus identifies, along with Deuteronomy 6:5, as the greatest biblical command—to love the Lord with all your heart, soul, mind, and strength (Mark 12:30).

HISTORICAL MATTERS

Mark in Search of an Ending

Mark's abrupt and unexpected ending on a note of fear did not entirely satisfy his readers any more than it does many people today. We do not know for sure whether Mark had a fuller ending that was lost, but we can be fairly confident that the stories that often are printed in Bibles today as Mark 16:9–20 were not original to him. They are very old but appear to be a compilation from the other Gospel stories, motivated by an understandable desire to give a more complete and positive ending. Matthew, Luke, and John each give us endings that fill out the story, though without the same dramatic feel.

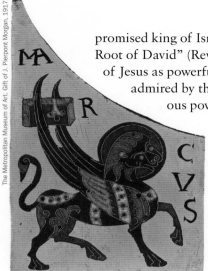

The Metropolitan Museum of Art. Gift of J. Pierpont Morgan, 1917.

promised king of Israel, he is called "the Lion from the tribe of Judah, the Root of David" (Rev. 5:5). The analogy of a lion is also helpful to think of Jesus as powerful and not to be toyed with. In Lewis's stories Aslan is admired by those around him, even with a hint of fear at his obvious power. Aslan is devoted to his friends and forceful with his enemies. He is both playful and majestic. So too is the Jesus we encounter in Mark's Gospel. The impression we get when reading Mark even two thousand years later is that this man Jesus was not someone who could be ignored. He forced people to pay attention to how they thought and acted.

Figure 7.5. Plaque with the lion symbol of Mark (1100)

And this is what a good reading of Mark should do for us. It is a call first to pay attention to who Jesus is. The answer that Mark gives is strong and beautiful: Jesus is the Son of God, the Son of Man, the Son of David, the one who frees people from bondage and then dies sacrificially to ransom a people for himself. Directly linked, the second call of Mark is to a life of discipleship. Because of Jesus's identity and actions, we cannot treat him as irrelevant or tangential to our personal lives. The presence of the Lion will not allow this. To be a Christian, Mark shows us, is to be a radical disciple. We will stumble and fail and misunderstand what God is doing. But we keep following with both fear and joy, just like Jesus's first disciples, who saw him die and rise again.

KEY VERSES IN MARK

- "Follow me," Jesus told them, "and I will make you fish for people." 1:17
- For even the Son of Man did not come to be served, but to serve, and to give his life as a ransom for many. 10:45

Christian Reading Questions

1. Trace the theme of the disciples' reactions to Jesus, noting how Jesus responds to them.
2. Read through Mark and make a list of the enemies of Jesus (demons and people) and what happens in their interactions. What does Mark teach us through this?

3. Read through the book of 1 Peter and make a list of similarities of language and theme shared with Mark's Gospel. Why do you think these similarities are present?
4. What emotions do you think Mark's abrupt ending would have evoked within his readers? Why do you think he ended his Gospel so suddenly?

CHAPTER EIGHT

The Gospel according to Luke

Orientation

Bible trivia question: Who wrote more of the New Testament than any other single person? The apostle Paul? Jesus's beloved disciple John? Both are good answers, but both are incorrect. Paul wrote more books of the New Testament than anyone else, and John wrote a lengthy Gospel. But the winner of the "Most Words Written by a Single Author in the New Testament" award goes to Luke, coming in with a solid 27 percent of the verbiage of the New Testament. (Paul has 23 percent, and John has 20 percent.) Luke, an educated gentile physician, who often accompanied Paul on his missionary journeys, wrote two lengthy and polished volumes that are crucial to the New Testament canon. These books are really two parts of one big story. The first book is Luke's contribution to the Fourfold Gospel Book, the Third Gospel account. The second volume, which we call the Acts of the Apostles, overlaps with the conclusion of his first book—the story of Jesus's post-resurrection ascension. Acts continues the story of Jesus by following the lives of his disciples and the growth of the Christian faith. Together these stories, which we refer to as Luke-Acts, give us fifty-two fascinating chapters, over a quarter of the New Testament writings.

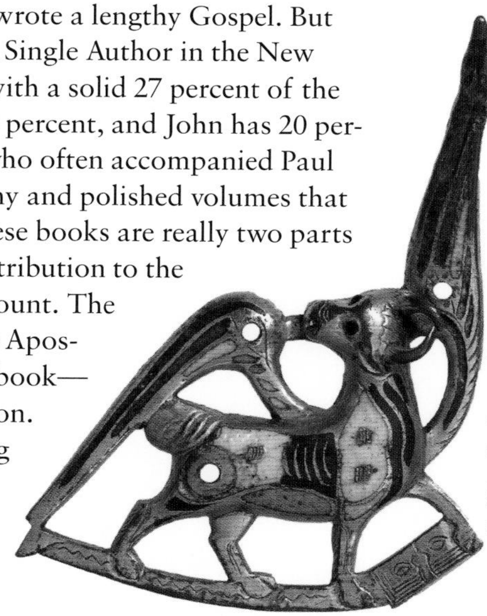

The Metropolitan Museum of Art. The Friedsam Collection, Bequest of Michael Friedsam, 1931.

Figure 8.1. An ox, the symbol of Luke's Gospel, from a book cover (1200–25)

Though Luke wrote a two-part story (Luke-Acts), throughout most of the church's history the Gospel according to Luke has not been read in direct tandem with Acts but rather has been clustered with its canonical Gospel siblings (Matthew, Mark, John). Early in the church's history the Fourfold Gospel Book was organized in a 3 + 1 pattern, with the Synoptic Gospels (Matthew, Mark, Luke) joined together with John. This is followed by a separate collection—Acts plus the **General Letters** and Paul's Letters (including Hebrews). This puts the Gospel according to Luke into closer connection with the other three Gospels than with his second volume, Acts. While there are important insights that come from reading Luke and Acts together, there are also advantages to thinking about Luke in conjunction with the other Gospels.

If we read Luke's Gospel account in dialogue with his canonical brothers, what kind of story does Luke give us? We can use three words to describe Luke: original, mimetic, challenging.

> *Original*—Around 40 percent of Luke's Gospel is not found in any of the other Gospels, including many beloved parables and stories. Luke is not merely rehashing Mark and Matthew, but rather makes many original contributions. The source of these materials seems to have come from Luke's own research.
>
> *Mimetic*—Luke tells his stories about Jesus in ways that deeply imitate and evoke key stories from Israel's history (**mimesis**). From the birth narratives to the post-resurrection road to Emmaus, Luke skillfully spices his stories with tastes of God's work in the world before Jesus, inviting his readers to taste and see that Jesus is truly the fulfillment of all of God's promises from the past.
>
> *Challenging*—Luke radically reverses his readers' values and expectations. Luke regularly shows Jesus turning the world upside down by valuing the poor, the outcasts, and the devalued, showing them filled with the Spirit and worshiping God truly.

Luke's story has three major sections, all centered on Jerusalem, which is known as the city of David and the center of Jewish worship and culture:

Luke 1:1–9:50: This section shows who Jesus is, beginning with his origins and focusing on his ministry of teaching and healing.

Luke 9:51–19:27: This section begins with Jesus resolutely setting a course to go to Jerusalem. This lengthy portion includes much of Luke's original and most memorable stories as Jesus faces increasing opposition by the Jewish leadership.

Luke 19:28–24:53: In this final part of Luke's story Jesus arrives in Jerusalem and spends his last week teaching his followers and interacting with his opponents. The book concludes with Jesus's trials, death, and resurrection, culminating with his appearance to several disciples, explaining how to understand all that God has done.

Exploration—Reading Luke

The Overture

■ READ LUKE 1:1–2:52 ■

These opening chapters are familiar to many people because of the oft-retold Christmas story. Many have heard the story of Mary and Joseph trekking to Bethlehem, unwelcome and without shelter, Mary giving birth to a son with animals all around, laying him to sleep in a feeding trough. Carols like "Away in a Manger" and "Silent Night," along with holiday images of angels and stars and shepherds, come straight from Luke 2.

But this Christmas-pageant part of the story is only that—part of the story. Taken together these first two chapters of Luke are less about Christmas night and more like the overture to a Broadway musical: they introduce the main themes and ideas, even if it is unclear what these themes and ideas mean and what the story will look like. In Luke's overture-like introduction we quickly learn that God is on the move and is about to fulfill the hopes of his people. Through a series of poems and songs we are told that God is about to turn everything upside down: a barren old woman and a virgin both become pregnant; a young, lowly girl is said to be most blessed of women and shows great faith, while a seasoned Jewish priest is struck dumb; unsavory shepherds are the first honored guests for the birth of a king;

LITERARY NOTES

The Structure of Luke

In comparison with Matthew and Mark, one distinct element in Luke's Gospel is the central role that Jerusalem plays in his account. The general narrative is the same, with a large overlap in events and stories with Matthew and Mark, but Jerusalem is particularly highlighted in the Third Gospel. Luke's story begins with narratives of events prior to Jesus's birth, which are largely centered on Jerusalem (1:1–2:25), and then the largest section of his Gospel is framed by reference to Jesus's intentional journey toward Jerusalem (9:51–19:27), culminating in the last week of Jesus's life there (19:28–24:53).

The births of John and Jesus (1:1–2:25)
Preparations for Jesus's ministry (3:1–4:13)
Jesus in Galilee (4:14–9:50)
Jesus's journey to Jerusalem (9:51–19:27)
Jesus in Jerusalem: his death and resurrection (19:28–24:53)

and a twelve-year-old boy astonishes the temple priests with his great wisdom. All of this and more create an expectation of wonder for the story that Luke is about to tell. This story is not boring. The main character, Jesus, is going to upend the world.

The Kingdom of God in Action

▧ READ LUKE 3:1–4:44 ▧

Luke's prologue focuses on the preparation and birth of Jesus followed by one story about the twelve-year-old Jesus in the temple (2:41–52). The story then jumps ahead about eighteen years (3:23) and provides additional stories about Jesus's preparation before he calls his first disciples.

Consistent across each of the Gospels is the appearance of John the Baptizer as the herald and forerunner of Jesus. Luke's reporting of John gives us more information on some points and less on others. We don't get any of John's interaction with Jesus regarding his baptism (3:21), but we are given more detail about the content of John's preaching. John was sent to preach "a baptism of repentance for the forgiveness of sins" (3:3), which is applied to specific life situations such as sharing one's goods (3:10–11), being honest in financial dealings (3:12–13), and not abusing one's authority and position (3:14).

After Jesus's genealogy traces him all the way back to Adam (3:23–38), we finally see Jesus in action and hear his voice. Jesus is shown to be Spirit-filled and powerful, successfully outwitting the devil's temptations (4:1–13), teaching with bold authority in the synagogue (4:14–30), rebuking and exorcising demons (4:31–37, 41), and healing people of all kinds of illnesses (4:38–40). All this activity is summarized as "the good news about the kingdom of God," which Jesus has come to bring (4:43). 📜

The Powerful Messiah at Work in Galilee

▧ READ LUKE 5:1–9:50 ▧

This long section constitutes the first major portion of Luke's account, offering a rapid-fire series of stories that describe Jesus's ministry in Galilee in the northern

RECEPTION HISTORY

Mary's Song in Western Music

When the scandously pregnant Mary visits her also unexpectedly expecting cousin Elizabeth, she receives a prophetic blessing. Luke records Mary's response in lyrical form, a song of praise rich with theological tones and foreshadowing (1:46–55).

This song came to be called the **Magnificat**, from the Latin form of what Mary says, "My soul magnifies the Lord." The Magnificat developed as a very important part of Christian worship, used in many parts of the church's various liturgies. Starting as early as the thirteenth century, the Magnificat inspired scores of musicians to set these words to music, resulting in numerous beautiful musical versions, including those of famous composers such as Josquin de Prez, Palestrina, Monteverdi, Pachelbel, Vivaldi, Bach, Mozart, Mendelssohn, and Tchaikovsky. Each composer uses the style of the time to express the emotion and power of Mary's words in musical form, thus deepening the experience of Luke's words among the worshipers.

Figure 8.2. Portrait of Antonio Vivaldi by unknown artist

International Museum and Library of Music / Wikimedia Commons

CANONICAL CONNECTIONS

The Genealogies of Jesus in Matthew and Luke

One of the many ways that both Matthew and Luke rewrite and expand Mark's Gospel account is by providing a genealogy of Jesus. This sequential list of Jesus's ancestors is an appropriate and expected part of a biography in the ancient world. A genealogy fills in a lot of important information about who Jesus is.

What is unexpected, however, is the variance between Matthew's and Luke's genealogies. Matthew traces Jesus's lineage back to Abraham. Luke is more ambitious and goes all the way back to Adam. But even more noticeably, the list of names is completely different.

Readers have long puzzled over this, and several solutions have been offered, such as seeing one as the genealogy of Mary (Luke) and the other of Joseph (Matthew), or one as a royal lineage (Matthew) and the other as physical descendants (Luke). A more likely solution is that Luke and Matthew give us the lineage of Joseph's two fathers, one by physical birth and one by adoption. We know that, according to the Jewish custom of levirate marriage, a widowed woman often married the relative of her deceased husband, thus providing a new father (see Deut. 25:5–10). It is possible that Joseph had two fathers (Heli and Jacob) and that Matthew and Luke give us their different lineages.

part of Israel, before Jesus begins his planned move south to Jerusalem (9:51).

This section begins with the calling of the first disciples—Simon Peter, James, and John—who would forever remain the innermost circle of Jesus's followers (5:1–11). In 6:12–16 Luke lists the group of twelve disciples appointed by Jesus from among the large group of followers. Between these two listings of disciples Luke tells a series of stories that position Jesus within Israel's tradition, while showing him to be unique and powerful: Peter's calling mimics the calling of Isaiah (5:1–11); the leper's cleansing is connected to the Mosaic commandments (5:12–15); a paralytic's healing is the occasion of Jesus proclaiming forgiveness of sins (5:17–26), which he says is why he has come (5:27–31); and Jesus explains the true meaning of the Sabbath, claiming to be the Lord of the Sabbath (6:1–11). All of this can be described with the metaphors of Jesus as the long-awaited bridegroom and the new wine that cannot be contained in old wineskins (5:33–39).

The second part of this section focuses on Jesus's authority as the Messiah. First, he is shown to be a powerful wisdom teacher (6:17–49). This is followed by a series of remarkable stories of Jesus's power over creation: Jesus heals the centurion's daughter from afar (7:1–10); he raises a widow's son and a synagogue leader's daughter from the

Figure 8.3. *The Annunciation* (1481) by Sandro Botticelli

dead (7:11–17; 8:49–56); he stills a violent storm by merely rebuking the wind and waves (8:22–25); he heals three seemingly unhealable people, a man possessed by a legion of demons (8:26–39), a hemorrhaging woman (8:42–48), and a demon-possessed boy (9:37–43); and finally, Jesus miraculously multiplies food for famished followers in the wilderness (9:10–17).

All of this confirms the claim made that Jesus is the God-sent Messiah (9:18–20) who is the glorious Son of God, honored by Moses and Elijah, who will bring about the new exodus (9:28–36).

Encouragement amid Dark Warnings

■ READ LUKE 9:51–13:35 ■

We have now entered Jesus's journey to Jerusalem (9:51–19:27), where Luke packs in many of the stories that are unique to his account. The first half of this journey is framed with references to Jerusalem (9:51 and 13:34–35). In between we hear teaching directly from Jesus more than stories about him.

The tone of this section focuses on a wide variety of stark warnings. The sense of urgency and the call to be alert are woven through a large number of images. These include warnings about counting the cost of following Jesus (9:57–62) while also being aware that this is a wicked generation heading for judgment (10:12–16; 11:29–32; 12:54–59; 13:1–5). In fact, a large part of Jesus's teachings here urge watchfulness because of the return of the Son of Man, who will bring judgment on the unrepentant. Jesus describes this as the return of unclean spirits (11:14–26), as woes on the Pharisees and scribes (11:37–52), as a foolish rich man losing his soul (12:13–21), like the unexpected return of a master

The Calling of Messengers

For early Christians, the Old Testament prophet Isaiah was particularly important. Isaiah is quoted, cited, and alluded to numerous times in the New Testament. This is because Isaiah looked forward to the restoration of God's reign on the earth, proclaimed by God's heralds (Isa. 40:1–11; 52:7) and brought about by the suffering servant (Isa. 52:13–53:12). This is precisely how Jesus came to be understood.

One fascinating connection between Isaiah and Luke is found in Isaiah 6:1–13 and Luke 5:1–11. These stories describe a sequence of parallel events: a person seeing the Lord in glory, responding with a request for the Lord to depart because of the person's self-aware sinfulness, and the gracious response of the Lord, who commissions the person to be his herald of light in the world.

This parallel is no accident and communicates to Luke's readers that the Lord Jesus's calling of Peter should be understood in light of the Lord God's calling of Isaiah, identifying the characters as parallel to each other. This connection is deepened when Jesus later uses God's words to Isaiah (Isa. 6:9–13) to describe his own ministry of teaching in parables (Luke 8:9–10).

Meals with Jesus

Luke records many stories of Jesus eating with various people. This is because of the great cultural significance in the ancient world of dining with others. In both the first-century Jewish and Greco-Roman cultures meals were more than mere calorie intake, but rather were events in which societal norms, ranking, and community were fostered and maintained. There was much to the ritual of social meals.

Luke uses the stories about Jesus at various meals to show how Jesus overturns humanity's distorted values in contrast with the values of the kingdom of God. Radically, Jesus eats meals with outsiders and notoriously "unclean" people (5:27–32; 19:1–10). He uses meals to promote the virtue of humility over pride (14:7–24). Ultimately, Jesus uses his final earthly meal (the "Last Supper") to speak of the coming kingdom of God and his own forthcoming death. At this last meal, he takes the role of a household slave, modeling the kingdom truth that the greatest ones are those who serve others (22:14–30).

Maker of Heaven and Earth

The first article of the Apostles' Creed rightly starts by affirming belief in God the Father. God is described as "almighty" and then as the "maker of heaven and earth." From within the biblical world this claim about who made the world is an important statement. Against any kind of polytheism, the Bible and Christian confession understand that there is only one God, who made everything in both the physical and spiritual realms; thus the Father of Jesus is the maker of all heaven and earth.

This confessional claim also has another important function outside the clear biblical witness. In the earliest centuries there were some forms of pseudo-Christianity that wedded biblical ideas with unbiblical ones about the creation and the material world. Both Marcionites and Gnostics looked on the physical world with disgust and as a hindrance to true, interior spirituality. These groups spoke of creation as satanic and imprisoning, including one's own body. Christianity, by contrast, firmly affirms the true goodness of all creation because it has all been made by God himself. Evil is not a created thing; it is the perversion and deficiency of the good that God has made, even as darkness is not a thing but the absence of light. As one theologian has helpfully put it, when Christians confess that God is the maker of heaven and earth, in saying no to **Marcionism** and Gnosticism, the church is saying yes to the whole material universe.[1]

Selling One's Possessions

In addition to Luke's emphasis on poverty and wealth, he makes radical statements about the need to sell one's possessions in order to be Jesus's disciple. One is to a rich leader (18:22) and the other two are more general statements (12:33; 14:33). While the monastic tradition provides an example of a group that has followed these commands literally, most Christians have not interpreted these verses in this way. We see this already within the pages of the New Testament, where there are many wealthy Christians, and some who sell some of their possessions to help the church, while still owning houses and businesses with no judgment from God (Acts 4:36–37; 10:1–2; 16:13–15). Sermons and commentaries from the first several centuries of the church show the same interpretation. Preachers as diverse as Origen, Chrysostom, Hilary of Poitiers, and Clement of Alexandria all interpret these sayings not as a requirement of self-imposed physical poverty but rather as a challenge to examine our hearts for greed and self-dependence. Money and possessions have a corrupting power that must be resisted. One way is to practice generous giving; for some, it may mean giving up everything. But in all things Jesus's teachings target the posture of the heart.

who finds his servants to be unfaithful (12:35–48), as a time coming with weeping outside of the kingdom feast (13:22–30), and as Jerusalem as a desolate city (13:31–35).

Yet this dark foreboding is peppered with words of encouragement to Jesus's followers. We see that Jesus gives power to his multitude of disciples to be his witnesses and overcome Satan (10:1–20). He calls his followers blessed because they are given the ability to believe in the Father and the Son (10:21–24). Jesus teaches his disciples how to pray to God as their Father, promising that they will receive what they ask for, even as a father gives good gifts to his children (11:1–13). Similarly, Jesus's disciples should not live in anxiety, because their Father will provide for their needs (12:22–34).

This juxtaposition of warnings and encouragement shows that Jesus has come as a sword that will divide the world into two groups: those who believe in him and those who don't (12:49–53). There is no middle ground.

Overturning Human Values

■ READ LUKE 14:1–19:27 ■

Jesus continues his long journey south to Jerusalem, and Luke records an interesting collection of interactions that Jesus had with people along the way. There are some stories that remind readers of Jesus's miraculous powers (14:1–4; 17:11–19; 18:35–43), but most of the stories instead focus on a different kind of wonder. With

parables and actions, Jesus repeatedly proves that the kingdom of God is going to look very different from human rule.

What are some of the differences in kingdom values? First on the list is wealth. The story of the great reversal of fates for the rich man and Lazarus (16:19–31) is shocking to any hearer and challenges our love of money and neglect of the poor. Jesus returns to this theme when interacting with a noble Jewish leader whom Jesus calls to give up all his wealth to become a disciple. When the man responds with grief rather than joy, Jesus shocks everyone by pronouncing that possessing wealth makes it extremely difficult to enter the kingdom of God. Rather, the truly rich are those who have given up whatever they must to become Jesus's disciples (18:18–30). This upheaval of human values is modeled in the memorable story and parable that culminates this section. The story details the conversion and salvation of the disreputable tax collector Zacchaeus. This wealthy man sees Jesus, and when he does his love and drive for wealth no longer control him. As a result, he gives away half of all he owns to the poor and recompenses fourfold any whom he had wronged (probably most people!). Jesus describes this response as evidence of a lost man being saved (19:1–10). The accompanying parable that concludes Jesus's journey to Jerusalem likewise focuses on wealth and how people respond to what they have been given. To those who honor God with their wealth and talents much will be given; to those who do not, just judgment is God's response (19:11–27). Jesus says all of this most simply with the statement that people cannot serve two masters, both God and money (16:13).

In addition to challenging the human obsession with wealth, Jesus shows that in God's kingdom those who are valued as worthy of most honor are often the opposite of those that human society honors. This often overlaps with wealth, as can be seen in the stories of the rich man and Lazarus and of Zacchaeus, but not always. Jesus uses the example of seating at a dinner party to confront humanity's propensity to boost personal honor rather than humbly seeking to bless society's dishonored ones (14:7–14). Some such people are highly praised by Jesus, contrary to their rank in human eyes. These include the widow whose faith in God makes her pray persistently (18:1–8), the tax collector whose humility and repentance grant him

Blessing and Breaking Bread

Great storytellers often leave a trail of verbal bread crumbs distanced just far enough between each piece so that observant readers will suddenly see the fragments and perceive the deep interconnection, the trail leading somewhere beautiful. Such is the case with Jesus taking, blessing, breaking, and giving bread three times in Luke. First is in 9:16 at the wilderness feeding. The exact same sequence is repeated at the Last Supper in 22:19. Finally, we hear the same words again when Jesus reveals himself to his disciples in Emmaus (24:30). Each of these events is deeply significant theologically. By repeating the precise sequence of words, Luke invites us to consider the interconnection between these three stories of God revealing himself to redeem his people. This then also provides the background for Luke's second volume, Acts, where he shows the church continuing this practice of breaking and sharing bread (Acts 2:42–46; 20:7–11; 27:35–36).

The One-in-Three Parables of Luke 15

Certainly one of the most famous portions of Luke is the parable of the prodigal son (15:11–32). This is a beautiful and powerful story of God graciously welcoming back a wayward son. However, to fully understand and appreciate this famous parable we need to pay attention to how Luke has set this parable in its literary context. The story of the prodigal (wasteful) or lost son is actually the climactic yet open-ended conclusion to a series of three interconnected parables. The set of three parables is introduced with the Pharisees grumbling about Jesus welcoming sinners and eating with them (15:2). Jesus responds with three escalating stories, each of which depicts God as rejoicing when something lost is found: one of one hundred sheep; one of ten silver coins; one of two sons. This proves crucial to the overall point of the last parable. While all three parables have the same structure (precious item lost, then found, then the finder rejoicing), the third parable has the *added twist* of the older brother who grumbles and complains at the father's gracious and joyful acceptance of the lost son. This addition to the sequence of stories becomes the main point. The Pharisees are the older brother, grumbling at Jesus's loving acceptance of broken and sinful people, thus putting themselves at odds with God himself.

HISTORICAL MATTERS

Short Zacchaeus and Ancient Physiognomy

The story of Zacchaeus (19:1–10) has long been a staple in Sunday school curricula. Countless children know the tale and song about this "wee little man" who climbed a sycamore tree to try to see Jesus. But even for adults it is a remarkable story that fits well with Luke's emphases on Jesus welcoming and saving notorious, sinful people who respond with faith to him.

Modern readers, however, are not likely aware that there is another way in which Jesus is radically overturning cultural values through this story. This centers on Zacchaeus's height and the ancient understanding of **physiognomy**. Physiognomy was the Greco-Roman cultural practice of judging someone's character based on their physical features. In this time smallness of stature was typically associated with smallness of spirit, even greediness. This accords with Zacchaeus's role as a wealthy tax collector. By emphasizing Zacchaeus's shortness and then showing Jesus's openhearted welcome and saving of this man, Luke highlights for us the radical and unexpected graciousness of God and how Jesus overturns social and cultural norms.[2]

a relationship with God while the holy Pharisee remains outside (18:9–14), little children who model what it means to enter the kingdom (18:15–17), and a blind beggar who comes to see God (18:35–42).

Jesus also shows through these stories that God loves to redeem and restore the lost, not condemn them. This theme is closely related to the topic of honor and shame. The stories of Zacchaeus (19:1–10), the ten lepers (17:11–19), and the tax collector (18:9–14) all show this. The series of parables in 15:1–32 most clearly shows this theme of joyful restoration instead of judgment. God is shown to rejoice over the now-found state of the lost sheep (15:3–7), the lost silver coin (15:8–10), and the lost son (15:11–24). The problem is that people—especially religious people who value external obedience—don't often share God's joy in this. To drive this point home, Jesus adds another part to the parable of the lost son: the story of the older brother who refuses to rejoice in the restoration of the lost son and brother (15:25–32). This serves as a challenge and invitation to reorient one's values toward what God loves and rejoices in.

As Jesus nears Jerusalem for the last week of his life, his conflict with the religious leaders is increasing. Luke shows us that this conflict is rooted in a different set of values and loves. This is summed up well in 16:14–15: "The Pharisees, who were lovers of money, were listening to all these things and scoffing at him. And he told them, 'You are the ones who justify yourselves in the sight of others, but God knows your hearts. For what is highly admired by people is revolting in God's sight.'"

The Authoritative Messiah

▨ READ LUKE 19:28–21:38 ▨

The final stage of Jesus's ministry has now been reached, and it takes place, not accidentally, in Jerusalem. Since the time of Israel's greatest king, David, Jerusalem has been the center of Israel's faith. The temple was built there, and Jews to this day make pilgrimage to their holy city. Jerusalem and its temple are also the center of the future hope for all Jewish people who are still looking for the return of the Davidic Messiah.

This is why Jesus, who knew himself to be the true Messiah, purposefully arrives in Jerusalem, prepared to complete the mission that God the Father has sent him to do. His entry into the city is intentionally symbolic. He arranges to go up through the Jerusalem gates riding on a colt. As he enters the city, his disciples and the massive crowds who have experienced his teaching and healing, and who believe him to be the promised king, cannot help but burst into spontaneous worship, laying their cloaks on the road before him in honor and shouting praise to God for the blessing of the return of the king (19:28–38).

This triumphal entry, which the church continues to celebrate to this day as Palm Sunday, is a picture of Jesus's regal glory. But this event also reveals the sad irony that even though Jesus came to rescue his people and reign as their king, many of the most religious Jewish people of the day did not rejoice. Instead, they were offended. Over the shouts of praise they command Jesus that his disciples must stop this inappropriate scene (19:39). Jesus responds that if his disciples are quiet, the stones themselves will cry out with praise (19:40), meaning that their actions are right and appropriate—he is the promised Son of David!

This story of a king being rejected by his subjects concludes not with Jesus shooting lasers out of his eyes or mocking his enemies but rather with Jesus weeping. With great compassion he sees the city of David as a place that is facing destruction because of the rebellion of its people. Because the

CANONICAL CONNECTIONS

The Transfiguration

Luke 9:28–36 records one of the most important yet often-neglected stories in the Gospels, what we call Jesus's transfiguration (also found in Matt. 17:1–8; Mark 9:2–8). As Jesus faces his final journey to Jerusalem and his impending crucifixion, he takes his closest disciples (Peter, James, and John) onto a high mountainside to pray. Throughout the Bible, mountains often are places where people see visions of God. In this case the disciples do hear God's voice, and the vision they see is of Jesus as glorious and radiating light. But he is not alone. He is conversing with two of the most important leaders of the Jewish Scriptures, Moses and Elijah (who also represent the Law and the Prophets).

This story is intriguing in many ways. One is the question of what Jesus would be talking about with Moses and Elijah. Luke makes a point to tell us, though its significance is somewhat lost in translation. Verse 31 says that they were talking about "his departure, which he was about to accomplish in Jerusalem." This is a sufficient translation, but it covers up a play on words that Luke's Greek text gives us. The word translated as "departure" is in Greek *exodos*, the same word used to describe God's saving work in bringing Israel out of bondage in Egypt through Moses (and where we get the title for the second book of the Bible). For those who understand the whole story line of the Bible, Luke is reminding us that we should understand Jesus's work as a rescuing of God's people, centered in and starting in Jerusalem.

Jewish leaders did not recognize that God himself was arriving in Jesus, the city itself will be destroyed (19:41–44). 👥

This is yet in the future. For now, Jesus is in Jerusalem, his place of rightful enthronement, for one last time before he will be killed. After this disputed entry into the city, Jesus focuses his time and teaching on the temple, the place where heaven kisses earth and God is present with his people. The actions and sayings that Luke records for us from 19:45 through 21:38 happen over the course of several days. Jesus's pattern was to go to the temple area early each morning to speak to the crowds and then to retire each night to the hill called the Mount of Olives (19:47; 21:37–38). Over the course of these long and tense days, what does Jesus say and do?

Jesus the king's first action is shocking. Rather than grabbing political power in the palace, Jesus exercises not his royal role but his priestly and prophetic callings. He goes to the center of Jewish worship, where the priests make daily sacrifices on behalf of God's people, and he disrupts and challenges their authority. With a zeal that matches any of the most dynamic Old Testament prophets, Jesus expels merchants and proclaims the corruption of the temple, calling the practices there thievery rather than prayer (19:45–46).

Not surprisingly, conflict with the established leaders in Jerusalem erupts. The crowds are fascinated by this vigorous teacher, but the priests, teachers of the law, and the Jerusalem leadership knew immediately that this troublemaker must be killed (19:47–48). First, they question the source of his authority, but he stumps them in this (20:1–8). Jesus then goes on the offensive with a pointed parable that shows him to be the faithful heir of God's kingdom and the leaders to be usurpers (20:1–18). Unlike Jesus's otherwise esoteric parables, this parable they fully understand he has spoken against them, thus stirring up their anger and resolve even more to silence him (20:19).

The infuriated leaders then try a different tactic: entrapping Jesus by his own words. First they try to trick him into offending either the Roman overlords or the Jewish conservatives over the issue of paying taxes (20:20–26). Jesus astonishes them with his brilliant answer (20:24–25). They are equally unsuccessful with a thorny theological question. Their attempt to entrap him between two different Jewish groups

Jesus the Sacrificial Priest in Luke

Early Christians recognized that each Gospel highlights particular aspects of Jesus's identity. This often was represented by the Four Symbols of the Evangelists (see chap. 5), with Luke traditionally associated with the image of an ox. This connection is meaningful because the ox represents the sacrifices required at the Jerusalem temple, drawing on Luke's strong emphasis on Jerusalem as the center of Jesus's ministry. For the church fathers, the theme of Jerusalem and the sacrificial ox helps readers understand Jesus's role as the true and final priest. Luke begins his account with Zechariah the priest performing his sacrificial temple duties in Jerusalem and ends with Jesus offering himself as the ultimate sacrifice there. In the closing scene Jesus, in true priestly fashion, raises his hands and blesses his gathered disciples even as he ascends into heaven and they return to the temple praising God (24:50–53; cf. Lev. 9:22). Jesus's role as God's high priest is developed extensively in the Letter to the Hebrews (Heb. 4:14–10:18), building on the Gospels' narrative depiction.

on the question of marriage in the resurrected state also fails miserably (20:27–40).

Figure 8.4. A scene of the entry into Jerusalem from a diptych with scenes from Christ's passion (ca. 1350–75)

Once again, Jesus goes on the offensive and poses to the leaders a theological dilemma that focuses on the mystery of a divine mediator between David and Yahweh, speaking of himself as the solution, David's Lord (20:41–44). They are unable to answer, and Jesus issues a dire warning that people should beware of such respected teachers of the law who seek praise and honor rather than the humble truth. Only punishment awaits them (20:45–47). By way of contrast, Jesus commends a lowly widow who is not seeking praise but rather who humbly gives to the Lord with a whole heart (21:1–4). This is the kind of person Jesus commends.

The remainder of Jesus's temple-based daily teachings focus not on the present but on the future, on a time when God will bring strong judgment on the unrighteous actions and attitudes of those who are leading and controlling the heart of Israel's worship. It is not pleasant to hear Jesus's teachings about this coming judgment. Beauty will become destruction, and peace will become war. Jerusalem, its people and its place, will be trampled and desecrated (21:5–27). But even amid this darkness Jesus offers hope to his disciples: these are the signs that redemption is drawing near (21:28), that God's kingdom is now fully at hand (21:31). The appropriate response to these images of judgment, then, is not despair but watchful care, anticipating Jesus's return (21:34–36).

With these daily doses of conflict with the religious leaders in the heart of Jerusalem, Jesus's die is cast. Sovereignly and intentionally he has fulfilled his role as God's prophet, knowing that the result will be his own destruction.

RECEPTION HISTORY

Denying Christ in the Early Church

In the intense persecution that the church experienced in the first several centuries, the matter of a person denying Jesus and then being restored into fellowship was hotly debated, particularly because of Jesus's own words that anyone who denied him would be denied before God (Matt. 10:33; Luke 12:9). Two groups in particular, the **Novatianists** and the **Donatists**, argued for a rigorous view of a "pure" church that did not forgive anyone who had denied Jesus. Over time, however, the church's leaders, including influential theologians such as Jerome and Augustine, argued vigorously that denying Jesus while being persecuted was a forgivable sin, not the unforgivable blasphemy of the Holy Spirit (Matt. 12:31–32; Luke 12:10). Ultimately, the winning argument in these debates was the story of Peter's own denial (Luke 22:54–62). Peter, the leader of the disciples and the leader of the early church, did fail and denied his association with Jesus. But unlike Judas Iscariot, Peter repented and was therefore restored by Jesus himself (John 21:15–23). Peter becomes the model of those who can be restored even after failure in the midst of persecution. To deny this restoration was, as Augustine argued, to steal medicine from the sick, and does not accord with Jesus's charitable nature.

The Fulfillment of a Crucified King

■ READ LUKE 22:1–23:56 ■

Up to this point Luke's story has contained moments of foreboding darkness—predictions of suffering and forewarnings of judgment. But here the story takes its darkest turn. This "crucial" section—meaning both central and crucifix-shaped—begins with Jesus being betrayed by one of his closest twelve companions (22:1–6) and ends with Jesus bloodied, bruised, and dead, his body sealed in a stone tomb, wrapped in linen cloths, and covered with spices (23:50–56). This was truly the most momentous twenty-four-hour period in history.

THEOLOGICAL ISSUES

The Resurrection of the Body

Christian theology has always affirmed the physical resurrection of Jesus's body. In the Apostles' Creed this first is mentioned in the second article with Jesus's resurrection and ascension into heaven. In the third article physical resurrection occurs again, this time with reference to all Christians joining with Jesus in his glorified state (cf. 1 Cor. 15:52; 1 Thess. 4:17).

This confessional affirmation means that, unlike either cynical or sentimental notions about the future, the Christian hope for the future is for a fullness of life in physical bodies on a renewed earth, where God himself is present (Rev. 21:1–22:5). The future for Christians will be both embodied and relational, centered on the Triune God. This ties the whole message of the Bible and Christian confession back to its beginnings: it is God who made all creation (Gen. 1), and therefore the first article of the Apostles' Creed affirms that God is the "maker of heaven and earth." The future bodily resurrection of believers is central to Christian faith as the consummation of God's whole story of creation and redemption.

Woven throughout these events, the repeated theme focuses on the kingdom of God. We see this first in the story of the Last Supper of Jesus and the twelve disciples. Luke, who often is sparse with details compared to Matthew and Mark, provides a rather lengthy account of Jesus's sayings on his last night with his disciples. Jesus chooses to celebrate the high Jewish holiday of Passover with his chosen family of faith, not his biological family, and he deepens the significance of this meal by expanding its meaning. This meal celebrating the past memory of the exodus of Israel from Egypt becomes a forward-looking celebration of the coming kingdom of God. Jesus speaks passionately and personally about his desire to celebrate this feast with his own disciples before the darkness of his suffering descends, because, he states, he will not eat this meal with them again "until it is fulfilled in the kingdom of God" (22:16), "until the kingdom of God comes" (22:18). When the disciples begin disputing among themselves who will be the greatest (presumably as they think about God's coming kingdom), Jesus contrasts God's kingdom with human kingdoms by stating that the servant and the lowly one will have great standing (22:24–27). The kingdom talk continues with the staggering statement that the Father has appointed Jesus over his kingdom and that Jesus is now doing the same for his disciples, so that they may dine with him and rule over all Israel (22:28–30).

The theme of Jesus as the king continues throughout the rest of the stories. When Jesus is betrayed and arrested, he must stand before the rulers of the area, first the Jewish leadership, then the Roman governor Pilate,

Figure 8.5. *The Last Supper* by Leonardo da Vinci. Da Vinci's famous painting is not meant to represent what a dinner in the area of first-century Palestine would have looked like, but rather depicts a meal setting of his own time. In the first century, diners would have reclined with pillows on the floor around low tables (triclinium in style).

and then Herod the king. In each case the dispute about Jesus's identity as the Messiah/King is forefront. The chief priests demand for him to be clear about whether he thinks he is the Messiah, and he answers affirmatively; he is the Son seated at the right hand of God (22:66–71). The priests use this as the opportunity to get him arrested by the Romans. Pilate asks him if he is the king of the Jews, and Jesus again responds positively (23:1–3). When Jesus is next dragged before Herod, the guards dress him in an elegant robe, mocking his claim to be king (23:11). Jesus finally is crucified, with the charge against him printed for all to see: "This is the King of the Jews" (23:38). The onlookers, both Jewish and Roman, mock him about this, challenging him to show his supposed power and save himself (23:35–37). The two criminals hung on either side of Jesus both speak to him about his role as king, one mocking him (23:39) and the other pleading for Jesus to remember him when Jesus comes into his kingdom (23:40–42). Finally, when Jesus's body is removed from the cross and prepared for a burial worthy of royalty, we are told this was accomplished through the power and influence of Joseph of Arimathea, a believer in Jesus who himself was "looking forward to the kingdom of God" (23:51). This dark twenty-four-hour story shows Jesus to be the crucified king. 🏺

HISTORICAL MATTERS

The Last Supper and the Passover Haggadah

Each year the Jewish people celebrate their deliverance from Egypt with a celebration called Passover. As instituted by God and then developed through tradition, this ritual meal retells the story of the exodus, complete with tactile and culinary experiences, including ceremonial hand washings, a set of questions and answers, bitter herbs, sweet wine, and unleavened bread. This ceremonious meal along with the liturgy of words became called the Passover Haggadah (or story). Of all the festivals Jesus could have chosen for his last visit to Jerusalem and the Last Supper, he chose the Passover celebration. Thus, for Christians this simultaneously imbues the Passover with abiding significance while also transforming it into the Christian celebration of the Lord's Supper. Jesus's Last Supper was a celebration looking back to the Passover, but he makes the ongoing remembrance of this meal a forward-looking picture of the new covenant he is offering to the world.

The Journey to True Seeing

■ READ LUKE 24:1–53 ■

This final chapter of Luke's Gospel is entirely unique—we know of these fascinating stories only because of his account. These stories are not only fascinating and unique but also essential: in this final chapter Luke ties together and pushes forward several truths that are central to the reason he has written his Gospel. Specifically, this chapter emphasizes that Jesus is the fulfillment of all the promises of God, and that in order to understand the message of the whole Bible one must see Jesus clearly. Along the way, readers are given one of the fullest accounts of Jesus's resurrection and post-resurrection activities (about the same length as John 20–21).

THEOLOGICAL ISSUES

I Believe in the Holy Spirit

One of the key Christian affirmations, as noted in the third article of the Apostles' Creed, is the belief in the Holy Spirit. The confession "I believe in the Holy Spirit" is simultaneously affirming several important aspects of what it means to be a Christian. First and foremost is the triune nature of God in three divine yet distinct persons—Father, Son, Spirit—as manifested in the three parts of the creed. Second, while the Spirit of God is clearly present from the first verses of Genesis, Christianity puts particular emphasis on the new work of the Spirit in the age of the church and the new covenant. It is the Spirit who baptized and empowered Jesus and then raised him from the dead (Matt. 3:16; Rom. 8:11). This same Spirit came upon the apostles at Pentecost and enabled them to preach with boldness and authority (Acts 2:1–47). In the era of the church, specifically, it is the Holy Spirit who reveals Jesus to the world (John 16:14), comforts and guides believers (John 14:26–27; 16:7–13), helps believers pray (Rom. 8:26), produces the fruit of godly character (Gal. 5:22–23), and enables believers to put to death sin in their lives (Rom. 8:13). The Holy Spirit gives gifts to Christians so that the church may function with power, wisdom, and love (1 Cor. 12:4–11; Eph. 4:12–13).

As dark and devastating as Luke 22–23 was, Luke 24 is alive and enlightening. Luke does not record the instant of Jesus's resurrection from the dead, but what happened as a result of this epic moment in history.

First, on the third day after his death, some of the women disciples (who are shown as more consistently believing than the male disciples) go to the place of Jesus's burial. They are shocked to find not a sealed cave, but rather the tomb opened and empty. They meet two angels who proclaim that Jesus is now among the living. These faithful women report this to the amazed apostles lingering in Jerusalem (24:1–12).

Second, on the same day, two of Jesus's disciples were making the seven-mile walk from Jerusalem to Emmaus (24:13). The resurrected Jesus caught up and walked with them, and he enters into a dialogue without revealing his identity. The hidden Jesus begins as the one who appears ignorant of recent events but soon becomes the teacher. He explains to them that all these events make total sense *if* one understands "Moses and all the Prophets" correctly, as all pointing to God's promised Messiah (24:25–27). Then, in a beautifully symbolic act, while Jesus is breaking bread to eat with them, God suddenly opens their eyes and they realize this man is not just any fellow believer; this is the risen Jesus himself (24:30–31)! Jesus vanishes, and these disciples run to the eleven apostles in Jerusalem to report what happened.

Third, building on the other two events, Jesus then appears to the apostles and disciples gathered in

Jerusalem. Naturally, they are shocked and doubt what they are seeing. Jesus graciously responds by speaking peace to them. When this is not enough to quell their fears, he eats a piece of broiled fish (24:36–43). With his identity and physical presence established, he once again explains to the stunned believers how everything that has happened to him is the promised fulfillment of all that God said and did in the past. As a result, he commissions them to go forth to every nation as his witnesses and proclaimers of repentance and forgiveness of sins (24:44–49).

This chapter ends in a way that strongly foreshadows and anticipates Luke's second volume, Acts. Jesus tells his disciples to stay in Jerusalem until they receive power from heaven, anticipating the giving of the Holy Spirit at Pentecost in Acts 2. He then gives them his last blessing while physically with them and is carried into heaven before their eyes. This long and eventful Gospel ends with Jesus's followers full of joy and worship, heading toward Jerusalem to be his witnesses (24:48–53).

It would be difficult to overestimate the importance of Luke 24 to Christian theology. This powerful conclusion to Luke's Gospel highlights the significance of Jesus's bodily resurrection, the necessity of God revealing himself so that people can understand the truth of the Bible's whole message, and the role of Christians as joyful witnesses to God's grace toward the whole world.

Implementation—Reading Luke as Christian Scripture Today

The Gospel according to Luke looks to the past, the present, and the future. Looking backward, Luke emphasizes repeatedly that

Figure 8.6. The Drogo Sacramentary (ca. 850) is an illuminated manuscript that includes this depiction of the ascension of Christ.

CANONICAL CONNECTIONS

Luke, 1 Corinthians 15, and the Resurrection Body

Toward the end of 1 Corinthians the apostle Paul discusses the mysterious reality of the resurrected body and physical human life after death (1 Cor. 15:1–58). He first proclaims that if Jesus did not physically rise from the dead, the entirety of Christianity is false, futile, and foolish (15:12–19). This raises a subsequent question: What will this resurrected body be like? Paul argues strongly that it will be a real body but will be different. Even as different animals have different kinds of bodies and as different celestial and earthly bodies differ from one another, so too the resurrected body will be different. It will be more than mere flesh and blood: a heavenly, immortal, imperishable, powerful, and glorious body (15:35–49).

Luke's stories about Jesus's interactions with his disciples after his resurrection manifest this same mysterious vision of what the resurrection body is. On the road to Emmaus Jesus is physically present, converses with people, sits down at a table, and breaks bread. Yet he also has the ability to vanish instantly (Luke 24:13–35). Then when he appears to his gathered disciples in Jerusalem, he invites them to touch him and see that he is not a ghost but a physical presence, seen ultimately by his ability to eat (24:36–43). And finally, in their presence he is lifted into heaven (24:50–53). All of this shows both the physicality and the spiritually new nature of the resurrection body promised to all believers, of which Jesus is the firstfruit and pioneer.

THEOLOGICAL ISSUES

The Theology of the Ascension

Luke 24:50–53 and Acts 1:6–11 tell us the story of Jesus ascending into the clouds in front of his disciples as his last time physically on the earth. A few other texts reference this event, usually tying it to Jesus's exaltation to sit in honor at the right hand of God the Father (John 20:17; Rom. 8:34; Col. 3:1; 1 Pet. 3:22).

Even though it has often been neglected in Christian theology, the doctrine of Jesus's bodily ascension to heaven is found in the ecumenical statements of faith including the Apostles', the **Nicene-Constantinopolitan**, and the Athanasian Creeds. The Feast of the Ascension is celebrated on the fortieth day after Easter in the Roman Catholic, Eastern Orthodox, and Anglican traditions, though not in most Protestant churches today.

The ascension is theologically weighty for many reasons. Jesus's ascension emphasizes, albeit mysteriously, that his incarnation and resurrection have forever changed the cosmology of the world. As the first human to receive a glorified body, Jesus entered into the presence of God in a spatial reality that is beyond our comprehension but that looks forward to the time and space of the new creation. At the same time, the ascension is essential to the ongoing work of Christ in the world. He stands before God as mediator and intercessor (see Acts 7:56; Rom. 8:34; 1 Tim. 2:5; Heb. 7:25; 8:6). Also, while Jesus's church is the means of his work in the world, the ascension highlights the distinction between Jesus and his church: residing in heaven, Jesus is the head of the church, but he is neither identical with nor coextensive with his earthly church.

through Jesus Christ God has fulfilled all of his many promises in the Jewish Scriptures. Looking to the future, Luke emphasizes that Christ's resurrection inaugurates a new era in history, the age of the Spirit, which looks forward to the time when Jesus will return to complete his work in the world. For the present Luke emphasizes the ongoing work of God in the world through the church that is faithful to Christ's teachings. This present work begins to unfold in Luke's second volume, the book of Acts, and continues to the present day. The Gospel of Luke serves as a guide to train the sensibilities, values, and habits of Christ's disciples as they engage and seek to transform individuals and, thereby, society itself. Jesus invites people into an alternative society/kingdom, where the outcast, the poor, the nobodies are valued and even exalted. To be a disciple is to enter into and participate in this way of being in the world.

KEY VERSES IN LUKE

- In the same region, shepherds were staying out in the fields and keeping watch at night over their flock. Then an angel of the Lord stood before them, and the glory of the Lord shone around them, and they were terrified. But the angel said to them, "Don't be afraid, for look, I proclaim to you good news of great joy that will be for all the people: Today in the city of David a Savior was born for you, who is the Messiah, the Lord." 2:8–11

- He came to Nazareth, where he had been brought up. As usual, he entered the synagogue on the Sabbath day and stood up to read. The scroll of the prophet Isaiah was given to him, and unrolling the scroll, he found the place where it was written: "The Spirit of the Lord is on me, because he has anointed me to preach good news to the poor. He has sent me to proclaim release to the captives and recovery of sight to the blind, to set free the oppressed, to proclaim the year of the Lord's favor." He then rolled up the scroll, gave it back to the attendant, and sat down. And the eyes of everyone in the synagogue were fixed on him. He began by saying to them, "Today as you listen, this Scripture has been fulfilled." 4:16–21

- He said to them, "How foolish you are, and how slow to believe all that the prophets have spoken! Wasn't it necessary for the Messiah to suffer these things and enter into his glory?" Then beginning with Moses and all the Prophets, he interpreted for them the things concerning himself in all the Scriptures. 24:25–27

Christian Reading Questions

1. Read through Luke 1–2 and note themes and ideas that Luke is trying to communicate. Then note ways in which these themes appear in other places in Luke's Gospel.

2. Note the many physical descriptions of characters in Luke's Gospel. How do you think Jesus's interactions with people with many different physical descriptions (e.g., Zacchaeus) shine light on the purpose of his ministry?

3. Listen to Johann Sebastian Bach's musical setting of the Magnificat, using translated lyrics. How do you think the music corresponds to the Magnificat as Luke wrote it in Luke 1:46–55, and what effect does it have on you as the listener?

4. Read Luke 4:16–30. What did Jesus mean by saying that the Scripture he read had been fulfilled today? What echoes of the Scripture that Jesus quotes here do you see throughout the rest of Luke's Gospel?

CHAPTER NINE

The Gospel according to John

Orientation

Throughout human history clever people have created riddles—paradoxical mysterious sayings that require ingenuity to solve, often with a veiled or double meaning. Consider this riddle: What is shallow enough for a child to wade in yet deep enough for an elephant to swim in? Answer: the Gospel according to John.

This paradoxical description is one of the main ways the Gospel of John has been described, going back to the church's earliest centuries. This riddle suits John well. On the surface the Fourth Gospel seems simple and straightforward. Compared to the Synoptic Gospels, John has fewer stories, and they are told more dramatically; the language (in Greek and in English) is simpler grammatically, using a smaller vocabulary; Jesus makes the clearest identity statements, saying things like "I and the Father are one." This is the book we often tell new believers to read, and rightly so. John is easy and engaging to read. Or so it seems.

The Metropolitan Museum of Art. The Cloisters Collection, 1977.

Figure 9.1. Plaque with John and the symbol of his Gospel, the eagle

When you start to pay closer attention and ask deeper questions, John turns out to be mysterious and multilayered. Pastors, theologians, and biblical scholars agree that John's apparent simplicity is a door into the deepest book of the New Testament. The Gospel according to John truly is shallow enough for a child to wade in while also being deep enough for an elephant to swim in.

Matthew's influence dominated for many centuries in the church, but eventually John took the lead. Theologians throughout history have distinguished the Fourth Gospel in several ways:

- If the Gospels are the firstfruits of Scripture, then John is the firstfruit of the firstfruits (Origen).
- The Synoptic Gospels address things from a physical perspective; John wrote a spiritual Gospel (Clement; Augustine).
- John is to be preferred to the others because "it will show you Christ and teach you everything you need to know" (Luther).

The Gospel of John soon became associated with the symbol of the eagle, king of birds, soaring high above the rest of Scripture and revealing deep theological truths from the heights.

Like the other Gospels, John is a biography and thus primarily consists of stories about the main subject, Jesus. While few specific stories overlap between John and the Synoptic Gospels (see chap. 5), the four Gospels are clearly describing the same Jesus and broadly telling the same story:

- Jesus, the Son of God, came into the world.
- He proclaimed that God was doing something new through him.
- This proclamation evoked two main responses: people believed and followed him, while the Jewish leadership opposed him.

- This opposition peaked in Jerusalem, where Jesus was arrested, tried, and crucified by the Roman government.
- But then Jesus rose from the dead and appeared to his disciples, emboldening them to form a new group of believers, calling others to believe in Jesus.

Inside and beyond this general story, each Gospel highlights certain theological themes to call believers to understand Jesus in a particular way and follow him accordingly. John makes his own purpose especially clear by telling us at the end of his story exactly why he wrote his Gospel: "Jesus performed many other signs in the presence of his disciples that are not written in this book. But these are written so that you may believe that Jesus is the Messiah, the Son of God, and that by believing you may have life in his name" (20:30–31).

So the Gospel of John gives us a series of stories, teachings, and signs recorded so that readers may truly believe that Jesus is the Messiah, the Son of God. Not everyone will believe, but those who do will enter into abundant life now and in the age to come.

John's purpose is that simple and that profound. Toward this goal, John highlights several key theological themes, including the fatherhood of God, the sonship of Jesus, and the role of the Holy Spirit. John is thoroughly trinitarian. The theme of eternal life also dominates John's Gospel, which is another expression of the Synoptic Gospels' language of the "kingdom of God/heaven." To enter into the kingdom is to enter into true and lasting life, and vice versa.

In all of this, the Gospel of John is simultaneously accessible and inscrutable. As the New Testament scholar N. T. Wright has been heard to describe it, "The Gospel of John is very much like my wife—I love her very much but I do not profess to understand her."

Exploration—Reading John

The Word Enters the World

■ READ JOHN 1:1–2:25 ■

Unlike the other Gospels, John begins with a highly theological prologue (1:1–18) that sets the tone for the whole book. John's introduction describes Jesus as eternal and divine (1:1–2), the agent of creation (1:3), the means by which people become God's children (1:12), truly human (1:14), the manifestation of grace and truth (1:17), and the only being who has ever seen God and made him fully known (1:18).

Figure 9.2. *Marriage at Cana* (1304–6) by Giotto di Bondone, Scrovegni Chapel, Padua, Italy

After this introduction we meet John the Baptizer, the forerunner who points to Jesus in all four Gospels. The prologue mentions the Baptizer as one sent from God "to bear witness about the light" (1:6–8). This Gospel's first story is about the Jewish leaders questioning John the Baptizer, and they receive a clear, if undesired, response: John is neither Elijah nor the Christ, but the powerful Christ is coming (1:19–28)! This Christ will be identified by the Holy Spirit descending on him like a dove; he will be the Son of God and the Lamb of God who takes away the sin of the world (1:29–34).

These details are nearly identical in all four of the Gospel accounts, but most similarities between John and the Synoptics end here, right at the beginning. What follows is a series of stories consistent with the tone of Jesus's ministry in the other Gospels but unique to John. First, we learn how the first four of Jesus's disciples—two brothers and two friends—began to follow him. Jesus shows supernatural knowledge that amazes these first disciples. They leave everything to follow him, perceiving that he is the Son of God, the true king of Israel (1:49), a rabbi/teacher (1:38, 49), and the fulfillment of the law and the prophets (1:45). Jesus calls these disciples to come and follow so that they will be able to truly see and understand (1:39). This is an invitation to all readers of John to come and learn from the rest of the book.

Two shocking stories follow—shocking for different reasons. First, in a very typical domestic scene, at a wedding ceremony with his family and disciples, Jesus performs a stunning miracle by turning vats of water into fine wine. John tells us that this sign unveiled Jesus's glory and bolstered the disciples' faith in him (2:11). We also learn that while Jesus is glorious, he is aware that his "hour has not yet come," hinting that he has work to do before he completes his mission (2:4).

The second shocking story overlaps with an event that we find in the Synoptics: Jesus disrupting the activities in the Jerusalem temple court (2:13–22;

Two Temple Cleansings?

An obvious difference between the Synoptic Gospels and John is the placement of the story of Jesus's prophetic cleansing of the temple. Matthew, Mark, and Luke tell this story during Jesus's last week of life in Jerusalem. John, on the other hand, shows Jesus performing this kind of action right at the beginning of his public ministry.

Many people believe that these differently placed stories describe the same event because it seems unlikely that the Jewish leaders would let Jesus disrupt the temple twice. The Synoptics place the story at the end of their accounts as part of their stylized narrative in which Jesus appears in Jerusalem only in the last week of his life, thus emphasizing that he was an outsider opposed by the Jewish leadership.

Others have suggested that Jesus performed this prophetic act twice, once at the beginning of his ministry (John) and once at the end (the Synoptics). There are differences between the stories, notably the accompanying crowds in the Synoptics who are proclaiming Jesus as king. This was the view of, for example, Augustine, who argued for two temple cleansings in his *Harmony of the Gospels*, and is probably the most common view throughout the church's history.

Regardless, the important question is how this story fits into the unique points that the Gospels are trying to make. For John, it is significant that Jesus has conflict with Jerusalem's religious leaders from the beginning and that Jesus claims that his own body will replace the temple of God (see also Jesus's discussion with the woman at the well in 4:20–24).

cf. Matt. 21:12–13; Mark 11:15–19; Luke 19:45–48). The crucial issue in this story is what John tells us about its meaning. The people who heard Jesus talk about destroying the temple assumed that he meant the physical temple building, but after Jesus's resurrection his disciples understood the far deeper meaning: Jesus was describing his own body, his own person, as the true temple of God (2:21–22).

Varied Reactions to Jesus

■ READ JOHN 3:1–4:54 ■

The next section contains four stories that teach specific truths about Jesus and show varied reactions to him. In each story there is a dialogue between characters followed by John's interpretive comments.

In the first story a Jewish Pharisee leader, Nicodemus, approaches Jesus to question him about his actions and speech (3:1–15). This is a reasonable challenge because, after all, Jesus is not a trained rabbi, yet he is calling disciples to follow him (1:35–51), he is reportedly performing miracles (2:1–12), and he is causing disruption and boldly challenging the authorities (2:13–22). Jesus answers, but not in the way Nicodemus anticipated. Instead, Jesus speaks with profound metaphor—about the Spirit

The Prologue as Table of Contents

In addition to its remarkable claims about Jesus's identity, John's prologue also lays out the main ideas that will be explored throughout his story:

Life—Jesus is offering life: true human flourishing with God for eternity (1:4).

Light and darkness—Jesus is the light coming into the dark world that misunderstands him and tries to oppose him (1:4–9).

Witness—The Gospel of John presents Jesus's ministry like a trial, where witnesses appear and judgment is rendered on the world for its unfaithfulness (1:7–8).

World—The world or cosmos serves as a character in John, and it clashes with Jesus at every turn (1:9–10).

Knowledge—Key to Jesus's teaching is that he alone truly knows God and gives this knowledge to his disciples (1:10, 18).

Seeing and believing—Deeply related to the emphasis on knowing, a vision metaphor is used by John to talk about the goal of the Gospel: belief in Jesus (1:14, 18).

Glory—Jesus is the true manifestation of God's majestic greatness (1:14).

Truth—Jesus is witness to who God truly is; he is truth incarnate (1:14, 17).

and being born again and the Son of Man being exalted—and then turns the tables on Nicodemus, asking him why *he* doesn't understand heavenly things even though he is a teacher in Israel (3:10). John then comments on this story by explaining that God sent Jesus not to condemn but to save the world but that those who love darkness will not come to the light (3:16–21).

In the second story John the Baptizer is also questioned, but by his own disciples. Compared to Jesus, John is being surpassed (3:22–36). The Baptizer sees himself clearly and knows his role is not *being* the light of the world but rather *witnessing to* the light of the world (1:8). He points to Jesus, the bridegroom and the Christ, and John finds his joy in Jesus increasing while he himself is decreasing in power and popularity. John the Gospel writer then comments on this story by describing Jesus as coming from heaven and being the authoritative agent of God on earth (3:31–36).

In the third story Jesus interacts with a person on the opposite end of the spectrum from Nicodemus the Pharisee: a sexually promiscuous Samaritan woman (4:1–38). Once again Jesus speaks of deep heavenly matters, and he challenges the woman's self-perception and heart-level desires. But unlike Nicodemus, this woman goes from skepticism to belief that Jesus is indeed a prophet. Her testimony leads her townspeople to welcome Jesus and eventually believe he is the Savior of the world (4:29, 42). In the commentary on this story, Jesus explains that his mission is to gather disciples from all over (4:31–38), and John reports that two groups of non-Jerusalemites had now welcomed Jesus, the Samaritans (4:39–42) and the Galileans (4:43–45).

Figure 9.3. Glass panel showing Jesus and the Samaritan woman at the well

THEOLOGICAL ISSUES

Life Everlasting / Eternal Life

The last line of the Apostles' Creed states that Christians believe in "life everlasting," coming from the biblical expression "eternal life," which is a favorite of John's Gospel. This confessional belief is intimately tied to the preceding line of the creed, "I believe in the resurrection of the body." This refers to the future promise that Christians will be raised from the dead in physical bodies to experience fullness of life with God in the new creation, freed from sin, bondage, and decay.

The English expressions "life everlasting" and "eternal life" communicate that the life believers experience with God will be unending. While this understanding is truly part of these expressions, it puts the emphasis in the wrong place. The focus of Jesus's promises about people entering into eternal life is on the *quality* of this new life more than its length. "Eternal life" is the flourishing life that accords with the new age (aeon) that Jesus is bringing into the world. A good explanation of what this eternal—or better, new age—life looks like is found in John 10:10: "I have come so that they may have life and have it in abundance."

To confess "I believe in the life everlasting" is to say that one trusts in the truthfulness of Jesus's teaching and that he has opened the way for people to enter into the full and abundant life that we were created for.

Challenge and Riposte, Shame and Honor

In many cultures shame and honor play a larger role than they do in modern Western civilization—more like a central commodity that can be traded, gained, or lost. Honor was the most valuable of possessions, providing stability and satisfaction in the communal society.

A major way honor was established or lost was through public interactions, especially for those who held positions of authority. Nicodemus's dialogue with Jesus was rooted in the basic honor-and-shame categories of the ancient world. By teaching with such authority, Jesus, who had no social status within Judaism (he was not a rabbi), presented a great challenge to the honor of the Jewish leaders like Nicodemus. Nicodemus did not come to Jesus as a seeker or learner, but as one investigating a rebellious, unlearned upstart. Customarily, Jesus should have been learning from Nicodemus and giving him honor. Instead, Jesus took the place of honor and challenged Nicodemus's honor for not understanding the things of God. This story shows that Jesus came to overturn human society, with the supposed honored ones being shamed and the shamed ones receiving honor.

Amphibology in John's Story

Amphibology is the term for communication that is double in meaning, a phrase that simultaneously means more than one thing. When the billboard advertisement for a casino reads, "She'll make you feel like twenty-one again," this is amphibology, with "feel like twenty-one" referring both to feeling young and to desiring to play the card game called Twenty-One.

Poetry also traffics extensively in amphibology; polyvalent wordplay makes poetry satisfying and rich.

So too with the profound Fourth Gospel. Amphibologies appear throughout John's story. For example, Jesus's phrases are regularly ambiguous and double in meaning: being born again / born from above (3:3); the Son of Man being lifted up—exalted or crucified? (3:14); living/flowing water (4:10); going to a place they cannot go (14:2–6).

Even Jesus's enemies unintentionally speak double meaning. The high priest Caiaphas said, "It is to your advantage that one man should die for the people rather than the whole nation perish" (11:50). John then notes that Caiaphas "did not say this on his own, but . . . he prophesied that Jesus was going to die for the nation, and not for the nation only, but also to unite the scattered children of God" (11:51–52).

Amphibology shows John's literary power while also serving an important theological point: people cannot understand heavenly things unless the Spirit reveals the truth. John's repeated amphibology is crucial to his theological presentation of Jesus as the true witness of God in his own world that does not understand him (1:10–11).

In the fourth story in this section Jesus returns to Cana in Galilee, where he performed his first miracle of wedding winemaking (2:1–12). Here he heals an official's son. John tells his readers that this is the second miracle that served as a witness to who Jesus is (4:54), thus tying together the events of chapters 2–4.

The Unveiling of Jesus as the Messiah

■ READ JOHN 5:1–10:42 ■

John 1–4 focused on Jesus's actions and interactions with people, framed with reference to his first and second signs (2:11; 4:54). John 5–10 provides a series of stories that show Jesus going in and out of Jerusalem in connection with Jewish holidays and festivals. The section of chapters 5–10 ends with Jesus returning to where the story began, with John's baptisms in the Jordan River (10:40–42; 3:22–24).

The first story (5:1–17) takes place on a Sabbath day, when Jews were forbidden from working. Jesus heals a paralyzed man, sparking greater conflict between Jesus and the religious leaders (5:16), a common theme in the Synoptic Gospels (e.g., Matt. 12:1–14). Most important is John's lengthy exploration of the theological implications of this, mostly coming in the form of Jesus's direct teaching (5:18–47). With powerful language Jesus makes two things clear: (1) as the Son of

God, Jesus has a special relationship with God the Father such that they share honor, authority, and mission (5:18–29); (2) all the world witnesses to Jesus's greatness—Moses in the past (5:39–47) and John the Baptizer now (5:32–38).

The second story (6:1–71) takes place during Passover, the most important Jewish festival and one of the three Passover celebrations occurring during Jesus's ministry (beginning with 2:13–25 and ending with 13:1–38), thus placing this story at the midpoint of Jesus's ministry. This story parallels the miraculous feedings in the wilderness and the walking on water in the other Gospels (Mark 6:31–52 and parallels), but, in typical Johannine fashion, it makes grand-scale theological statements. Once again Jesus challenges his hearers by making claims that are difficult to understand and hard to accept. He claims to be greater than Moses, that he has come directly from heaven as the true bread of life, and that to enter into life people must feed on his flesh and drink his blood! The result, not surprisingly, is that many people choose to stop following and believing in Jesus (6:60–66), to which he simply responds, "No one can come to me unless it is granted to him by the Father" (6:65).

The third movement in this section (7:1–52) revolves around another important Jewish festival, the Feast of Booths, in which the Jewish people celebrated the harvest and remembered the booths/tents they lived in after their escape from Egypt. The events of chapter 7 follow the tension that Jesus caused in chapter 6 by making such bold claims about himself. Here Jesus returns to Jerusalem, knowing that his work there is unfinished, but he does so secretly because the Jewish leaders are plotting his murder (7:1–13). Then, suddenly, he stands up in the temple and begins preaching (7:14–24), challenging the leaders for trying to kill him because he healed a man on the Sabbath (cf. 5:1–17). John shows that the response to Jesus was deeply divided: some people in the crowd believed that he was a prophet or the Christ (7:31, 40–41), while others were confused (7:25–27, 35–36, 41–43), while the leaders were angry and frustrated that they could not arrest him (7:32, 45–52). In an interesting turn, even Nicodemus, who previously had challenged Jesus (3:1–15), was beginning to wonder about Jesus (7:50–52).

Cyril of Alexandria and the Internal Connections of Scripture

One of the most brilliant commentators of the ancient world was the patriarch Cyril of Alexandria, Egypt (ca. 378–444). Among his many important works is his large commentary on the Gospel of John, written around 425–428.[1] Central to his ability to be such a good commentator was that he had most of Scripture completely memorized from his years of meditation and study. As a result, whenever he read any text of Scripture he could immediately recall other texts that used the same words or phrases. For example, when commenting on John 5:35, where John the Baptizer is called "a burning and shining lamp," Cyril connects this with other passages throughout Scripture that refer to lamps and burning and shining, such as Psalm 132:17, Exodus 27:20–28:1, and Luke 12:49.[2] This unified reading of Scripture based on the internal connections among texts was the typical pattern of patristic commentary and preaching, something that has been largely lost in the modern era.

The Woman Caught in Adultery

The memorable and famous story about Jesus protecting the woman caught in adultery probably is not original to John's Gospel. In our modern Bibles this story is printed as John 7:53–8:11, but the earliest and most reliable manuscripts do not contain these verses. Nonetheless, the story apparently is very old and accords with Jesus's character and ministry: he is gracious to a shamed woman while challenging the religious authorities' hypocrisy. Early in the church's history some people inserted this story into John's Gospel, maybe from another source or from other oral memories about Jesus, certainly with sincere and good intentions. This textual variant (see chap. 2) became a part of the church's tradition in art and memory.

Figure 9.4. Panel with Christ and the woman taken in adultery

Jesus's bold claims about himself continue in 8:12–59. He is the light of the world (8:12); his father is God himself (8:19), whereas the Jewish leaders have the devil as their father (8:44), even though they claim to be Abraham's children (8:39); and he is greater than Abraham because he existed before Abraham did (8:56–58). From a Jewish perspective, Jesus's words are confusing (8:21–22) and then deemed downright blasphemous. As a result, the Jewish leaders decide he is demonic and try to kill him by stoning (8:52, 59), but he slips away.

The next story takes place once again on a Sabbath day, when Jesus performed a remarkable and rare kind of miracle: the healing of someone blind from birth (9:1–7). This striking miracle raised questions and commotion (9:8–12). So the neighbors took the formerly blind beggar to the Pharisees for investigation. The result was a great dispute: some said that Jesus must be wrong because he did (healing) work on a Sabbath; others reasoned that God must be behind such a miracle; while the Pharisees, feeling the pinch of these arguments, desperately claimed that the man was never actually blind (9:13–18). So the Pharisees called in the man's parents and questioned him again, still not getting the results they wanted. The healed man turned the tables on their argument and challenged their lack of understanding and belief. They cast him out of the synagogue completely (9:18–34). Jesus finds the healed man and invites him to believe fully in him (9:35–38). Jesus goes on to explain that he—not the Pharisees—is the good shepherd, the one who cares for God's people, providing for them, protecting them, and even laying down his own life for them (10:1–18). In this Jesus claims once again that he uniquely shares God's identity and mission in the world.

This long section of chapters 5–10 ends with the Feast of Dedication (today called Hanukkah), during which the Jews celebrated their recapturing of the temple during the Maccabean period. The Jewish people were divided about whether Jesus was from God or demonic (10:19–21)—the only two real options—and so when he shows up in Jerusalem for this festival, they ask him plainly if he is the Christ (10:24). His response is once again clear and bold: "I and the Father are one" (10:30) and "The Father is in me and I in the Father" (10:38). Those who heard him understood the depth of his claim, that he was making himself divine, which in their eyes was nothing short of blasphemy (10:33). Such claims could create only two choices: either believe in Jesus (10:42) or try to arrest and kill him for his blasphemy (10:31, 39). Jesus again withdrew north to the wilderness.

Resurrection and Opposition

■ READ JOHN 11:1–12:50 ■

These two chapters conclude the first part of John's Gospel (the Book of Signs, 1:19–12:50) and prepare readers for the second half (the Book of Glory, 13:1–20:31). John chooses to conclude this section with one of the most important miracles of Jesus's ministry: the raising of Lazarus from the dead (11:1–44). This story is intimate and complex, full of deeper meaning, while also being the final catalyst that causes Jesus's own death.

Jesus was not an aloof celebrity; he was loved by many people, and he loved many in a close and personal way. John tells us of two sisters and a brother (Mary, Martha, and Lazarus) in the village of Bethany with whom Jesus had a special relationship. Lazarus became ill and died, causing great grief and putting Mary and Martha in a precarious social situation. Jesus delayed his arrival in Bethany, because he knew that God was going to do something amazing and beautiful. When Jesus finally got near the village, Martha and Mary came to Jesus separately, both confused and grieving, wondering why Jesus did not come earlier and heal Lazarus (11:21, 32). Filled with compassion and grief himself, Jesus went to the tomb and, in front of everyone, raised Lazarus from the dead by calling him to walk out of his cave tomb (11:43–44). In response to this undeniable wonder, the Pharisees and Jerusalem priests convene and decide that Jesus must be killed. Otherwise, they fear, there may be an uprising of belief in Jesus that causes the Roman rulers to crush the Jews completely (11:45–57). Theologically, the resurrection of Lazarus points toward Jesus's own resurrection (20:1–29) and makes clear that Jesus himself is the source of resurrection and life for everyone who believes and follows him (5:25–29; 11:25–26).

John 12 transitions the story from Jesus's ministry to his last week of life. The time of year is the Passover, the third Passover festival recorded by John and used to frame Jesus's activities (2:13; 6:4; 12:1). Once again

Los Angeles County Museum of Art / Wikimedia Commons

Jesus speaks and acts boldly, and once again this causes a very mixed reaction. Jesus claims to have the same authority and honor as God the Father (12:26–36, 44–50). Lazarus's sister Mary humbly washes Jesus's feet with expensive ointment as a sign of love and gratitude, while Judas gets angry at this supposed waste of money (12:1–8). Many Jews, both from Judea and Greek Jews from afar, both lowly people and even some priests, understand Jesus as the king of Israel, the Christ who is worthy of praise and honor (12:12–21, 42). But the chief priests are furious and plan to kill Lazarus in addition to Jesus (12:9–11).

Figure 9.5. *The Raising of Lazarus* by Rembrandt

Mary and Martha

Mary and Martha (sisters of Lazarus) appear twice in the New Testament. In Luke 10:38–42 the sisters respond differently to Jesus. Martha is busy with household preparations and becomes upset that Mary is sitting and listening to Jesus. Jesus does not condemn Martha, but he commends Mary for choosing "what is better." Both service and contemplation are good, but Mary is engaged in the more fruitful activity.

These two sisters also appear in a pair of stories in John 11:1–12:8. Jesus comes to their village once again and turns their grief into joy by raising their brother from the dead. Afterward, Martha serves a meal while Mary washes and anoints Jesus's feet with a precious perfume.

The appearance of these characters in both Luke and John raises an interesting question about a Christian reading of the canon: Should our interpretation of Mary and Martha in Luke inform how we understand them in John? There are similarities in the stories, with Martha serving in both accounts and Mary sitting at Jesus's feet. Interpreters have often taken this difference between the sisters in Luke and read it into John's story, where Martha runs out to meet Jesus but Mary stays in the house weeping.

While it is not wrong to read these stories in parallel, we should also let each Gospel writer tell his own story. John does not seem to draw the same distinction between Mary and Martha that Luke does. Both sisters say nearly the same thing to Jesus after their brother's death (John 11:21, 32), and both welcome him into their home, albeit with different actions.

The Knowledge of God

Knowledge of God is a central concept within the Judeo-Christian worldview, the Bible, and Christian theology. According to biblical teaching, it is possible to know God because he has chosen to reveal himself. In the Greek philosophical and religious world, to know the divine meant to contemplate the ultimate reality. Within the Jewish and Christian traditions, however, knowing God is more relational, hearing and obeying in a covenantal relationship.

The Gospel of John contributes very strongly to the Christian understanding of what it means to know God. In addition to frequently speaking about knowing God, in John Jesus highlights the intimacy of the knowledge of God, where the Father, the Son, and the Spirit indwell one another in a mutual knowledge and revelation. Also, knowledge of God is deeply ethical, with an indwelling relationship between knowing God and doing his will: knowing God is evidenced by keeping his commandments (especially love), and one's moral desires affect one's knowledge (7:17).

Jesus Teaches His Friends

■ READ JOHN 13:1–17:26 ■

Jesus chose to come to Jerusalem for the last time during the Passover festival, the foremost Jewish holiday, commemorating the exodus from Egypt through Moses. At the heart of this festival is a family meal that symbolically retells the significance of the exodus. The weighty chapters of John 13–17 are known as the **Upper Room Discourse**. Jesus used this Passover meal to teach his disciples core truths of the Christian faith.

The first noticeable thing about this last night of teachings from Jesus is that John does not record the most influential part of this event: the bread-breaking and wine-sharing that became known as the Lord's Supper. John's method instead is to assume that his readers are familiar with this widespread practice. This frees John to emphasize a complementary theme central to following Christ: sacrificial love for one another.

The theme of sacrificial love and relational unity dominates the Upper Room Discourse. It begins with Jesus's model of servanthood in washing his disciples' feet (13:2–20), which he explains clearly as the example that his disciples should follow (13:14–15). Jesus continues by giving what he calls a new commandment—new but rooted in God's law—that his people love one another in the same way that he has loved them (13:34), which is how the world will recognize Christians (13:35). This sacrificial love for others is the ultimate love (15:12–17). The Upper Room Discourse concludes with the same theme in what is referred to as Jesus's **High Priestly Prayer** (17:1–26). In this prayer Jesus asks his Father to protect his disciples and to create among them a unity mirroring that of the Father and Son (17:20–26). 🔗

LITERARY NOTES 📖

The Seven Signs in John

One of the dominant themes in John is that Jesus performed many actions that served as signs. These signs show that Jesus is sent from God and exercises divine power on the earth. John concludes his Gospel by saying that the whole reason he has written his story is to record these many signs so that people might believe that Jesus is the Messiah, the Son of God, and thereby have eternal life (20:30–31).

It is no accident that John records *seven* specific signs that point to Jesus's divinity, with seven being an important symbolic number in the Bible. He explicitly identifies the first two, and readers are expected to extrapolate and count the remainder of the signs that lead up to Jesus's last week of life:

1. changing water into wine (2:1–11)
2. healing of the nobleman's son (4:46b–54)
3. healing of the lame man (5:2–47)
4. feeding of the five thousand (6:1–15)
5. walking on water (6:16–21)
6. healing of the man born blind (9:1–41)
7. raising of Lazarus (11:1–44)

All **seven signs in John** occur in the first half of the book. However, many scholars suggest the final and greatest sign to be Jesus's death, burial, and resurrection (chaps. 19–20).

Cleveland Museum of Art / Wikimedia Commons

Figure 9.6. Fragment of the top of a column depicting the mourning Mary and Martha

I Believe in the Holy Catholic Church

One of the lines from the Apostles' Creed that may seem odd to many Christians is the confession "I believe in the holy catholic church." This is because the Roman branch of Christianity has long used this same word, "catholic," as part of its name, the Roman Catholic Church. The reason they started using this word as a description and the reason we still use it in the creeds is that "catholic" simply means "universal." That is, the Roman tradition started using this expression to describe the Christian understanding that was agreed on by all Christians (like the Apostles' Creed). This is no longer the case, of course, in that there are some significant disagreements among the Eastern Orthodox, the Roman, and the Protestant traditions.

At the same time, all of these branches of Christianity still share much in common (more than their differences), and all would say that ultimately there is one true church, the body of believers in Jesus across all time and space.

This is the benefit of confessing one holy and universal church. This confession reminds Christians that our identity as people is first and foremost our identity as believers, as those who have been made part of Christ's body, the church. The unity of believers is deeper than social, ethnic, gender, educational, economic, and even denominational differences. This unity even transcends the great barrier of death, with the understanding that Christians who are alive and dead are united in Christ. There is one Lord, one faith, one baptism, and, ultimately, one church (Eph. 4:4–6).[3]

John's Metaphors and Jesus's Parables

One of the distinctive marks of Jesus's teaching is that he regularly used parables—figures of speech, analogies, and allegorical stories (see chap. 4). When Jesus's parables are analyzed, the Gospel of John typically is excluded because Jesus's teaching style as presented in John seems so different from the Synoptics.

It is true that the familiar Synoptic parables about the kingdom are not found in John. However, Jesus's teaching in John is no less parabolic. All throughout John, Jesus teaches with images, metaphors, and figures: Jesus is the bread, the gate, the way, the light, the vine. The difference is that in the Synoptics Jesus's parables focus on the kingdom while in John Jesus's parabolic teaching centers on who he is.

Parables in all four Gospels have the same purpose and effect, however. By using parabolic images Jesus shows himself to be speaking of heavenly matters that people on earth cannot understand unless God reveals them.

Inside this bookended emphasis on love and unity among believers, Jesus gives instructions on two other themes: overcoming the hateful world, and the Holy Spirit's role in the new age. Jesus foretells his betrayal (13:21–30) and teaches his disciples to expect hatred from the world, just like the world hated him (15:18–16:4). Christians should not be disheartened, however, because Jesus has overcome the world (16:33). This emphasis on suffering in the present age intersects with the theme of the Holy Spirit. Jesus promises his disciples that he will not leave them alone in the world, but that the Father will send the Spirit of truth (14:15–18). The Holy Spirit will teach and remind Jesus's disciples what Jesus has said (14:26; 16:13) and also testify to and convict the world because of its rejection of Jesus (16:8–11).

Jesus's Death and Resurrection

▓ READ JOHN 18:1–20:31 ▓

Every Gospel emphasizes Jesus's death and resurrection as central to its message, and John is no exception. Yet each Gospel relays different details and highlights diverse theological themes. John's story in chapters 18–20 is particularly marked by conflict and violence.

Under Roman rule, the Jewish people were not allowed to exercise capital punishment, and so after the priests questioned Jesus (18:19–24) they handed him off in hopes that Pilate would execute him. But when Pilate questioned Jesus he found him innocent according to Roman law, and in fact he was daunted by the claims that Jesus was the Son of God

(19:8). Pilate attempted to release Jesus, but the Jewish leadership pressured him into executing Jesus for treason (19:12–16). So Jesus is crucified with a mocking accusation above his head: "King of the Jews" (19:17–22). He died and was buried, attended to by a couple of wealthy men who had become disciples: Joseph of Arimathea and Nicodemus (19:38–42), the teacher who had first questioned Jesus (3:1–15).

John 18–20 alternates between locations to tell its story. A garden frames the beginning and ending of this section. At this time, gardens were walled and curated spaces that only the wealthy and royalty could maintain. In the privacy of such a garden Jesus was betrayed and arrested (18:1–14), and later was buried, resurrected, and first appeared to Mary Magdalene (19:38–20:18), who initially mistook him for the gardener (20:15). It is also outside the high priest's house where Peter follows Jesus but then denies being a follower (18:15–18, 25–27).

The dialogues occurring indoors are also important, especially Jesus's interaction with the Roman governor, Pontius Pilate (18:28–19:11). In this exchange Jesus acknowledges that he is truly a king, but his kingdom is from above (18:33–38). After his resurrection Jesus suddenly appears to the disciples who have locked themselves in a room for fear of being killed (20:19–29). In this final interchange

Love One Another

The theme of love is undoubtedly central to the Gospel of John, with words for "love" occurring more than fifty times, and Jesus continually teaching about the love that the Father and Son have for each other and about God's love for his people. Additionally, Jesus tells his disciples that the summary of his command is that they love one another (13:34–35).

Some three hundred years after John's writing, St. Jerome recorded a well-known tradition about the apostle John:

> The blessed evangelist John remained in Ephesus until extreme old age, when he could scarcely be carried to church anymore in his disciples' arms. When he was no longer able to utter many words, he used to say no more than "Children, love one another" at each of their assemblies. In the end the assembled disciples and brethren grew tired of always hearing the same thing, and they said, "Master, why do you always say that?" John replied with the worthy statement, "Because it is in the Lord's commandment, and if that alone is done, it suffices."[4]

And the Son? The *Filioque* Debate

All the branches of orthodox Christianity have greatly valued the many ways in which the Gospel of John has contributed to our understanding of the Trinity. There is a great disagreement, however, between the Eastern and Western branches of Christianity on what is called the ***filioque* clause**. *Filioque* is Latin for "and the Son," and the debate concerns whether the orthodox creeds should say that the Holy Spirit proceeds from the Father alone (the Eastern view) or from both the Father *and the Son* (the Western view). This difference has an impact on how the relationship of the persons of the Trinity is understood, so it is no mere intellectual debate.

The Gospel of John plays a key role in this discussion. In John 15:26 Jesus speaks about the Spirit coming from the Father (with no mention of Jesus sending). However, in John 16:13–15 Jesus says the Spirit will take what he says and declare it to the disciples, thus implying the Son's role also in sending the Spirit. Additionally, in John 20:22 Jesus breathes the Spirit on his disciples. Most strongly, John 16:7 indicates that Jesus is involved in the sending of the Spirit after his resurrection.

Unfortunately, the difference of opinion on the *filioque* clause has caused a major rift between the Roman Catholic and Eastern Orthodox branches of Christianity going back at least to the eleventh century, interwoven as the debate is with questions of whether popes have the authority to insist on the inclusion of this phrase in the creeds.

Jesus's "I Am" Statements

One of the most notable ways that John presents Jesus is through Jesus's famous "I am" statements. There are two types of "I am" statements, both of which occur seven times.

Seven times Jesus says, "I am X," with the predicate X being some weighty theological metaphor:

1. I am the bread of life (6:35)
2. I am the light of the world (8:12)
3. I am the gate (10:9)
4. I am the good shepherd (10:11)
5. I am the resurrection and the life (11:25)
6. I am the way, the truth, and the life (14:6)
7. I am the true vine (15:1)

On another seven occasions Jesus uses the same "I am" phrase with no noun afterward to refer to himself: 4:26; 6:20; 8:24, 28, 58; 13:19; 18:5–8.

In both cases Jesus is intentionally tapping into a deep and important Old Testament root. "I am" is a primary way that God reveals himself to Moses, especially in Exodus: God is the father of Abraham, Isaac, and Jacob (Exod. 3:6), and he tells Moses to tell the Israelites that the great "I am" is coming to rescue them (Exod. 3:14). Jesus's "I am" statements are connected to the metaphors of bread, light, vine, and so on, and in each case it is not the "I am" part that is found in the Old Testament but rather these powerful theological images. Thus, Jesus identifies himself with these key ideas and statements from Israel's history: he is bread from the exodus, the light from Isaiah, the shepherd from Jeremiah and Ezekiel, the way that Isaiah prophesies.

before John's epilogue (21:1–25) Jesus speaks peace to his frightened disciples and, as promised, breathes the Holy Spirit on them, empowering them as the agents of God's forgiveness in the world (20:19–23; cf. Matt. 28:16–20). Jesus welcomes his disciples to confirm his embodied resurrection, pronouncing a blessing on those who in generations to come will believe and follow him without this physical witness (20:24–29).

John concludes his Gospel story with a clear statement about why he has written this lengthy and elaborate Gospel biography: to provide a record of some of the many signs Jesus performed so that his readers may believe that Jesus really is the risen Christ (Messiah), and that through this belief they might experience true and full life (20:30–31). Aware of this purpose statement, we can reread the Gospel and see John's emphasis on Jesus's authority and unity with the Father, along with Jesus's revelation of God's true nature.

The Relationship of the Gospel of John to the Letters of John and the Book of Revelation

Five New Testament books are traditionally understood to have been written by the apostle John: the Fourth Gospel, the three letters we call First, Second, and Third John, and the Apocalypse, or book of Revelation. Providing definitive dates and chronology for each of these is difficult. According to tradition, John lived long, and it appears that each of his writings comes from a mature stage in his ministry, particularly addressing theological and moral problems that arose in the later decades of the first century.

Apart from questions about the historical connections within this Johannine literature, we can observe fruitful canonical connections—ways in which these writings share themes and enlighten one another.

For example, Revelation and the Gospel of John both paint a picture of the world that is rooted in a sharp dualism between

the heavenly and the earthly realms. Revelation and John are written in different genres (see chap. 29, on Revelation), so they speak differently, but both share a fundamental worldview that contrasts two realms of reality: heaven (God) and earth (humanity).

For another example, it is often helpful to read the letters of 1–3 John side by side with the Gospel of John. The language and themes are often the same, such as their shared emphasis on light versus darkness (John 8:12; 12:46; 1 John 1:5–7; 2:9–11), the Holy Spirit as Paraclete or Counselor/Advocate (John 14:16, 26; 15:26; 1 John 2:1), and the centrality of loving one another (John 13:34; 15:12; 1 John 3:11–16; 4:7–12; 2 John 5).

The Epilogue

■ READ JOHN 21:1–25 ■

John 20:30–31 feels like an appropriate ending to this Gospel story, with its clear statement of the purpose for writing. The Gospel of John concludes, however, with an epilogue (21:1–25) consisting of three little stories that tie up loose ends and prepare the reader for the rest of the New Testament. This epilogue is separate from the rest of the story yet continues with the narrative and two key characters, Peter and the Beloved Disciple.

The epilogue's first story is set where the story began (1:35–51), outside Jerusalem, with the disciples engaged in their lifelong occupation of fishing (21:1–14). After an unsuccessful night on the water, the disciples see Jesus—though they do not recognize him—and he causes a miraculous catch of fish (153 large fish, to be precise). Through this event the disciples realize they are with the risen Jesus. They get to shore, and he shares bread and fish with them. This whole story is intentionally ripe with allusions to the other Gospels. The calling of Peter, Andrew, James, and John in Luke 5:1–11 is clearly being referenced in John's story, as are the wilderness feedings of bread and fish (Matt. 14:13–21; 15:32–39; Mark 8:1–10; Luke 9:10–17; John 6:1–15), and Luke 24:13–49, where Jesus's identity becomes clear only when he reveals himself through reminiscent actions.

John's next epilogue story (21:15–19) flows from the previous one and focuses on Jesus's restoration of Peter. Three times Peter denied Jesus by a charcoal fire (18:15–18, 25–27), and now three times by the fire Jesus presses Peter with the vision of being a loving shepherd of God's people. This is a painful and potentially shameful situation for Peter, but Jesus graciously reinstates him to his place of leadership, ending with the same call that Peter first received: "Follow me."

The third and final story (21:20–23) deals with the two key characters, Peter and the Beloved Disciple. This story is, frankly, a little odd. It concerns a misunderstanding of words between Peter and Jesus that was later misinterpreted by the other disciples. Specifically, the issue seemed to be that some Christians came to believe that Jesus had promised that the Beloved Disciple would not die before Jesus returned to the earth. But this little vignette clarifies that Jesus did *not* promise this. Why has John included this story here? One possibility is that this last story was added by John's faithful disciples as the conclusion of his book shortly after he died. This could explain why the story is included—to correct a wrong rumor—and this would also make sense of 21:24, which refers to the faithful testimony of the Beloved Disciple in the third person. This would make this section comparable to the reports of Moses's death at the end of the Pentateuch (Deut. 34:1–12). We cannot know for certain. What is clear, however, is how the final verse of this

153 Fish?

John 21:11 contains a very curious detail. When the postresurrection Jesus revealed himself to his disciples through a great catch of fish, John tells us that there were exactly 153 fish. Why does this detail matter?

The short answer is that we don't know. Christians have pondered this detail for millennia and have offered a variety of answers—from reflections on how 153 is a triangular number, to arguments about 153 being the number of species of fish known at the time, to simplistic answers about fishermen's propensity to count their catch.

What is clear is that before the modern era most Jews and Christians thought a lot about the symbolic use of numbers and names. In fact, an important connection between numbers and names is called *gematria*, where the numeric value of words is calculated and symbolic significance seen in the connection.

Some contemporary scholars have revisited these ancient ideas and suggest that John would have indeed intended something by referencing 153 fish. Suggestions include that 153 is the *gematria* value of "sons of God" (John 1:12, connecting the epilogue to the prologue), and that the number 153 is connected to the prime number 17, which itself is a combination of 10 (representing the law) and 7 (representing the gifts of the Spirit), and is also connected with what we know was an important early Christian number, 18. Regardless, it is true that the ancient world commonly used numbers symbolically, and this may have included John's 153 fish.

beautiful Gospel story serves as a great summary of the whole Fourfold Gospel Book: "And there are also many other things that Jesus did, which, if every one of them were written down, I suppose not even the world itself could contain the books that would be written" (21:25).

Implementation—Reading John as Christian Scripture Today

We don't need to wonder how John would want us to implement his Gospel. He makes clear at the end of his story and then again in the final words of the epilogue that he has written his Gospel biography "so that you may believe that Jesus is the Messiah, the Son of God, and that by believing you may have life in his name" (20:31). The proper response to the Gospel of John is to engage in honest self-reflection, to let the weight of Jesus's claims work in our lives. The true and eternal life that all humans long for is offered by Jesus (see 10:10), the only one through whom we can know God. All other desires, pursuits, and loves pale in comparison to the eternal life that Jesus offers.

Jesus declares a blessing on his disciples for believing when they saw his pierced side and punctured hands, but he was already thinking of you and me: "Blessed are those who have not seen and yet believe" (20:29). The invitation that Jesus gave to his first believing disciples he now gives to all the hearers of John's Gospel: "What are you seeking? Follow me. Come and see! You will see greater things than these!" (see 1:35–51).

The Gospel of John is to the Fourfold Gospel Book what Deuteronomy is to the Pentateuch—the volume in the collection that is the summary, the apex, the culminating and clarifying book. John's traditional association with the symbol of the eagle is clear in light of the high-flying theology and Christology of this Gospel. The use of John as the starting place for many Christians and seekers also makes sense: John's stories are engaging and entertaining, and there is no question that Jesus is being presented to readers as the incarnation of God himself on the earth.

KEY VERSES IN JOHN

- In the beginning was the Word, and the Word was with God, and the Word was God. 1:1
- Jesus told him, "I am the way, the truth, and the life. No one comes to the Father except through me." 14:6
- Jesus performed many other signs in the presence of his disciples that are not written in this book. But these are written so that you may believe that Jesus is the Messiah, the Son of God, and that by believing you may have life in his name. 20:30–31

John and the Synoptics, DC and Marvel

It has been observed that (with a few exceptions) in the world of superheroes, Marvel Comics tells stories of humans ascending to the divine, while DC Comics is about gods learning what it is like to be human. Together these speak of the different journeys of ascent and descent.

We may compare this to the Synoptics and John. One recognized difference is that in the Synoptics Jesus's journey is depicted as from the earth to heaven, while in John's Gospel Jesus comes from heaven to earth before returning there (see the prologue and many of Jesus's dialogues). In all four accounts Jesus is the God-man, but the journey is highlighted in a different direction.

Christian Reading Questions

1. Read John's prologue (1:1–18) several times, noting its major themes. Trace these themes throughout the rest of John's Gospel.

2. Read through each of the seven signs in John. How do you think each of these signs reveals different aspects of Jesus's character and divine power?

3. Read through 1 John. What themes are prevalent throughout the letter? How do these themes compare and contrast with the themes in John's Gospel?

4. Why do you think John's Gospel is so different from the Synoptics? What value does it add to the Fourfold Gospel Book?

CHAPTER TEN

The Acts of the Apostles

Orientation

The book of Acts is an action-packed drama, full of God's signs and wonders, incredible conversions, amazing provisions, and the unfolding plan of God. But above all, Acts testifies to the life-altering, world-changing person of Jesus Christ. He is the Lord of all, appointed as the Savior and Judge of all. As the apostles proclaim his name, they reveal to the world the only name under heaven by which people may be saved.

Acts is the bridge of the New Testament, taking us from the earthly ministry of Jesus in the Gospels to the heavenly ministry of Jesus as he works through his Spirit, and as his Spirit works through his apostles. In this sense, the Acts of the Apostles is misnamed. It should be called the Acts of the Ascended Christ Jesus.

Acts is also the bridge of salvation history, as we see God pour out his Spirit on believing gentiles, as well as Jews, in fulfillment of Old Testament prophecy. In the course of this narrative we see the people of God reconfigured so that it is no longer limited to ethnic Israel with its laws and customs, but is now opened up to all people from all nations who are willing to confess Jesus as the Messiah of God and receive the forgiveness of sins in his name.

Finally, Acts is the bridge between the relatively unimportant region of Judea to the very center of world power and influence, Rome, the capital of the empire. By the end of the story we see the message of Christ boom out of Jerusalem, travel through the

---

HISTORICAL MATTERS

The Historical Origins of Acts

Author: Luke the physician

Date: Around AD 62

Location: Rome

Setting: Luke writes to Theophilus and others like him who need to know the next part of the story after Luke's Gospel.

Mediterranean world, and become a global movement.

Exploration—Reading Acts

"You Will Be My Witnesses"

■ READ ACTS 1:1–14 ■

Luke begins the second volume of his history of the Jesus movement with a dedication to Theophilus (cf. Luke 1:1–4), reminding him of the first volume's account of all that Jesus did and taught and the convincing proofs he gave of his resurrection over forty days (1:1–3).

After the dedication, Luke offers a seamless connection to his Gospel, with the story overlapping with the end of the Third Gospel, picking it up just prior to the ascension of Jesus (Luke ends with the ascension). In Luke, Jesus had said that he would send what the Father promised (referring to the Holy Spirit) and that the disciples were to wait in Jerusalem until they were empowered by the Spirit (24:49). In Acts, Jesus says the same thing but is more explicit this time, indicating that the disciples will be baptized with the Holy Spirit (1:4–5). Having received the Holy Spirit, they will become Jesus's witnesses in Jerusalem, Judea and Samaria, and to the ends of the earth (1:8).

Jesus then ascended to heaven, and two angels told the apostles that he would return in the same way, thus confirming their expectation that Jesus would one day come again from the clouds (1:9–11). The apostles returned to Jerusalem, where they stayed together in prayer (1:12–14).

The Twelfth Man

■ READ ACTS 1:15–26 ■

Next Luke offers an insight into the postascension regrouping of the apostles. Peter continued his leadership among the disciples of Jesus by arguing from Scripture that Judas had been destined to betray Jesus, thus implying that even this devastating event was not beyond God's control, but in fact happened according to plan. He also insisted that Judas had to be replaced so that the apostles would number twelve. Since the apostles were to be witnesses, the twelfth man had to have been a follower of Jesus from the time of his baptism to his ascension—the full scope of Jesus's earthly ministry (1:15–22). They cast lots to choose between Joseph and Matthias, with the latter elected to join the apostles (15:23–26).

LITERARY NOTES

Acts 1:8 and the Structure of Acts

This verse is programmatic for the whole book, as Jesus says that when the Spirit comes upon the disciples, they will be his witnesses in Jerusalem, Judea and Samaria, and to the ends of the earth. The structure of Acts follows that outline as the apostles are first empowered by the Spirit and then witness about Christ first in Jerusalem (chaps. 1–7), then farther out from Jerusalem in Judea (chaps. 8–12), through Asia Minor and Europe (chaps. 13–28), with the book ending in Rome (chap. 28). As for Rome, the capital of the empire, representing the "ends of the earth," it may mean that Rome represents the whole world, or that from Rome all the earth will hear the apostles' witness about Jesus because of its influence and capacity for the dissemination of their message.

HISTORICAL MATTERS

How Did Judas Die?

The account of Judas's death in Acts seems quite different from the one found in Matthew 27:1–10. According to Matthew, Judas hanged himself after returning the thirty pieces of silver that the chief priests and elders paid him to betray Jesus. In Acts 1:18 Peter says that Judas acquired a field with his blood money, fell headfirst, and his body burst open. The two accounts are difficult to reconcile, but not impossible. Matthew says that the chief priests used Judas's money to buy a field, which is not too dissimilar from saying that Judas bought the field. And if Judas hanged himself, it is possible that after a period of hanging, his body fell and split open (this was Augustine's view). A more recent view is that Matthew is deliberately drawing on Jeremiah 18:1–4; 19:1–13; 32:6–15. This would then be an imaginative account that Matthew offers, tying Judas's death to biblical prophecy.

The Arrival of the Spirit

■ READ ACTS 2:1–47 ■

Luke wastes little time showing the fulfillment of Jesus's promise to the apostles. As Jesus indicated (1:8), the Spirit soon came upon the apostles, and it happened on the day of Pentecost. Like a rushing wind coming from heaven, the Spirit caused tongues of fire to appear on each one as he filled them and empowered them to speak languages they didn't already know (2:1–4).

Because it was Pentecost, Jews living in other regions and nations had gathered in Jerusalem. Each one heard the apostles speaking in their own language, and they were amazed by this. But it was confusing, and some claimed that the apostles were drunk (2:5–13).

This is when Peter gives his first speech after having received the Spirit, and it is tremendously important for the themes of Acts. Of course the apostles were not drunk, he said, but by appealing to the prophet Joel he argued that what they had witnessed was evidence that the promised Spirit of God had been poured out on them (2:14–21; cf. Joel 2:28–32).

But Peter's Pentecost sermon ultimately was not about the Spirit, but about Christ. Jesus had been attested by signs and wonders and was delivered up to death according to God's plan. But God raised him from the dead, fulfilling the prophecy of Psalm 16:8–11. Whereas David is dead and buried, the true Messiah did not stay dead, and the apostles are witnesses to the resurrection of Jesus (2:22–32). Indeed, Jesus has been exalted to the right hand of God—the position of honor for God's anointed king—and it is from this exalted position that Christ has poured out the Holy Spirit (2:33–35). The pouring out of the Spirit, then, is proof that Jesus is both Lord and Messiah (2:36).

CANONICAL CONNECTIONS

Messianic Expectation in the Psalms

While the apostles drew on several Old Testament texts to demonstrate that Jesus is the Messiah, God's anointed king, Psalms 2, 16, and 110 were especially important. Peter draws on the latter two in his Pentecost sermon. In Acts 2:25–28 we find a lengthy quote from Psalm 16:8–11, in which the messianic figure will not be abandoned to death in **Hades**, but will know the paths of life. This is used to demonstrate that Jesus's resurrection from the dead confirms his messianic status. In Acts 2:34 Peter cites Psalm 110:1 to show that King David looked ahead to a time when God (the LORD) would call the Messiah (David's Lord) to sit in the position of highest honor, at God's right hand. Jesus's ascension to heaven is regarded as the fulfillment of this prophecy, therefore again affirming that Jesus is the Messiah.

The logic of Peter's sermon is that the apostles' ability to speak other languages is evidence that the Spirit has been poured out, and this is in turn evidence that Jesus is the Messiah. In other words, Peter's Pentecost speech is actually about the messianic status of Jesus.

The members of Peter's Jewish audience were cut to the heart by his message and were instructed to repent and be baptized in the name of Jesus Christ for the forgiveness of their sins. They will then receive the Holy Spirit themselves, according to the promise of God (2:37–40; cf. Isa. 44:3). About three thousand people were baptized that day and were added to the Jesus community. They became devoted to the teaching of the apostles, to their new fellowship together, and to prayer (2:41–42).

The newly enlarged community was marked by apostolic signs and wonders, sharing their goods with those in need, and meeting together in the temple and in their homes. They were joyful and sincere as they praised God and increased in number every day (2:41–47).

The Walters Art Museum. Acquired by Henry Walters, 1903.

Figure 10.1. Pentecost (Acts 2:1–4) depicted by William de Brailes (thirteenth century)

The Witnessing Begins

■ READ ACTS 3:1–26 ■

Luke demonstrates what a huge difference the Spirit makes to the apostles' ministry. After the arrival of the Spirit and Peter's declaration of Jesus's messiahship, the apostles began to fulfill their mandate as witnesses to Christ. While praying in the temple, Peter and John were approached by a man, born lame, looking for money. Peter told him to get up and walk in the name of Christ in a manner reminiscent of Jesus's similar feats (3:1–6; cf. Mark 2:1–12). Immediately the man walked and praised God, and all who knew him could see what had happened and were filled with awe (3:7–10).

The astonished crowd prompted Peter to preach about Jesus. After rebuking them for killing Jesus, and once again affirming the apostles' witness to his resurrection, Peter attributed the healing miracle to Jesus, the source of life (3:11–16). Peter called the crowd to repentance by once again connecting the life, death, and resurrection of Jesus to the promises of God in Scripture (3:17–23, 26; cf. Deut. 18:15–19). Even their repentance fulfilled promises (3:24–25; cf. Gen. 12:3; 18:18; 22:18; 26:4).

Persecution Begins

■ READ ACTS 4:1–37 ■

Now Luke shows his readers what to expect in the face of bold preaching about Jesus. Peter's sermon drew the ire of the priests, temple police, and Sadducees. Peter and John were seized, while the number of Jesus's followers had reached five thousand (4:1–4). The next day, before Annas the high priest and others, Peter and John testified that the healing of the lame man was achieved by Jesus of Nazareth, who was crucified and resurrected. Salvation can be found only in his name (4:5–12).

Seeing their boldness and the man who had been healed, the Jewish leaders could not say anything against Peter and John. But they determined not to let the message of Jesus spread any further and ordered Peter and John not to speak in his name (4:13–18). Peter and John defied them directly, claiming obedience to God rather than to men (4:19–20). They reluctantly released Peter and John, who went back to their community praising God's sovereign hand (4:21–31). The new community continued to share all things as they listened

RECEPTION HISTORY

Continuationism vs. Cessationism

Related to a question raised above (see the sidebar "Description vs. Prescription"), this debate concerns whether miraculous signs such as we see in Acts *continue* in the present age or have *ceased* to occur with the end of the apostolic age. On the one hand, it seems that Acts describes a period in salvation history in which God worked amazing feats that served as signposts for the inauguration of the age of the Spirit (in support of **cessationism**). On the other hand, God is not limited and can perform miracles today if he so chooses without compromising the salvation-historical importance of the signs recorded in Acts (in support of **continuationism**).

to the apostles' testimony of the resurrection of Christ, and no one was in need (4:32–37).

Lying to the Holy Spirit

■ READ ACTS 5:1–11 ■

In a fairly bizarre account, Luke portrays the sharing community corrupted when Ananias and Sapphira felt that they needed to lie about their giving. While there would have been nothing wrong with keeping some of their money for themselves, they pretended to give all the proceeds for a property sale to the apostolic community (5:1–2). Peter knew what had happened and rebuked Ananias for lying (not for keeping the money), which was tantamount to lying to God (5:3–4). Sadly, this rebuke led to Ananias's immediate death. Three hours later the same thing happened to his wife, provoking fear in all who heard about it (5:5–11).

Persecution Ramps Up

■ READ ACTS 5:12–42 ■

Over the next few chapters, Luke shows the escalation of persecution against the preaching apostles. They continued to perform signs and wonders, healing the sick and lame, and drawing a great crowd (5:12–16). This once again raised the ire of the high priest and others, who arrested the apostles (5:17–18). But an angel set them free and instructed them to go and preach in the temple (5:19–21a).

Meanwhile the high priest convened a meeting of the Sanhedrin and ordered for the apostles to be brought to them—not knowing they had escaped prison. After discovering their absence, the Sanhedrin learned that the apostles were now teaching in the temple and had them brought before the Sanhedrin (5:21b–27). The high priest reminded the apostles that they were forbidden to teach in Jesus's name, but Peter restated that they must obey God rather than men, and he also reminded them of the message they preached (5:28–32).

This response rather upset the Sanhedrin, but Gamaliel, a famous Pharisee and teacher (of Paul, among

THEOLOGICAL ISSUES

Why Did Ananias and Sapphira Have to Die?

This account in Acts 5 seems particularly harsh to modern readers. Why did the sin of lying about their real-estate proceeds lead to the deaths of Ananias and Sapphira? After all, many lies have been uttered by Christians since then, and no one has been struck down by God for it (as far as we know!). The most satisfying answer is that Acts describes a unique period in the history of salvation, which explains many of the weird and amazing things that occur in the narrative. The fate of Ananias and Sapphira reminds us that the penalty for all sin is death (cf. Gen. 3; Rom. 6:23). While God normally shows mercy by not bringing death at the moment of sin, he nevertheless is the judge of all who gives and takes life as he pleases. The deaths of Ananias and Sapphira underscore God's heightened activity through this key phase of salvation history.

HISTORICAL MATTERS

The Sanhedrin

In every city in ancient Israel there was a court of twenty-three judges that adjudicated disputed matters. This was known as a Sanhedrin. In Jerusalem sat the Grand Sanhedrin, with seventy-one members, which acted as a supreme court, accepting appeals from cases judged by the smaller courts and legislating all manner of Jewish religious and political matters.

Shutterstock / ruskpp

Figure 10.2. *Stephen, a Martyr for Christ* by Gustave Doré

others), tried to reason with them. He reminded the Sanhedrin that movements come and go, and if the apostles do not enjoy God's support, they will fail. But if they are of God, the Sanhedrin will not be able to stop them (5:33–39). After agreeing with Gamaliel's logic, they flogged the apostles, again forbade them to preach in the name of Jesus, and let them go. Rejoicing that they had suffered for the name of Jesus, the apostles promptly ignored the prohibition and continually taught about Jesus (5:40–42).

Persecution Becomes Lethal

■ READ ACTS 6:1–8:3 ■

Next we see the growing persecution reach a lethal level. With the increase of the Jesus movement, a problem developed in the community regarding care for widows. The apostles delegated responsibility for this to seven men, while they remained focused on teaching and prayer (6:1–6). One of the seven servants was Stephen, who performed signs and wonders like the apostles did. As such he drew opposition and foul play: a conspiracy against him led to his arrest, and he was taken to appear before the Sanhedrin (6:8–15).

When asked if the false accusations against him were true, Stephen launched into a remarkable speech that traces the history of God's people from Abraham to Joseph to Moses to Israel to David to Solomon (7:1–50). The speech shows that although God had been faithful to his promises throughout Israel's history, there has always been a rebellious element of people who rejected him (7:39–43). Stephen then linked his accusers and the Sanhedrin to this rebellious element, claiming that they resist the Holy Spirit and killed the promised Righteous One, Jesus (7:51–53). 👥

Stephen's speech enraged the Sanhedrin, and they dragged him out of the city and stoned him. While Stephen calls out to the Lord Jesus to receive his spirit, the narrative introduces Saul, who soon becomes the major figure in the book of Acts (7:54–60).

The death of Stephen seemed to trigger something in Saul, who led a severe persecution against the church, scattering believers throughout Judea and Samaria (8:1). While Stephen was still being buried, Saul launched on a tirade against the church, dragging men and women off to prison (8:2–3).

Ministry outside Jerusalem

■ READ ACTS 8:4–40 ■

Luke helps his readers to see that prophecy can be fulfilled in unexpected ways. Because of Saul's persecution, the apostles began to spread out beyond Jerusalem, just as Jesus had predicted (1:8). Philip preached in Samaria, performing great signs there (8:4–8). Simon, a former sor-

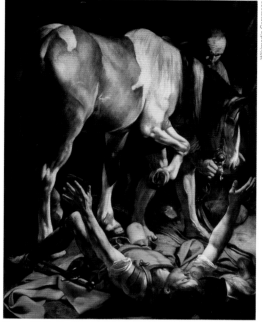

Figure 10.3. *The Conversion on the Way to Damascus* by Caravaggio

cerer, became a believer but tried to buy the apostles' ability to bestow the Spirit, for which he was strongly rebuked (8:9–25).

Outside Jerusalem, Philip met an important Ethiopian eunuch who was reading Isaiah out loud in his chariot. Philip explained the prophecy of Isaiah 53:7–8 to him, demonstrating its fulfillment in Jesus. The eunuch believed and was baptized, after which Philip miraculously disappeared and began preaching near Caesarea (8:26–40).

Saul Meets the Risen Christ

■ READ ACTS 9:1–31 ■

As a historian, Luke knows that truth is stranger than fiction, and what he records next is one of the most unexpected events in history. As the leader of the persecution against the church, Saul continued his mission to destroy it. But while he made his way to Damascus to hunt down believers, a heavenly light surrounded him. A voice asked, "Saul, Saul, why are you persecuting me?" Saul asked who had spoken to him, and the speaker identified himself as Jesus, the one whom Saul was persecuting. Saul lost his vision after this encounter and was led into Damascus (9:1–9).

The Lord told Ananias, a disciple in Damascus, to help Saul. After Ananias's initial refusal, the Lord told him that Saul was his chosen instrument to preach Christ to the gentiles, kings, and Israelites. Ananias laid his hands on Saul, who then regained his sight and was baptized (9:10–19).

After some time, Saul began preaching Jesus in the synagogues in Damascus, causing great confusion because people knew him as the persecutor of the church. Nevertheless, Saul grew in his strength and abilities and became the target of a conspiracy to kill him. But Saul escaped Damascus by being lowered in a basket through an opening in the city walls (9:20–25).

Saul went to Jerusalem for the first time since becoming a follower of Jesus, and the disciples there were afraid of him. But Barnabas took him to the apostles and explained to them how Saul had met the risen Christ, whom he now preached. The apostles accepted Saul and protected him from attempted murder in Jerusalem by taking him to Caesarea and sending him home to Tarsus (9:26–30). Since Saul, the great persecutor, had now become one of them, the church enjoyed a period of peace and growth (9:31).

Gentiles Come to Faith

■ READ ACTS 9:32–11:30 ■

Luke isn't done with surprises yet, as the focus switches back to Peter. His fame was growing as he healed a bedridden man and raised a dead woman (9:32–43). Meanwhile, Cornelius, a centurion in Caesarea, was instructed by an angel to send for Simon Peter in Joppa (10:1–8). At the same time, Peter had seen a bizarre vision about eating unclean food that had left him confused (10:9–16). Then Cornelius's men met Peter and took him to Caesarea with them. Cornelius told Peter what had happened, and Peter then realized that his vision about unclean food was designed to teach him that God does not show favoritism (10:17–35). Peter related his testimony about Jesus to this gentile audience, and the Holy Spirit came upon them and they were baptized (10:36–48).

Word about these gentiles spread to Jerusalem, leading to some criticism of Peter, who was not supposed to associate with such people. But Peter related to them what had happened, including his vision from God, their response to his preaching, and their reception of the Spirit. Peter reasoned that if God had given the gift of the Spirit to gentiles, they should not be discriminated against. His hearers were persuaded and declared that God has given repentance to the gentiles (11:1–18).

A large number of gentiles came to faith in Antioch, so the church in Jerusalem sent Barnabas to serve them there. Needing help with this work, Barnabas went to Tarsus to find Saul, and the two of them served together for a year in Antioch. It was there that the disciples of Jesus were first called Christians (11:19–25).

Persecution from King Herod

■ READ ACTS 12:1–25 ■

Luke's narrative now reminds us that joy is often mixed with tragedy. King Herod executed James, the disciple of Jesus and brother of John, and arrested Peter (12:1–5). An angel of the Lord rescued Peter from Herod and delivered him safely to other believers (12:6–19). Herod, after delivering a speech and being acclaimed by the crowd as a god, was struck down by an angel of the Lord and died (12:20–23). Meanwhile, the word of God flourished (12:24–25).

Paul's First Missionary Journey

■ READ ACTS 13:1–14:28 ■

Luke reaches a major turning point in the narrative, as Paul's mission to the gentiles will dominate the book from here to the end. The Holy Spirit commissioned Barnabas and Saul to embark on a mission to the gentile world. Their first stop was Cyprus—an island in the Mediterranean, and Barnabas's home country—where they preached in the Jewish synagogues along with John Mark, who also was from Cyprus and was Barnabas's cousin. This led to a conflict with Elymas, a sorcerer connected with Sergius Paulus, a proconsul who answered to the Roman senate. Saul—now referred to as Paul—cursed Elymas for his wickedness, causing him to go blind. As a result, Sergius Paulus believed and was astonished by their teaching about the Lord (13:1–12). He was the first Roman official to become a disciple of Jesus.

The missionaries sailed from Cyprus to Perga, on the south coast of modern-day Turkey. Though John Mark abandoned the mission here, Paul and Barnabas continued into the interior to Pisidian Antioch, in the region of Galatia (central Turkey).

HISTORICAL MATTERS

Who Was King Herod?

The King Herod mentioned in Acts 12 is Herod Agrippa I, the son of Aristobulus and the grandson of Herod the Great. Herod Agrippa ruled over Judea in AD 41–44 and was zealous for Judaism, which perhaps explains his violence toward the Jerusalem church, as he may have seen it as a heretical sect threatening orthodox Judaism. The account of his death in Acts 12 is similar to that offered by the Jewish historian Josephus. Herod's two daughters are mentioned later in Acts: Drusilla (24:24) and Bernice (25:13).

HISTORICAL MATTERS

Why Was Saul Called Paul?

It is sometimes assumed that Saul changed his name to Paul when he became a follower of Jesus, but this is incorrect. Luke continues to call him Saul well after this encounter with Christ and begins to refer to him as Paul only during his first missionary journey (Acts 13:9), which is approximately fourteen years after Saul began to follow Christ. Born in the Roman province of Tarsus, Saul would have been given two names at his birth: his Jewish name, Saul, and his Roman name, Paul. So why does Saul become known as Paul during his first missionary journey and from that point on? There are two plausible reasons. One is that he may have ingratiated himself with the Roman proconsul on Cyprus—Sergius *Paulus*. The more important reason is that once this missionary journey had begun, Saul had become Paul—the apostle to the gentiles. His special commission to reach the gentiles would explain why he became known exclusively as Paul.

Paul preached his first recorded sermon in the synagogue there, arguing that Jesus is the promised descendant of King David whom God made the Savior of Israel (13:13–23). He outlined Jesus's ministry, death, and resurrection, showing him to be the fulfillment of the messianic expectations of Psalms 2 and 16. Forgiveness of sins is now given through faith in Jesus (13:24–41).

Paul and Barnabas gained quite a following in Pisidian Antioch, and the whole town gathered to hear them on the following Sabbath. But this inspired jealousy among some of the Jews, who rebutted Paul. Citing Isaiah 49:6, Paul turned to gentile ministry, with many coming to faith. But the Jews stirred up persecution against Paul and Barnabas, pushing them on to their next destination (13:42–52).

Also in the region of Galatia, Paul and Barnabas spoke in the synagogue in Iconium, with many Jews and Greeks believing. But again they faced Jewish persecution, causing them to move on to Lystra and Derbe nearby (14:1–7). In Lystra Paul healed a lame man, causing the crowds to worship Paul (as Hermes) and Barnabas (as Zeus). But they rejected their worship and pointed them to the living God, from whom all good things come. Later, opponents turned the crowds hostile, and Paul was stoned and left for dead outside the town (14:8–20).

After preaching in Derbe, Paul and Barnabas returned back through Lystra, Iconium, and Antioch, encouraging and strengthening the new believers in those places. They then sailed back to Syrian Antioch, their home base, and reported to the church all that God had done to save the gentiles during their mission (14:21–28).

CANONICAL CONNECTIONS

Paul's Letter to the Galatians

Though there is some debate as to whom exactly Paul's Letter to the Galatians is written, the most likely answer is that it addresses the churches that were planted on his first missionary journey, through the center of modern-day Turkey. This region was known as Galatia, but the boundaries of Galatia were subject to change, so that some historians think that Pisidian Antioch, Iconium, Lystra, and Derbe fell outside it. But given that those towns were part of Galatia (at least at one stage) and that we have no record of Paul planting churches elsewhere in Galatia, it remains most likely that this is to whom Paul writes his Letter to the Galatians—one of his earliest letters, if not the earliest.

The Jerusalem Council

■ READ ACTS 15:1–35 ■

With some success in the gentile mission, Luke now draws attention to its implications for the wider church. In Antioch some men from Judea arrived saying that gentiles needed to be circumcised in order to be saved. Paul and Barnabas debated them and eventually went to Jerusalem in order to speak to the apostles about the issue (15:1–5).

The apostles and elders in Jerusalem gathered to discuss the matter. Peter reminded them of his experience with Cornelius and concluded that God no longer distinguishes between Jews and gentiles. Both Jews and gentiles are saved through the grace of the Lord Jesus (15:6–11). Paul and Barnabas recounted all that God had done among the gentiles during their mission to Cyprus and Galatia (15:12). Finally, James spoke in support of gentile inclusion, drawing on Amos 9 and Isaiah 45, concluding that the gentiles should not be burdened with the law of Moses, but that they should abstain from certain things that might cause Jewish believers to stumble (15:13–21).

Then the apostles and elders composed a letter to be sent to the church in Antioch, confirming their resolutions about gentile inclusion and requirements. This news was well received (15:22–35).

Paul's Second Missionary Journey

■ READ ACTS 15:36–18:22 ■

Once apostolic agreement was reached about the gentiles, Paul decided to revisit the churches established on their first missionary journey, but he had a falling out with Barnabas over John Mark, who had deserted them in Perga (cf. 13:13). Barnabas took Mark to Cyprus, while Paul left Antioch with Silas, traveling through Syria and Cilicia and encouraging the churches (15:36–41). On their way back through Galatia, they met a disciple named Timothy, who would go on to be a very important companion for Paul. Timothy joined the missionary group (16:1–5).

The Spirit limited where they could go after that until Paul had a vision of a man from Macedonia who pleaded with him to preach there. In this way, Luke reminds us that Paul's mission unfolds according to God's plan. So they set out for Macedonia—the first time the gospel would be preached in Europe. The first convert in Europe was Lydia, a woman in Philippi (16:6–15).

After an incident in which Paul cast out a spirit from a fortune-telling girl, Paul and Silas were apprehended for disturbing the city. They were stripped, beaten, and imprisoned (16:16–24). At midnight an earthquake gave them an opportunity to escape prison, but they didn't take it. The jailer thought they had escaped while he had slept and was about to take his own life for dereliction of duty when Paul called out and assured him they were still there. The

THEOLOGICAL ISSUES

Why Was Timothy Circumcised?

With all the debate in the Jerusalem and Antioch churches about whether gentiles should be circumcised, it may be surprising that Paul has Timothy circumcised. After all, Paul was one of the key leaders to insist that gentiles did not need to be circumcised (see also Galatians). In Acts 16:3 we are told that Timothy was circumcised "because of the Jews who were in those places," which most likely means that his circumcision was done for missionary purposes. Contrary to the mistaken belief that gentile believers had to be circumcised—a view that Paul opposed in his Letter to the Galatians—Timothy did not get circumcised for spiritual or salvation reasons. Rather, it was done in order to gain access to the Jewish communities in which Paul and Timothy would serve.

LITERARY NOTES

When "They" Becomes "We"

Luke does not directly include himself in the narrative of Acts, but his presence in the story is felt when he starts describing the actors in the story with "we" instead of "they." Up until 16:8, the entire narrative of Acts is portrayed with "they." But in 16:9 it switches to "we" and remains that way until the end of the book. This means that Luke became Paul's traveling companion in Troas (the location of 16:8–10). It also means that from 16:9 through 28:31 Luke is a personal eyewitness of the events he narrates.

jailer was so stunned by this act of mercy that he believed in the Lord and was baptized along with his whole family (16:25–34). The next day, after learning that Paul and Silas were Roman citizens, the magistrates escorted them from the jail, and they went to Lydia's house before leaving the city (16:35–40).

Next, the missionaries arrived in Thessalonica, where Paul's synagogue preaching was initially well received by Jews and Greeks. But once again some Jews became jealous, and a mob started a riot in the city. They attacked Jason's house, where the missionaries were staying, but didn't find them and so dragged poor Jason to the authorities (17:1–9). Later, Paul and Silas left for Berea, where the Jews listened carefully to what they said, examining the Scriptures. Many Jews and gentiles believed. But some troublemakers from Thessalonica came down to Berea, causing Paul to leave town (17:10–15).

At this critical juncture Luke depicts Paul going head-to-head with the Greek intelligentsia. Paul traveled to Athens alone and began reasoning with people in the synagogue and the marketplace. He debated with philosophers who took him to the **Areopagus** to give him a hearing there. Paul then preached his famous Areopagus address, in which he drew on the Athenians' obvious religiosity to speak of a god they did not know. This god is actually the true God, who made all things and has controlled all of human destiny. He has overlooked previous ignorance but now commands all people to repent because a day of judgment is coming in which Jesus,

Figure 10.4. Areopagus

whom God raised from the dead, will judge the world. The mention of resurrection from the dead divided Paul's audience, but some people became believers, including Dionysius of the Areopagus (17:16–34). In this way, Luke demonstrates that even in the epicenter of Greek thought and religion Paul's message gained a hearing and was taken seriously.

Leaving Athens, Paul traveled to Corinth and connected with Aquila and Priscilla, two Jews from Rome who were tentmakers like Paul. After Silas and Timothy joined him there, Paul began preaching full time, going first to the Jews then to the gentiles. Many believed and were baptized (18:1–8).

The Lord encouraged Paul in a vision, and he remained in Corinth for a year and a half—the longest he had been in any one place on his missionary journeys so far. The Jews made a case against Paul to the proconsul Gallio, but he quickly dismissed the case (18:9–17)—reminding us that Paul posed no threat to Roman authority. After a quick stop in Ephesus, Paul made his way to Caesarea, Jerusalem, then home to Antioch (18:18–22).

Paul's Third Missionary Journey

■ READ ACTS 18:23–19:41 ■

Paul once again set out through Galatia and other regions to strengthen the churches he'd planted on previous missions (18:23). In the meantime, Apollos, an eloquent Jew accomplished in the Scriptures, had arrived in Ephesus and was teaching about the Lord, but his knowledge was not complete. Priscilla and Aquila explained to him what was missing, and Apollos went on to Achaia (i.e., Greece) and had a great ministry there (18:24–28).

After Apollos had left, Paul arrived in Ephesus, where he would stay nearly three years—longer than in any other location on

Shutterstock / Jana Janina

Figure 10.5. Areopagus

Figure 10.6. Apollo's temple at Corinth

HISTORICAL MATTERS

The Significance of Ephesus

Paul's first visit to Ephesus was during his second missionary journey, but he did not have time to stay. He probably was struck by the strategic importance of this city during that short visit, causing him to go straight there on his third missionary journey and to stay there longer than in any other missionary location. Ephesus was the third-largest city in the Roman Empire, after Rome and Alexandria, and was the major hub of Asia Minor. The majestic temple of Artemis, one of the seven wonders of the ancient world, made Ephesus a major destination for spirituality and also for economy, as it also served as the bank for the region. With travelers constantly coming to and from Ephesus, and with its strong regional influence, Paul hoped that his ministry there would facilitate the rapid spread of his message throughout the eastern Roman Empire. Indeed, it seems that the church in Colossae, one hundred miles east of Ephesus, was planted exactly in this way.

CANONICAL CONNECTIONS

Paul's Letter to the Ephesians

Most likely written in Rome during his house arrest, Paul's letter to the church in Ephesus is one of his most majestic. However, given his extensive ministry in Ephesus over nearly three years, it is striking that the letter bears no personal references and no personalized greetings. Together with the fact that early manuscripts do not include the phrase "in Ephesus" in 1:1, this suggests that the letter was originally written to circulate among the churches in western Asia Minor. Since Ephesus was the major hub of that region, the letter became associated with that city. The themes of the letter fit very well with the spiritual interests of Ephesus, but these were characteristic of the region surrounding Ephesus too.

any of his missionary journeys. Paul instructed some believers who had not learned about the Holy Spirit, and he spoke for three months in the synagogue. After experiencing some opposition there, Paul used a hall where he taught every day for two years (19:1–10).

God performed extraordinary miracles through Paul, and some Jewish exorcists tried to emulate him. The seven sons of Sceva got into some trouble when an evil spirit overpowered them because they did not have the authority to cast it out (19:11–17). On the other hand, former magicians gave up their practices and burned their pagan books (19:18–20). By recording these events, Luke shows us that Paul is not just some magician who could perform the parlor tricks of his day. Even pagan magicians recognized that his power came from God, which led them to give up their deceptions.

While Paul made plans to continue his missionary journey, a riot was instigated by Demetrius, a silversmith. Since craftsmen in Ephesus made their living from forging silver shrines for the local goddess Artemis, Paul's message that discredited the gods was bad for business. The whole city erupted in a frenzy and poured into the amphitheater. Paul wanted to address the crowd but was not allowed to for his own safety as the crowd chanted "Great is Artemis of the Ephesians!" for two hours straight. Finally, a city clerk settled the crowd and dismissed the assembly (19:21–41).

Paul's Last Lap Around

■ READ ACTS 20:1–38 ■

After the drama in Ephesus, Paul went to Macedonia one more time, this time for three months only. On his way back to Antioch, he traveled back through Macedonia again because of a plot against him and paused in Troas (20:1–6). On the Lord's day, Paul preached for an extended stint, during which a young man named Eutychus fell asleep and then to his death out a third-story window. After raising him from the dead, Paul continued to talk until dawn (20:7–12). The incredible feat of raising the dead reminds us that Paul's ministry is powered by Jesus himself, as his miracles emulate those of his Lord.

To avoid spending more time in Asia, Paul sailed past Ephesus and sent for the elders of the church there to meet him nearby in Miletus (20:13–17). He gave an emotional farewell speech that reminded them of his ministry among them through thick and thin, and he announced his plans to go to Jerusalem—not knowing what fate would befall him there. But one thing he did know: this would be the last time they would see one another (20:18–25). Paul had faithfully dispensed his responsibility to teach them the whole plan of God, and he now charged them to shepherd the church of God and to watch out for false teachers who will come among them (20:26–35). After this they prayed together, embraced, and kissed. Then Paul embarked on his ship (20:36–38).

© Baker Publishing Group

Figure 10.7. Theater at Ephesus

Big Trouble in Jerusalem

■ READ ACTS 21:1–23:35 ■

Here the narrative—and Paul's life and ministry—reaches a major turning point as he goes to Jerusalem for the last time. Paul and his companions sailed through the Mediterranean and eventually made it to Caesarea, on the western coast of Judea, and stayed there with Philip the evangelist (21:1–9). There the prophet Agabus warned Paul that if he went to Jerusalem, he would be bound and handed over to the Romans (21:10–12). While many pleaded with Paul not to go to Jerusalem because of this warning, he declared his readiness to suffer and die for the Lord Jesus. And so they went (21:13–16).

They were warmly welcomed by the believers in Jerusalem, and they reported all that God had been doing among the gentiles through Paul's missionary activity (21:17–19). The Jerusalem brothers reported many thousands of believers there, but also some misinformation about Paul's ministry, with some believing that he had been instructing Jews to abandon their Jewish customs that reached back to Moses. Therefore, they instructed Paul to shave his head as a ceremonial observance so that these believing Jews would be appeased. Regarding the gentiles, the letter of the **Jerusalem Council** still stood (21:23–25).

Paul took their advice, but while he in the temple, some Jews from Asia recognized him and stirred up a riot that involved the whole city. They grabbed Paul and dragged him out of the temple (21:26–30). But the Roman commander intervened, and the Jews stopped beating Paul. In the confusion, the commander ordered Paul to be taken into the Antonia barracks on the northwestern wall of the temple complex (21:31–36).

But in classic Pauline style, he sensed an opportunity to preach and asked if he could address the crowd on the steps to the Roman barracks. He then addressed the crowd and, speaking in Aramaic, gave his testimony. He recounted his Jewish credentials, his period as a persecutor of the church, his encounter with the risen Christ on the way to Damascus, and his commissioning from Christ himself to preach to the gentiles (21:37–22:21).

Once Paul mentioned ministry to the gentiles, the crowd lost their composure and erupted again. The Roman commander brought Paul inside the barracks, where they prepared to flog him. But Paul appealed to his **Roman citizenship** (which forbade such treatment without a trial), and the commander relented (22:22–29).

The next day, the Roman commander called for the Jewish Sanhedrin to gather in order to hear Paul's case. After clashing with the high priest, Ananias, Paul managed to divide the group by appealing to the resurrection of the dead. Since one part of the Sanhedrin consisted of Pharisees (who believed in resurrection) and the other part Sadducees (who did not believe in resurrection), a dispute broke out among them that became violent. Paul was once again taken to safety inside the Roman barracks (22:30–23:11).

A serious conspiracy formed against Paul in which forty Jews swore that they would not eat until they had killed him. In a rare mention of Paul's family, Luke reports that Paul's nephew heard of the plot against him and reported it to the Roman commander (23:12–22). In response to this threat the commander ordered 470 soldiers to give Paul safe passage to Caesarea overnight. He composed a letter for the Roman governor of Judea, Felix, explaining the situation (23:23–35).

On Trial in Caesarea

■ READ ACTS 24:1–26:32 ■

During the next two years, Paul would remain in Caesarea as a prisoner awaiting a proper hearing. When Felix, the governor of Judea, received Paul and the commander's letter, he agreed to give him a hearing once his accusers had come down from Jerusalem (23:31–35). Ananias the high priest and others went down to Caesarea to present their case against Paul. They claimed that Paul was an agitator among Jews throughout the Roman Empire (24:1–9). Paul then had an opportunity to defend himself, concluding that the real reason he was on trial concerned the resurrection of the dead (24:10–21).

Felix was well informed about the Way (i.e., Christianity), and after several days he began to listen to Paul speak about Christ often, hoping that Paul would try to bribe him. After two years had passed, Felix was replaced by a new governor, Festus, while Paul remained in prison (24:22–27). Festus restarted Paul's trial, at which point Paul exercised his right as a Roman citizen and appealed to Caesar. Festus therefore was bound to send Paul to Rome (25:1–12).

Before that happened, however, Paul appeared before King Agrippa and his sister Bernice, who were visiting Festus in Caesarea. Festus had explained Paul's situation to Agrippa, who consequently wished to hear Paul himself (25:13–22). Festus declared that Paul had done nothing deserving of death, but he had appealed to Caesar and therefore was to appear before Agrippa in order to establish proper charges against him to be heard by the emperor in Rome (25:23–27). 🜚

Paul was then given ample opportunity to speak. He again recounted his testimony—how he had lived as a

Paul's Conversion Experience Recorded Three Times

While it is common to refer to Acts 9 when considering Paul's encounter with the risen Christ, that incident is actually recorded three times in Acts: 9:1–18; 22:1–16; 26:1–18. It is important to study all three accounts for a fuller understanding of the events they narrate, because each retelling adds details not previously included. It is also worth noting that 22:1–16 and 26:1–18 are reported by Paul himself (mediated through Luke as narrator). As such, he sets his experience on the Damascus road in the context of his life narrative, demonstrating the amazing turnaround that Christ wrought in his life, while also showing that Christ is the fulfillment of God's plans in salvation history and in Paul's own life.

Pharisee, persecuted followers of Jesus, and then was confronted by the risen Christ on the way to Damascus. Jesus himself sent Paul to the gentiles that they might turn from darkness to light and receive the forgiveness of sins (26:1–18). Paul did just as he had been instructed by Christ, and for this reason the Jews had tried to kill him. But Paul affirmed that everything he had preached was supported by the prophets and Moses, who foretold the suffering and resurrection of the Messiah, offering light to all peoples (26:19–23).

Festus declared Paul to be out of his mind because of his great learning (!), but Paul calmly replied that he was speaking publicly the truth about things that had happened, not in a corner (26:24–26). He then challenged King Agrippa about his own beliefs, receiving a swift rebuff from the king. Paul, however, declared his desire for all those listening to him to believe (26:27–29). Finally, the king told the governor that Paul had done nothing deserving death and could have been released had he not appealed to Caesar (26:30–32).

Onward to Rome

■ READ ACTS 27:1–44 ■

Luke recounts the last episode of his narrative, as Paul finally heads for Rome, but his journey is far from smooth sailing. Paul and some other prisoners were put under the keep of a centurion named Julius, who was charged with delivering them safely to Rome. After switching ships in Myra (on the south coast of modern-day Turkey), their travel progressed slowly due to weather and was becoming dangerous (27:1–9). Paul warned of impending doom, but the centurion Julius followed the captain's preference to continue (27:10–12).

A fierce wind picked them up near the Mediterranean island of Crete and drove them along out of control (27:13–17). Battered by a fierce storm, they began to jettison the ship's cargo and tackle. For several days they lost sight of sun and stars as the storm continued to rage, and they all began to lose hope of survival (27:18–20).

After rebuking his fellow travelers for not heeding his warning, Paul encouraged them with knowledge of a message he received from an angel. There would be no loss of life, only of the ship. God's will was for Paul to appear before Caesar, so there was no reason to fear (27:21–26).

After they had drifted in the Adriatic Sea for two weeks, Paul urged everyone to eat for their survival, and all 276 on board were encouraged by his words (27:27–38). Finally, land appeared, but they struck a sandbar, which caused the ship to begin to break apart. Everyone had to jump overboard, some swimming and others floating on debris, until all reached land safely (27:39–44).

A Brief Respite in Malta

■ READ ACTS 28:1–10 ■

The shipwrecked survivors learned that they had landed on the Mediterranean island of Malta, and they were shown extraordinary kindness and hospitality there. But after Paul was bitten by a viper, the people concluded that he was a murderer condemned to death by the gods. When Paul shook off the viper and suffered no ill effects, they changed their minds and decided he was a god (28:1–6).

The key leader of the island, Publius, showed Paul and Luke hospitality, and Paul healed his ill father. After this, all the sick of the island came to Paul for healing. After a pleasant and restful spell on Malta, the voyagers continued on to Rome (28:7–10).

Rome at Last!

■ READ ACTS 28:11–31 ■

After three months on Malta, they made it to the Italian coast at Puteoli and walked from there to Rome. News about Paul's arrival in Rome was well known by the believers there, who came to meet them and encourage them. Upon entering Rome, Paul was put under house arrest (28:11–16).

Paul called together the leaders of the Jews in Rome and recounted the most recent parts of his story to them. He then proclaimed his message of Jesus Christ to them, resulting in some being persuaded while others were not. Given Jewish resistance to the Christ, Paul drew on Isaiah 6:9–10 to underscore his ministry to the gentiles. Two years passed with Paul under house arrest in Rome as he continued to proclaim the kingdom of God and the Lord Jesus Christ (28:17–31). Luke concludes his narrative here, without letting us know what happened to Paul after his Roman house arrest.

CANONICAL CONNECTIONS

Paul's Last Letters

During Paul's imprisonment(s) in Rome, he most likely composed the Letters to the Ephesians, Philippians, Colossians, Philemon, Timothy, and Titus. If that is correct, it means that more than half of Paul's thirteen New Testament Letters were composed in the last few years of his life, while in Rome.

HISTORICAL MATTERS

So, What Happened Next?

Why does the narrative end with Paul's house arrest in Rome? What happened to Paul next? Why not finish the story? It is possible that Luke died before he finished writing. It is also possible that once Paul had preached in Rome, the book *was* complete, since the agenda of Acts 1:8 had been fulfilled—so long as Rome is interpreted as the "end of the earth." Acts is not, after all, a biography of Paul—though it does read that way after Acts 15. As for what happened to Paul after Acts 28, we know that he underwent a much more severe imprisonment before being beheaded by Emperor Nero sometime in the mid-60s. We don't know if he went straight from house arrest to this more severe imprisonment, or if there was an intervening period. According to 1 Clement 5 (AD 96), Paul fulfilled his ambition to preach in Spain (Rom. 15:24, 28). If true, it must have happened after his house arrest and before his more severe imprisonment.

Implementation—Reading Acts as Christian Scripture Today

While readers may differ over *how* Acts is relevant for church life today, no one can dispute that it *is* exceptionally relevant. In Acts we witness the very birth of the church, and we see that its DNA is the Lord Jesus Christ, who died for our sins, was raised from the dead, and has ascended to sit at God's right hand. He is the messianic king who reigns through his Holy Spirit and works through frail, faulty, sinful human beings to execute his extraordinary will.

Acts offers profound assurance that God is working in the world and through history. Here we see a turning point in God's plans and in the history of salvation, ushering in a new era in which we continue to live even now. God's people, who in centuries past waited patiently to see such plans come to fruition, would not have been disappointed. And we can take comfort in the fact that Christ will one day return just as he ascended in order to complete the story once and for all.

Finally, Acts reminds us that God works through trial, suffering, and persecution. Indeed, severe persecution of the newborn church was its prompt to multiply. The same remains true today. We must not become disillusioned when God seems silent or does not immediately deliver us from hardship. The night is darkest before the dawn. We cannot tell what rich blessings await us at daybreak. Joy comes in the morning.

KEY VERSES IN ACTS

- But you will receive power when the Holy Spirit has come on you, and you will be my witnesses in Jerusalem, in all Judea and Samaria, and to the end of the earth. (1:8)
- God has raised this Jesus; we are all witnesses of this. Therefore, since he has been exalted to the right hand of God and has received from the Father the promised Holy Spirit, he has poured out what you both see and hear. 2:32–33
- After there had been much debate, Peter stood up and said to them: "Brothers and sisters, you are aware that in the early days God made a choice among you, that by my mouth the Gentiles would hear the gospel message and believe. And God, who knows the heart, bore witness to them by giving them the Holy Spirit, just as he also did to us." 15:7–8
- Therefore, having overlooked the times of ignorance, God now commands all people everywhere to repent, because he has set a day when he is going to judge the world in righteousness by the man he has appointed. He has provided proof of this to everyone by raising him from the dead. 17:30–31
- To this very day, I have had help from God, and I stand and testify to both small and great, saying nothing other than what the prophets and Moses said would take place—that the Messiah must suffer, and that, as the first to rise from the dead, he would proclaim light to our people and to the Gentiles. 26:22–23

Christian Reading Questions

1. Consider the sidebar "Description vs. Prescription," near the beginning of this chapter. Brainstorm the pros and cons of each position.

2. Why are the resurrection and ascension of Jesus so important in Acts?

3. Compare Paul's sermon in Pisidian Antioch (Acts 13:16–41) with his Areopagus speech in Athens (Acts 17:22–31). How are these talks different? What might account for these differences?

4. Compare and contrast the three accounts of Paul's encounter with the risen Christ in Acts 9:1–18; 22:1–16; 26:1–18. How do they differ? What do you learn from these differences?

CHAPTER ELEVEN

The Apostle Paul's Life and Teaching

Paul's Importance

After Jesus, Paul is the most influential figure in the history of Christianity. The combination of his extraordinary life and ministry with his even more extraordinary writings made him a force that changed the world—and he continues to change it two thousand years later. His radical conversion and transformation were astonishingly profound. His extensive ministry established churches throughout the Mediterranean world. His grit, humility, love, and absolute trust in Christ made him a stellar example for all Christians everywhere at all times.

Paul's writings are profound, dense, challenging, and inspiring. They reveal a pastor-theologian who shares the knowledge of God in Christ so that people will believe and become mature in the faith. His letters made an indelible imprint on the early church, and on every generation of the church since. They continue to inspire in-depth study and debate, as well as radical living for the glory of Christ. When we put his teaching together with

Figure 11.1. *San Pablo Apóstol* by El Greco

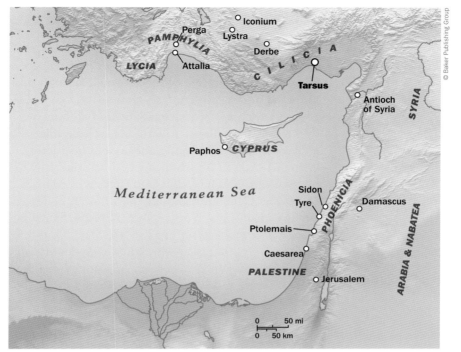

Figure 11.2. Location of Tarsus

his life, we see a remarkable gift to the church whose importance is beyond measure.

Paul's Life

Paul was born around AD 6 in Tarsus, an important city that had been part of the Roman Empire from 64 BC. Located on the southeast coast of modern-day Turkey, Tarsus was the capital of the Roman province Cilicia and was known for its university. It was home to the famous Stoic philosopher Athenadorus, who taught the Roman emperor Octavian. ⓘ

Paul was born a Roman citizen (Acts 21:39), but we don't know why he was born into such privilege. He was also born a Jew in the tribe of Benjamin (Phil. 3:5), likely named after the most famous Benjaminite, King Saul. Thus as a Jew and a Roman citizen, he had two names: Saul and Paul. He would have spoken Hebrew

© Baker Publishing Group

INTRODUCTORY MATTERS ⓘ

Sources for Paul's Biography

The main source for Paul's biography is the Acts of the Apostles, in which Paul's story is told from the stoning of Stephen through to Paul's house arrest in Rome. However, all history is selective, and Acts is no different. Thus it is very important to pay close attention to Paul's Letters. Paul does not narrate his life in his letters (though there is a partial narration in Gal. 1:13–2:10), but his letters contain incidental comments that parallel or supplement Acts. A key example is Paul's three years in Arabia, which is not mentioned at all in Acts, being found only in Galatians 1:17. Beyond the New Testament, the first-century letter 1 Clement (AD 96) contains information that helps to resolve a question that Acts leaves open, namely, what happened after Paul's house arrest in Rome. There are also second-century works dedicated to Paul, such as the Acts of Paul, and the Acts of Paul and Thecla, but these are not regarded as historically reliable.

or Aramaic at home while growing up, but he was also fluent in Greek, the lingua franca of the empire at that time. These two facets of his heritage—a Jew born as a citizen of Rome—would dramatically shape his future ministry. ⓘ

As a teenager, it seems that Saul (and his family?) moved from Tarsus to Jerusalem. He became a Pharisee and trained under the famous instructor Gamaliel (Acts 22:3), advancing beyond other Jews of his own age (Gal. 1:14). But Saul later diverged from his teacher Gamaliel regarding the followers of Jesus. While Gamaliel urged peace (Acts 5:34–39), Saul was filled with a zealous rage against "the Way" (Acts 8:3; 9:1; 26:11). It is not clear why Saul was so out of step with his mentor and teacher, but Acts implies that his rage was triggered by Stephen's speech and stoning (Acts 7).

While Saul was trying to destroy the church, the risen Jesus Christ appeared to him on the road to Damascus and asked why Saul had been persecuting him (Acts 9:1–9). This encounter radically transformed Saul's life and theology. He had been persecuting followers of Jesus, but now would become one himself. He had been a violent man, but now would become the object of violence. As a Pharisee, he believed in the resurrection of the dead on the last day, but now he believed that the last day had already come with the resurrection of Jesus. And since he had been persecuting the followers of Jesus, the fact that Jesus said that Saul was persecuting *him* meant that Jesus and his followers shared a special union—to persecute them was to persecute him. This would develop into Paul's central theological motif of being "in Christ." ⓘ

Instead of going to the synagogues in Damascus to speak against Jesus and to capture his followers, Saul now spoke in favor of Jesus as the Messiah and encouraged his followers—though they were shocked by the 180-degree turnaround of their greatest persecutor (Acts 9:19b–22). In time he would become their greatest missionary, theologian, and pastor.

After some time in Damascus, Saul went to Arabia for three years (Gal. 1:17). We know nothing

ⓘ INTRODUCTORY MATTERS

What Did It Mean to Be a Roman Citizen?

Unlike citizenship today, people in the Roman Empire were not given citizenship just because they were born in the empire. Citizenship was given if both parents were Roman citizens, but it also could be granted by generals and emperors. Roman citizenship was a status of political and legal privilege, available only to free people (not slaves). Male Roman citizens were given several privileges and protections that were defined by the Roman state, while Roman women experienced a more limited range of privileges. For instance, women were not permitted to vote or to stand for public office. Paul drew on his rights as a Roman citizen to stand trial in Rome before the emperor. He was executed by the sword, since Roman citizens were not permitted to be crucified.

ⓘ INTRODUCTORY MATTERS

Was Paul "Converted"?

Some scholars have questioned whether it is appropriate to describe Paul's experience following his encounter with the risen Christ as "conversion." After all, he recognized Jesus to be the Jewish Messiah, in keeping with Jewish expectation, and Paul himself remained a Jew. He did not abandon Judaism but understood Christ as the fulfillment of it. On the other hand, it is obvious that Paul's life was radically transformed and certain central beliefs were altered. Furthermore, he regarded Jews who rejected Jesus as falling out of step with God. A Jew who rejected Christ rejected the correct trajectory of Judaism. In this sense, "conversion" is an appropriate description of a Jew who accepts Christ, including Paul.

Figure 11.3. *The Conversion of Saul* by Simeon Griswald

about this period except that by the end of it the king of Arabia, Aretas IV, wanted Saul arrested (2 Cor. 11:32). Given that he had inspired such trouble, it is fair to assume that Saul had been preaching in Arabia just as he had in Damascus.

Saul's first visit to Jerusalem after encountering the risen Christ occurred after this three-year period in Arabia, via Damascus. There the apostles greeted him and sought to protect him, for his life was already in danger. They sent him back to his home city of Tarsus (Acts 9:26–30; Gal. 1:18–24). Thus began the second undocumented period of Paul's life, lasting for about ten years.

After significant growth in the church in Antioch (Syria), Barnabas went to Tarsus to find Saul in order to get his help for the work to be done in Antioch (Acts 11:19–26). During a year of ministering in Antioch, Saul and Barnabas made a brief trip back to Jerusalem in order to deliver relief to the disciples in Judea in the wake of a severe famine (Acts 11:27–30).

It had been about fourteen years since Saul's encounter with the risen Christ on the road to Damascus. Now it was time to embark on his first missionary journey to the gentile world. Saul left Antioch

INTRODUCTORY MATTERS

Paul's Incubation Period

There are two periods of "silence" in Paul's life after his conversion, only one of which is recorded in Acts, and it is passed over quickly. We may not, therefore, appreciate the significance of these periods, which together account for about thirteen years. We tend to imagine that after encountering Christ, Paul immediately became the apostle to the gentiles with all his apostolic wisdom and knowledge already in place. The truth is that Paul had a lengthy period of incubation. It took time to process the implications of the newly discovered truth that Jesus was the Christ, risen from the dead. Though already learned in the Scriptures, Paul had to reread them in light of Christ. He had to reshape his eschatological framework. He had to learn how to articulate the gospel to Jews and to gentiles. He had to learn what it meant to be "in Christ." None of these things happen automatically (even with the Spirit!), and we should not be surprised that Paul needed time to work it all out.

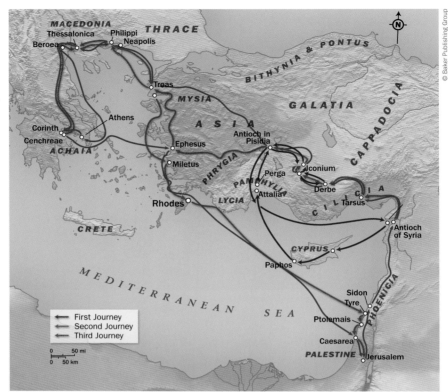

Figure 11.4. Paul's three missionary journeys

INTRODUCTORY MATTERS

Why Did Paul Go to the Jews First?

Paul believed that the Jewish people ought to be told first that Jesus is the Christ, since theirs are the promises concerning the Christ to come. As he says in Romans 1:16, the gospel is the power of God for salvation for everyone who believes, first to the Jew, and also to the Greek. But there was also a strategic reason for preaching in the synagogues in each location before preaching to the gentiles. In each synagogue there were Jews who were ready to receive the news of the Christ. They knew the Scriptures, the promises of God, and the covenants. When they accepted Christ, they became ready-made leaders for the new churches that formed.

with the help of Barnabas and his cousin John Mark (Acts 13:1–3, 5b). Their first stop was the Mediterranean island of Cyprus, Barnabas and John Mark's home country, before going into the region of Galatia, in what today is central Turkey (Acts 13:4–14:23). It is during this mission to the gentile world that Saul became known as Paul (his Roman name) and was known that way henceforth.

Paul's first missionary journey was modest compared to his next two, both in time spent and in distance traveled. But it was important for several reasons. Most important was Paul and Barnabas's testimony that gentiles were accepting Christ and receiving the Spirit. This experience informed the Jerusalem Council as they deliberated about the inclusion of gentiles in the church (Acts 15). It also established patterns that Paul would follow going forward. For instance, on this journey he developed the practice of going to the Jewish synagogues first before preaching to the gentiles. This pattern would continue throughout Paul's missionary activity. ⓘ

We also see Paul's letter-writing ministry develop as he sought to encourage (and/or rebuke) the churches he planted, while being absent. His Letter to the Galatians (arguably his earliest) was written to the churches that began as a result of the first missionary journey. Nearly all of Paul's letters to churches had the same intent: to strengthen the young churches that came into being through his missionary activity. He also established the pattern of selecting elders to pastor these churches so that they were not reliant on Paul. 📖

Paul's second missionary journey was much more ambitious. After revisiting the Galatian churches first (Acts 15:36–41), he and Silas went into Europe for the first time, preaching in Macedonia and Achaia (modern-day Greece). Churches were formed in Philippi, Thessalonica, and Berea, though persecution against them began to increase (Acts 16:1–17:15). Paul preached his famous Areopagus speech in Athens, to mixed reception (Acts 17:22–34), and then went to Corinth.

Though Paul's speech at the Areopagus was important for demonstrating his engagement with gentiles (compare his synagogue sermon in Pisidian Antioch [Acts 13:16–41]), his ministry in Corinth became the most important element of Paul's second missionary journey (Acts 18:1–17). In Corinth, Paul first demonstrated his priority to target strategic cities. Corinth was a significant seaport that saw multitudes coming and going through the city. While that created several problems for the church, since the city's debauched culture seeped in, Paul no doubt saw Corinth as an opportunity to have his message spread far and wide, carried along by his converts there. Paul spent more time in Corinth than any other place so far on his missionary journeys (eighteen months), and he wrote 1 and 2 Thessalonians there (Romans too, but a few years later, on his third missionary journey).

On his way from Corinth back to Syrian Antioch, Paul made a brief stop in Ephesus, on the western coast of modern-day Turkey. The city no doubt made an impression on him, because his third missionary journey saw him go straight there and remain there for nearly three years—the longest he spent in any city during his missions (Acts 19:1–41).

Paul stayed in Ephesus for the same reason he had earlier stayed in Corinth—its wide influence. It was a hub for the whole of Asia Minor, it was the

LITERARY NOTES

Paul as Letter Writer

Compared to ancient practice, most of Paul's Letters are quite long—Romans is around 7,100 words, while Cicero averaged around 300 words per letter. His letters are more like literary works than normal letters, with much planning and careful argument exhibited. But they generally follow the expected structure: salutation, thanksgiving, main body, and final greetings. Many scholars have connected Paul's Letters to ancient rhetoric—the study of formal public speaking. While there is no evidence that Paul had formal rhetorical training, he demonstrated great rhetorical skill and use of language. Paul's letter writing shows significant argumentation, which was a hallmark of rhetoric, and he uses known rhetorical devices and forms. But his letters cannot be classified strictly according to standard rhetorical forms—and indeed ancient formal speeches mixed such forms anyway.

The Temple of Artemis

Artemis was the goddess of fertility and was very popular in the region of Ephesus. The temple of Artemis was one of the seven wonders of the ancient world and was a very impressive structure, twice the size of the Parthenon in Athens, with 127 marble columns, each one sixty feet tall. Apart from being the most important site for the worship of Artemis, the temple served as a major bank for the region and thus was the center of religion and commerce.

How Many Times Was Paul Imprisoned?

The book of Acts records three Pauline imprisonments: overnight in Philippi (16:16–34), two years in Caesarea (24:27), and two years in Rome (28:30). But in 2 Corinthians 11:23 Paul refers to his *many* imprisonments, which would fit the three mentioned in Acts except that 2 Corinthians was written before his imprisonments in Caesarea and Rome had occurred. In other words, Acts reports only one imprisonment (in Philippi) having occurred before he wrote 2 Corinthians in AD 57, meaning that there must have been other imprisonments that Acts does not record. Tradition holds that Paul was imprisoned in Ephesus. (It is still possible to visit the traditional site of that imprisonment, a cave in a mountainside near Selçuk, Turkey.) Though there is almost no biblical evidence for that (see 1 Cor. 15:32), it is entirely possible. Given that "many imprisonments" would normally indicate more than two, there probably was at least one other imprisonment that we do not know about.

third-largest city in the Roman Empire, and it saw thousands of travelers passing through as they visited the temple of Artemis and conducted business there. Paul anticipated that his message would spread throughout the region by focusing on Ephesus, and he was right (Acts 19:10). A key example is found in the church at Colossae. Paul never went there, but one of his converts in Ephesus was from Colossae and planted the church there. Paul's Letter to the Colossians acknowledges this fact (Col. 1:5b–8).

After leaving Ephesus, Paul traveled again through Macedonia and Achaia, spending three months in Greece (probably mostly in Corinth [Acts 20:1–3]). On this third missionary journey, Paul wrote 1 Corinthians (in Ephesus), 2 Corinthians (in Philippi), and Romans (in Corinth)—his three longest letters. He knew that this was his last journey to this part of the world (Acts 20:25), as he set his path to Jerusalem.

Though being warned about the dangers facing him in Jerusalem, Paul was determined to go there, counting his own life as nothing (Acts 20:22–24). His presence at the Jerusalem temple caused a violent riot, and the Roman soldiers had to intervene on Paul's behalf (Acts 21:26–36). With a plot set against his life, the Romans sent Paul to Caesarea with the protection of hundreds of soldiers in order to appear before Felix, the governor of Judea (Acts 23:12–24).

Felix did not know what to do with Paul, who sat in prison in Caesarea for two years. Felix was replaced by Festus (Acts 24:27), who took Paul more seriously. He would have released Paul except that Paul had used his right as a Roman citizen to appeal to Caesar (Acts 25:11; 26:30–32). Festus was thus obliged to give him safe passage to Rome in order to appear before the emperor. Given Paul's ambition to reach Rome, it is possible that he appealed to Caesar in order to get there. He knew that Festus would be obliged to send him there, and this move not only got him out of prison but also helped him to fulfill his agenda.

A disastrous sea voyage saw Paul, his traveling companions, and the crew shipwrecked on the Mediterranean island of Malta, where they stayed for three months and were treated to kind hospitality (Acts 28:1–10). Eventually Paul made it to Rome and was placed under house arrest for two years (Acts 28:11–31).

At some point in the mid-60s, Paul was beheaded in Rome by order of the emperor. But there is some ambiguity as to what happened after his house arrest and before his beheading. It is possible that he went straight from house arrest to a more serious form of imprisonment and then to his death. But it is also possible, and perhaps more likely, that after his house arrest Paul traveled to Spain. This had been his ambition (Rom. 15:24) and was attested by early sources, most importantly Clement of Rome. Clement was bishop in Rome at the end of the first century, so he would have had good knowledge of what happened to the apostles in Rome. He wrote in 1 Clement 5 (AD 96) that Paul had "reached the farthest limits of the west."[1] Though Clement's wording is a little unclear, the most likely reading is that he affirms Paul's Spanish mission. It is also the historic tradition of the church in Spain that it had been founded by the apostle Paul. After preaching in Spain, Paul must have been arrested again, and this time he faced a severe imprisonment leading to his death.

It was during his time in Rome (and perhaps Spain) that Paul composed more than half of his New Testament letters: Philippians, Ephesians, Colossians, Philemon, 1 and 2 Timothy, and Titus. The first four, known as the **Captivity Letters**, would have been penned during Paul's house arrest. The last three, known as the **Pastoral Letters**, may have been written during his brief free period between the house arrest and re-arrest.

Paul's biography is the most complex in the New Testament—more so than Jesus's as reported in the Gospels, and much more so than Peter's, John's, or anyone else's. But knowing the basic outline of his life and ministry is enormously helpful for reading his letters. So to assist in this task, the following brief chronology is offered. The only firm dates in this chronology are Paul's time in Corinth in 50–52—since the proconsul Gallio (mentioned in Acts 18:12) was in Corinth in 51–52—and the fire of Rome in 64. Paul's dates are figured out from these two fixtures (especially the former).

Paul's Chronology

1. Early Ministry	Date (AD)
Birth	ca. 6
Conversion and commissioning	ca. 33
Period in Arabia	ca. 33–35
First visit to Jerusalem after conversion	ca. 36
Ministry in Cilicia and Syria	ca. 36–46
Famine collection from Antioch taken to Jerusalem	ca. 46

2. First Missionary Journey	ca. 46–47
From Antioch to Cyprus	ca. 46
From Cyprus to Perga and Pisidian Antioch	ca. 46
To Iconium, Lystra, Derbe—cities of South Galatia	ca. 46
Return to Perga, then by ship to Syrian Antioch	ca. 47

3. The Apostolic Council in Jerusalem	ca. 48
Galatians written around this time	ca. 48

4. Second Missionary Journey	ca. 49–52
Overland from Syrian Antioch through Galatia	ca. 49
Churches in Philippi, Thessalonica, and Berea	ca. 49
The visit to Athens	ca. 49
Eighteen months in Corinth	50–52
1 and 2 Thessalonians written in Corinth	50
A quick trip to Ephesus	52
Return to Syrian Antioch	52

5. Third Missionary Journey	ca. 52–57
From Syrian Antioch through Galatia to Ephesus	ca. 52
Three years in Ephesus	ca. 52–55
1 Corinthians written in Ephesus	ca. 54
Leaves for Macedonia	ca. 55
2 Corinthians written in Philippi	ca. 56
Three months in Corinth, where Romans was written	ca. 57
Bids farewell to the Ephesian elders in Miletus	ca. 57
Sails to Caesarea, then on to Jerusalem	ca. 57

6. The Caesarean and Roman Imprisonments	ca. 57–??
Imprisoned by the governor Felix in Caesarea	ca. 57–59
Sails for Rome, spends three months in Malta	ca. 59–60
House arrest in Rome	ca. 60–62
Philippians, Ephesians, Colossians, Philemon written	ca. 62
Visit to Spain?	ca. 63–??
1 and 2 Timothy, Titus written	ca. 63–65
Great fire of Rome and persecution of Christians	64
Paul is executed	ca. 65?

Paul's Teaching

Paul is the premier theologian of the New Testament, and after Jesus he is the most important theologian in the history of the Christian church. His teaching has influenced every major thinker in the history of Christianity, and his letters continue to generate vigorous discussion. Paul's writings lit the spark of the Protestant Reformation and profoundly shaped Western culture and its intellectual tradition. Today, Paul is a staple of every church's preaching calendar and is the favorite author of millions of Bible readers around the world. It is simply impossible to overestimate the impact and significance of this remarkable man's teaching.

But it is important to remember that Paul is not a professional theologian, writing for an academic audience. Paul is first and foremost a missionary and pastor. His writing always serves his missionary and pastoral objectives. It is striking how much theologizing Paul does in order to address his missionary and pastoral concerns, but his teaching must always be read in those contexts. He does not do abstract, **systematic theology** for its own sake, and it is easy to imagine him objecting to such a notion.

Having said that, we acknowledge that Paul *is* a systematic theologian in the sense that his theological thinking has a particular shape and logic. It is possible to piece together his thinking on various topics since there is an overarching coherence to his thought (despite the opinion of some commentators). In this way, we might say that Paul's theology is systematic, but it is not presented systematically. It is always presented and packaged in missionary and pastoral concerns.

The center of Paul's theology is the person and work of Jesus Christ. Christ is the fulfillment of God's promises that a descendant of David would rule forever at God's right hand. He is God's anointed king, not just over Israel, but over the entirety of humanity. He was appointed Messiah through his resurrection from the dead and ascension into the heavens. But while he is the powerful, ruling king, Christ is also the humble servant who died for the sake of his enemies. He is the very demonstration of God's love for humanity, enabling all people—both Jews and gentiles—to be reconciled to God.

Although the ascended Christ is seated in the heavens with his heavenly Father, he is not a remote figure. In fact, all those who believe in Christ have become one with him by the power of the Spirit. Believers are "in Christ," and Christ is in them. This means that our relationship with Christ is intensely personal rather than mechanistic, and that our fellowship with God is one of mutual indwelling. It also means that all believers are connected to one another, since each person in union with Christ is a member of his body. Every blessing that God bestows on his people comes in and through Christ. ⓘ

INTRODUCTORY MATTERS ⓘ

What Is Union with Christ?

"Union with Christ" is the term we use to describe Paul's theology of being joined to Christ. It is reflected in his very common idioms "in Christ," "with Christ," "through Christ," and so forth. It is also seen through various metaphors such as the body of Christ, clothing, the temple, and the church as the bride of Christ. Union with Christ is best understood through four images: union, participation, identification, incorporation. *Union* refers to a profound spiritual connection to Christ through mutual indwelling by the Spirit. *Participation* refers to sharing in the key events of Christ's narrative, such as his suffering, death, burial, resurrection, ascension, and glorification. *Identification* refers to shifting our allegiance from Adam and the realm of sin and death to Christ and his realm of righteousness and peace. *Incorporation* refers to being members together in a corporate entity shaped by Christ. All of God's blessings are bestowed to believers through our union with Christ (Eph. 1:3).

What Is the Role of the Law?

Paul's understanding of the law of Moses can appear self-contradictory, since he proclaims that believers are not under the law (Rom. 6:14), while he also says that we uphold the law (Rom. 3:31). While Paul clearly does not expect gentile believers to maintain the customs of the Mosaic law (Gal. 5:1–6), he also sometimes quotes the law directly as authoritative for all (Eph. 6:2). The most likely resolution of these apparent tensions is as follows: Paul believes that Christ has fulfilled the righteous requirements of the law (Rom. 10:4; Gal. 3:13); believers uphold the law by being in Christ. When a new covenant is created, it is accompanied by a new law, and the new covenant of Christ is ruled by the law of love, not the law of Moses (Gal. 6:2). Nevertheless, the law of Moses reflects God's moral character. For this reason, it is profitable to know the law and sometimes even to apply it directly.

The New Perspective on Paul

Paul continues to inspire rigorous study and debate. The most famous controversy surrounding Paul in recent decades is known as the **New Perspective on Paul**. Associated with scholars such as E. P. Sanders, J. D. G. Dunn, and N. T. Wright, its basic premise is that the type of Judaism that Paul critiques is different from what Protestants have typically assumed. Judaism was not a "salvation by works" religion, but rather relied on God's grace. The problem with law-keeping Jews in Paul's day was that the law identified them as God's people, which was a source of pride and boasting. Therefore, Paul's critique of such Jews is more about how to identify the people of God: they are identified by faith in Christ and by having the Spirit, not by keeping the law of Moses. There is much to affirm about the New Perspective—especially its reminder that Paul was very concerned about Jew-gentile issues—even if some of its conclusions warrant further discussion.

If the center of Paul's theology is the person and work of Christ, the Holy Spirit is the one through whom Christ is joined to his people. Where the Spirit dwells, there dwells Christ. The presence of the Spirit among believers is also evidence that God does not show partiality but instead dwells among any who will confess Christ as Lord. The Spirit intercedes for us with groans that words cannot express, and he produces his fruit in the lives of believers, taking the place of the law of Moses of the old covenant. The Spirit is also a deposit guaranteeing an inheritance to come, meaning that through the Spirit believers are connected to a glorious future in the presence of God. ⓘ

The resurrection of Christ inaugurated an overlap of the ages, since it signaled that the new age had already dawned—before the old age has yet passed. This is because resurrection belongs to the end of time, to judgment day. Christ's resurrection from the dead declares him righteous in the face of judgment and secures God's verdict now of all who are in Christ. Thus the resurrection has created a "now and not yet" eschatological framework that gives shape to all of Paul's theology. Believers are to live as new creations in Christ who belong to the new age, no longer enslaved by the powers that dominated the old age.

Because Christ sets his people free from the dominion of sin and death, he is their savior. By dying for sins on the cross, he canceled the debt that stood against us, and by rising from the dead, he secured our righteous status before God. He has inaugurated a new age of righteousness and peace into which believers have access by rising with Christ. Dying with Christ ends their allegiance to the old age, and rising with him secures their eternal life in the new age. Because of this, salvation is most assuredly by God's grace and cannot be achieved by human works or boasting. ⓘ

As the Savior, Christ has overpowered the authorities and forces of darkness that rule over this present age and influence those who do not know Christ. He has publicly put those powers to shame, having canceled their hold on humanity, and having been seated above them in all authority. While we do not yet see Christ's dominion over evil, sin, and death, his return will reveal his universal victory in glory.

In the meantime, the church must remember who it is, having been set apart for Christ as his bride, and living in the daylight rather than in darkness. Believers must put away all shameful acts and attitudes that are unfit for the people of Christ, as his Spirit works in and among them. While no believer will reach perfection in this lifetime, the church is called to be holy, while remembering that the grace of God is sufficient for all.

The church of God consists of believing Jews and gentiles, who are now unified in Christ Jesus. Nevertheless, Israel remains the recipient of the promises of God, and no one should forget Israel's privilege: salvation is first for the Jew, then for the gentile. God is completely sovereign over Israel's trajectory, even when it appears that the majority of Israel has rejected their Messiah. This partial hardening is so that the gentiles may come in, and is not necessarily indefinite. ⓘ

In order to live in a manner pleasing to God, believers are reminded of who they are in Christ: their old selves have died with Christ and their new selves have been raised with him. We are taught to imitate our heavenly Father as his children. And we are to set our eyes on things above, where Christ is seated, rather than on things below. By keeping in step with the Spirit, believers will reap according to the Spirit. But if we sow according to the flesh, we will reap death and destruction.

Finally, the goal of all things is the glory of God in Christ. In the end, Christ will be glorified by all creation to the glory of his heavenly Father. And an astonishing hope awaits us, as Christ will share his glory with his people. We will be glorified with him, if indeed we have suffered with him.

Implementation

Paul wrote, "Imitate me, as also I imitate Christ" (1 Cor. 11:1). That may seem like an impossible task to most of us. Who could possibly imitate Paul or live up to the standard he has set? And yet there is much to learn from Paul and much that can be implemented

INTRODUCTORY MATTERS ⓘ

The Way Paul Does Ethics

Paul's approach to ethics is always theological. That is, his instructions about how to live are grounded in theological truths about God, Christ, and what it means to be the people of God in Christ. His letters demonstrate this as their "practical" sections spell out the implications of their "theological" sections. A good example is Paul's Letter to the Ephesians, in which the first three chapters contain his main theological arguments and the second three chapters draw out their implications for living. This means that Paul cannot be described as a moralist. He does not prescribe moral actions just because they are the right things to do. He begins with the truth of who we are in Christ and draws that out to sketch a vision of the Christian life.

in our daily lives here and now. Our lives may look entirely different from Paul's in so many ways, and yet there are principles gleaned from him that we can instill in ourselves.

The most radical principle is that Christ Jesus is Lord of all, and our lives must be lived in full submission to and trust in him. Likewise, Paul shows us that we will never exhaust the richness and beauty of Christ. Instead of moving on from Christ to something else, we must move deeper *into* him.

We can learn from Paul that it is right to live for glory, as long as it is not *our* glory. By living for the glory of Christ, we are living into our design, fulfilling our God-given mandate as his creatures made in his image. Our joy is found in the glory of Christ, not our own glory, but just as we share in the sufferings of Christ, so we will share in his glory. To him be the glory forever and ever!

Christian Reading Questions

1. Create a mental image of Paul's three missionary journeys and his final journey to Rome. Find a map of the Mediterranean region and attempt to draw the route of each journey.

2. Now make a list of Paul's thirteen New Testament letters. Can you connect each one to the journeys you've drawn? Think of the destination of each letter as well as where Paul was when he wrote each one.

3. Scan Paul's Letters for every time he mentions the "gospel" that he preaches. How does he describe this gospel?

4. Read Romans 6 carefully. Put into your own words why it is not appropriate for believers just to keep on sinning.

CHAPTER TWELVE

The Letter to the Romans

Orientation

Widely regarded as the most important letter ever written, the Letter to the Romans is Paul's most comprehensive explanation and defense of the gospel he preaches. Romans was hugely influential for the Protestant Reformation, with its major themes of justification by faith, union with Christ, and life by the Spirit profoundly shaping Reformation theology.

Paul's gospel is the power of God for the salvation of everyone who believes. Jews and gentiles alike are under sin, but God shows mercy by presenting Christ as a sacrifice that makes believers right with God. By dying with Christ, believers have escaped slavery to sin and death and now have life in the Spirit. This message is consistent with God's plans spanning history, including his relationship with Israel. Paul's gospel leads to a transformed life of love and worship.

HISTORICAL MATTERS

The Historical Origins of Romans

Author: Paul

Date: AD 57

Location: Corinth

Setting: Paul is on his third missionary journey near Corinth as he writes. He intends to go to Jerusalem and then begin a mission to Spain. He intends to visit the church in Rome on his way to Spain, and this letter is sent in preparation for that visit.

HISTORICAL MATTERS

The Church in Rome

The Letter to the Romans is one of only two letters that Paul addressed to churches he did not know personally (Colossians is the other). We do not know how the church in Rome first came into existence, but its origins may have gone all the way back to the first Pentecost after the resurrection and ascension of Christ, when three thousand Jews from around the Roman world repented and believed (Acts 2:1–41). We are told that there were visitors from Rome among the crowd that heard Peter's Pentecost speech (Acts 2:10). Thus it is possible that among the three thousand new converts some were Romans who later went home and established the first church there. Usually Paul wrote to encourage the churches he had planted himself, but in this case he hoped to establish a new relationship with the church through his letter.

The Son of God

When Paul says that Jesus Christ has become the Son of God by the resurrection of the dead (1:4), he is not saying that Jesus was not already God's divine Son. Rather, "Son of God" language in the Old Testament often refers to God's Messiah, his anointed king, as seen especially in Psalm 2:7. That is why Paul points out that Jesus was a descendant of David, which the promised Messiah had to be. It is his resurrection from the dead that declares the messianic status of Jesus, as the apostle Peter likewise claimed (cf. Acts 2:24–36). Thus the gospel for which Paul is set apart (Rom. 1:1) is a message centrally concerned with Jesus's having been declared God's anointed king.

The Structure of Romans

The letter falls into four quite distinct sections. Chapters 1–4 address justification by faith; chapters 6–8 deal with union with Christ and the work of the Spirit; chapters 9–11 are about the history of salvation and Jew-gentile relationships; chapters 12–16 unpack the practical exhortations of the letter. The only possible nuance to that structure is to divide chapter 5 into two, so that justification by faith is addressed up to 5:11 while treatment of union with Christ and the work of the Spirit begins in 5:12.

Exploration—Reading Romans

The Gospel Is the Power of God for Salvation

◼ READ ROMANS 1:1–17 ◼

The letter begins with an extended introduction of the author. Paul the apostle has been set apart for the gospel of God (1:1), which was promised by God, centers on Jesus Christ, and involves Christ's appointment to be the Son of God through his resurrection (1:2–4). Paul has been called to see the gentiles come to faith in this Christ (1:5–6).

Because of his apostolic commission to preach Christ to the gentiles, Paul wants to visit the believers in Rome, whose faith is known around the world (1:8). Paul is faithful in prayer for them (1:9–10) and wants to visit them for their mutual encouragement (1:11–12). Though previously prevented from visiting them, Paul is eager to preach the gospel to

Figure 12.1. The forum in Rome

them in Rome (1:13–15). Paul is not ashamed of the gospel that he has been commissioned to preach, since it is the power of God for salvation (1:16a). This message will save all who believe, whether Jew or gentile, because it reveals the righteousness of God (1:16b–17).

Gentile Guilt before God

■ READ ROMANS 1:18–32 ■

All people need to hear the gospel that Paul preaches, and he begins by showing the gentiles' need for salvation. God's wrath is being revealed even now against those who reject the truth about him (1:18). God has allowed all people to know something about him, such as his invisible attributes and eternal power (1:19–20), but they did not glorify him as God, and instead turned to various idols (1:21–23). Consequently, God gave them over to the desires of their hearts as they worshiped God's creation instead of the Creator (1:24–25).

The desires of the gentiles' hearts involved sexual impurity, including homosexual relations (1:26–27). God gave them over to these destructive desires and to the corruption of their minds (1:28). As a result, they have been filled with all kinds of evil and wickedness (1:29–31). Though being aware that God will condemn such practices, they continue to do them and encourage others to do so too (1:32).

Jewish Guilt before God

■ READ ROMANS 2:1–29 ■

While the previous section about gentile guilt would have been affirmed by Jewish readers of Paul's day, the next section points the finger at Jews. If they judge gentile unbelievers, they condemn themselves because they do the same things (2:1–3). Instead of repenting of their sins, Jews have hardened their hearts and are storing up wrath for themselves (2:4–5).

God will judge each person according to their deeds: eternal life will be given to those who seek good, glory, honor, and immortality, but wrath and anger to those who reject the truth and righteousness (2:6–8). The same judgment will be extended to both

RECEPTION HISTORY

A Fourth-Century Overview of Romans

Ambrosiaster's commentary on Romans is part of the oldest surviving Latin commentary on the Pauline Letters. It was widely circulated and influenced many other thinkers such as Augustine. In his opening remarks on Romans Ambrosiaster gives a succinct introduction to the whole book, describing Paul's letter as having four main points: (1) the nature of the human race as consisting of two parts: those who exist by nature and a second, favored group who were given the law; (2) human beings did not submit to God even though nature revealed him, resulting in humanity's rejection; (3) therefore, God preferred the Jews to the non-Jews in the world; (4) however, when the Jewish people rejected the Christ, they departed from the law that God had given them and so became like gentiles. Now, both Jews and gentiles have only one hope: the mercy of God appropriated not through the law but by faith in Christ.

This overview influences the way Romans was interpreted throughout much of the church's history in the West but also differs at points from some later interpretations within both Catholic and Protestant traditions.[1]

William of St. Thierry's Exposition of Romans

William of St. Thierry (1085–1148) was a French Cistercian monk who wrote several works during his life at the abbey in Signy between 1135 and 1148, including his *Exposition on the Letter to the Romans*. William had been a student at the cathedral school of Rheims before becoming a monk, and this training is reflected in a couple of ways in which his close reading of Romans is different from typical Cistercian readings. First, the favorite book for **exegesis** in the Cistercian tradition was definitely Song of Songs. Monks did not often comment on letters like Romans; this was something that reflected the different mode of school training. Second, William shows a knowledge of and preference for the Greek text at many points over the Latin Vulgate, believing it to have superior readings. This reflects his use of Rufinus's influential translation of Origen's Greek commentary on Romans.

Despite these differences, William reflects the beauty of the monastic tradition's reading of Scripture through and through. His goal is not academic but devotional and personal. His exposition is full of joy and delight, repeatedly reflecting on God's grace. Many times in the midst of his detailed exegesis he shifts seamlessly to address God directly, breaking into prayers such as, "Lord Jesus, beautiful above the sons of men . . ."[2]

Figure 12.2. Statue of St. Paul holding a sword in front of the Basilica of Saint Paul outside the Walls in Rome

Jews and gentiles, for there is no favoritism with God (2:9–11). Even having the law (as the Jews do) is not a great advantage in judgment because Jews must obey it, not just hear it, and gentiles can know the right way to live by their hearts and consciences (2:12–16).

Jews who know God's will and law, and who seek to teach the ignorant, ought to teach themselves too (2:17–21a). While they teach against theft, adultery, and idolatry, do they keep themselves from such things (2:21b–23)? Rather, God's name is dishonored by Jewish disobedience (2:24). By the same token, the Jewish practice of circumcision is beneficial only if a person keeps the law (2:25). Indeed, the "true Jew" is so inwardly, with a "circumcision of the heart" by the Spirit (2:26–29).

The Whole World Stands Condemned

■ READ ROMANS 3:1–20 ■

Though Jews are just as liable for God's judgment as gentiles, Paul stresses that there are nevertheless great advantages for the Jew, for they have been entrusted with the very words of God (3:1–2). Though some of his people have been unfaithful to him, God remains faithful to his people, which highlights his righteousness (3:3–4).

Paul then explores a possible objection to the judgment of God, anticipating that someone will say that because their unrighteousness highlights God's righteousness, they should not be judged (3:5–7). But he simply dismisses the suggestion by saying that their condemnation is deserved (3:8).

Then comes the main point of the chapter, as Paul combines the guilt of gentiles (1:18–32) with the guilt of Jews (2:1–29) and concludes that Jews and gentiles alike are all under sin (3:9). He supports the point with the series of quotations from Psalms and Isaiah (3:10–18) that together declare, "There is no one who does what is good, not even one" (3:12). The law further underscores Paul's point, since it renders the whole world subject to God's judgment (3:19). No one will be justified through the law, since the law simply further reveals human sin (3:20).

Justification by Grace

■ READ ROMANS 3:21–31 ■

Having established the universal guilt of humanity, Paul turns to address the only solution open to us. Apart from the law, which condemns, the righteousness of God has been revealed through faith in Jesus Christ (3:21–22a). Because it is received by faith in Christ, this good news applies equally to Jew and gentile alike (3:22b). All people have sinned and fall short of the glory of God (3:23), and likewise all are justified freely through redemption in Christ Jesus (3:24).

Redemption in Christ brings justification, and this is achieved by his sacrifice in blood, which is received by faith (3:25a). In other words, the offering of Christ's body in his crucifixion is the sacrifice that achieves atonement, or propitiation. This sacrifice takes effect for all who trust in Christ.

This sacrifice also demonstrates the righteousness of God, since he had previously allowed sin to stand without being properly dealt with (3:25b). God might have been charged with unrighteousness because sin had not been fully punished. But Christ's sacrifice fully dealt with the sin of humanity, thus vindicating God's righteousness—sin was properly judged in that sacrificial offering. Thus, Christ's atoning sacrifice declares the righteousness of God as well as the righteousness of all people who trust in Christ (3:26).

Because righteousness can be granted only through faith in Christ's atoning sacrifice, Paul

THEOLOGICAL ISSUES

The Righteousness of God

The key idea in Romans 3:21–26 is the revelation of the righteousness of God in Christ. But there is a very important issue debated by commentators that affects our interpretation of this passage. In the original Greek the "righteousness of God" could mean God's *own* righteousness (his upright character, etc.), which is revealed through Christ, or it could refer to righteousness that *comes from* God, which is given to believers in Christ. Whatever the correct reading, however, both ideas are present in the text anyway. God's own righteousness is demonstrated by offering Christ as an atoning sacrifice for sin (3:25–26). And his righteousness is given to all who believe in Christ (3:22). Whatever conclusion is reached about the meaning of the "righteousness of God," both options are communicated within the text.

THEOLOGICAL ISSUES

Expiation or Propitiation?

In 3:25 Paul writes, "God presented him [Christ] as an atoning sacrifice in his blood, received through faith, to demonstrate his righteousness, because in his restraint God passed over the sins previously committed." The Greek word translated as "atoning sacrifice" (a neutral term) has been hotly debated for more than half a century. The key issue is whether the word refers to **expiation** or **propitiation**. "Expiation" means that guilt is removed through sacrifice. "Propitiation" means that God's wrath is diverted away from the sinner by sacrifice. In other words, does the sacrifice remove human guilt, or does it redirect God's wrath away from humanity? One objection to the latter is that it might portray God as an angry, unreasonable deity like those found in Greco-Roman religion. But it is clear that the God of the Bible is not like those gods, and yet rightly he expresses wrath toward sin and evil. If propitiation is accepted as the meaning here, God's character is not to be likened to other gods, whose anger is often self-serving and capricious.

Figure 12.3. *Sacrificio di Isacco* by G. B. Pittoni

dispels any temptation to boast in one's standing. A person is justified by faith in Christ's accomplishment, not in any personal accomplishment (3:27–28). There is no higher standing for Jews over gentiles, since all are justified by the same faith in the same Christ (3:29–30). Perhaps ironically, justification by faith does not nullify the law but rather upholds it (3:31).

CANONICAL CONNECTIONS

Abraham and David

Most of Romans 4 revolves around Paul's discussion of Abraham, with David introduced in a supporting role. The overarching point of this chapter is that both Abraham and David were justified by God apart from their deeds (Gen. 15:6; Ps. 32:1–2). It was their faith that made them right with God. In this way, their example supports Paul's broader point that God justifies those who have faith, not those who uphold the law of Moses (3:21–31). These two figures are enormously important in Israel's history and are towering figures in the Old Testament. But Abraham is especially important for the argument because his justification occurred *before* he was circumcised (circumcision would later represent the requirements of the law of Moses). This clinches Paul's argument that justification cannot be dependent on circumcision, and therefore cannot be dependent on **works of the law** in general.

It Has Always Been by Faith

■ READ ROMANS 4:1–25 ■

Having made the bold claim that it is only by faith in Christ that people can be declared righteous, Paul defends this point by appealing to the examples of Abraham and David. He argues that both were justified by faith (not works), which shows that it has always been by faith. Therefore, Paul's message is not something brand new.

Abraham had nothing to boast about, because he believed God and it was credited to him for righteousness (4:1–3). His righteousness was bestowed to him as a gift, not as payment for his good works (4:4–5). David likewise depended on the gift of righteousness, rather than being owed it because of good deeds. In fact, his not-good deeds were forgiven and not charged to his account (4:6–8).

Paul then pivots to show that righteousness by faith is open to everyone, whether Jew or gentile.

Since Abraham was given righteousness through his faith *before* he was circumcised, righteousness cannot depend on that Jewish practice (4:9–10). Rather than receiving righteousness through circumcision, circumcision became a sign of the righteousness that Abraham already had through faith (4:11). As such, Abraham truly is the father of all (as his name means), because both the circumcised (Jews) and noncircumcised (gentiles) can follow in the footsteps of his faith (4:12).

The reason why righteousness must be by faith, and not by circumcision or any other kind of human qualification, is that faith depends on the promise of God. God's promise to Abraham that his dependents would inherit the world did not come through the law (4:13). A person who depends on the law empties the promise of its meaning (4:14–15). But the promise requires faith, not law, which means that it must be according to God's grace—his pure gift. And if it is by grace, then all who have the faith of Abraham may share in the promise (4:16).

Paul then zeroes in on the nature of Abraham's faith in God. He believed God's promise that he would become the father of many nations, even though he was old and Sarah's womb was dead (4:17–19). Because Abraham believed—even against the plain facts of biology—God credited him with righteousness (4:20–22). In the same way, anyone who believes God, who raised Jesus from the dead, will be credited with righteousness (4:23–24). Christ died for our trespasses and was raised for our justification (4:25). Just as God brought life from Sarah's dead womb, so he brings life out of Jesus's dead body. Jesus himself received life again, but also all who believe in him.

Peace with God

■ READ ROMANS 5:1–11 ■

In the previous two chapters Paul has established that believers are declared righteous by faith. Now, because of that, he says, we therefore have peace with God (5:1). Instead of being God's enemies, believers are now restored to him in peaceful harmony. This peace with God brings access to the grace that enables believers to stand before him, and it results in rejoicing (5:2).

Such rejoicing even takes place amid sufferings, which develops endurance within the suffering believers (5:3). Endurance likewise fosters character, which brings about hope (5:4). Hope is a certain expectation and will not let us down, because God's love has already been given to us through the Holy Spirit (5:5).

The love of God now becomes Paul's focus. His love for humanity is proved by the fact that Christ died for us while we were still God's enemies (5:6–8). And having been declared righteous through Jesus's blood, believers will be rescued from facing God's wrath (5:9), which, as Paul has already argued, would otherwise justly come to all humanity. If God was willing to reconcile us to him even while we were his enemies, we can be confident that he will save us from the coming judgment (5:10), which is another cause for rejoicing (5:11).

Adam vs. Christist

■ READ ROMANS 5:12–21 ■

So far, Paul has shown how his gospel is consistent with God's previous activity reaching all the way back to Abraham. Now Paul shifts to show an even bigger picture by comparing Christ to the very first man, Adam. Sin and death entered the human world through Adam and spread to all people (5:12). Though the law, which makes sin all the more obvious, had not yet come, sin was already in the world and death reigned from the time of Adam to the lawgiver, Moses (5:13–14).

The comparison with Christ is a negative one. Adam's one sin brought widespread judgment and condemnation into humanity. But after widespread human sin, the gift of righteousness comes through Jesus Christ (5:15–16). While death reigned through Adam's one sin, those who receive Christ's grace and righteousness will reign through Christ (5:17). While one trespass leads to universal condemnation, one act of righteousness offers universal righteousness and life (5:18–19). When the law finally did come, trespasses increased because the law made it possible to catalog and keep a record of sin. But when sin increased, grace increased all the more (5:20). In short, the reality is that in Adam's world, sin and death reigned. But in Christ, grace and righteousness will reign (5:21).

Figure 12.4. Mosaic of Adam and Christ by the Franciscan friar Jacobus in the Baptistery of Saint John in Florence

Shall We Continue in Sin?

■ READ ROMANS 6:1–23 ■

Paul then anticipates a key question in light of all he has said so far. If salvation is by grace, why not continue in sin? Indeed, if increased sin magnifies God's grace, why not sin all the more (6:1)? His short answer to the question is *No!* (6:2a). But then he launches into the longer answer.

The longer answer begins with his own question: "How can we

who died to sin still live in it?" (6:2b). The remainder of the chapter unpacks the significance of this question. First, Paul reminds his readers that their baptism into Christ connected them to his death (6:3). And if connected to Christ in his death, they are also connected to him in his resurrection, resulting in "newness of life" (6:4–5).

Being connected to Christ in his death means that the "old self" has been crucified, making the sinful body powerless. This means that believers are no longer slaves to sin (6:6–7). And since Christ died to sin once and for all, death no longer has any power over him. This means that believers are also dead to sin and alive to God in Christ (6:8–11). His status of life and conquered death becomes ours because we have been connected to him.

Being dead to sin, believers must not allow sin to reign in their bodies. Having been set free from sin, they should not give sin any control again. All parts of their body and person should be offered as weapons to serve God in righteousness, rather than weapons for unrighteousness (6:12–14).

Finally, Paul returns to the original question. Should we sin because we are under grace? The short answer is the same: *No!* (6:15). Though once slaves to sin, believers have been set free from sin in order to become slaves to righteousness and to God (6:16–23).

Married to the Law

■ READ ROMANS 7:1–13 ■

Being united to Christ in his death also has implications for the way believers relate to the law of Moses. Paul argues that the law is like a marriage partner: you're bound together until death. But if you have died with Christ, you are no longer "married" to the law (7:1–3). Instead of belonging to the law, believers now belong to God. While the law once provoked sinful passions that bring death, believers are now released from the law and live by the Spirit (7:4–6).

But the problem with the law is not the law's fault. The problem with the law is that it points out sin, and once a person starts thinking about sin, it springs to life (7:7–8). Though the law was meant for life, it resulted in death because of sin, even though the law itself is holy, just, and good (7:9–12). In the end, death is sin's fault—not the law's fault—but through the law sin became truly "sinful" (7:13).

THEOLOGICAL ISSUES

Dying and Rising with Christ

The idea of dying with Christ and rising with Christ is enormously important for Paul's overall theology but is often overlooked or misunderstood by many reading him today. When someone comes to faith in Christ, they become connected to him so that his death becomes their death, and his resurrection becomes their resurrection. This is why Paul can say that the old person has died; he or she has "died with" Christ. And that person has new life because they have been raised with Christ too. This dying and rising with Christ has enormous implications for Christian salvation, identity, and conduct. Believers must no longer live according to the old person who was enslaved to sin, since that person is now dead. The new person in Christ is not enslaved to sin and ought to live as a slave to righteousness instead.

The Internal Battle

■ READ ROMANS 7:14–25 ■

Paul then moves to a first-person account of struggling with sin. The passage is hotly debated because, while it sounds like Paul is simply describing his own experience, many commentators believe that he is speaking as a "non-Christian" version of himself, or perhaps a "pre-Christian" version.

Whoever it is speaking here, he is a slave to sin and continues to do the things he hates because of sin living in him (7:14–17). Nothing good lives in his flesh, so even if he desires to do the right thing, he has no ability to do it and is forced to practice evil (7:18–20). Though he delights in God's law, his body prefers the law of sin (7:21–23). He needs rescue from this body of death, and thankfully is rescued by God through Jesus Christ our Lord (7:24–25).

Life in the Spirit

■ READ ROMANS 8:1–17 ■

For those in Christ, there is no condemnation, because the Spirit has set them free from sin and death (8:1–2). God condemned sin by sending Jesus in the flesh to die as a sin offering, thus fulfilling the law's demand (8:3–4). Instead of living according to the flesh, which leads to death, believers now live according to the Spirit, which leads to life (8:5–7). Those living according to the flesh are unable to please God; believers are not in the flesh, but rather are in the Spirit and therefore belong to Christ (8:8–9). The Spirit who lives in believers is the same one who raised Christ from the dead, and will raise the dead in Christ too (8:10–11).

By the Spirit believers will put to death the misdeeds of the body, just as all of God's children are led by the Spirit (8:12–14). Indeed, the Spirit enables believers to cry out to God as their Father and confirms them as his children (8:15–16). As God's children, they are also his heirs and coheirs

---

THEOLOGICAL ISSUES

Who Is the "I" in Romans 7:14–25?

The debate about this passage stems from the fact that Paul sounds like he is just dropping into a first-person narrative, without any reason to think that he is talking about someone other than himself. But at the same time, what he says about himself seems to contradict his own arguments in Romans 6 and 8. For example, he calls himself a slave to sin (7:14), but in 6:17 he says that believers are no longer slaves to sin (cf. 8:2). There are several other examples in which 7:14–25 seems to

jar with Paul's affirmations in chapters 6 and 8. Put together, they offer compelling evidence that the "I" in 7:14–25 is *not* the Christian Paul. Whether it is Paul before conversion, or someone else, does not really matter. The testimony provides an account of how life under the law only condemns the sinner to death. But thanks be to God for his rescue through Jesus Christ our Lord (7:25)!

with Christ. And as Christ's coheirs, believers will share in his suffering as well as his glory (8:17).

The Glory to Come

■ READ ROMANS 8:18–39 ■

These truths lead Paul to reflect on his attitude toward suffering. Whatever sufferings are endured in this life, they are nothing compared to the glory that is coming (8:18). The creation itself anticipates the glory of the children of God and eagerly awaits its own liberation in concert with them (8:19–22). The Spirit living within believers is the firstfruits of what is to come; he connects us to the glorious future in Christ and helps us to anticipate it with patient hope (8:23–25). In the meantime, the Spirit intercedes for us, expressing to the Father our deepest longings without words (8:26–27). ⌇

Whatever happens in this life, Paul affirms the good purposes of God at work through it all (8:28). After all, he predestined believers to be conformed to Christ, which is their ultimate good (8:29). Those he predestined he also called, justified, and will glorify (8:30). If God is willing to do all of this, as well as offer up his Son, will he not grant everything to his children (8:31–32)? No one can rob them of their standing with him, since God is the one who justifies and Christ is the judge of all—and he is already on their side (8:33–34). This means that no one and nothing can separate us from the love of God in Christ (8:35–39).

What about Israel?

■ READ ROMANS 9:1–33 ■

With the end of chapter 8, Paul concludes his main exposition of the gospel he preaches, ending on the high note of the future glory of the children of God in Christ. With chapter 9, he turns to address a potential major problem for his argument. It is the question of why Israel has largely rejected Christ. Since Paul has been at pains to show that his gospel is consistent with the plans and workings of God throughout history, Israel's rejection of Christ raises some serious issues. He spends the next three chapters addressing them.

Paul begins by expressing his personal anguish for his own people, the Israelites, and even wishes he could

The Fate of Creation

Paul's discussion of the present frustration and future liberation of creation ties to the whole sweep of biblical expectation. In Genesis 3:14–19 the created order is corrupted because Adam and Eve rebelled against God. But Isaiah 66 looks to a new heavens and a new earth, with the reversal of the effects of humanity's fall and creation's curse. In 2 Peter 3:12–13 the new heavens and earth will come after the old have been dissolved with fire. Revelation 21:1–2 also pictures a new heavens and new earth, with the old having passed away. But Paul's vision of the future is a *renewal* of the created order rather than its replacement. However, it is best to view the language of 2 Peter 3 and Revelation 21 as dramatic rhetoric meant to convey the radical cleansing of creation, with sin being completely eradicated. Ultimately, there will not be two creations but one. The creation will be renewed to such an extent that it will seem brand new.

trade places with them, willing to be cut off from Christ himself if they would turn to him (9:1–3). They have been God's special people, as the recipients of the covenants, the law, the temple, and the promises of God. Indeed, even Christ himself is descended from them (9:4–5).

Israelite rejection of Christ raises the question as to whether God's word failed them. But in answer to that, Paul again reaches back behind Israel to father Abraham. Abraham's true children are those who are "children of the promise," rather than simply Abraham's physical descendants (9:6–8). This point is illustrated by Abraham's sons. Isaac, born of Abraham's wife, Sarah, is Abraham's true son (not Ishmael, born of the slave girl Hagar) because Isaac comes through God's promise to Abraham and Sarah rather than through human effort (when Abraham slept with Hagar in order to force the promise to fruition himself). The same applies to Isaac's son Jacob (9:9–13).

Since Abraham's children are established by the promise of God, rather than by human credentials, it raises the question of God's justice. Is God unjust? Paul's short answer is *No!* (9:14). As God told Moses, he will have compassion on whom he chooses, and as with Pharaoh, he will harden whom he chooses (9:15–18). It is God's prerogative—as *God*—to choose whom he will. This way, it all depends on God's mercy rather than on human will (9:16).

This then raises the next question: If it is all up to God's will, not human will, why are we held accountable (9:19)? Paul's answer here is more blunt: "Who are you, a mere man, to talk back to God?" (9:20). In the end, God has every right to do as he pleases with the people he has created. Perhaps in order to display his power, mercy, and glory, he has chosen some for mercy and not others (9:21–23). The upshot of this is that he has called some from the Jews and some from the gentiles (9:24–26); indeed, as the prophet Isaiah taught, only a remnant of Israel will be saved anyway (9:27–29). So, then, some gentiles have received righteousness through faith, while some Israelites have not received it because they tried to attain it through the law (9:30–33).

CANONICAL CONNECTIONS

Election in Israel's History

Throughout Romans 9 Paul draws on three key eras of Israel's history to demonstrate that God has always operated through election. God did not choose all of Abraham's offspring to be God's children, but only those according to his promise. The same is true for Isaac's sons, since God chose Jacob not Esau (9:7–13; cf. Gen. 21:12; 18:10, 14; 25:23; Mal. 1:2–3). The next era is God's rescue of the Israelites from captivity in Egypt, when he tells Moses that his mercy is shown to whomever he chooses, while he hardens Pharaoh for his own purposes (9:14–18; cf. Exod. 33:19; 9:16). The third era is the prophets' expectation of the future work of God in gathering a people for himself. According to Hosea, God will call people who are not his people, and according to Isaiah, only a remnant from within Israel will be saved (9:25–29; cf. Hosea 2:23; 1:10; Isa. 10:22–23; 28:22; 1:9).

The Way to Salvation

■ READ ROMANS 10:1–21 ■

Paul's heart desires that Israel be saved (10:1). But while they have zeal for God, they don't have understanding (10:2). Instead of understanding and accepting God's righteousness through faith, Israel has attempted to establish its own righteousness through the law (10:3). But only Christ has fulfilled the law, and so righteousness can be accessed only through faith in him (10:4–7). All that is required for salvation is the confession and belief that Jesus is the resurrected Lord (10:9–10). Everyone who does so will be saved, whether Jew or Greek (10:11–13).

But how can people believe this message if they've not heard it? In order to hear it, there must be someone to preach it, and to preach it they must be sent (10:14–15). But the reality is that hearing does not equal believing, and many in Israel will defy the message even while many gentiles accept it (10:16–21).

Has God Rejected Israel?

■ READ ROMANS 11:1–36 ■

The next question that Paul tackles is whether God has rejected his people. Again, the short answer is *No!* (11:1). The longer answer is that there is a remnant from within Israel who will be saved, which has always been the case in the history of Israel (e.g., in Elijah's day), and Paul himself is an example of such (11:2–5). The salvation of a chosen remnant again underscores that it is by grace, because it is not determined by human action or will (11:6). Only the chosen remnant will find the truth, while the rest of Israel will be hardened (11:7–10).

This leads to yet another question: Has Israel stumbled too far, beyond recovery? The short answer is, again, *No!* (11:11a). The longer answer is that the salvation of the gentiles will make Israel jealous, in hope that some will believe (11:b–15). But there is no room for gentile arrogance in all of this, as Paul reminds them that they are like wild olive branches that have been grafted into a cultivated olive tree (11:17–21). And if they were grafted in, they can also be cut off again, while the natural branches can always be grafted back in (11:22–24). So, Paul affirms that Israelite unbelief actually serves the gentiles, since it gives them the opportunity to come to faith in Christ (11:25–32). Finally, the conclusion of this long section of chapters 9–11 sees Paul caught up in praise mode, as he utters a **doxology** dedicated to the inscrutable wisdom of God (11:33–36).

Where the Rubber Meets the Road

■ READ ROMANS 12:1–21 ■

The whole of chapters 1–11 has seen Paul in theology mode, unpacking his gospel and answering several possible objections and questions along the way. Now, finally, in chapter 12 he turns to address the implications of all this for Christian living. In view of the amazing mercies of God (articulated throughout chaps. 1–11), believers ought to offer themselves as living sacrifices to God, resisting the world's ideology while being transformed in their minds in order to know the will of God (12:1–2). This call to self-sacrifice and to the knowledge of God's will serves as the frame for the remainder of the letter. It will shape all that follows.

A consequence of having a transformed mind is to not think too highly of oneself, but instead to have an understanding of being part of the body of Christ. Believers belong to one another, and each one's gifts are to be used in service of the whole (12:3–8). Believers are to love one another deeply, show honor as appropriate, and be filled with zeal, rejoicing, and patience as they share with those in need (12:9–13). They should live in harmony, blessing their enemies, being humble and honorable, and allowing God to take justice on those who oppress them (12:14–21).

Submit to the Authorities

■ READ ROMANS 13:1–10 ■

Another aspect of living with a transformed mind involves one's attitude toward authorities in power. Even though Emperor Nero, a ruthless tyrant, was the ruler of Rome at the time of Paul's writing, Paul nevertheless instructs his readers to submit to all governing authorities (13:1a). While this instruction might seem to put all the power in the hands of oppressive

Figure 12.5. Model of ancient Jerusalem and the second temple

rulers like Nero, Paul quickly adds that all authorities are subject to God's will (13:1b), which pushes believers to submission to rulers out of their submission to God but at the same time relativizes Nero's power. In other words, even a supreme ruler like Nero is actually under God's authority. He is not sovereign, contrary to what any Roman emperor might have thought.

The instruction to believers to submit is serious because rebellion actually opposes God himself, the one who institutes all authorities (13:2). Lack of submission will bring God's judgment, since rulers ordinarily reward good conduct; if people live well, they should have nothing to fear (13:3–4a). But if they are lawbreakers, authorities may wield disciplinary action that ultimately expresses God's wrath (13:4b). Believers ought to submit out of conscience too, not just out of fear of wrath (13:5).

As part of their submission to the authorities, believers must pay taxes, which support the work of the authorities (who ultimately serve God) (13:6). Indeed, they ought to pay whatever is owed to anyone, including respect, honor (13:7), and love (13:8–10).

Live as in the Day

■ READ ROMANS 13:11–14 ■

Another aspect of living with a transformed mind is to realize what time it is (13:11). The night is nearly over and the day is near, so believers ought to live according to the light (13:12). The metaphors of night and day, darkness and light, are used eschatologically to convey that this current period of world history is coming to an end. The day of the Lord's coming will change everything, and believers are to live in light of that day. This means that activities that belong to this dark world should be shunned by believers, including sexual impurity and jealousy (13:13). Believers are to "put on Christ," like a garment, and reject the desires of the flesh (13:14).

Love Bears All

■ READ ROMANS 14:1–15:13 ■

One of the challenges for the church is for its members to get along with one another in the face of minor disagreements. Perhaps as an extension of owing love to one another (13:8), Paul encourages his readers to

RECEPTION HISTORY

What about the Nazis?

Reading Romans 13:1–7 inevitably raises questions about dictator states, especially with regimes such as Hitler's Nazi Germany, within living memory. Does Paul mean for Christians to submit even to evil tyrants such as Hitler? It's hard to say that Paul would exclude bad rulers like Hitler, given that as Paul wrote, Nero sat on the throne—one of the most evil rulers in Roman history. Many German Christians and churches gave their allegiance to Hitler for precisely this reason: they believed that his authority came from God. While Paul expects Christian submission to rulers because God has given them authority, that fact also relativizes their power. Nero did not have absolute authority; his authority was given by God. This means that when there is a conflict between obeying God and obeying rulers, it is clear that believers ought to obey God, as Daniel did (Dan. 3). This kind of reasoning also led many faithful Christians such as Dietrich Bonhoeffer and Karl Barth to resist and oppose Hitler's rule.

accept those who are weak in faith without getting caught up in disputable matters (14:1). One important such issue for first-century churches was the matter of food. The person of "strong" faith can eat anything, while the one with "weak" faith restricts their eating (14:2). (See the sidebar "Food Sacrificed to Idols" in chap. 13.)

On whichever side of this issue someone comes down, they should not look down on those who hold a different opinion. It's a disputable issue, and God has already accepted believers on both sides of it, so we should not judge one another (14:3–4). Another example is the issue of days, like the Sabbath; some believers will want to observe the Sabbath while others will not (14:5). But again, believers ought not judge, since each will behave in good conscience before God, to whom we all belong (14:6–8). Christ died to claim us as his own, so it is not fitting that we judge one another. Rather, each will need to give an account to God, the true judge (14:9–12).

Instead of judging, believers should love one another. While Paul himself knows that no food is "unclean," no one should cause the stumbling of a brother or sister who holds a different opinion. Their freedom in eating should be put under the higher priority of love (14:13–21). Whatever someone believes about such issues should be between them and God, and no one should act against conscience (14:22–23).

The fact that Christ came not for himself but for the sake of others sets the model for believers to follow; this means that the strong will carry others' weaknesses and will seek to please their neighbors (15:1–4). Living in harmony with one another will lead to the glory of God and Christ (15:5–6). And just as Christ has accepted them—both Jews and gentiles—so believers must accept one another (15:7–12). At this point, before turning to conclude his letter, Paul pauses to bless his readers with God's hope, joy, and peace (15:13).

Wrapping Up

■ READ ROMANS 15:14–33 ■

Paul begins to conclude his magisterial letter by reminding his readers of his special calling as a servant of Christ for the gentiles. He has written to them boldly out of his commission that the gentiles might become an acceptable offering to God (15:14–17). By the miraculous power of the Holy Spirit, Paul has preached the gospel all the way from Jerusalem to Illyricum (the northwest of Greece). His aim is still to preach Christ wherever Christ is not known (15:18–21).

Paul's busyness in preaching Christ throughout these regions has prevented him from visiting Rome thus far. But now he wishes to visit the

Roman church on his way to Spain for the purpose of enjoying their fellowship and to gain their support for his mission (15:22–24). At the end of his third missionary journey, Paul is now traveling to Jerusalem for the sake of poor believers there, for whom the churches throughout Greece have offered material support (15:25–27). After that job is completed, Paul will stop in Rome on his way to Spain (15:28–29). In the meantime, Paul covets their prayers for his safety in Jerusalem and that he would be able to see them in Rome as he intends (15:30–32). And once again, Paul blesses his readers with God's peace (15:33).

Figure 12.6. Medallion with St. Paul from an icon frame (ca. 1100)

Final Greetings

■ READ ROMANS 16:1–27 ■

For a church that Paul had not yet visited, he sure knew a lot of people there! The final chapter of Romans is dedicated to final greetings. He begins by commending his spiritual sister Phoebe, from the church in Cenchreae, near Corinth in Greece. It seems she is planning a visit to Rome, since Paul encourages his Roman readers to welcome her when she comes (16:1–2).

Paul greets Prisca and Aquila, who risked their lives for Paul and who host a church in their home in Rome (16:3–5). There are also the Jewish believers, Andronicus and Junia, who had shared imprisonment with Paul (16:7). Various other believers and fellow workers are greeted on behalf of all the churches of Christ (16:8–16).

The church in Rome is instructed to avoid people who create unnecessary divisions and obstacles, who deceive people with their smooth talk (16:17–18). The Romans enjoy a good

HISTORICAL MATTERS

Paul's Plans Are Fulfilled, but Not in the Way He Anticipated

Paul tells the Romans that he has many times been prevented from visiting them, and now intends to go there on his way to Spain (15:22–24). Clearly Paul has wanted to visit Rome for some time, and now his plans are moving in that direction. According to Acts 21–28, Paul did indeed make it to Rome, but not the way he had planned. When he visited Jerusalem after writing this letter, a riot broke out in the temple as some Jews objected to Paul's presence there. He was then taken into Roman custody for his protection, and then sent down to Caesarea Philippi to await trial. After two years under arrest there, he called on his privilege as a Roman citizen to appeal to Caesar, and the authorities were obligated to provide him safe passage to Rome. So Paul did achieve his goal of visiting Rome, but his journey there was under Roman guard, and his time there was under house arrest, ultimately leading to his execution.

LITERARY NOTES

Final Greetings in Paul's Letters

It is often tempting to skip over the final greetings of a letter, but these sections can offer many insights. First, they remind us how relational Paul was, and how many people were important to him. Second, usually they contain historical bits and pieces that help us to stitch together Paul's travels, ministry, and the letters' relationship to the narrative of Acts. Third, they often harbor hidden exhortations and theological comments buried within the greetings, which readers will miss if they just skip this part of the letter.

reputation among the churches and should be wise and innocent (16:19). As Eve was promised in the garden that her offspring would strike the serpent's head (Gen. 3:15), so God will soon crush Satan under their feet (16:20).

Finally, we see that Paul is accompanied by Timothy, Lucius, Jason, and Sosipater, who also send their greetings. Paul evidently used an **amanuensis** (scribe) named Tertius to compose the letter, who also greets the church in Rome (16:22). Paul's last words in the letter ascribe glory to God by way of a doxology that is centered on God's revelation to the gentiles (16:25–27).

The Converting Power of Romans

Throughout history Romans has had a great impact on the church's leaders, many of whom credit their own conversion to paying attention to this letter. Augustine (354–430), the most influential theologian in the Western church, heard a voice telling him to pick up the Scriptures, so he opened and randomly read Romans 13:13–14, upon which he felt his soul was flooded with light and he was converted and baptized. Martin Luther (1483–1546), the founder of the Protestant Reformation, was studying Romans in a newly produced Greek edition (instead of Latin), and when he read Romans 1:17, he came to see that it was through grace and mercy that God justifies us. He experienced for the first time deliverance from his guilt and bondage, and this set in motion his vision to reform the church. John Wesley (1703–91), the great preacher involved in the Great Awakening and the founder of Methodism, was converted when he heard someone reading in a chapel service the preface to Luther's commentary on Romans. Wesley later wrote, "While he was describing the change which God works in the heart through faith in Christ, I felt my heart strangely warmed. I felt I did trust in Christ, Christ alone, for salvation; and an assurance was given me that He had taken away my sins, even mine, and saved me from the law of sin and death."[3]

Implementation—Reading Romans as Christian Scripture Today

The Letter to the Romans is a glorious exposition of the gospel and how the gospel changes everything. Though the whole world stands condemned before God, he graciously gives right standing to all who have faith in Christ. Believers have died with Christ, escaped slavery to sin, and are heirs of the glory of God—both Jews and gentiles. In response to God's mercies, believers will live with transformed minds, engaged hearts, and love for one another.

Historically, different parts of Romans have been favored at different times, whether it is chapters 1–5, focusing on justification by faith; chapters 6–8, focusing on union with Christ; chapters 9–11, focusing on Jew-gentile relations; or chapters 12–16, focusing on the Christian life. The challenge for the church today is to embrace the *whole* message of Romans. Rather than reducing the gospel to justification by faith, or union with Christ, we must understand that the gospel includes all such things.

The gospel goes well beyond Christ's atoning sacrifice and righteousness by faith. We must also see that the way God saves us is by uniting us to Christ in his death and resurrection. It involves deliverance from evil powers, especially sin and death, and lifts us up to share in the glory of God by the power of the Spirit.

Likewise, the implications of the gospel go well beyond simply faith and salvation. Because of God's mercies toward us, believers are to be marked by love for one another, obedience to authorities, compassion toward weakness, and other-person centeredness. Ultimately, believers will marvel at the glory of God in Christ.

KEY VERSES IN ROMANS

- For I am not ashamed of the gospel, because it is the power of God for salvation to everyone who believes, first to the Jew, and also to the Greek. 1:16
- The righteousness of God is through faith in Jesus Christ to all who believe, since there is no distinction. For all have sinned and fall short of the glory of God. 3:22–23
- For if we have been united with him in the likeness of his death, we will certainly also be in the likeness of his resurrection. For we know that our old self was crucified with him so that the body ruled by sin might be rendered powerless so that we may no longer be enslaved to sin, since a person who has died is freed from sin. 6:5–7
- For I am persuaded that neither death nor life, nor angels nor rulers, nor things present nor things to come, nor powers, nor height nor depth, nor any other created thing will be able to separate us from the love of God that is in Christ Jesus our Lord. 8:38–39
- I ask, then, has God rejected his people? Absolutely not! For I too am an Israelite, a descendant of Abraham, from the tribe of Benjamin. God has not rejected his people whom he foreknew. 11:1–2a
- Therefore, brothers and sisters, in view of the mercies of God, I urge you to present your bodies as a living sacrifice, holy and pleasing to God; this is your true worship. Do not be conformed to this age, but be transformed by the renewing of your mind, so that you may discern what is the good, pleasing, and perfect will of God. 12:1–2

Christian Reading Questions

1. Pretend you are a Jewish reader (or perhaps you are!). Try to think of as many objections as you can to Paul's gospel message. Now skim through the letter and try to find Paul's answers to those objections. What do you find?

2. Most interpreters break the letter up into four sections. What do you think these sections are, and what are their main themes?

3. What exactly does Paul think will happen with Israel in the end (Rom. 9–11)?

4. Trace the theme of love through Romans 12–16. Why is it such an important theme in the letter?

CHAPTER THIRTEEN

The First Letter to the Corinthians

The Historical Origins of 1 Corinthians

Author: Paul

Date: AD 53–54

Location: Ephesus

Setting: Paul is responding to matters that the Corinthians wrote to him about (their letter is lost). Paul has also heard reports about trouble among the Corinthians.

"First" Corinthians

Although this letter is known as "First" Corinthians, the letter itself reveals that it is not the first one Paul wrote to the church in Corinth (1 Cor. 5:9). He has already written to them addressing various problems, and they have written back to him. The letter we call First Corinthians is actually his second letter to that church, while the first letter has not survived.

Orientation

The Corinthian church is really messed up. They are plagued with division, sexual immorality, idolatry, arrogance, worldliness, and many other things. But above all, they lack the most important thing—*love*. Paul's pastoral response to the situation in Corinth produces one of his greatest literary treasures, his "first" letter to the Corinthians.

Because of the many problems in the church in Corinth, the letter gives us stunning insights into Paul's pastoral ministry as he addresses one problem after another. But the letter is not simply a collection of rebukes and encouragements; the whole thing is deeply theological in nature, as Paul applies theological truths to the church's failings and blind spots.

In particular, the letter provides us with some of the most striking reflections on the significance of the cross and the resurrection of Christ. These twin themes bookend the letter, with the cross of Christ dominating its early chapters and the resurrection of Christ gloriously expounded at the end of the letter. Indeed, 1 Corinthians 15 is the richest and most important discussion of

Figure 13.1. Location of Corinth

Christ's resurrection and the resurrection of believers in the entire New Testament. 📖

Perhaps the letter's most striking element is how Paul never questions the genuine salvation of his readers. From the beginning of the letter, where he describes them as "the church of God at Corinth," "those sanctified," and "called as saints" (1:2), to the end, where he reaffirms his love in Christ for them all (16:24), the Corinthians are regarded as genuine believers, even though some of their faults and shortcomings are nothing less than shocking. This tells us a lot about the gospel that Paul preaches. Even extreme moral and spiritual failure does not disqualify believers from what is promised to them in Christ. Of course, they must repent and

© Baker Publishing Group

HISTORICAL MATTERS

Paul and the Church in Corinth

Paul visited Corinth for the first time on his second missionary journey in AD 50, after venturing into Europe—Philippi, Thessalonica, Berea, Athens, then Corinth (Acts 18). His ministry there lasted about a year and a half and established the Corinthian church. This letter is written during Paul's third missionary journey, while he was located in Ephesus in AD 53 or 54. After his time in Ephesus (and after writing this letter), Paul revisits Corinth as part of his third missionary journey.

LITERARY NOTES

The Strange Structure of 1 Corinthians

Scholars have long struggled to understand the structure of 1 Corinthians. The usual solution is to see it as addressing a random collection of topics determined by the Corinthians' letter to Paul. While there are several different topics, there does appear to be a logic that holds it all together: the theme of the *body*. The letter addresses divisions within the body (the church; 1:10–4:21), sex and marriage (involving physical bodies; 5:1–7:40), food sacrificed to idols (food is for the body; 8:1–11:1), and instructions for corporate worship (when the body, the church, gathers; 11:2–14:40). And the letter begins with the crucifixion of Christ's body (1:18–25) and ends with the resurrection of his body and the bodies of believers (chap.15). Thus, the "body" (understood as Christ's actual body, believers' physical bodies, and the church as the body of Christ) could account for the structure of 1 Corinthians.

Corinthian Culture

More than any of Paul's other letters, 1 Corinthians requires some understanding of the culture of the city in which the church lived. Corinth was notorious for its immorality and worldly perspectives and practices. The city was located at the foot of a high mountain, known as the Acrocorinth, at a strategic location for shipping where the Ionian and Aegean Seas are separated by a short stretch of land that connects the Peloponnese to mainland Greece. Because of its location, Corinth was an important hub for commercial, military, and transportation activity. And as such, it gained a reputation for its vice, sexual corruption, and religious temples. According to Aristophanes (ca. 450–385 BC), "to act like a Corinthian" meant "to commit fornication." Plato (428–348 BC) referred to the description "Corinthian girl," which was a euphemism for a prostitute. And according to Strabo's account (7 BC), the temple of Aphrodite located on the Acrocorinth was home to one thousand temple prostitutes. Needless to say, the new church in Corinth had a lot of cultural baggage to overcome in order to live as the holy people of God.

Figure 13.2. Road in ancient Corinth with Acrocorinth in the background

The Proper Understanding of Christ in Ambrosiaster

In his early Latin commentary on 1 Corinthians (probably fourth century) Ambrosiaster pays attention to how Paul describes God and Christ in the opening words of the letter (1:1). Paul uses both the names "God" and "Christ" separately to show that "Christ is God but not the Father, or that Christ is the Son although the Father is also God, and that they are not identical." By this, Paul is refuting the false apostles who do not understand Jesus Christ correctly in this way. Ambrosiaster says that many sects arose that preached Christ wrongly and that "their dried-up branches are still with us today."[1]

follow Christ with their whole lives, but Paul does not question their standing with God. This makes the letter a tremendous encouragement to the church today—as it has been throughout history—which wrestles with its own versions of failure in various respects.

Exploration—Reading 1 Corinthians

Divisions in Corinth

■ READ 1 CORINTHIANS 1:1–17 ■

Paul describes his readers as "the church of God at Corinth," "those sanctified in Christ Jesus," and "called as saints" (1:2)—descriptions that will resonate throughout the letter as Paul calls them to live up to their identity in Christ. He also thanks God that they "do not lack any spiritual gift" (1:7) and that God will make them "blameless in the day of our Lord Jesus Christ" (1:8), again anticipating themes that he will soon address.

Then Paul immediately launches into one of the many problems afflicting the church in Corinth. There are divisions and rivalries among them, represented by various factions: a Paul faction, an Apollos faction, a Cephas faction—even a "Christ" faction (1:10–12)! Paul's critique of this attitude is summed up in the question "Is Christ divided?" (1:13). His logic is that Christ is the one who unites people, not divides them.

He also rejects the thought of a "Paul" faction, reminding the Corinthians that he was not crucified for them, and that they were not baptized into his name (1:13). The point is that Christ is the one who should have their full allegiance, and that there is no room for factions. Paul is very relaxed about whom he baptized in Corinth—a possible badge of the "Paul" faction—and reminds them that Christ sent him to preach the gospel, not to baptize people, especially not into Paul's name (1:14–17).

Figure 13.3. *Christ on the Cross* by Eugène Delacroix

The Foolishness of the Cross

■ READ 1 CORINTHIANS 1:18–31 ■

Paul then zeroes in on one of the main themes of the letter: the contrast between worldly "wisdom" and the "foolishness" of the cross. The Corinthians are spiritually gifted (1:7) and seem to value outward signs of strength and power—like the world around them. But God has inverted worldly wisdom by the message of Christ crucified, because this act of apparent weakness is, in fact, the power and wisdom of God. Thus, "God's foolishness is wiser than human wisdom, and God's weakness is stronger than human strength" (1:18–25).

The Corinthians themselves are not wise from a worldly point of view, but God chose what is foolish, weak, insignificant, and despised in the eyes of the world to shame the strong (1:26–28). This is so that no one may boast, because Christ is the true wisdom from God, as well as "our righteousness, sanctification, and redemption" (1:29–31). It is Christ alone who makes the Corinthians the church of God (1:2); it has not been achieved by them in any way. This whole section is designed to undermine the Corinthians' confidence in worldly strength and wisdom, by demonstrating that God overpowers worldly strength through the weakness of the cross of Christ. This message of the cross turns everything upside down.

Wisdom Talk

■ READ 1 CORINTHIANS 2:1–16 ■

The theme of crucifixion continues as Paul reminds the Corinthians of the way he taught them—not with impressive techniques, but with the message of Christ

CANONICAL CONNECTIONS

Isaiah 29:14

In 1:19 Paul cites Isaiah 29:14 to show the fundamental opposition between human wisdom and the word of the cross. The Isaiah text is part of a woe oracle in which various human practices are condemned and God will judge the "wisdom of the wise." Paul draws on this text to announce that God's judgment and salvation are already taking place among the Corinthians, and those who still value human wisdom have not understood God's judgment of such wisdom through the cross.

THEOLOGICAL ISSUES

Cruciformity

A central theme through chapters 1–4 is the idea of **cruciformity**. This refers to a way of living, thinking, and relating that is shaped by the cross. The cross of Christ turns everything upside down. The word of the cross is foolishness to the world, but it is the power of God (1:18). Believers are not powerful from a human perspective, but boast in the Lord (1:26–31). Paul does not use impressive speaking techniques, but came in weakness (2:1–5). God's servants are no one, yet God works through them to build his church (3:1–17). Through all of these themes runs the idea that God's power is seen in human weakness. This is how the cross of Christ saves humanity: though appearing as weakness, God worked through it powerfully. The Corinthians' problem is that they value human strength, power, and glory, but Paul's encouragement is that they need to become shaped by the cross.

CANONICAL CONNECTIONS

Who Has Known the Mind of the Lord?

When Paul cites Isaiah 40:13 in 2:16, he gives it a christological twist. In its original context the anticipated answer to the question "Who has known the mind of the Lord?" is "No one." However, Paul follows up the citation with "But we have the mind of Christ" (2:16b). The point here is that without Christ we cannot know the Lord's mind, but with the mind of Christ it is possible to know it because he has revealed it. This feeds into the wider context to support the idea that the person of the Spirit, the spiritual person, can evaluate all matters in accordance with the Lord, whereas those without the Spirit of Christ are bound to human wisdom and therefore cannot understand the wisdom of the cross (2:10–15).

crucified (2:1–2). His manner reflected his message, speaking in weakness rather than with impressive words, though with the Spirit's power (2:4–5).

Instead of speaking according to the standards of worldly wisdom, Paul speaks "God's hidden wisdom," which is a riddle that God kept secret from the beginning. This riddle is revealed to people by God's Spirit, but without the Spirit it is impossible to know the secret ways of God (2:6–16). This section relates to the message of the cross, which seems like foolishness to the wise but secretly is the power of God for salvation (1:18). Only by the Spirit can people understand that message and receive it.

Belonging to Christ

■ READ 1 CORINTHIANS 3:1–23 ■

Unfortunately, the Corinthians are not acting in line with the Spirit, so Paul needs to address them as "people of the flesh" and as "babies in Christ" (3:1–2). Their worldliness is evident in the strife and division among them, some saying they belong to Paul, others to Apollos (3:3–4; cf. 1:10–17). Instead of being competitors in a Corinthian popularity contest, Paul and Apollos are coworkers with God (3:8–9). Paul planted the church in Corinth, and Apollos followed up, but God is the one who brought the growth (3:5–7). This highlights how silly it is to favor one or the other, when it is God who ought to receive the credit.

Paul views himself as a master builder who laid the foundation for God's building—the church in Corinth—and the foundation that he laid is none other than Jesus himself (3:10–11). Whatever is built on top of that foundation will one day be judged. If poor-quality materials are used for building, they will perish. But if high-quality materials are used, they will withstand the judgment (3:12–15). This means that the quality of the ministry among the Corinthians will be tested. Since they themselves are the building, Paul is raising the question of what sort of quality building they are becoming.

Paul reminds the Corinthians of their status before God: they are God's temple, and so the Spirit of God lives in them. God's temple is holy, and so they are holy (3:16–17). While the letter will go on to reveal that they are living in a less than holy way, this is nevertheless their status before God, and they need to live up to that identity. Part of doing so means that they will no longer embrace the wisdom of the world. And if they let go of the wisdom of the world, they will not boast in their human leaders, such as Paul and Apollos (3:18–22a). Instead, he says that "everything is yours" because they belong to Christ and Christ belongs to God (3:22b–23). In this way, Paul concludes the section that began with divisions in the church (1:10); the ultimate conclusion is that they belong to Christ, not to their tribal factions.

Managers of the Mysteries of God

■ READ 1 CORINTHIANS 4:1–21 ■

Paul and Apollos are to be regarded as servants of Christ and managers of the mysteries of God, who are expected to be faithful in their management (4:1–2). The Lord, not people (not even Paul himself), will judge their work, and this will take place when Christ comes again. He will reveal the secret intentions of all, which highlights why he, not people, is the judge, since people are unable to see what is hidden within (4:3–5).

The Corinthians' favoring of one leader over another is regarded by Paul as an expression of superiority, as though they are in a position to judge between them. But in fact, whatever strengths the Corinthians may have, they have received from the Lord. There is therefore no room for boasting or for any smug sense of superiority (4:6–7).

Paul then launches into a bit of a sarcastic critique of the Corinthians' sense of superiority: "You are already full! You are already rich! You have begun to reign as kings without us" (4:8). In contrast to the "superior" Corinthians, the apostles are in last place, condemned to die, fools for Christ, weak, and dishonored (4:9–10). They are hungry, thirsty, poorly clothed, and homeless (4:11). But like Christ, the apostles bless when reviled, and respond graciously when slandered (4:12–13). The fact that the Corinthians behave in the opposite fashion shows how much *un*like Christ they really are.

But Paul quickly drops the sarcasm and replaces it with family love. He writes as the Corinthians' spiritual father, warning them as his children (4:14–15). Like a father, he reminds the Corinthians that he is coming soon and will sort out their big talkers. It is up to them which side of the spiritual father they want to see—he can bring his rod for disciplining them, or he can come gently and lovingly (4:18–21).

The Problem of Sexual Immorality

■ READ 1 CORINTHIANS 5:1–13 ■

Instead of arrogance, the Corinthians should be experiencing grief because of the sin among them that Paul has heard about. Their sexual immorality is worse even than that of the pagans, with one of the Corinthians sleeping with his stepmother (5:1–2)! For the sake of his restoration, the man doing this must be handed over to Satan, which probably means that he should be expelled from the Christian community (5:3–5, 13). Indeed, the believers should not associate at all with those who claim to be brothers or sisters and yet are sexually immoral, greedy, idolatrous, abusive, or drunkards (5:11–13). Instead, such people should be expelled from the fellowship for the sake of restoration.

The Problem of Legal Disputes

■ READ 1 CORINTHIANS 6:1–11 ■

Sexual immorality is only one of many problems within the Corinthian church. They are also taking one another to court, allowing secular powers to sort out their internal disputes. But believers one day will participate in Christ's judgment of the world, and even of angels—surely at least one of them ought to be wise enough to judge internal matters appropriately (6:1–6).

Believers should prefer to be wronged and cheated, but instead the Corinthians do wrong and cheat one another (6:7–8). This is inherently evil, and Paul warns them of the severe consequences of such evil—"the unrighteous will not inherit the kingdom of God"—listing examples of such people (6:9–10). The Corinthians used to be like this, but in Christ they have been washed, sanctified, and justified by the Spirit of God (6:11). Again they must remember their status before God and act accordingly.

Why Sexual Immorality Is a Problem

■ READ 1 CORINTHIANS 6:12–20 ■

Turning back to one of the big problems in Corinth, Paul first critiques the popular notion of unrestricted freedom. Not everything you *can* do is good for you or others (6:12). Specifically, he says that the reason that sexual immorality is wrong is that the body is for the Lord, not for sexual immorality (6:13), and the body will be resurrected (and therefore has an eternal aspect) (6:14). But the big point here is that "your bodies are a part of Christ's body." You cannot then take a part of Christ's body and join it with a prostitute. Instead of becoming one with a prostitute, believers are joined to the Lord in one spirit (6:15–17). Because of this, believers must "flee sexual immorality." Such sin is against one's own body, which is a temple for the Holy Spirit to dwell in. Believers were bought by God for a price—the death of his Son—so they ought to honor him with their bodies (6:18–20).

Marriage and Singleness

■ READ 1 CORINTHIANS 7:1–40 ■

In response to issues that the Corinthians wrote to Paul about, he unpacks his thoughts on marriage and singleness in chapter 7. Because of the temptation to sexual immorality (addressed in the last chapter), people should get married and fulfill their spouse's sexual needs. But Paul is clear that this is a concession, not a command, because it is even better to be single, as he is (7:1–9).

Married people should not separate from their spouses (7:10–11, 39–40). But if an unbelieving spouse leaves the marriage, the believer is no longer bound to the marriage. But the believer should stay married to their unbelieving spouse if the latter is willing to stay married (7:10–16).

Whatever their situation, believers should learn to be content rather than try to upgrade their status or situation. The calling of the Lord is their upgrade to status and situation, so that the slave called by the Lord is the Lord's freedman. He does not need to become free in the eyes of the world to know true freedom in Christ. In the end, believers belong to God, so they should not become slaves of people—meaning that they should not be slaves to human standards and systems (7:17–24).

This principle applies to marriage. If you're single, there's no harm in staying so. If you're married, stay married. But if you're single and get married, it's no sin (7:25–28, 36–38). The underlying point is that "the time is limited," which Paul reinforces with apocalyptic imagery: "this world in its current form is passing away" (7:29–31). This means that Paul wants believers to think more about the big picture of what God is doing rather than to get bogged down in their own personal circumstances. While Paul doesn't deny the importance of getting married, or of a slave receiving freedom, these things can easily consume our attention. Instead, believers should see that the end is coming. In this light, married people are necessarily tied up with pleasing their spouse, but the single person is able to focus on pleasing the Lord (7:32–34).

About Food Sacrificed to Idols

■ READ 1 CORINTHIANS 8:1–13 ■

It seems an abrupt change of topic, but Paul turns now to another issue that the Corinthians had written to him about (7:1): food sacrificed to idols. In the Corinthians' world, meat sold at market often was dedicated to a pagan idol or god before it was sold. This raised a question of conscience for believers: Should they eat such meat, or would doing so compromise their devotion to Christ?

Paul spends three chapters addressing this question and the issues underlying it, but he begins with a key principle: "Knowledge puffs up, but love builds up" (8:1). This principle relates to the question at hand by saying that, on the one hand, there is a *"right" answer* to this question, but, on the other hand, we also need to ask what the *most loving action* will be.

The first part of Paul's answer is to state that idols are nothing, since there is only one God (8:4–6). But not everyone understands this point, and perhaps they were accustomed to idolatry in their former lives (8:7). For them to eat such food might cause a problem for their conscience because of their previous experiences with idolatry. So the truth is that food is irrelevant, and idols are nothing. But this knowledge should not cause others to stumble (8:8–9; cf. 8:1). If you eat food sacrificed to an idol, will your action cause a fellow believer in Christ to ruin their conscience? Thus, Paul concludes, "If food causes my brother or sister to fall, I will never again eat meat" (8:10–13). In this way, the principle laid out in 8:1 is applied: love is more important than knowledge. You may know that an idol is nothing, and that eating food sacrificed to an idol is nothing, but if your eating is unloving toward others, don't do it.

HISTORICAL MATTERS

Food Sacrificed to Idols

At temple dining halls people ate meat that had been offered to idols as part of their worship. At markets much of the meat for sale also had been offered to idols, though sometimes it was difficult to know whether that was the case. In large cities Jews often had their own markets in order to avoid buying meat that might have been sacrificed to idols. Jewish teachers of the time debated about what to do when a Jew was offered meat without knowing whether it had been offered to an idol; they would avoid eating it if they suspected idolatry. Paul's approach to the issue, however, is more nuanced and takes into account social considerations, other people's consciences, and, above all, love.

Learning from Paul's Example

■ READ 1 CORINTHIANS 9:1–27 ■

Paul illustrates the central principle of love through his own life. As an apostle, he is entitled to various privileges, including being married and being supported financially in his work of ministry (9:1–14). But he has not

Figure 13.4. *Moses Striking the Rock* by Tintoretto

used these privileges because he wants to preach the gospel free of charge (9:15–18). Though he is free, he chooses to make himself a slave for the sake of others (9:19–23).

Freedom and privilege are not the most important values; rather, serving others in love is the highest good. Paul's life sets an example for the Corinthians when they are considering whether to submit their knowledge to the principle of love (cf. 8:1).

Learning from Israel's Past

■ READ 1 CORINTHIANS 10:1–11:1 ■

The third chapter addressing the question and issues of food sacrificed to idols is the most confusing. The big point is that Israel ate and drank the same food and drink, provided to them by the Lord, but still sinned in various ways and therefore were judged. The food you eat is not what will make you right with God, and food will not prevent you from being judged by God!

Though the people of Israel were "baptized into Moses" and ate the same food given to them by God, God was not pleased with most of them, and so they were struck down (10:1–5). Paul stresses that Israel's disobedience stands as an example for believers today; they committed idolatry and adultery, they

CANONICAL CONNECTIONS

Learning from the History of Israel

In 10:1–22 Paul offers a typological reading of Israel's exodus (vv. 1–2), wilderness wandering (vv. 3–4), and **apostasy** (v. 5), drawing a parallel between Israel's experience and that of the church (v. 6). Though the recipients of God's grace, the Israelites rebelled and were judged; so believers today should not rebel against God—committing sexual immorality, testing Christ, and complaining—and so find themselves subject to his judgment (vv. 7–10). Israel's experience is an example and warning for believers (vv. 6, 11).

complained and grumbled, and when tested they failed the test (10:6–11). The warning is, "Whoever thinks he stands must be careful not to fall" (10:12). There is no room for spiritual complacency or overconfidence. Testing will continue to happen, but God will not allow you to be tempted beyond what you can bear (10:13). 📜

Back to the Corinthians' problem now, Paul warns them to "flee from idolatry" (10:14), just as they are to flee sexual immorality (6:18). Though idols are nothing, eating food sacrificed to idols suggests complicity in idolatry after all. This is not because idols are anything, but because behind all idolatry are the forces of evil. So eating food sacrificed to idols is participation with demons, just as sharing in the Lord's Supper is a **participation with Christ** (10:16–22). This seems like a strange backflip from the earlier point that food is nothing, and people can eat whatever they want (8:8).

But Paul then harmonizes the two points. The key principle comes back into play: "No one is to seek his own good, but the good of the other person" (10:23). Believers can eat anything sold in the meat market because "the earth is the Lord's and all that is in it" (10:25–26; cf. Ps. 24:1). They can eat meat if served by an unbelieving neighbor, but if the neighbor makes a point that the meat was sacrificed to an idol, the believer should not eat it—but this is for the sake of the unbeliever. From the unbeliever's point of view, eating such meat is a participation in the worship of idols, and so the believer must not engage in it. But if it is just meat, with no further significance in the mind of the host, the believer may go ahead and eat it. In other words, if the unbeliever is inviting you to commit idolatry, you must reject it. But if they are just inviting you to share a meal together, there is no problem.

The lengthy answer to the question about food sacrificed to idols is complex and often leads to confusion, but the conclusion is very clear: "Whether you eat or drink, or whatever you do, do everything for the glory of God." This means giving offense neither to outsiders nor to the church of God. Instead, just as Paul seeks to benefit others, the Corinthians should follow Paul as he follows Christ (10:31–11:1). In all of this, the principle that Paul began with in 8:1 will be fulfilled: love builds up, so do whatever is most loving to others.

CANONICAL CONNECTIONS

Baptized into Moses?

Moses did not baptize anyone, so what does Paul mean when he says that "all passed through the sea, and all were baptized into Moses in the cloud and in the sea" (10:1–2)? Since Paul is drawing parallels between Israel and Christians in this passage, he likens the salvation of Israel out of Egypt under the leadership of Moses to the salvation of believers out of sin and death under the leadership of Christ. Passing through the Red Sea was the decisive moment of Israel's liberation from slavery in Egypt, and on the other side of the sea Israel became God's people through the covenant mediated by Moses. God then led Israel through the desert by the cloud representing his presence. In the same way, baptism today symbolizes deliverance from slavery to sin (cf. Rom. 6:1–14), and once delivered from sin, believers enter a new covenant relationship with God through Christ. For these reasons, being "baptized into Moses" points forward to Christ.

Head Coverings in Worship?

▦ READ 1 CORINTHIANS 11:2–16 ▦

If the previous three chapters seemed confusing, the next topic addressed by Paul raises the bar even further: **head coverings** in the congregation, men and women, and the Trinity. Paul begins by mixing all three topics together. Christ is the head of every man, man is the head of the woman, and God is the head of Christ (11:3). Men and women should pray and prophesy in a way that honors their head (11:4). This means that men should pray and prophesy without a head covering, while women should wear a head covering. 🏺

Paul then focuses on the mutual dependence between men and women, and their dependence on God (11:7–12). He concludes that it is obviously proper for women to pray with a head covering, and vice versa for men (11:13–16). While many of these issues, and the arguments that Paul makes, seem completely alien to us in the twenty-first century, his main point is that how we adorn ourselves—what we wear—has symbolic value and should reflect godly attitudes and relationships. Much of the passage is highly cultural in its application, but this underlying principle still pertains to corporate worship in the church today.

The Lord's Supper in Worship

▦ READ 1 CORINTHIANS 11:17–34 ▦

Worshipers' head coverings are not the only thing to be mindful of when the Corinthians gather. Sadly, their factionalism affects their time together, and their practice of the Lord's Supper is very problematic. Instead of sharing a meal of thanksgiving that remembers the Lord and demonstrates love one to another, they have been abusing the practice (11:17–22).

Paul then reminds the Corinthians of the significance of the Lord's Supper. He repeats the oral tradition of Jesus's words that was handed down to him (probably from the apostle Peter): "This is my body, which is for you. Do this in remembrance of me," and "This cup is the new covenant in my blood. Do this, as often as you drink it, in remembrance of me" (11:24–25; cf. Luke 22:19–20). The supper is meant to "proclaim the Lord's death until he comes" (11:26); it is not meant to replace the Corinthians' dinner or further enhance the divisions between them.

The Corinthians need to take a good hard look at themselves. Abusing the Lord's Supper is sin, and eating and drinking without consideration of the body (meaning the Corinthian congregation) will incur judgment

Figure 13.5. Stained-glass window in the Cathedral of Brussels depicting Jesus and the twelve apostles at the Last Supper

(11:27–32). Instead, they should welcome one another and enjoy this special expression of their fellowship together in Christ (11:33–34).

Spiritual Gifts in Worship

■ READ 1 CORINTHIANS 12:1–31 ■

Paul then turns to his important discussion about **spiritual gifts**, which begins with the assertion that everyone who recognizes that Jesus is Lord has the Spirit of God (12:1–3). It's possible that the Corinthians did not think that all believers had the Spirit, given their preoccupation with impressive gifts and divine displays. So Paul claims the opposite: regardless of gifting or outward displays, everyone under Jesus's lordship has the Spirit.

All believers share the same Spirit, but the Spirit gives different gifts to different people. The variety of gifts means that there will be different ministries and activities within the church for the common good: some will speak messages of wisdom or knowledge; others will exercise gifts of faith, or healing, or miracles, or prophecy; and so forth (12:4–11).

These differences in gifts and roles within the church lead Paul to reflect on the issue of unity and diversity within the body of Christ. The "body" image is an excellent one for discussing unity and diversity, because by definition a body must be one

THEOLOGICAL ISSUES

What Are "Spiritual Gifts"?

While translations render it "spiritual gifts," the Greek word that Paul uses in 12:1 literally means "spiritual things" or perhaps even "spiritual people." But the topic of "gifts" is confirmed in 12:4: "There are different gifts, but the same Spirit." This shows us that "spiritual gifts" are simply gifts or abilities given by the Spirit. They are not necessarily miraculous in nature (though some are). Their "spiritual" quality comes from their origin in the Spirit of God, who imparts these good things to people for the benefit of the whole church.

entity. But at the same time, a body has many different parts, all of which are necessary for the proper functioning of the body. All the parts of the body need one another—all are indispensable (12:12–26).

The body of Christ has been designed and arranged by God, so there should be no jealousy or divisions within it—all operate as he has planned for the greater good. This includes some to be apostles, others to be prophets, others to be teachers, and so on. Not all are apostles, or prophets, or teachers, and that is okay. All individuals are members of the body of Christ (12:27–31).

All You Need Is Love

■ READ 1 CORINTHIANS 13:1–13 ■

Ultimately, the guiding principle for the use of spiritual gifts is the same as that for food sacrificed to idols: the answer is *love*. Paul's famous "love chapter" is set in the context of how believers should behave when they are gathered together, and how they should treat one another.

It doesn't matter simply how gifted someone is. A person may have the gifts of tongues, prophecy, understanding, knowledge, and even abundant faith, but without love, it is all for nothing (13:1–3). Love is characterized by patience, kindness, forgiveness, truth, belief, hope, and endurance. It is not characterized by envy, boastfulness, rudeness, selfishness, or unrighteousness (13:4–7). While the functions of many gifts, such as prophecy, tongues, and knowledge, will come to an end, love never ends (13:8–12). In fact, faith, hope, and love—the characteristic hallmarks of the believer—will each remain, but the greatest of these is love (13:13).

Pursue Spiritual Gifts That Build Up Others

■ READ 1 CORINTHIANS 14:1–40 ■

Resuming his discussion about gifts in the church—though he never actually left it—Paul encourages the Corinthians to pursue love and to desire the gifts that build up others. Prophecy is a better gift than speaking in tongues, because it builds up the church instead of just the individual (14:1–12). But anyone who does have the gift of speaking in tongues should pray for the gift of interpretation too so that they can share their gift with the

RECEPTION HISTORY

The Danger of Prophetic "Nothings"

In his commentary on 1 Corinthians 13:1–2 Ambrosiaster reflects a way of reading that is very typical in the Christian tradition: connecting one text of Scripture with many other similar teachings. Paul says that if he prophesies without love, he is nothing. Ambrosiaster connects this with many similar examples in the Bible: Balaam, Caiaphas, the disobedient king Saul, Judas, and even the devil, who knows the mysteries of heaven but they do him no good. Ambrosiaster goes on to explain from this verse that knowledge without love is no good, as seen in the examples of Tertullian and Novatian, who started well but fell into schism, even as the Pharisees did. He concludes that even the casting out of demons is worthless "unless the person who does these things has been determined to behave well," to be a person of love.[2]

Women in the Church

Under the theme of orderliness, Paul instructs women to remain silent in the churches. If they have a question, they should ask their own husbands at home (14:34–35). This difficult text will offend many today and is rejected outright by some biblical scholars as not being original to the letter. Whatever one's interpretation, a few points are worth keeping in mind. First, the word translated as "silent" can simply mean "quiet" rather than indicating strict silence. This is important because, second, Paul clearly does not expect women to be silent. He has already instructed them (alongside men) as to how to pray and prophesy within the congregation (11:5–16). They will have a voice in the congregation through prayer and prophecy at least. So why should women be "quiet" in the congregation? Some speculate that there was a problem with the women in Corinth—perhaps, for example, they were unusually aggressive or unruly. Others have suggested that it is simply part of the expected orderliness that would characterize the Jewish synagogue (14:40). Whatever the case, the overarching principle is to be respected: the congregation is to act in an orderly fashion with the intent of building up one another in love.

HISTORICAL MATTERS

Witnesses to the Resurrection of Christ

First Corinthians 15:5–8 is a very important account supporting the historicity of Christ's resurrection appearances. Jesus's resurrection appearances to Cephas (Simon Peter) and the other main disciples are well recorded in the Gospels, but it is important to realize that 1 Corinthians was written before Matthew, Mark, Luke, and John. Thus, 1 Corinthians 15:5–8 stands as the earliest historical record of the eyewitness accounts of the resurrection of Jesus. The group of five hundred witnesses is known only here. But Paul adds that most of them are still alive (at the time of writing), implying that the Corinthians can go ahead and check out their claims for themselves.

congregation (14:13–17). Paul himself would rather speak five intelligible words than ten thousand in a tongue, because those five words can build up others (14:18–19). The same principles of love and building up others should direct the orderliness of their gathered meetings (14:20–40).

The Glorious Resurrection from the Dead

■ READ 1 CORINTHIANS 15:1–58 ■

The theological conclusion of the letter is also its glorious high point. At first it may not seem clear how it relates to the rest of the letter, but that will become evident as we move through it. Paul begins by articulating the gospel that the Corinthians have already accepted and that has already saved them: Christ died for our sins according to the Scriptures, and he was buried, and he was raised on the third day according to the Scriptures (15:1–4). Paul then lists various important witnesses of the resurrection of Christ: Cephas (Simon Peter), the twelve main disciples, a group of five hundred others, Jesus's brother James, all the apostles, and finally Paul himself (15:5–8).

Apparently, yet another problem in Corinth was that some denied that there would be a resurrection of the dead at the end of time, which was a mainstream Jewish and biblical conviction (cf. Dan. 12:1–2; John 11:24). But Paul easily overturns this error by appealing to Jesus's resurrection from the dead, which he has already asserted to be a historical fact. The argument is simple: If Christ has been raised from the dead, how can some say that there is no resurrection from the dead (15:12–13)? And then their denial of resurrection (and hence Christ's resurrection) creates all kinds of other problems. If Christ has not been raised, their faith is useless because they are still in their sins. Those who have already died in Christ are lost, and believers should be pitied more than anyone (15:14–19).

Instead, Christ has indeed been raised, and this is a theological necessity for overcoming the problem of death in the world. Since death came into the world through a man (Adam), so resurrection must come through a man, Jesus (15:21–22; cf. Rom. 5:12–21). Jesus is the firstfruits of the resurrection, guaranteeing that others will follow. This image is taken from the world of agriculture, in which the firstfruits preceded the main harvest, not only guaranteeing that a harvest was going to follow but also indicating the quality of the harvest to come. Jesus's resurrection stands as the firstfruits of the resurrection of all believers, since it guarantees their resurrection and demonstrates the nature of their resurrection—it will be like his (15:20, 23).

When those who belong to Christ are finally resurrected, then comes the end, when all God's enemies will be abolished, the last of which is death itself (15:24–28). Without the hope of resurrection, baptism for the dead is useless, as is suffering for the gospel message. In fact, if this life is all there is, we ought to just enjoy ourselves, because tomorrow we will die and it will all be over (15:29–34).

Paul then anticipates the inevitable question: How are the dead raised, and what sort of body will they have (15:35)? Drawing again on an agricultural issue, he answers his own question with the image of a seed. A seed will grow only by

RECEPTION HISTORY

The Resurrection and Its Implications in Chrysostom

The famous preacher John Chrysostom (347–407) regularly preached through books of the Bible, including forty-four homilies on 1 Corinthians. Five of these (numbers 38–42) were dedicated to 1 Corinthians 15, Paul's famous exploration of the resurrection.

Chrysostom emphasized that the resurrection—Jesus's resurrection and thereby other humans' resurrections—was truly physical and not just spiritual. In this, Chrysostom was consciously refuting the **heresy** of **Manichaeism**, which interpreted the resurrection as only a freedom from sin, not as bodily in nature.

Chrysostom also taught that in the future resurrection not all resurrected bodies will be equal in glory. There will be a hierarchy of honor, with those who practiced an ascetic lifestyle—martyrs, virgins, monks, hermits—being at the highest level. For Chrysostom, this was an important argument for promoting ascetic Christian practices, especially in his city of Antioch, which officially was Christian but marked by what he perceived as many urban vices and few godly people.[3]

CANONICAL CONNECTIONS

God Has Put Everything under Christ's Feet

In the context of what will happen at the end of this age, Paul discusses the fact that Christ must reign until all his enemies have been put under his feet. In support of this, in 15:27 he cites Psalm 8:6: "God has put everything under his feet." This psalm addresses the elevated position in which God has established humanity—a little lower than the divine, crowned with glory and honor (8:4–5). God has established humankind's rule over his creation and has put everything under their feet (8:6). Paul uses Psalm 8:6 with reference to Christ because he represents the apex of humanity, and indeed he is the "last Adam" (15:45). As the apex of humanity, Christ fulfills Psalm 8:6 and the mandate given to humanity to rule over all creation, including death—the last enemy (15:26).

THEOLOGICAL ISSUES

Baptism for the Dead?

Paul refers to the practice of baptism for the dead, saying that if there is no resurrection, such a practice makes no sense (15:29). We don't know what this practice is, but it might refer to the following scenario. If someone became a Christian but died before they could be baptized, a baptism would be held for them symbolically after their death. Again, this is mere speculation, so we don't know for sure. Also, we don't know whether Paul endorses such a practice. Even if he does not (which seems most likely), his point still stands: without resurrection, such a practice would be nonsensical.

first dying. Then it grows into what it is meant to produce. The current body (the seed) is corrupted, dishonorable, weak, and natural. But the resurrection body will be incorruptible, glorious, powerful, and spiritual (15:36–44). Paul then returns to the Adam-versus-Christ idea, saying that our "seed" existence bears the image of Adam, but in the resurrection we will bear the image of Christ (15:47–49).

The resurrection bodies of believers must be of a different nature from their current bodies, because "flesh and blood cannot inherit the kingdom of God" (15:50). When the last trumpet sounds, believers' bodies will be transformed in the blink of an eye and will be raised incorruptible (15:51–53). At this point, death will finally be defeated, swallowed up in victory (15:54–57).

All of this ultimately addresses the Corinthians' lives, since the resurrection of the dead ought to inspire them to excel in the work of the

Figure 13.6. Plaque showing the resurrection of Christ by Jean Limosin

Lord. Such labor will not be in vain, because their resurrection means that the fruit of their labor will be enjoyed for all eternity (15:58). The resurrection of the dead also puts the Corinthians' other problems into perspective. They should not be living for this world, indulging the flesh or behaving as though they belonged to this world. Instead, they are to look forward to their future resurrection from the dead and find their glory in Christ.

Final Instructions and Greetings

■ READ 1 CORINTHIANS 16:1–24 ■

The Corinthians are expected to contribute to the collection that Paul is gathering for the believers in Jerusalem, who currently were suffering from famine (16:1–4). Paul explains his plans to visit Corinth again on his third missionary journey, after an extended stay in Ephesus (16:5–9). He alerts the Corinthians to the possible visits by Timothy and Apollos (16:10–12; cf. 4:17). Various other instructions and greetings follow (16:13–20), and Paul concludes this incredible but difficult pastoral letter with an expression of his love in Christ for all the Corinthians (16:24).

Implementation—Reading 1 Corinthians as Christian Scripture Today

The Corinthians' multiple problems led to multiple gifts to the church in the form of 1 Corinthians. The letter is a rich tapestry of pastoral and theological insights that teaches how to live in light of the cross of Christ and in the hope of the resurrection from the dead. It combines strong rebuke with warm affection, and practical instruction with profound theology. It is exciting, frustrating, challenging, and uplifting.

There are several lessons that the church today can learn from 1 Corinthians. Those of us living within Western culture—which in many ways resembles that of Corinth—will see how important it is to resist the attitudes of the world around us. The way of the cross teaches us to value humility, weakness, and service to others rather than arrogance, human power, and self-glorification. The church is the holy temple of God and must repent of ungodliness and immorality, even if those assault us in every direction.

Believers today need to embrace the priority of love over freedom. In the United States in particular, freedom is often regarded as the highest possible virtue, but 1 Corinthians teaches that love is more important than freedom. We should be prepared to let go of our freedoms for the sake of loving others.

Finally, the church needs to hold on to the hope of glory. The way of the cross, the way of humble service and suffering, will one day give way to the full splendor of resurrection glory in Christ. The defeat of death, the end of mortality, and the triumphant immortal and glorified body constitute the hope that enables us to serve and love, by the power of the Spirit.

KEY VERSES IN 1 CORINTHIANS

- For the word of the cross is foolishness to those who are perishing, but it is the power of God to us who are being saved. 1:18
- Don't you yourselves know that you are God's temple and that the Spirit of God lives in you? If anyone destroys God's temple, God will destroy him; for God's temple is holy, and that is what you are. 3:16–17
- Now about food sacrificed to idols: We know that "we all have knowledge." Knowledge puffs up, but love builds up. 8:1
- If I speak human or angelic tongues but do not have love, I am a noisy gong or a clanging cymbal. If I have the gift of prophecy and understand all mysteries and all knowledge, and if I have all faith so that I can move mountains but do not have love, I am nothing. And if I give away all my possessions, and if I give over my body in order to boast but do not have love, I gain nothing. 13:1–3
- When this corruptible body is clothed with incorruptibility, and this mortal body is clothed with immortality, then the saying that is written will take place: "Death has been swallowed up in victory. Where, death, is your victory? Where, death, is your sting?" 15:54–55

Christian Reading Questions

1. Read 1 Corinthians 1:18–25 and think about modern objections to the message about Christ. In what ways is that message regarded as foolish? How does it cause people to stumble today? And how does the wisdom of God address those concerns?

2. Read 1 Corinthians 3–4. Note all the characteristics of Paul's ministry among the Corinthians.

3. What principles in 1 Corinthians 8–10, addressing food sacrificed to idols, might apply to contemporary issues within the church?

4. Think through 1 Corinthians 12–14. How well does the church today apply the instructions and principles laid out there?

CHAPTER FOURTEEN

The Second Letter to the Corinthians

Orientation

Second Corinthians is the hidden gem of Paul's writings. Regularly overshadowed by its sister letter, 1 Corinthians, it deals with some of the same themes and same problems as that letter but offers a deeper and more personal account of what it means to do genuine Christian ministry.

Because the Corinthians are once again questioning the value of Paul's ministry—in comparison with other, more impressive preachers—Paul argues that the mark of a true apostle and servant of Christ is sharing in the sufferings of Christ. The cross of Christ turns worldly values upside down, so that outward impressiveness is the wrong standard by which to value the ambassadors of Christ.

While the message of Christ is a treasure that brings reconciliation to God, those messengers who carry it are but fragile jars of clay. Indeed, because this message involves the humility and self-sacrifice of Christ, it is fitting that those who carry the message should match it. The humility,

HISTORICAL MATTERS

The Historical Origins of 2 Corinthians

Author: Paul

Date: AD 56–57

Location: Philippi

Setting: This is Paul's fourth letter to the Corinthians (the first and third are lost). The Corinthians had responded well to his third letter, but some of Paul's opponents have stirred up trouble.

LITERARY NOTES

The Four Letters to Corinth

The letter that we call 2 Corinthians is actually the fourth letter that Paul wrote to the church in Corinth, while 1 Corinthians is the second letter. This is clear from references within both letters (1 Cor. 5:9–11; 2 Cor. 2:3–4, 9; 7:8, 12). If the four letters are labeled A, B, C, D, then B = 1 Corinthians and D = 2 Corinthians, while A and C are lost.

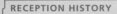
The Structure of 2 Corinthians

This letter has a kind of "defense and challenge" structure, shaped around Paul's defense of himself (1:12–2:13), his defense of his new-covenant ministry (2:14–7:16), his challenge to the Corinthians to give generously to the needy Jerusalem church (8:1–9:15), his defense of himself against the **super-apostles** (10:1–12:13), and his challenge to the Corinthians to be prepared for his next visit to them (12:14–13:13). This "defense and challenge" structure gives 2 Corinthians a polemical feel as the Corinthians challenge Paul and he challenges them in return.

RECEPTION HISTORY

The Call to Detach Oneself from the World

Basil the Great (fourth century) was one of the Cappadocian fathers, the bishop of Caesarea, and the founder of a monastery. His instructions for the monastery, later called "The Rule of St. Basil," greatly shaped **monasticism** in the Eastern church for many centuries.

Basil's monastic sensibilities are evident in his comments on 2 Corinthians 1:8. In this text Paul says that he was so burdened by suffering that he despaired of living any longer. Basil applies this to the lifestyle of renouncing all love for the world. The way to learn to emulate Paul in not loving the world is to start by detaching oneself from all external goods: "property, vainglory, life in society, useless desires."[1] This renunciation of the world follows the example of Jesus's holy disciples like James and John, who left their boats and business. It can also be compared to Matthew, who walked away from his tax-collecting business, not caring about the dangers that would fall on him and his family at the hands of the magistrates for failing to complete his tax duties. According to Basil and his monastic rule, this is what it means to be a dedicated disciple like Paul.

sufferings, and afflictions that Paul endures in order to make Christ known are the true commendations of his ministry. If the Corinthians cannot see that, they have not really understood the message of the cross.

Exploration—Reading 2 Corinthians

Comfort in Afflictions

■ READ 2 CORINTHIANS 1:1–11 ■

After a brief greeting from Paul and his cosignatory, Timothy (1:1–2), the letter moves immediately into a doxology that praises God as the God of all comfort (1:3). God's comfort in the face of affliction enables Paul and his coworkers to comfort others facing affliction (1:4). Paul's afflictions come to him because he shares in the sufferings of Christ, which is his way of talking about the suffering that his ministry in Christ's name brings to him (1:5). But this means that Paul's afflictions are *for* the Corinthians, since he suffers in ministry for their sake (and for the other churches he planted). But likewise, any comfort he receives from God leads to their comfort (1:6a). And the Corinthians need to be comforted because they share in the same sufferings that Paul suffers (1:6b). As they share in suffering, they will share in comfort (1:7).

Paul then recounts a particular affliction in Asia (perhaps in Ephesus?) that nearly led to death, but he and his companions put their trust in God who raises the dead, and who delivered them from death this time (1:8–10a). As they continue to put their trust in God, Paul asks the Corinthians for their prayers (1:10b–11).

A Complicated Relationship

■ READ 2 CORINTHIANS 1:12–2:11 ■

Paul reflects on his sincere interactions with the Corinthians, and he hopes that his writing now will help them to understand him better (1:12–14). Apparently there has been some confusion in Corinth regarding Paul's travel plans. Paul had planned to visit them on the way to Macedonia and again on the way back from Macedonia to Judea (1:15–16). The problem is, Paul did not stick to this plan. But he defends himself on this point, saying that he was not of two minds when the original plans were made. Rather, his "yes" means "yes" and his "no" means "no" (1:17–18), just as God's promises are "yes" in Jesus Christ (1:19–20).

The change of plans was to spare the Corinthians another "painful visit" (1:23–2:3). In a previous letter (now lost), Paul wrote to the Corinthians out of an anguished heart to make known his love for them (2:4). By the same token, the Corinthians ought to reaffirm their love for any person among them who has caused them pain. After discipline, the group should forgive and comfort such a person (2:5–8). In such a way, the Corinthians will demonstrate good character and obedience to Paul, following his example (2:9). Whomever the Corinthians forgive, Paul will likewise forgive (2:10–11).

The Nature of Ministry

▓ READ 2 CORINTHIANS 2:12–3:6 ▓

The difficulties of ministry are in view in this section as Paul reveals his frustrated desire to find Titus (2:12–13), and the humbling nature of his ministry. As part of Christ's **triumphal procession**, Paul views himself as Christ's captive (2:14), as though conquered by his army and paraded through the streets, as the Romans would do to their conquered foes. Christ uses Paul to spread his "aroma" in every place. The message that Paul preaches will be received either as "the fragrance of Christ" or "an aroma of death." Those who receive it as a fragrance will receive life, while those who receive it as a death stench will be led to death (2:15–16). This is the nature of Paul's ministry; it is not self-serving but leads to good things and bad (2:17).

Paul's ministry cannot be commended by normal human recommendation. Instead, the Corinthians are Paul's commendation, for they testify to the work of Christ by the Spirit that has come through Paul's ministry among them (3:1–3). It is not that Paul and his coworkers are so competent; rather, God has equipped them to be ministers of a new covenant (3:4–6).

New-Covenant Ministry

▓ READ 2 CORINTHIANS 3:7–18 ▓

Having raised the topic of the new covenant in the previous section, Paul now reflects on the key

HISTORICAL MATTERS

Roman Triumphal Processions

Being led "in Christ's triumphal procession" (2:14) imagines Christ as a conquering general or emperor leading a victory march through the streets of Rome. Such victory marches paraded defeated leaders at the rear of the procession. They were bound, sometimes naked, and the crowd mocked and abused them. Usually the captives were executed at the end of the procession. Paul's use of this image fits his depiction of true apostleship: the triumph of Christ over the formerly unbelieving Paul will lead to his mockery, abuse, and ultimately to his execution.

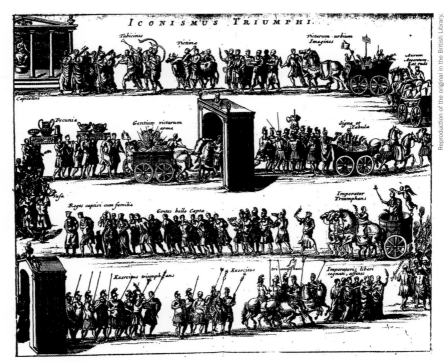

Figure 14.1. Depiction of a Roman triumphal procession from Basil Kennett, *Romae Antiquae Notitia; or, The Antiquities of Rome* (London, 1699)

differences between old and new covenants. The old covenant, with its Ten Commandments chiseled on stone, was glorious but brought death and condemnation because the law of Moses condemns sin. The ministry of the Spirit, however, is even more glorious and brings righteousness instead of condemnation (3:7–11).

The following, somewhat confusing section compares not only the old and new covenants but also the people under the old and under the new. Moses's ministry differs from Paul's, and believers differ under each ministry. The old covenant and ministry hide something under a veil, but the new covenant and ministry reveal what was hidden. This refers to the glory of God in Christ, which is fully revealed under the new.

Unlike Moses, who had to veil his face to hide the glory of the old

Figure 14.2. *Moses* by Michelangelo Buonarroti, ca. 1513–15

covenant from the Israelites, Paul acts with boldness (3:12–13). Paul says that whenever the old covenant is read, a metaphorical veil remains over it. This "veil" is removed only in Christ. In other words, the truth about the fulfillment of the old covenant in Christ is hidden until he reveals it (3:14). In the same way, a veil hangs over the hearts of those under the old covenant until the Lord removes it so that they can see clearly (3:15–16). The Spirit, whom Paul calls the Lord, unveils our faces so that we may look directly at the glory of the Lord and are transformed into that same glory (3:17–18).

Treasures in Jars of Clay

▨ READ 2 CORINTHIANS 4:1–18 ▨

Continuing the theme of his new-covenant ministry, Paul reflects on some principles that shape it. He does not give up; he does not use shameful practices or distort the truth; he acts in a way that everyone can approve (4:1–2). But those who reject the gospel have been blinded from seeing the light of the glory of Christ, which has illuminated Paul's heart (4:3–6).

The knowledge of God's glory in Christ is powered by God himself, not by Paul. That treasure is "stored" in the "clay jar" of his human body, which is afflicted and persecuted but not destroyed (4:7–9). Paul says that he carries the death of Jesus in his body, so that Jesus's life may be displayed. This means that those who preach the gospel continually face death because of the dangers of preaching it, but their mortal danger serves to make Jesus known, so that the life found in Christ is made known through their dying (4:10–12). In any case, the God who raised Jesus from the dead will raise those in Christ, and in the meantime the Corinthians benefit from Paul's ministry (4:13–15).

Knowing these truths means that Paul does not give up. Though the outer "shell" of the body is deteriorating day by day, the inner, spiritual person is continually renewed (4:16). Whatever troubles he encounters in this life, they

Figure 14.3. Clay jars

The Truth Triumphs in India

Many Indian coins are inscribed with the words *Satyamev Jayate* (truth alone triumphs), adopted as the national motto for independent India in 1950. This saying is shorthand for a mantra from the ancient Sanskrit Vedic Hindu text called the Mundaka Upanishad. The mantra goes on to say that through truth the divine path is laid out, and by this sages can find the ultimate treasure of enlightenment.

In reflecting on 2 Corinthians 4:1–6, Jacob Cherian contrasts this traditional Indian understanding of enlightenment with what Paul says about the revelation of God's light through Jesus Christ. The Christian task in every culture, then, is to "boldly and clearly declare the truth of the gospel to each person's conscience." Within Indian culture, the mandate is to preach the truth of the gospel, "the *gnana* (knowledge) that will free people and provide true enlightenment" in a way that is culturally sensitive and humble, empowered by the Holy Spirit.[2]

THEOLOGICAL ISSUES

Christ Became Sin?

Second Corinthians 5:21 is a very compressed statement that summarizes how sinners may be reconciled with God (see also 5:20). It refers to the sinless Christ becoming "sin for us" so that believers might "become the righteousness of God." When Paul states that Christ became "sin," it does not undermine Christ's sinless status. Rather, he is regarded by God as bearing the sin of humanity so that reconciliation between God and humanity can take place. Without the removal of sin, reconciliation is impossible. By the same token, those who are "in him" are regarded as righteous before God, because we share in the righteousness of Christ.

produce in him "an absolutely incomparable eternal weight of glory" (4:17). This life, with its temporary troubles, is passing away. But the glory that is to come is eternal and far outweighs current light afflictions (4:18).

The Eternal Dwelling

■ READ 2 CORINTHIANS 5:1–10 ■

Speaking of what is eternal, Paul turns here to reflect on differences between life here and now and the life to come. He describes our current body as an "earthly tent," which will be destroyed and replaced with a heavenly "eternal dwelling" (5:1). This heavenly eternal dwelling corresponds to the "spiritual" resurrection body that Paul discusses in 1 Corinthians 15:44–49. Paul longs for this better heavenly body so that "mortality may be swallowed up by life"—a future expectation that has been guaranteed by the down payment of the Spirit (5:2–5). As a result, this current period, before receiving the resurrection body, is lived by faith not sight, seeking to please Christ, since all will appear before his judgment seat to be repaid for deeds done in this life's body (5:6–10).

The Nature of Ministry

■ READ 2 CORINTHIANS 5:11–6:13 ■

Because of these things, Paul conducts his ministry accordingly. He aims to persuade people, compelled by the love of Christ. After all, Christ's death for all means that believers no longer live for themselves but rather for him (5:11–15). Paul does not view people from a worldly perspective, since anyone in Christ has become a new creation (5:16–17). And because God reconciles us to himself through Christ, Paul's ministry is one of reconciliation, he and his coworkers working as God's ambassadors (5:18–20). At the heart of that reconciliation is the message that Christ took the place of sinners so that sinners could become righteous in God's sight (5:21). Believers should therefore receive the grace of God, for now is the time for salvation (6:1–2).

Paul and his team are commended as God's ministers by their many sufferings and afflictions, but also their godliness, alongside the work of the Spirit, the word of truth, and the power of God (6:3–7). Their lives are marked by a series of contrasts too: glory and dishonor, slander and truth, dying and yet living, having nothing while possessing everything (6:8–10). They have not withheld their affection from the Corinthians, though the sentiment has not been mutual (6:11–13).

Genuine Repentance

■ READ 2 CORINTHIANS 6:14–7:16 ■

Believers are to be cleansed from all kinds of impurity (7:1), which will include inappropriate partnerships with those who do not believe (6:14–18). This does not mean that believers need to avoid unbelievers altogether, but that they need to be careful to not be influenced too much and end up going in the wrong direction. After all, the thrust of this section is that believers will be cleansed from impurity.

Paul and his team have done no wrong to the Corinthians, who they hope will make room for them in their hearts (7:2–4). Although he had upset them by one of the four letters he sent the Corinthians, they responded appropriately in genuine repentance about the things Paul had rebuked them about (7:5–12). The Corinthians also showed hospitality to Titus, Paul's beloved coworker, giving Paul further reason to rejoice about how the Corinthians are acting in love (7:13–16).

The Collection

■ READ 2 CORINTHIANS 8:1–9:15 ■

Paul changes topic now and tells the Corinthians about the believers in Macedonia, who, despite trials and poverty, gave generously in support of other believers in need (8:1–6). As a test of their love, Paul asks the Corinthians also to join in the practice of giving (8:7–8). Though he does not command them to do this, he reminds them that Christ, who was rich, became poor so that they could become rich (8:9). In other words, Paul helps the Corinthians to see how the gospel can be interpreted economically.

CANONICAL CONNECTIONS

The Day of Salvation

In 2 Corinthians 6:2 Paul cites Isaiah 49:8 regarding "an acceptable time," "the day of salvation" in which God helps his people as a sign of a messianic age to come. In the style of a Jewish **pesher**, Paul cites his text, then adds an interpretive comment that relates to his own day: "now is the acceptable time; now is the day of salvation" (6:2b). Paul regards the present era of Christ as the fulfillment of this Isaianic prophecy; it is the messianic age toward which Isaiah looked, with salvation available through Christ by the grace of God (6:1).

CANONICAL CONNECTIONS

Dwelling with God

In 2 Corinthians 6:16b–18 Paul draws on several Old Testament texts in order to support his point that believers constitute the temple of the living God, which must be kept pure from idolatry (6:15–16a). These texts are sourced from Leviticus 26:12; Isaiah 52:11; 2 Samuel 7:14 and together are used to claim that believers are the people of God. They are his sons and daughters and belong to him. They therefore must remain separate and undefiled in a way fitting for God's people. The wider point that this supports is Paul's call for believers to avoid partnerships with unbelievers, who are represented by the impurity that idols would bring into the temple (6:14–16).

Jesus laid his life down for the sake of others, and so believers ought to express the same love and commitment with their resources.

But in the matter of giving, what's important is that their heart and attitude are right, not how much they can give (8:10–12). But if they have more than they need, it is good to meet others' needs, who will do the same if the tables are turned in the future (8:13–15). In all of this, Paul and his colleagues have been careful to do the right thing in handling this large collection, and they have been careful to be *seen* to do the right thing too (8:16–24).

After reminding the Corinthians of the commitment to give that they had already made (9:1–5), Paul encourages them to give according to their heart. They should not give reluctantly, because God loves a cheerful giver (9:6–7). And God will bless them in their giving, so that they have all they need and will be spiritually enriched (9:8–12). Indeed, the Corinthians' generosity will result in others glorifying God as they pray for the Corinthians with deep affection (9:13–15).

Ministry of the Knowledge of God

■ READ 2 CORINTHIANS 10:1–18 ■

Having dealt with the issue of generosity and giving, Paul turns to another extended discussion of the nature of his ministry (chaps. 10–12). The first section (10:1–11) addresses meekness and strength. Paul appeals to the Corinthians by the meekness of Christ so that he would not need to be too strong in person when rebuking certain people. Those people think that Paul and his coworkers behave "according to the flesh"—that is, their ministry tactics resemble the tactics of this world (10:1–2). But Paul assures them that, though living in the flesh, they do not conduct their ministry by it. Their agenda is to demolish arguments that are set against the knowledge of God, taking every thought captive for Christ (10:3–6).

Paul reminds the Corinthians that they all belong to Christ, who gave Paul authority to build up believers rather than to tear them down. His letters are not intended to terrify them—they are meant to strengthen—but if he needs to be equally strong in person, he will be (10:7–11). Paul's ministry cannot be measured against normal standards but only according to the parameters set by God (10:12–13). Self-commendation means nothing; only the commendation of the Lord means anything (10:14–17).

Paul vs. the Super-Apostles

■ READ 2 CORINTHIANS 11:1–12:13 ■

Continuing the theme of his ministry, Paul likens himself to a best man who has arranged a marriage for his best friend (Christ) and a pure virgin (the Corinthians). He is jealous for them in a godly way, wanting them to remain pure for the groom (11:1–2). He is worried that, like the very first wife, Eve, the Corinthians will be deceived by Satan and led away from devotion to Christ (11:3). Specifically, Paul is worried that the Corinthians accept all too easily "another Jesus," preached by someone else. In fact, such preachers preach a different Jesus and a different gospel, by the power of a different spirit. In other words, they are false teachers (11:4).

Paul calls these false teachers "super-apostles," apparently because they are outwardly impressive, especially in their rhetorical skills. Though Paul is not a trained speaker, he is knowledgeable and has taught the Corinthians everything they need to know (11:5–6).

Given the Corinthians' fondness of worldly impressiveness, Paul wonders out loud whether he did the wrong thing by humbling himself before them. Unlike trained speakers, Paul did not charge money for speaking to them and in fact relied on support from other churches so as to not be a burden to the Corinthians (11:7–11).

Whatever the Corinthians think, Paul will continue the way he has because he does not want the super-apostles to have any opportunity to regard themselves on the same playing field as Paul (11:12). Then he comes straight out and says it: they are false apostles, deceitful workers, and only in disguise as sent by Christ, just like Satan, who masquerades as an angel from God (11:13–15).

Paul then begins an extraordinary section in which he "boasts" about his credentials as an apostle. But while the super-apostles boast "according to the flesh," Paul's boasting is upside down: he boasts about his weaknesses and his sufferings. He and the super-apostles share Jewish heritage (11:22), but Paul, a genuine servant of Christ, outdoes them in his sufferings (11:23–33). The reason that Paul's sufferings enable him to boast is that his message is a message of the

Figure 14.4. Lunette fresco of the apostle Paul's shipwreck in the Church of St. Paul's Shipwreck, Valletta, Malta

What Is the Third Heaven?

Interpreters have long puzzled over Paul's reference to the **third heaven** (12:2). Most likely this refers to the highest segment of the heavenly realms, according to his cosmology. In ancient understandings of the cosmos, the heavenly realms had levels, with God occupying the highest level—the third level of the heavens. It is possible that Paul is talking about an out-of-body experience of this highest level of the heavens.

Paul then talks about his **thorn in the flesh**, which was given so that he would not take pride in himself. It is unclear what this thorn in the flesh is, except that it is "a messenger of Satan" that torments him to keep him humble (12:7b). In answer to Paul's prayers that his thorn be removed, God assured him that his grace is sufficient and that his power is exerted through human weakness (12:8–9a). All of this is to say that Paul's weaknesses and sufferings allow Christ's power to shine (12:9b–10). He concludes that he is not inferior to the super-apostles, and the Corinthians should have known it (12:11–13).

Paul's Thorn in the Flesh

Interpreters debate Paul's reference to his "thorn in the flesh" (12:7). Suggestions range from physical ailments such as failing eyesight, to moral weaknesses such as sexual temptation, through to spiritual problems such as guilt for deeds done in his previous life before Christ. There are three clues. First, it is a thorn "in the flesh," suggesting something physical or moral (since for Paul "flesh" usually refers to the sinful nature). Second, it is "a messenger of Satan," which may rule out a physical option, since something like blindness is not evil. Third, God's answer to Paul's repeated request to have this thorn removed is "My grace is sufficient for you" (12:8–9). The mention of grace suggests that Paul's thorn may have been something moral. Grace offers forgiveness in the face of moral temptation and failure. Nevertheless, all of this is speculative, and if Paul struggled with a moral problem, it is not possible to identify what it was.

cross (1 Cor. 1:18), which is foolish and weak from a worldly perspective. Paul's sufferings are consistent with such a message.

Paul's boasting continues, but now he turns to visions and revelations. This is a sort of half boast, where he talks about "a man in Christ" who was somehow "caught up to the third heaven" (12:1–5). Most likely he is talking about himself, but he speaks in the third person because he doesn't want to boast about something that the Corinthians can't assess for themselves (12:6–7a).

Getting Ready for His Third Visit to Corinth

■ READ 2 CORINTHIANS 12:14–13:13 ■

Paul indicates his plans to visit Corinth again, but he will not burden the Corinthians when he comes—after all, he does not want what they have; he wants *them* (12:14–18)! All he has said in this letter is for the purpose of building up the Corinthians, but he anticipates that when he comes, there may be some conflict (12:19–21). Indeed, Paul will come in the power of Christ in order to deal with them (13:1–4). The Corinthians should check themselves to make sure they really are following Christ, and they should also check Paul and his crew (13:5–8). But above all, Paul is writing for the Corinthians' growth and maturity as believers (13:9–13).

Implementation—Reading 2 Corinthians as Christian Scripture Today

If the Pastoral Letters (1–2 Timothy, Titus) reveal Paul's expectations of church leaders, and 1 Thessalonians demonstrates his pastoral love, 2 Corinthians offers Paul's most profound theological reflections on the nature of his ministry. The authenticity of his ministry is evident by his suffering and afflictions because he shares the sufferings of Christ and is afflicted as Christ's captive. The treasure of the knowledge of God in Christ is carried in the frail clay jar of his earthly body, indicating that outward appearance is of little importance, but what is inside is everything. The Corinthians are wrong to prize the impressive super-apostles over the humble and afflicted Paul because it shows that they do not yet understand the implications of the cross for Christian ministry.

The tone and the heart of this letter have much to say to today's church at large, but especially to those who engage in pastoral ministry. It corrects worldly views about success, power, and popularity in ministry. It reminds us that genuine Christian ministry is a ministry of the cross that shares in the sufferings of Christ as gospel treasure is conveyed through frail and broken vessels.

While modern-day "super-apostles" abound, being outwardly impressive in various ways, 2 Corinthians reminds us not to value the quality and integrity of ministry according to worldly standards. Perseverance in affliction and humility in suffering are the marks of ministry shaped by the message of reconciliation to God. Rather than being ashamed of his weaknesses, Paul glories in the fact that they amplify the power of Christ. May the same be true of the ambassadors of Christ today.

HISTORICAL MATTERS

Paul's Three Visits to Corinth

Only two of Paul's visits to Corinth are recorded in Acts (18:1–17; 20:2), though in this letter he tells the Corinthians that he is planning a third visit (12:14). There are two options for resolving this. First, Paul never made a third visit to Corinth, despite his intention to go there again. Second, and more likely, the visit to Greece in Acts 20:2 refers to his third visit to Corinth, meaning that there was a second visit that is not recorded in Acts—his "painful visit" (2:1). He may have made a quick trip across the Aegean Sea to Corinth from Ephesus when he was based there for nearly three years on his third missionary journey. This would have been an emergency pastoral visit, given all the problems in Corinth, prompted by one of their letters to him. After his three years in Ephesus he went to Philippi in Macedonia, where he wrote 2 Corinthians, informing them of his plans for a final third visit.

KEY VERSES IN 2 CORINTHIANS

- But thanks be to God, who always leads us in Christ's triumphal procession and through us spreads the aroma of the knowledge of him in every place. For to God we are the fragrance of Christ among those who are being saved and among those who are perishing. 2:14–15
- Therefore we do not give up. Even though our outer person is being destroyed, our inner person is being renewed day by day. For our momentary light affliction is producing for us an absolutely incomparable eternal weight of glory. 4:16–17
- Therefore, we are ambassadors for Christ, since God is making his appeal through us. We plead on Christ's behalf: "Be reconciled to God." He made the one who did not know sin to be sin for us, so that in him we might become the righteousness of God. 5:20–21
- For you know the grace of our Lord Jesus Christ: Though he was rich, for your sake he became poor, so that by his poverty you might become rich. 8:9
- I will most gladly boast all the more about my weaknesses, so that Christ's power may reside in me. 12:9b

---

Christian Reading Questions

1. Trace the theme of boasting throughout the whole of 2 Corinthians. What does Paul boast in and why?

2. Four letters and three visits. It's all a bit confusing. Map out Paul's interactions with the church in Corinth in relation to his missionary journeys as recorded in Acts.

3. Summarize the argument of 2 Corinthians 5. How do the themes of this chapter relate to the rest of the letter?

4. Try to articulate the ways in which churches today need to learn from Paul about the nature of ministry. What are churches doing right? What needs to be corrected?

CHAPTER FIFTEEN

The Letter
to the Galatians

Orientation

Galatians shows us what righteous anger looks like. Paul is angry at the Galatian churches because they are threatening to abandon the true gospel. Nowhere else do we see him so upset, even with other churches that have made some ridiculously large blunders (think of the Corinthians!). The heat generated in this letter comes because the gospel itself is under attack, and where there is no gospel, there is no salvation. Paul even worries that some of the Galatians might not be saved at all. But the strength of Paul's anger tells of his great love for the Galatians. He is upset because he cares about them and their salvation. The letter is the rebuke from a loving pastor who wants his people to come to their senses before it is too late.

The heart of the problem is that the gentile Galatians think that they must become Jews under the law in order to be good Christians. This is symbolized by their desire to become circumcised. Paul rails against this thinking because all they need is Christ. They do not need to become Jewish, submit to the law, or get circumcised. If they think that these things are necessary, they have rejected the true gospel of Christ and have lost Christ by trying to add to him. It is a very strong letter that even records Paul's rebuke of the apostle Peter for similar reasons.

HISTORICAL MATTERS

The Historical Origins of Galatians

Author: Paul

Date: AD 49

Location: Most likely Antioch

Setting: The churches planted during Paul's missionary journey have been misled to believe that they need to become like Jews in order to be good Christians.

Figure 15.1. Province of Galatia

If the letter was polemical in Paul's day, it continued to be so in the centuries that followed. Martin Luther famously depended heavily on Galatians in shaping the theology of the Protestant Reformation. His lectures on Galatians were first published in 1519 and showed his moving toward what would become Protestantism. His second commentary on Galatians (1535) is a defense of his settled theological position. In Galatians, Luther saw that adding anything to faith in Christ is a distortion of the truth. The medieval Roman Catholic Church required many things added on to Christ for salvation. But to add to the gospel was to detract from it and would lead people into slavery instead of freedom. The issues were different from Paul's day, but the principle remained the same.

Exploration—Reading Galatians

The Real Gospel from a Real Apostle

◾ READ GALATIANS 1:1–2:10 ◾

From the very beginning, the Letter to the Galatians stands out from Paul's other letters. Paul defends his apostleship in the very first verse, as he asserts that he was appointed an apostle directly by Jesus Christ and God the Father, not by men (1:1). This is a sign of what will follow.

But even more striking is the complete absence of a thanksgiving for the Galatians. Every other letter to the churches includes Paul thanking God for them (with the exception of 2 Corinthians, where we find praise offered to God instead), but he does not thank God for the Galatians. This is an ominous beginning!

Instead of a thanksgiving, Paul begins with a straight-out rebuke. The Galatians have turned to a different gospel from the one Paul preached to them (1:6–7), and this is nothing short of disastrous. Anyone, even Paul himself or an angel from heaven, who preaches a different gospel will be accursed (1:8–9). This is how serious the Galatians' error is: to turn

LITERARY NOTES

The Structure of Galatians

Galatians falls into two halves, with chapters 1–3 addressing justification by faith and chapters 4–6 addressing sonship and freedom. Within the first half, Paul accuses the Galatians of abandoning the true gospel that was preached to them (chaps. 1–2) and explains why God's promises come by faith, not through law (chap. 3). Within the second half, he writes of the privilege of becoming sons and heirs of God (chap. 4) and the freedom that comes from the Spirit and love (chaps. 5–6). This structure gives the letter the feel of sorting out problems and misunderstandings first, leading to the positive, celebratory outcomes of the gospel.

away from the true gospel is to turn away from Christ himself and removes any hope of salvation.

The true gospel, the gospel that Paul preached to the Galatians, is not of human origin, and Paul received it directly from Christ himself (1:11–12). This then leads Paul to remind the Galatians of his own experience of the revelation of Christ and his apostolic ministry that followed (1:13–2:10). Before he was an apostle, Paul was an enemy of the faith, zealously persecuting God's church (1:13–14). But God revealed Christ to him on the road to Damascus in order that Paul would preach him to the gentiles (1:15–16a; cf. Acts 9:1–19). Paul makes a point of the fact that he did not consult with anyone for approval, but instead spent three years in Arabia and Damascus before meeting any of the apostles in Jerusalem (1:16b–17). Then Paul did meet and stayed with Cephas (Peter) and James the brother of Jesus (1:18–19). Paul then disappeared into Syria and Cilicia, unknown to the churches in Israel except by reputation: this former persecutor of the faith now proclaims it himself (1:21–24).

After a period of fourteen years (his time in Arabia, Damascus, Cilicia, and Syria combined), Paul went to Jerusalem again and met with the leaders of the church there (James, Cephas [Peter], and John) to discuss his ministry to the gentiles. This issue arose because some "false brothers" had infiltrated them, saying that gentiles needed to adopt Jewish practices, trying to steal their freedom in Christ (2:3–4). On the contrary, the leaders in Jerusalem recognized that Paul had been entrusted with the gospel for the sake of the gentiles, and they added nothing to his message (2:6–10).

Trouble in Antioch

■ READ GALATIANS 2:11–21 ■

Though Paul acknowledged the God-given authority of the leaders in Jerusalem, this did not make the leaders immune from error, as becomes clear in the following account of Paul's rebuke of Peter. When Peter came to Antioch, where Paul was based at the time, Paul "opposed him to his face because he stood condemned" (2:11). Peter's mistake may seem a little strange at first, but Paul understood that it threatened to undermine the gospel itself.

The problem was that Peter had been freely associating and eating with gentiles, but once a group of

Luther and Erasmus on Peter and Paul

Small differences in the interpretation of biblical texts can be indicative of larger theological commitments. This is the case regarding Luther and Erasmus on Galatians 2:11, where Paul opposes Peter to his face at Antioch. Erasmus, like several interpreters before him, believed that the disagreement between Peter and Paul at Antioch constituted a *dissimulatio*, a pretend argument being used to teach the Galatians a theological lesson. Peter was not actually doing something wrong, but rather was playing a part. Luther, following Augustine, instead believed Paul's confrontation was not staged but in fact constituted a real conflict over the truth of the gospel. Both Erasmus and Luther referenced Galatians 2:11 in their correspondence with each other before the publications of their opposing works, *The Freedom of the Will* (Erasmus, 1524) and *The Bondage of the Will* (Luther, 1525), as a reason for their writing these theological treatises. Erasmus hoped that their theological debate would restore the divided European church. Luther, however, interpreted his work as a line in the sand about the truth of the gospel. Erasmus was sorely disappointed.[1]

Figure 15.2. German postage stamp depicting Martin Luther

Jewish believers came from Jerusalem, he stopped associating with them and spent time only with other Jewish Christians. The so-called **circumcision party** evidently insisted that all believers be circumcised, whether Jewish or gentile, and refused to have fellowship with uncircumcised gentiles, even though they all believed in Christ. But Paul saw this as a deviation from the gospel, because it is only by faith in Christ that people are saved. Circumcision is not required, so by insisting on circumcision these believers were altering the gospel (2:12–14). This is the point that Paul goes on to unpack through the rest of the letter.

All believers, whether Jew or gentile, are justified by faith in Christ, not by works of the law (2:15–16). Indeed, no one can be made right with God through works of the law, as it points out that all are sinners (2:17). Instead, the law puts people to death (since sin requires the sentence of death), and so Paul can say, "I have been crucified with Christ"; Christ was crucified to take on the **curse of the law** (see ahead in 3:13), which means that in Christ the penalty of death that the law requires has already been paid. Since Paul has been crucified with Christ, he no longer lives as the old Paul, but now lives by faith in Jesus (2:20). Indeed, if righteousness can be achieved through the law, there was no need for Christ to die (2:21).

The True Sons of Abraham

■ READ GALATIANS 3:1–26 ■

The most complex, but also the most important, part of the letter is found in chapter 3. The main agenda is to argue that it is by *faith* that people are made the children of Abraham. It is not through works of the law, or from being a descendant of Abraham, that the true children of Abraham are recognized.

After lambasting the Galatians for their foolishness (3:1), Paul asks if they received the Spirit by the law or by believing. Of course, the intended answer is by believing, but this leads to his next question: If they began the

Christian life by the Spirit, do they intend to continue in the flesh (3:2–3)? The implicit point is that the Christian life begins with faith and the Spirit, and so it continues by faith and the Spirit. Believers do not transition to law and flesh in place of faith and Spirit.

It is by faith that believers received the Spirit, and this is like the faith of Abraham. Those who have the same faith as Abraham are the true children of Abraham (3:5–7). This reality was foretold in Scripture through God's promise to Abraham that all nations would be blessed through him. The gentiles coming to faith in Christ, having the same faith as Abraham, is the fulfillment of this promise to Abraham (3:8–9; cf. Gen. 12:1–3).

In contrast to faith in Christ, some rely on the works of the law. But such people are under a curse because they fail to keep the law, and so they are condemned by the law. No one, then, can be justified by trying to keep the law, because all fail to keep it (3:10–11).

The crucifixion of Christ represents his taking on himself the curse that the law demands for those condemned by the law. By "becoming a curse for us," Christ redeems those under the curse of the law (3:13). This means that everyone who has failed to live up to God's standards will be made right with God (justified), because the penalty that God's law demands for sin has been dealt with by Christ on the cross.

This is also why Paul previously said that he has been crucified with Christ and no longer lives as the old Paul (2:20). The old Paul, who stood condemned under the law, is now dead because he died with

Works of the Law?

Paul rails against "works of the law" as the key to being right with God (e.g., 2:15–16; 3:2–3). We are justified only by faith in Christ. But there is debate as to what he means by "works of the law." Are these works primarily about obedience to the law of Moses and living in an upright way? Some argue that Paul has in mind things that define people as being Jewish rather than gentile. That would explain the focus on circumcision, which is regarded as a "badge" of membership in the covenant to Israel. In other words, are the Galatians trusting in their good deeds to be right with God or are they trusting in their "Jewishness" to be right with him? Probably the answer includes both ideas. The works of the law involve obedience and good deeds, as well as Jewish identity as members of the covenant of Israel. The point of being justified by faith in Christ, however, is that no human credentials—of performance or identity—can make someone right with God.

CANONICAL CONNECTIONS

The Faith of Abraham

Though Abraham did not have a perfect track record, he believed God's promise to him and it was "credited to him as righteousness" (Gen. 15:6; Gal. 3:6). God had promised to bless Abraham with land and that his descendants would become a great nation. All people of the earth would be blessed through him (Gen. 12:1–3). Abraham worried that he had no descendants and his body was old (Gen. 15:1–3), but the Lord promised that an heir would come from Abraham's own body and his offspring would be as numerous as the stars (Gen. 15:4–5). Paul draws on Abraham's trust in God's promise as the model for how people are made right with God. It is by trusting his promise. So, in his day, believers were to trust in God's promise that those who accept Christ will be made right with him. Those who have the faith of Abraham are the true sons of Abraham (3:7).

The Walters Art Museum. Acquired by Henry Walters with the Massarenti Collection, 1902.

Figure 15.3. *The Prophet Abraham* by Niccolò da Foligno

Christ. The new Paul is now released from that condemnation and is no longer bound by the demands of the law. The cross therefore expresses the love of Christ and the grace of God (2:20–21). And all of this fulfills the promise to Abraham that the gentiles would be blessed. Through faith in Christ, believers are blessed by receiving the Spirit (3:14).

The promises made to Abraham were not set aside when the law came, 430 years later. This means that the blessings promised to Abraham and his seed (who is Christ) cannot come through the law, but rather through the original promise that God made (3:15–18). This in turn raises the question of why the law was given in the first place. Paul says that its purpose was to point out transgressions and sins so that it would ultimately point to Christ. When Christ came, all could be justified by faith in him, escaping the imprisonment of the law. The law functioned as a guardian, or babysitter, over God's people for a time. But now God's people have become mature sons of God in Christ Jesus, and there is no further need for a babysitter (3:19–26).

Sons and Heirs

■ READ GALATIANS 3:27–4:7 ■

All who are baptized into Christ have been clothed with Christ (3:27). Christ is like a garment worn by believers, and there is no meaningful distinction between them anymore: Jew, Greek, slave, free, male, female—all are "one in Christ Jesus" (3:27–28). This does not mean that all differences between people are erased, but that all are on the same footing with Christ and with one another. Their differences no longer divide.

Belonging to Christ, believers become part of Abraham's seed, which previously Paul had said was Christ alone (3:16). By belonging to Christ, people share in the promises to the seed, who is Christ, so the seed of Abraham (singular) becomes the seed of Abraham (plural) through trust in Christ (3:29).

Paul then reflects on the difference between an heir as a child and an heir as an adult. As a child, an heir is no different from a slave, under the authority of guardians and babysitters. In the same way, the people of God were slaves under the law—though heirs, still under

RECEPTION HISTORY

"The Elements of the World": A Sri Lankan Reading

In Galatians 4:3, 9, Paul refers to the *stoicheia* (translated variously as "elements," "principles," or "powers") of the world. Paul designates these entities that once served as wardens over the Galatians as being weak and worthless now that God has sent Christ to redeem his people out from under their bondage (4:4–6). In every era there is the potential for cultural *stoicheia* to get woven into one's Christian theology and practice in an unhealthy way.

Some Sri Lankan Christians today have become aware that certain aspects of their Christian understanding may have more to do with the influence of Western Christian cultural elements (*stoicheia*) than with the core of Christianity itself. These Christians continue to wrestle with how the spiritual import of these cultural forces informs their unique identity as Sri Lankan Christians, which as powers no longer define their identity in Christ.[2]

the authority of a babysitter. But then the Son of God came to enable others to be adopted by God. Adoption means that now we are sons of God—adult sons, not children—and so we are no longer under the babysitter of the law. And since we are sons, the Spirit of God's Son is in our hearts calling out "*Abba*, Father!" This means that we know God as Father from our hearts, not just from our adopted status. Believers are no longer slaves to the law, or anything else, but are sons of God and heirs of God (4:1–7).

Back to the Galatians

■ READ GALATIANS 4:8–20 ■

The Galatians used to be slaves, but now that they have become known by God, should they turn back to slavery? Because they are insisting on the observation of Jewish ritual customs, Paul wonders if he has wasted his energy on the Galatians (4:8–11). This is an extraordinary thing to say, something that he says to no other congregation—not even the messed-up Corinthians!

Though the Galatians first received Paul as an angel of God ("angel" means "messenger"), he worries that he has become their enemy (4:14–16). Paul describes himself like a mother in labor pain, waiting for his child to be born—that is, waiting for Christ to be formed in the Galatians (4:19). They have not yet "arrived," and this causes Paul anguish and distress.

Two Covenants, Two Mothers

■ READ GALATIANS 4:21–31 ■

Paul launches into an extended, and sometimes confusing, illustration that employs typology—things of old point forward to things today. The illustration is about the two sons of Abraham: Ishmael, born of the slave Hagar; and Isaac, born of Abraham's (free) wife, Sarah. Paul points to these two mothers and draws a parallel to two covenants. The covenant of Moses, established at Mount Sinai, corresponds to Hagar and bears children born into slavery. And this also corresponds to the Jerusalem of Paul's day, whose citizens are in slavery to the law of Moses (4:21–25).

But "the Jerusalem above is free, and she is our mother" (4:26). Paul refers to the heavenly Jerusalem, which does not bear children into slavery. Then he quotes from Isaiah 54:1 to make the point

---

THEOLOGICAL ISSUES

Sons of God . . . But What about Women?

When Paul describes believers as "sons of God in Christ Jesus" (3:26; 4:6–7), he is not being sexist. His intention is not to exclude women, but rather to press a theological point. Later in chapter 4 he will discuss two sons born to Abraham: one from the slave woman Hagar and the other from his barren wife, Sarah (4:21–31). By calling believers "sons," Paul is drawing a connection with the sons of Abraham. Those who believe in the promise are the true sons of Abraham, unlike those born of the flesh. Moreover, God sent "the Spirit of his Son into our hearts" (4:6). That is, the Spirit of Jesus is in us, which makes us sons of God. Our sonship is a sharing in the sonship of Jesus. This is why Paul refers to all believers as sons, even though these "sons" are male and female.

Figure 15.4. *Hagar in the Wilderness* by Camille Corot

The Metropolitan Museum of Art. Rogers Fund, 1938.

that it is the barren woman who will bear many children (4:27). Abraham's wife, Sarah, was barren and yet miraculously gave birth to Isaac, whose line brought many descendants for Abraham. This was in fulfillment of God's promise to Abraham, and this is the key difference between Hagar's and Sarah's sons. Hagar's son was born naturally, as a result of the flesh, but Sarah's son was born miraculously, as a result of the promise (4:28). Christians are children of the free woman, not of the slave (4:31). That is, they are born of the promise of God to Abraham (the first covenant), not born under the law (the second covenant).

All of this underscores the fact that these gentile Galatians do not live under the covenant of Moses and therefore are not required to keep its law. Rather than being slaves to the law, they are the free sons of Abraham and ought to live as such.

Freedom!

■ READ GALATIANS 5:1–15 ■

Christ sets slaves free, so the Galatians should not put themselves under the law and become slaves again (5:1). Only faith in Christ can justify someone and make them right with God. Getting circumcised cannot do that, nor can adopting any Jewish practice prescribed by the law of Moses (5:2–6). In fact, the issue is much more serious than whether a believer should get circumcised or not; Paul puts it bluntly: "You who are trying to be justified by the law are alienated from Christ; you have fallen from grace" (5:4). Again, unlike his rebuke of any other congregation, Paul questions whether the Galatians are saved at all. But this is not because they are any worse in character or morality; it is because they have started to alter the gospel message itself. And as Paul said earlier, anyone who preaches a different gospel is accursed (1:8–9).

Paul wonders who has been preaching this false message to the Galatians, and he expects that they will be punished for it (5:7–10). He even wishes that they would "mutilate" themselves (5:12)! This is a play on the word for circumcision, since these teachers have insisted that gentiles become circumcised. It is an unusually harsh statement, but one that shows how serious their false message is. It harms other people, and Paul expects that there will be consequences for these messengers too.

The Galatians have been called to freedom in Christ, not slavery to the law. But freedom should not be used as an excuse for sin; instead, it is an opportunity for them to love one another (5:13–15).

Spirit vs. Flesh

■ READ GALATIANS 5:16–26 ■

Having argued in detail about the place of the law, justification by faith, and the sonship of believers, Paul turns now to address the way believers ought to live. After beginning with the Spirit (3:3), believers are to continue by the Spirit and not the flesh. If they walk by the Spirit, they will not be driven by what the flesh wants (5:16). These two are opposed to each other, with works of the flesh being things such as sexual immorality, idolatry, jealousy, factionalism, and so forth. People who live according to the flesh as their characteristic mode of existence will not inherit the kingdom of God; that is, they reveal themselves not to be the children of Abraham after all (5:17–21).

But walking by the Spirit will produce the Spirit's fruit, such as love, patience, faithfulness, self-control, and so forth (5:22–23). If you belong to Christ, the flesh has been crucified with him along with its passions and desires, and so believers are to keep in step with the Spirit instead of following what the flesh wants (5:24–25).

This whole discussion about the Spirit versus flesh is the outworking of the theological issue that has occupied most of the letter. Believers received

The Law of Christ

Love is the "law" of Christ. This is clear from the context of Galatians, but it also connects to the law of Moses and what Jesus says about the law. The Ten Commandments (itself a summary of the whole law) can be summarized as love for God and love for neighbor. Indeed, this is exactly how Jesus summarized the law (Matt. 22:34–40). Believers are not required to submit to the law of Moses, because its demands have now been fulfilled in Christ (3:10–13), but the intent of the law can be lived out by loving God and loving neighbor. This is why Paul says that carrying one another's burdens fulfills the law of Christ (6:2). It is love in action.

Israel and God, the Church and Christ

Orthodox Christian confession has always maintained the divinity of Jesus Christ; he is "God from God" (**Nicene Creed**). In the modern era several scholars have studied the ways in which the New Testament presents this divine Christology in light of the simultaneous Christian commitment to monotheism. There is only one God, yet Jesus is also God. How does the New Testament understand this complex idea?

Richard Bauckham has argued that the New Testament shows that Jesus "shares the divine identity" through his actions.[3] Larry Hurtado has argued that the idea of worship is central, and that the New Testament shows that the worship and devotion that should alone be given to God is also given to Jesus.[4] Chris Tilling has suggested that neither of these ideas is sufficient to understand the New Testament's divine Christology.[5] The strongest argument, Tilling proposes, is that Jews understood there to be a special *relationship* between God and Israel, and that Paul uses this same language to describe the relationship of Christ to the church. That is, the language used in the Old Testament and Second Temple Jewish texts to describe the unique relationship between God and Israel is now used in the same way to describe the relationship between the risen Christ and believers, creating a powerful parallel. This, then, shows that for Paul and the rest of the New Testament, Jesus is divine; to call him "Lord" is not an accident or coincidence, even as God is called "Lord."

the Spirit by faith, not by works of the law. After beginning with the Spirit, they do not finish by the flesh (3:2–3). This was Paul's way of introducing the role of faith, not works of the law, in establishing right standing with God. And so, since believers received the Spirit by faith, not through works of the flesh, now they are to continue in that same path, following the Spirit, not the flesh.

The Law of Christ

■ READ GALATIANS 6:1–10 ■

Though Paul has spent much of the letter arguing that Christians do not need to submit to the law of Moses, he says that carrying one another's burdens will fulfill "the law of Christ" (6:2). This is a play on the term "law," since technically there is no "law" of Christ. But no doubt Paul means that *love* is "the law of Christ."

Such love will mean that believers will want to help a fellow believer who is going astray. They are to restore such a person gently (6:1). They will carry one another's burdens and assess themselves honestly, without comparison to one another (6:2–5). What you reap is what you sow. The person who "sows to his flesh" will reap destruction. That is, the one who lives according to the flesh will experience the destructive consequences of that way of life. But the one who lives according to the Spirit will reap eternal life (6:6–8). Believers should do good for all, as opportunities arise (6:9).

Final Encouragements

■ READ GALATIANS 6:11–18 ■

Paul warns the Galatians one more time about those who are trying to get them circumcised. The truth is that even those who are urging circumcision don't keep the law properly but want to boast in the Galatians' "flesh." But Paul will not boast in anything except the cross of Christ; the world has been crucified to him and he to the world. In the end, neither circumcision nor lack of circumcision is relevant—"what matters instead is a new creation" (6:12–15). The crucial point is whether someone has been made anew in Christ and through the Spirit. Keeping the law, getting circumcised, or anything else misses that point.

Implementation—Reading Galatians as Christian Scripture Today

Dramatic. Bold. Fiery. These are just some ways to describe Paul's Letter to the Galatians. It is intense, for sure. But more important than these is the clear call for the preservation of the true gospel. Faith in Christ alone is how people are reconciled to God. It is not through belonging to a particular people group, observing certain customs, or obeying difficult rules. Christ became the curse of the law for us, so that we might not be condemned for our failure to keep God's standards.

Moreover, those who trust in Christ are the inheritors of the promises to Abraham and have become the children of God. And as God's children, believers are free and should not submit again to slavery. But their freedom is to be used for love, not for excess, as they walk by the Spirit rather than by the flesh.

Galatians continues to instruct the church centuries after the Protestant Reformation, and millennia after the problems in Galatia. Though circumcision and keeping the law may not be debated within the church as they once were, the principles behind Paul's letter still stand. To add anything to the gospel is to lose the gospel. To add anything to Christ is to lose Christ.

KEY VERSES IN GALATIANS

- But even if we or an angel from heaven should preach to you a gospel contrary to what we have preached to you, a curse be on him! 1:8
- Christ redeemed us from the curse of the law by becoming a curse for us, because it is written, "Cursed is everyone who is hung on a tree." 3:13
- There is no Jew or Greek, slave or free, male and female; since you are all one in Christ Jesus. 3:28
- I say then, walk by the Spirit and you will certainly not carry out the desire of the flesh. For the flesh desires what is against the Spirit, and the Spirit desires what is against the flesh; these are opposed to each other, so that you don't do what you want. 5:16–17
- Carry one another's burdens; in this way you will fulfill the law of Christ. 6:2

Christian Reading Questions

1. Read Galatians 1:13–2:10 and compare it with Acts 9:1–30; 15:1–35. What parallels do you find? What tensions exist between the two?

2. Put into your own words the argument of Galatians 3. Give special attention to how the promises to Abraham relate to the law of Moses and how Jesus's death fits in.

3. What is the difference between "the present Jerusalem" and "the Jerusalem above" (Gal. 4:25–26)?

4. What does it mean to "walk by the Spirit" (Gal. 5:16)? Pay attention to the wider context of chapter 5.

CHAPTER SIXTEEN

Ephesus

Pisidian
Antioch

Miletus

PHRYGIA

Iconium

Lystra

The Letter
to the Ephesians

Orientation

Ephesians is a majestic letter. The great Protestant Reformer John Calvin
regarded it as his favorite book of the Bible. Samuel
Taylor Coleridge, the English poet and literary
critic, described it as "one of the divinest composi-
tions of man." Leading twentieth-century biblical
scholar F. F. Bruce called it "the quintessence of
Paulinism," while contemporary commentators regard it as one of the most significant documents ever
written.

    Ephesians has played a pivotal role in the
theology of the church throughout the ages, providing major contributions to themes such as union

HISTORICAL MATTERS

The Historical Origins
of Ephesians

Author: Paul, but this is disputed (see
the sidebar "The Authorship of
Ephesians")

Date: AD 61–62

Location: Most likely Rome

Setting: Paul is imprisoned, mostly
likely in Rome.

LITERARY NOTES

The Authorship of Ephesians

Ephesians claims to be written by Paul (1:1; 3:1), and for most
of church history this was not disputed. Currently, however,
many scholars regard the letter as **pseudonymous** (it claims to
be written by Paul but actually was written by someone else).
Doubts about authorship have been raised on linguistic, stylis-
tic, and theological grounds. While the language of Ephesians
is somewhat distinct when compared to Paul's "undisputed"
letters, it is not so different as to necessitate a different author.

We do not have enough of Paul's writings to make a scientific
judgment about that. Theologically, the letter is similar to
Colossians (also disputed), but its emphases are quite different from Romans and Galatians. While the issues are complex,
Ephesians is better regarded as an authentic, late writing that
complements Paul's earlier writings by setting the work of
Christ in a cosmic, universal context.

Figure 16.1. Location of Ephesus

with Christ, **predestination**, salvation, grace, the church, Jew-gentile relations, marriage, and **spiritual warfare**. This short letter has left a huge legacy. 🏺 🏺 📖

HISTORICAL MATTERS

In Captivity

Ephesians is one of the Captivity Letters, having been written during one of Paul's imprisonments (see 3:1; 4:1; 6:20). He wrote the letter late in life, around AD 61–62, most likely during his imprisonment in Rome. If, however, Ephesians was written while Paul was imprisoned in Ephesus itself or Caesarea, then its dates would be around 55 or 58, respectively. Paul spent three years in Ephesus (52–55), longer than any other location, on his third missionary journey (Acts 19).

HISTORICAL MATTERS

Ephesus

Ephesus was on the western coast of modern-day Turkey. It was the capital city of the Roman province of Asia, and the third biggest city in the empire at the time. It was also a religious hub, being home to the famed temple of the goddess Artemis (Acts 19:27)—one of the seven wonders of the world—and was the center of the imperial cult for worship of the emperor. Even though the letter probably was not written for the Ephesians only, the city's religious and political importance affected the entire region.

Exploration—Reading Ephesians

Every Spiritual Blessing in Christ

■ READ EPHESIANS 1:1–14 ■

After a standard greeting (1:1–2), Paul begins an extended doxology that is introduced and summarized by verse 3: "Praise be to the God and Father of our Lord Jesus Christ, who has blessed us in the heavenly realms with every spiritual blessing in Christ" (NIV). The heavenly realms and spiritual blessings are a key focus of the letter. Moreover, these blessings come us to "in Christ"; union with Christ is a central theme. Several blessings are mentioned in the doxology, including predestination, adoption, redemption, forgiveness of sins, and the Holy Spirit. These blessings are bestowed on us "in him" (1:4–13).

The doxology includes what are arguably the theme verses of the letter: "He made known to us the mystery of his will, according to his good pleasure that he purposed in Christ as a plan for the right time—to bring everything together in Christ, both things in heaven and things on earth in him" (1:9–10). Everything in heaven and earth is brought together in Christ. Christ is the centerpiece and central coherence of the entire cosmos, which finds its purpose and goal in him.

At Ephesus

Since the best and earliest manuscripts do not include the phrase "at Ephesus" in the opening address, "To the faithful saints in Christ Jesus *at Ephesus*" (1:1), the letter probably is not written to the church in Ephesus directly. This would explain why there are no personal references, no mention of problems in the church, and nothing else that indicates that Paul is addressing a particular congregation. Since Paul spent three years in Ephesus on his third missionary journey (Acts 19), it would be strange not to greet his friends if the letter was meant for that church in particular. Instead, Ephesians reads as a general letter that can easily be circulated to multiple congregations (cf. Col. 4:16). Most likely, the letter was sent to churches in Asia Minor in the general vicinity of Ephesus, and over time it became associated with the most important city of that region, which is why later scribes added "at Ephesus" to the text.

In Christ

"In Christ" can mean a variety of things, depending on the context. Sometimes it means that God has acted "in Christ" for us, with Jesus as the mediator of God's will. Sometimes it describes people ("my brother in Christ"); this is Paul's way of saying that someone is a Christian. The phrase "in Christ" is only one way that Paul indicates one of his most important themes: union with Christ. This theme can be understood through four terms: union, participation, identification, and incorporation.

At three points in the doxology we see that these spiritual blessings are "to the praise of his glorious grace" and "to the praise of his glory" (1:6, 12, 14). God's plan for the salvation and blessing of humanity has praise as its ultimate goal. In the end, believers are part of a grand plan that results in the praise and glory of God in Christ.

Psalms and Isaiah

Paul alludes to several psalms and Isaiah to show that believers are united to God's anointed king in his victory over God's enemies. Christ is now enthroned in heaven, seated above competing rulers, authorities, and powers (1:20–22; 4:8; cf. Pss. 110:1; 8:6; 68:18). When the people of Christ take their stand against these powers (6:10–17), they do so with the **armor of God** and of his Messiah, as seen in Isaiah 11:5; 52:7; 59:17.

Adoption as Sons and Daughters

In English translations, Ephesians 1:5 has long been translated with some version of "adopted as a son" or "adopted to sonship." This accords with the practice of Roman law whereby the inheritance was passed through the male line. In the late twentieth and early twenty-first centuries there has been greater recognition of the difficulties this kind of translation creates for female readers. Claire Powell describes it this way: "Nowadays it may be somewhat confusing for women to read this" language of adoption as sons. Paul's point is not meant to exclude women. Rather, Paul's point in calling salvation "adoption" is to say that through Jesus believers obtain "the privileged relationship of the beloved child to a committed parent." In Christianity, the inheritance of God is given to all who believe, male and female, slave and free, rich and poor. Therefore, it is probably clearer in modern culture to use "children" as some translations like the NRSV now do: "adoption as his children."[1]

The Structure of Ephesians

The letter divides neatly into two halves, with the first half (chaps. 1–3) offering a profound theological treatise centered on God's reconciling work in Christ. God brings salvation by making spiritually dead people alive with Christ. As a consequence, Jews and gentiles—formerly enemies—are brought together in Christ. The second half (chaps. 4–6) applies the theological argument of the first half to the life of the church, households, and individual believers. While there are still some major theological insights to be found in this half of the letter, it is primarily about living together as members of Christ's body, while resisting the spiritual forces of evil.

Prayer

■ READ EPHESIANS 1:15–23 ■

Paul then prays that God would give his readers "the Spirit of wisdom and revelation in the knowledge of him" (1:17). He wants them to know the riches of their glorious inheritance and God's power that raised Jesus Christ to his right hand, above all (1:18–21). God has put all things under Christ's feet and made him head of the church, his body (1:22–23).

We see here the importance of *knowledge*: wisdom, revelation, knowing God better, and knowing God's power are important for believers. We also see the exalted Christ towering above all competing spiritual forces.

Salvation

■ READ EPHESIANS 2:1–10 ■

The argument of the letter properly begins in chapter 2, with the assertion that prior to Christ, all people were "dead in [their] trespasses and sins" (2:1). Walking according to the world and the ruler of the air (the devil), all people live for the gratification of the flesh (2:2–3). This is a hopeless situation, since spiritually dead people are unable to please God or reach out to him on their own.

God alone can change the situation. He makes people alive with Christ, raising them up and seating them with him in the heavenly place. The mechanism for salvation is participation with Christ. His resurrection becomes our resurrection, his ascension becomes our ascension, and we go from being dead and buried to being seated with God in heaven. Since it is God's work that makes us alive with Christ, it is by grace we are saved, through

Figure 16.2. Statue of Artemis

faith (2:4–9). Our works cannot achieve salvation; rather, we become God's workmanship, "created in Christ Jesus for good works" (2:10).

Reconciliation

■ READ EPHESIANS 2:11–22 ■

The vertical reconciliation with God in Christ has horizontal implications, which Paul spells out for Jews and gentiles (2:11–22). The gentiles were far off, strangers to Israel and God's promises (2:11–12). But now Christ has made the two (Jew and gentile) one by making peace through the cross (2:13–16).

While at one time the gentiles had only limited access to the presence of God in the temple, now they are built together with believing Jews into a holy temple, in which God dwells by the Spirit (2:18–19). This is an extraordinary reversal of fortune for gentiles; now in Christ they are coheirs and equal partners with believing Jews.

Mystery Revealed

■ READ EPHESIANS 3:1–21 ■

Paul reflects on his own role in proclaiming Christ to the gentiles, and how God has revealed a formerly hidden secret: in Christ the gentiles are coheirs and partakers of the promise (3:1–6). The "promise" likely refers back to God's promise to Abraham that all peoples of the earth would be blessed through him (Gen. 12:1–3). A big question mark left hanging at the end of the Old Testament is how exactly the peoples of the earth will be blessed through Abraham. Paul's point is that in Christ

THEOLOGICAL ISSUES

Participation with Christ

Our *participation* with Christ is seen clearly in 2:1–10 as Paul says that believers have been made alive *with Christ*, raised *with Christ*, and seated *with Christ* in the heavenly realms. By faith believers are connected to Christ so that we participate in the events of his narrative. We hitch our wagon to his wagon, so that where he goes we go too. He pulls his people through death, resurrection, and ascension, so that believers can say we have been put to death with Christ, raised to new life with Christ, and elevated with Christ to the heavens. Participation is a key mechanism in the way that God saves his people.

CANONICAL CONNECTIONS

The Mystery of Christ

Related to the Jew-gentile theme is the unveiling of the "mystery" of Christ (Eph. 3:3–7). This refers to how God would fulfill his promises to Abraham, that all peoples would be blessed through him (Gen. 12:3). The Old Testament does not directly answer how this will happen but says only that it *will* happen in the fullness of time, and so it remained a mystery as to how God would do it. Though Paul does not spell this out in Ephesians, he sees gentile salvation in Abrahamic terms in Romans 4 and Galatians 4. The fact that Jews *and* gentiles can now be God's people through faith in Christ answers the mystery that was left unexplained for generations past. Now it is clear how the gentiles will be blessed through Abraham: through faith in Christ.

CANONICAL CONNECTIONS

Peace between the Nations

When Paul discusses the reconciliation of Jews and gentiles in 2:13–17, he alludes to Isaiah 57:19, which points to a future peace between the nations, Israel, and God. This is a common theme in Isaiah (2:2–4; 11:10; 19:24–25; 45:14, 22; 51:4–5; 52:10; 55:5; 56:6–7; 60:11; 66:18–23) and sometimes is connected to the idea of a new creation (66:18–23). Paul regards the union of Jew and gentile as the creation of a new person (2:15), and the new-creation theme is seen throughout Ephesians (2:10; 3:9; 4:13, 22, 24).

THEOLOGICAL ISSUES

Incorporation

Incorporation is a major motif in Ephesians 4, as Paul speaks about believers as parts of the *body of Christ*. Our individual union with Christ means that we are also united to one another. As incorporated members of Christ, each body part has a role to play to serve the overall body.

Ecclesiology: The Theology of the Church

Ephesians presents the most developed theology of the church (**ecclesiology**) in the New Testament. Beginning with salvation by grace through faith (2:1–10), Paul moves immediately to the reconciliation of Jew and gentile (2:11–22). In chapter 4 the church is described as the body of Christ, with Christ as its head (4:15–16) and with other parts of the body performing different functions, such as apostles, prophets, evangelists, and pastor-teachers (4:11). There is *unity* and *diversity* within the church: a body is obviously one, but a body also has different parts, working together for the proper function of the body. In 5:22–33 the church is regarded as the bride of Christ. The bride metaphor is common in the Old Testament, speaking of the marriage between God and Israel (e.g., Jer. 2:2; Ezek. 16; Hosea 1–3). It is striking that the image now refers to Christ as the husband and the church as the bride. Marriage emphasizes Christ's love and devotion to the church. He dies for her (5:2) and is her savior (5:23). He continues to nourish and care for her (5:29) and wants to present her pure and holy (5:26), beautiful and glorious (5:27).

Ephesians and Colossians

Why is Ephesians so similar to Colossians? Is one an expansion of the other? Is one a summary of the other? Are they written by two different people—Paul and an imitator? An interesting fact is that the Old Testament quotations and allusions found in Ephesians are missing in Colossians. Perhaps this means that Paul wrote Colossians first and then decided to expand it for a general audience and with deeper scriptural support. While there does seem to be a genetic relationship (siblings or cousins?), the two letters are also somewhat independent of each other. They have differences in purpose, audience, and some content.

that question has now been answered. Now that all people are saved through faith—and not through membership in the nation of Israel—the gentiles will be blessed in Christ.

The Body of Christ

■ READ EPHESIANS 4:1–32 ■

Paul begins the second half of the letter by stressing the unity of the body of Christ. We share in the one body, one Spirit, one hope, one Lord, one faith, one baptism, and one God and Father of all (4:1–6).

But the attention then turns to the necessary diversity within the body. From his ascended and victorious position, Christ gave grace to each one as he apportioned it (4:7–10). In particular, he gave the apostles, prophets, evangelists, pastors, and teachers (4:11). Their role is to equip the saints for the work of ministry, which is building up the body of Christ (4:12). The goal of all this is that the body will attain unity and maturity, with members no longer being little children who are tossed around by false teaching and human craftiness (4:13–14).

As members of the body, believers are to put off the old self and replace their former practices and attitudes with godly alternatives that will build others up. Instead of lying, believers should speak the truth (4:25); instead of stealing, they should work and give to others (4:28); instead of being consumed by bitterness and malice, they should be kind, compassionate, and forgiving (4:31–32).

Walking in Love, Light, and Wisdom

■ READ EPHESIANS 5:1–17 ■

Children imitate their father, and so believers are to walk in love, just as Christ loved us and gave himself up for us (5:1–2). Paul leans further on the "walking" metaphor as he highlights the incompatibility of deeds of darkness for the children of God (5:3–14). Believers are now light in the Lord and ought to walk as children of light (5:8–9). Not only will they take no part in the works of darkness, but also they will expose them (5:11). Believers are to consider carefully how they walk, choosing to walk in wisdom (5:15), redeeming the time, and understanding the will of the Lord (5:16–17).

Filled with the Spirit

■ READ EPHESIANS 5:18–6:9 ■

Rather than getting drunk on wine, believers are to be filled with the Spirit (5:18). The Spirit-filled life consists of speaking to one another in psalms, hymns, and spiritual songs, giving thanks to the Father, and submitting to one another (5:19–21).

Submission becomes the pivot point into the household code of Ephesians, and Paul spells out a series of asymmetrical relationships, with wives submitting to husbands, children obeying their parents, and slaves obeying their masters. Husbands are to love their wives as Christ loves the church, fathers are to instruct their children without provocation, and masters are to remember that they too have a master in heaven (5:22–6:9).

Spiritual Warfare

■ READ EPHESIANS 6:10–20 ■

The concluding section of the letter acknowledges that believers' battle is not against flesh and blood, but against the spiritual forces of darkness (6:10–12). Believers are to take up the whole armor of God to stand against evil, donning the belt of truth, the breastplate of righteousness, the sandals of peace, the shield of faith, the helmet of salvation, and the sword of the Spirit, which is the word of God (6:13–17).

These well-known images of the Roman soldier also have a background in Isaiah, as the Lord and his Messiah battle their enemies. The armor of God is shared with his people so they are fully equipped to take their stand.

THEOLOGICAL ISSUES

Married to Christ

Our *union* with Christ is emphasized in 5:22–33, where Paul connects human marriage to the marriage between Christ and the church: Christ is the husband, and the church is the bride. He gave himself up for her, and he nourishes and cherishes her. When Paul cites Genesis 2:24 in 5:31, saying that a man will leave his parents and be united to his wife and the two will become one, Paul says that he is actually talking about Christ and the church (5:32).

THEOLOGICAL ISSUES

Mutual Submission?

Some interpreters regard 5:21, "Submit to one another out of reverence for Christ" (NIV), as teaching *mutual submission* being required between husbands and wives, parents and children, and slaves and masters. Others interpret "submit to one another" to refer to submission as appropriate according to each set of relationships (wives to husbands, children to parents, and slaves to masters) and therefore not as an endorsement of mutual submission.

Shutterstock / Sanit Fuangnakhon

Figure 16.3. Statue of a Roman soldier

High Impact

Ephesians had a significant impact on the early church, seen in the letter's many quotations in early Christian literature and its influence on Christian liturgy and piety through the centuries. At the end of the fourth century, John Chrysostom declared that it is full of Paul's sublime thoughts and doctrines. Ephesians also played a significant role in the theology of the Reformation. John Calvin preached a series of forty-eight sermons on the letter from May 1558 to March 1559. Through Calvin and others the letter has wielded significant influence on the Reformed tradition of Protestantism.

Final Greetings

■ READ EPHESIANS 6:21–24 ■

Ephesians closes with a short greeting that does not mention any of Paul's readers by name. The only person named is Tychicus, whom Paul apparently sent to deliver the letter.

Implementation—Reading Ephesians as Christian Scripture Today

The theological contribution of Ephesians is hard to overstate. It presents a view of the cosmic Christ, with Jesus as the central reconciling figure of the entire cosmos, with all human history seen within a divine plan that spans before creation to its consummation, and with all people caught up in the intersection between worldly and spiritual forces.

While the Protestant tradition has tended to focus on themes like justification by faith and the atoning death of Jesus, Ephesians pushes us to reflect on complementary themes such as the importance of union with Christ, Jesus's ascension to the right hand of the Father, and the reality of spiritual warfare.

The letter provides a clear exposition of salvation by grace through faith, and the reconciliation of Jew and gentile in Christ. The nature of the church as the body of Christ is instructive, as is the household code. All of these issues continue to shape the church's theology and practice in profound ways.

KEY VERSES IN EPHESIANS

- Blessed is the God and Father of our Lord Jesus Christ, who has blessed us with every spiritual blessing in the heavens in Christ. 1:3
- But God, who is rich in mercy, because of his great love that he had for us, made us alive with Christ even though we were dead in trespasses. You are saved by grace! 2:4–5
- Therefore, be imitators of God, as dearly loved children, and walk in love, as Christ also loved us and gave himself for us, a sacrificial and fragrant offering to God. 5:1–2
- Put on the full armor of God so that you can take your stand against the schemes of the devil. For our struggle is not against flesh and blood, but against the rulers, against the authorities, against the cosmic powers of this darkness, against evil, spiritual forces in the heavens. 6:11–12

Christian Reading Questions

1. Read the doxology in Ephesians 1:3–14 and contemplate how each spiritual blessing mentioned there is mediated to believers through Jesus Christ. How do the blessings come "in him"?
2. Articulate the logic driving the argument from Ephesians 2:1 to 4:16. How does "salvation by grace through faith" construct the body of Christ?
3. Read Colossians and make a list of similarities and differences between it and Ephesians.
4. Read Galatians and notice the differences in purpose, tone, and argument between it and Ephesians.

The Letter to the Philippians

Orientation

If Galatians is Paul's angry letter, Philippians is his letter of pure joy. It is full of sweet affection, genuine appreciation, and heartfelt love. Paul holds the Philippians close to his heart, as they have proved themselves to be his genuine partners in the gospel, showing their concern for him in various ways. And though Paul is in chains as he writes, possibly close to death, he is still able to say, "Rejoice in the Lord always!"

This letter is famous for its hymn concerning Christ's humility and exaltation: Jesus demonstrated true humility by lowering himself for the sake of others, then God lifted him above all others. It is also known for Paul's critique of "confidence in the flesh," in which he lists his own credentials as a faithful Jew but then dismisses them as rubbish compared to knowing Christ. The righteousness that comes from God is based on faith in Christ, not on human credentials and qualifications.

HISTORICAL MATTERS

The Historical Origins of Philippians

Author: Paul

Date: AD 61–62

Location: Rome

Setting: Paul is imprisoned in Rome, under **imperial guard**.

HISTORICAL MATTERS

Philippi

Paul visited Philippi on his second missionary journey (AD 49 or 50), in his first visit to Europe. It was then part of Macedonia, but now is located in northern Greece. Paul went there because of a vision he had of a Macedonian man pleading with him to come (Acts 16:6–10). This letter was written while Paul was in captivity (1:7, 13–14, 17) in Rome (4:22), around 61–62.

262

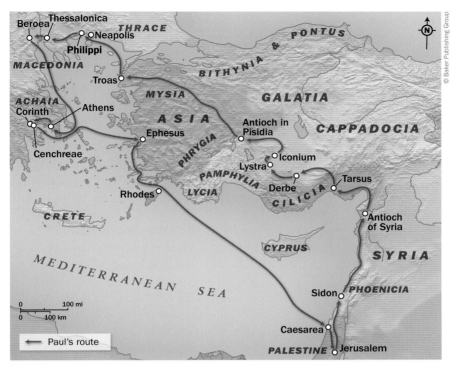

Figure 17.1. Location of Philippi

Exploration—Reading Philippians

Partnership in the Gospel

▓ READ PHILIPPIANS 1:1–11 ▓

The greeting of this letter focuses on servanthood, as Paul and Timothy are described as "servants of Christ Jesus," and among their readers in Philippi the **overseers** and deacons are singled out for special mention (1:1). This focus continues into the thanksgiving (1:3–11) as Paul emphasizes the theme of partnership. Paul gives thanks for all the Philippians because of their partnership in the gospel (1:3–5). They are in Paul's heart as his partners in grace, "both in my imprisonment and in the defense and confirmation of the gospel" (1:7). He misses them deeply (1:8), and he prays that the Philippians will continue to grow in love, knowledge, and discernment, in order to be pure and blameless in the day of Christ, filled with righteousness through Christ to the praise and glory of God (1:9–11). 📖

© Baker Publishing Group

LITERARY NOTES

The Structure of Philippians

This joyous letter has its tone set with Paul's effusive thanksgiving for the Philippians (1:1–11). He then addresses the priority of the gospel for Paul (1:12–26) and the importance of the Philippians conducting themselves in a manner worthy of the gospel (1:27–2:18). In Timothy and Epaphroditus, Paul commends two stellar servants of the gospel (2:19–30), while urging that false teachers must be resisted and opposed (3:1–21). The letter concludes with final exhortations, thanksgiving, and greetings (4:1–23).

A Picture of Paul's Life

Throughout the history of the church some parts of the Bible have had a more widespread impact than others. The Sermon on the Mount or Romans, for example, is easier to find in the history of interpretation than Amos or Jude. Despite its theological riches, one is hard-pressed to find a lot of commentaries or sermon series on Philippians. There are parts of Philippians that are obviously very important, especially the Christ hymn in 2:5–11, but in general, much of Philippians was overlooked as a candidate for commentary.

However, when one steps back and considers the picture of who Paul was and what his ministry was like throughout the church's history, it turns out that Philippians provides a central and beautiful picture. In Philippians we see the joyful apostle who is in chains (1:3–20), the one who is expecting death as gain because it means being with Christ (1:21–23), the zealous Jew who has left this identity behind in comparison to knowing the risen Christ (3:1–14), the one who understands our citizenship to be in heaven (3:20), and the one who has learned to be content in all circumstances (4:11). This picture of Paul's life has inspired and shaped the lives of God's people throughout history.[1]

He Emptied Himself

That Jesus "emptied himself" (2:7) when he became a man has caused much debate over the centuries. Some have understood this self-emptying, or *kenosis* (from a Greek word translated as "emptied"), to mean that Jesus gave up his divinity when he became human; that is, he stopped being God in order to be man. But the early church rejected this understanding, asserting that Jesus gave up his *divine privileges* in order to become human but never stopped being fully God. Instead of enjoying his position of "equality with God" (2:6), Jesus humbled himself to become a man, a servant, and to die (2:7–8).

To Live Is Christ, to Die Is Gain

◼ READ PHILIPPIANS 1:12–30 ◼

Paul is imprisoned because of Christ, and he regards this as good for the gospel, since everyone (including the whole imperial guard) knows why he is in chains (1:12–13). This has given confidence to others in their preaching, though not all preach with pure motives (1:14–17). But Paul's only concern is that Christ is preached, whatever the motivation (1:18).

As for Paul himself, he hopes that Christ will be honored in his body, whether by going on living or by his death (1:20). If he goes on living, it is for Christ; if he dies, it is his personal gain (1:21). He would prefer to die and be with Christ, but he thinks he will continue living for now for the sake of others (1:22–26).

As for the Philippians, as citizens of heaven, they are to live in a way that is worthy of the gospel of Christ (1:27). This means being united in one spirit, wrestling together for the faith, and not giving in to fear (1:27–28). Sharing with Paul in the same struggles, it has been granted to the Philippians to suffer for Christ as well as to believe in him (1:29–30).

Show Humility, Like Christ

◼ READ PHILIPPIANS 2:1–11 ◼

If the Philippians experience encouragement, consolation, fellowship, affection, and mercy because of being in Christ, Paul wants them to be united in spirit and purpose (2:1–2). For this to work, believers must not act out of selfish ambition, but in humility they are to look to the interests of others (2:3–4).

Unlike false modesty, genuine humility involves lowering oneself in order to lift up others, as Christ demonstrated in his own life. He gave up the privileges of equality with God in order to become a man, in order to serve humanity by his death on a cross (2:5–8). But as Jesus himself taught, those who lower themselves will be exalted, and so God highly exalted Jesus, giving him the name above every name (2:9). Every knee will bow at his name, and every tongue will confess that Christ is Lord (2:10–11). This is a picture of the day on which the glory of Jesus is finally revealed to all, and all beings in heaven and earth will bow their knees in response to his majesty. 📜

Shining Like Stars in the World

▩ READ PHILIPPIANS 2:12–30 ▩

Paul encourages the Philippians that God is working out his will and purpose in their lives, and so they ought to live accordingly (2:12–14). In so doing, as the children of God they will shine like stars in a crooked and perverted world (2:15), holding on to the word of life (2:16).

Stellar examples of believers who shine like stars in the world include Timothy and Epaphroditus, both of whom demonstrate Christlike humility in their concern for others (2:19–30). Timothy genuinely cares for the Philippians' interests, while Epaphroditus nearly died from his illness but was more concerned that the Philippians were worrying about him.

Knowing Christ

▩ READ PHILIPPIANS 3:1–21 ▩

Paul warns against those who insist that gentile believers must be circumcised (3:2). Rather than putting confidence in the flesh (as with circumcision), believers worship by the Spirit (3:3). In comparison to these false teachers, Paul has more reasons for confidence in the flesh than anyone, since he is "a Hebrew born of Hebrews," a Pharisee, formerly a zealous persecutor of the church, and blameless in law keeping (3:4–6). But all of this is nothing compared to knowing Christ (3:7–8).

Instead of relying on the flesh, such as human achievements or Jewish identity, Paul has lost all things but is found in Christ (3:8–9). And in Christ, he has a righteousness that comes from God, not from outward, fleshly practices (3:9). Instead of pursuing further religious qualifications, Paul simply

CANONICAL CONNECTIONS

Isaiah's Servant of the Lord

The Christ hymn in 2:5–11 contains several overtones of Isaiah's servant of the Lord, who "poured out his life unto death" (Isa. 53:12 NIV). This person is highly exalted (Isa. 52:13; Phil. 2:9), takes the form of the servant (Isa. 52:14; Phil. 2:7), and is exalted by God (Isa. 53:12; Phil. 2:9). Isaiah even includes the phrase "every knee will bow, every tongue will swear" (Isa. 45:23; Phil. 2:10–11). Clearly, the hymn regards Jesus as the fulfillment of Isaiah's prophecy of this servant of the Lord.

THEOLOGICAL ISSUES

Confidence in the Flesh

Paul opposes "the dogs," "the evil workers," "those who mutilate the flesh" (3:2). These unflattering terms refer to people who insist that gentile believers should be circumcised and put under the law of Moses. In other words, they think that gentiles need to become Jews in order to follow Christ. He calls this idea "confidence in the flesh," since it relies on physical, outward practices to be right with God. Paul opposes this view in several of his letters, but here he gives it special treatment by drawing attention to his own credentials in Judaism. Although highly qualified in Judaism, he regards these things as meaningless, and in fact as a loss, in comparison to knowing Christ (3:7–8).

THEOLOGICAL ISSUES

Being Found in Christ

Paul lost all things so that he may gain Christ and be "found in him" (3:9). The qualifications in Judaism that once defined him are no more, and Paul is now defined by Christ. His life and identity are found in Christ. He will therefore share in the sufferings of Christ and become conformed to his death (3:10). These ideas indicate Paul's theology of participation with Christ: he has been connected to Christ through faith, and he shares not only in Christ's righteousness and resurrection but also in his sufferings and death. Just as Christ himself became humble to the point of death and then was exalted (2:5–11), so Paul regards his own life taking the same cruciform shape—the way of humiliation, suffering, and death must precede resurrection and exaltation (3:10–11).

RECEPTION HISTORY

Paul, Augustine, and Conversion Narratives

One of the most famous and influential books in Western civilization is Augustine's *Confessions*. If you haven't yet read it, you should. The *Confessions* describes in a very personal and powerful way Augustine's conversion from various philosophies and immoralities to Christianity. Augustine was not the first (or the last) to write such a **conversion narrative**—an autobiographical story of how someone came to see the world differently—but because of his great influence on subsequent history and theology, Augustine's skillful and engaging version had a big impact.

The only person whose conversion had an even bigger impact on the history of the world is the apostle Paul. "Saul" who became "Paul" went from being a zealous and intellectual Jewish leader who tried to kill Christians to becoming Christianity's boldest advocate and the author of more New Testament books than anyone else.

Philippians 3:4–14 contains a microversion of Paul's conversion story (see also Acts 9:1–18; 22:6–16; 26:12–20). In language that could not be more stark or shocking, Paul describes his former life within Judaism (in which he was something of a rock star) as dung and garbage compared to his personal relationship with (knowledge of) Jesus Christ. This vision of radical conversion and commitment to Christ has influenced millions of Christians ever since, providing language to frame the experience of coming to know and follow the risen Christ.

desires to know Christ more deeply, being shaped by his resurrection, sufferings, and death (3:10).

Paul has not yet fulfilled his goal, but he continues to push toward "the prize promised by God's heavenly call in Christ Jesus" (3:12–14). The Christian life is one of constantly moving forward toward this goal, and all mature believers should think in this way (3:15). They should live like Paul, not like the enemies of the cross, who are focused on earthly things and will one day be destroyed (3:17–19).

Instead of being focused on earthly things, believers are citizens of heaven (cf. 1:27) and so "eagerly wait for a Savior from there, the Lord Jesus Christ" (3:20). With loyalty to heaven rather than earth, believers have their eyes fixed there in anticipation of Christ, who will transform their bodies to be like his when he returns (3:21).

Rejoice in the Lord!

■ READ PHILIPPIANS 4:1–9 ■

Paul longs for his readers to stand firm in the Lord, remembering the things he has just talked about (4:1). This will have some implications for everyday life, such as reconciling differences, as Paul wants the two women Euodia and Syntyche to do (4:2–3). Whatever circumstances we might face (and remember that Paul is in prison as he writes), there is reason to "rejoice in the Lord always" (4:4). Believers have no reason for worry, and they ought to entrust their concerns to God in prayer (4:6), who will give peace to our troubled hearts (4:7).

Standing firm in the Lord also means focusing on things that are true, honorable, just, pure, lovely, commendable, excellent, and praiseworthy—following Paul's example (4:8–9).

Figure 17.2. Theater at Philippi

Real Partnership

■ READ PHILIPPIANS 4:10–20 ■

Paul does not hesitate to make his love and appreciation known to the Philippians. They have shown genuine concern for him (4:10) and provided for his needs (4:15–18). While appreciating the Philippians' generosity toward him, he knows how to make do with whatever he has, having learned "the secret of being content" (4:11–12). God supplies Paul's needs (4:13) and will look after the Philippians too (4:19).

Final Greetings

■ READ PHILIPPIANS 4:21–23 ■

The letter concludes with greetings from those with Paul, including "those who belong to Caesar's household," which seems to refer to believers who work for Caesar managing his vast estates (4:22).

Implementation—Reading Philippians as Christian Scripture Today

The letter to the Philippians gives us insight into Paul's heart for people and into what it means to share in partnership in the gospel. Paul does not draw on the Philippians' resources as a disinterested fundraiser, but considers their sharing with him as an expression of love—love for Paul and love for Christ. It encourages us today to consider financial and prayer support for missionaries and other Christian workers as a genuine expression of partnership in their ministry.

CANONICAL CONNECTIONS

A Fragrant Offering

Paul's description of the Philippians' gift as a fragrant offering, an acceptable sacrifice, pleasing to God (4:18) connects to Old Testament ceremonial texts such as Exodus 29:18, in which a sacrificial animal presented to the Lord as a burnt offering is pleasing to him. But here Paul uses such language for a monetary gift, not an animal sacrifice. It seems that, for Paul, Israel's sacrificial system has been transformed and applied to the Christian church so that believers are able to make offerings pleasing to the Lord in more general ways. These are not offered for cleansing from sin (like burnt sacrifices in the Old Testament), but nevertheless are given out of a desire to please the Lord.

Philippians also points to the surpassing glory of the exalted Christ, who humbled himself, suffered, and was lifted up. Believers will share in that same pattern of suffering before glory, and that gives us reason to rejoice in all situations. Though we may suffer, as Paul was indeed suffering when he wrote the letter, we know that suffering is followed by glory.

Moreover, it is through faith in the exalted Christ that we receive righteousness from God. It is not gained through Jewish identity, or any other qualifications or human achievements, but only in Christ. Being found in Christ is the ultimate key to our sense of identity, which can no longer be found in external factors or human status.

KEY VERSES IN PHILIPPIANS

- For me, to live is Christ and to die is gain. 1:21
- Do nothing out of selfish ambition or conceit, but in humility consider others as more important than yourselves. 2:3
- I also consider everything to be a loss in view of the surpassing value of knowing Christ Jesus my Lord. Because of him I have suffered the loss of all things and consider them as dung, so that I may gain Christ and be found in him, not having a righteousness of my own from the law, but one that is through faith in Christ—the righteousness from God based on faith. 3:8–9
- Rejoice in the Lord always. I will say it again: Rejoice! 4:4

Christian Reading Questions

1. Put into your own words what Paul means when he says "to live is Christ and to die is gain" (Phil. 1:21). What might this look like in your own life?

2. Read Philippians 2:1–11, 19–30; 4:10–19 and reflect on what it means to demonstrate true humility in our relationships with others.

3. What might be modern equivalents of Paul's "reasons for confidence in the flesh" (Phil. 3:4–6)?

4. Trace the theme of partnership throughout Philippians. What exactly is partnership, according to Paul, and what does it involve?

CHAPTER EIGHTEEN

The Letter to the Colossians

Orientation

Colossians is often overshadowed by its better-known sister, Paul's Letter to the Ephesians. Since the letters are similar in various ways, Ephesians tends to get the spotlight because it is more comprehensive, teaches salvation by grace, and addresses the nature of the church. But this is unfair, because Colossians has its own message of great importance for the church: Christ is supreme over all creation, and he is fully sufficient for genuine spirituality. No other letter offers as powerful a rebuttal against false forms of spirituality than the Letter to the Colossians.

Exploration—Reading Colossians

The Fruit of the Gospel

▓ READ COLOSSIANS 1:1–14 ▓

Paul and his cosignatory, Timothy, greet the Colossians (1:1–2) and describe their

---

CANONICAL CONNECTIONS

The Historical Origins of Colossians

Author: Paul, but this is disputed for similar reasons as is Ephesians

Date: AD 61–62

Location: Rome

Setting: Paul is imprisoned in Rome, under imperial guard.

LITERARY NOTES

Comparing Colossians and Ephesians

- Colossians (1,583 words) is considerably shorter than Ephesians (2,425 words).
- The two letters share a similar structure, and both can be divided into distinct halves (Col. 1–2; 3–4; Eph. 1–3; 4–6).
- Both were written while Paul was imprisoned (mostly likely) in Rome, around AD 61–62.
- Both give emphasis to participation with Christ, the supremacy of Christ, and the reconciliation of the cosmos in Christ.
- The two letters share several similar phrases.
- Ephesians includes many more references to the Old Testament than does Colossians.
- Both letters' authorship is disputed for similar reasons (see the sidebar "The Authorship of Ephesians" in chap. 16).

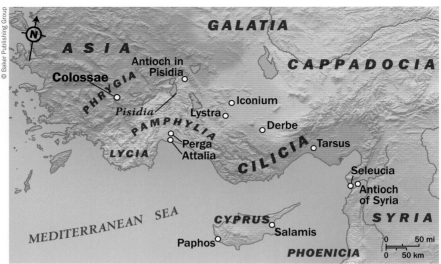

Figure 18.1. Location of Colossae

thankfulness to God for the Colossians' *faith*, *hope*, and *love* (1:3–5)—the hallmarks of the Christian life (cf. 1 Cor. 13:13). Their hope comes from the word of truth, the gospel, which has been bearing fruit among them since it came to them (1:5–8).

Paul and Timothy have been diligent in prayer for the Colossians, asking that they would know God's will and walk worthily of the Lord—continuing to bear fruit, growing in their knowledge of God, and being strengthened by God's power (1:9–11). This strength is for patient endurance as they give thanks to the Father for rescuing them from the domain of darkness and for bringing them into the kingdom of the Son. In the Son, believers are redeemed through the forgiveness of their sins (1:12–14).

The Supremacy of Christ

■ READ COLOSSIANS 1:15–20 ■

Paul launches the argument of the letter with a stunning hymn to the supremacy of Christ. The hymn may have been Paul's own creation or he may have adopted it. Either way, the supremacy of Christ seen in the Christ hymn will play a role in the argument of the letter, as Paul asserts that Christ is superior over any false forms of spirituality or worship.

The Structure of Colossians

Though shorter than Ephesians, Colossians has a similar structure, with the first half (chaps. 1–2) presenting the main theological argument, that Christ is supreme and sufficient, and that the so-called **Colossian heresy** is completely undermined by Christ. This heresy is based on the **elements of the world**, but believers have died with Christ to such things. The second half of the letter (chaps. 3–4) unpacks the implications of dying and rising with Christ: believers are to live in line with things above, where Christ is, rather than earthly things below.

Colossae

Colossae was a small town that once was more important, about one hundred miles east of Ephesus, near the bigger centers of Hierapolis and Laodicea. Paul never visited Colossae, but his message spread there from Ephesus through the Colossian believer Epaphras (also known as Epaphroditus).

Christ is the image of the invisible God, the firstborn over all creation (1:15), meaning that he is the ultimate human in the image of God, he reveals the invisible God to humanity, and he is the Son who will inherit everything.

Everything in creation was made through Christ, including seen and unseen powers. He is preeminent over all things and holds everything together (1:16–17). And he has a special relationship with the church as its head and as the firstborn from the dead (1:18). The fullness of God dwells within Christ, and through him God reconciles everything to himself (1:19–20).

The Christ hymn offers a spectacular view of Christ and his supremacy over all creation, which was made through him and for him (1:16).

Reconciliation through Christ

■ READ COLOSSIANS 1:21–2:3 ■

Though alienated from Christ in mind and action, the Colossians have now been reconciled to him through his death so as to be blameless before him (1:21–22). But they must hold on to the hope of the gospel, of which Paul has become a servant (1:23).

As a servant of the gospel Paul suffers many afflictions, which he describes as "completing in my flesh what is lacking in Christ's afflictions" for the church (1:24). This cannot mean that Christ's death was somehow deficient in reconciling people to God (Paul would be the last person to say such a thing), but the message must be proclaimed in order to take effect in people's lives. That's where Paul's suffering comes in.

Paul makes known "the mystery hidden for ages and generations but now revealed to his saints" (1:26), which is Christ among the gentiles (1:27). Paul wants all to understand Christ, since "in him are hidden all the treasures of wisdom and knowledge" (2:2–3). This adds to Paul's unfolding argument that Christ is sufficient for worship and life.

Against the "Colossian Heresy"

■ READ COLOSSIANS 2:4–23 ■

The main purpose of the letter is seen in this section, as Paul critiques forms of spirituality and worship that are based on philosophy and religious practices. Paul wants no one deceived by clever arguments (2:4) or taken captive by philosophy or human traditions (2:8).

Instead, the Colossians are to continue as they began, by growing in Christ (2:6–7). The fullness of God's nature is in Christ, and believers are filled by him (2:9–10). This means that no other form of spirituality can compete with Christ—the fullness of God is in him, and he is in you! There is no greater spiritual "fullness" than God himself.

Believers' spirituality is determined by their participation with Christ. They have been "circumcised in him," "buried with him," and made "alive with him" (2:11–13). These things mean that believers are set apart for God through Christ (spiritual "circumcision"), have spiritually died with Christ and been raised with him. Participation with Christ in these things means that believers have become new people. Other forms of spirituality and worship have nothing to offer in comparison to new life in Christ.

HISTORICAL MATTERS

The Colossian Heresy

In Colossians 2 Paul warns against a form of worship that involves a range of spiritual and religious practices that seem to combine Jewish and pagan elements. Scholars refer to this as the "Colossian heresy," though outside this letter we know of no such religious practice that combines such elements. It could be that this was a religion or philosophy unique to Colossae, described only in this letter, or it could simply describe a mishmash of religious and spiritual practices that existed in Colossae at the time (without constituting a religious or philosophical system).

THEOLOGICAL ISSUES

Elements of This World

The "elements of this world" (2:8, 20) refer to the building blocks of the physical, material realm. Food, drink, outward rituals make up our physical world, but all will perish with use (2:22). Since believers have died and risen with Christ, they are no longer confined to the elements of the world for their spiritual sustenance. And so they should not follow rules that depend on these elements as a way of achieving spiritual fulfillment.

Sins have been forgiven and debt has been erased through the cross of Christ (2:14). And through it Christ has also "disarmed the rulers and authorities and disgraced them publicly" (2:15). This means that Christ's death not only conquered the problem of human sin but also conquered the competing spiritual powers that stood against him.

As a result, believers should not submit to any regulations that are not based on Christ—food and drink, observance of Sabbath or festival, ascetic practices, worship of angels, or visionary experiences (2:16–18). While some people have an inflated view of their spirituality, they have lost hold of Christ. But those attached to him continue to grow in him with the growth that God gives (2:19).

Having died with Christ (cf. 2:12) to the elements of this world, believers should not listen to rules that are related only to the worldly elements (2:20–22). Some people may think that such rules increase their spirituality, but ultimately these are useless (2:23).

Look to Things Above

■ READ COLOSSIANS 3:1–17 ■

Participation with Christ has direct bearing on the Christian life. Having been raised with Christ, believers are to "seek the things above, where Christ is, seated at the right hand of God" (3:1). The elements of the world (2:8, 20) are not what believers should be preoccupied with, but rather they ought to be higher-minded. Believers have already died, and now their lives are bound up with Christ (3:3–4).

Since believers have died to the elements of the world (2:20), and all that goes with that, they are to "put to death what belongs to [their] earthly nature" (3:5). They once lived according to sexual immorality, impurity, lust, evil desire, and idolatrous greed, but it is no longer appropriate to live that way (3:5–7). Nor is it right to engage in anger, wrath, malice, slander, filthy language, and lying (3:8–9). Those things belong to the old self, but believers have "put on the new self," which is being shaped in the image of God (3:9–10). This flows from participation with Christ; having died and risen with him changes everything in this life. And in him the old divisions between people are gone (3:11).

Figure 18.2. *Christ Ascension*, icon from Michurin, Bulgaria

Burgas Art Gallery / Wikimedia Commons

Instead of being characterized by their former way of life, God's chosen ones will be characterized by compassion, kindness, humility, gentleness, patience, forgiveness, love, and peace (3:12–15). Their community will be permeated by the word of Christ as they encourage one another through singing and gratitude, doing everything in the name of Christ (3:16–17). Dying and rising with Christ completely transforms lives.

Christ in the Home

▓ READ COLOSSIANS 3:18–4:1 ▓

This is a brief household code compared to that of Colossians' sister letter, Ephesians (cf. Eph. 5:22–6:9). As in Ephesians, here we observe a set of asymmetrical relationships in which wives submit to husbands, children obey parents, and slaves obey masters, while husbands love their wives, fathers do not exasperate their children, and masters treat their slaves justly (3:18–4:1). There is no theological justification offered for this arrangement (again in contrast to Ephesians), but perhaps Paul did not consider it necessary to give one—though modern readers would have appreciated it!

The focus on slaves is also interesting. They are given more attention than others in the household code. Though we might prefer Paul to condemn slavery, instead he instructs slaves to obey their human masters in everything, and with integrity (3:22–23). But since slaves were not paid for their labors, Paul reminds them that they will "receive the reward of an inheritance from the Lord," since they "serve the Lord Christ" (3:24). This is an extraordinary statement, because slaves were not entitled to inheritances in the Roman world; it means that believing slaves are, in fact, regarded as the legal sons and daughters of God.

Making Known the Mystery of Christ

■ READ COLOSSIANS 4:2–6 ■

The last section of the letter (before the final greetings) encourages prayer and mindfulness toward outsiders (4:2–6). Being devoted to prayer, the Colossians are to remember Paul and his coworkers in their work of proclaiming the mystery of Christ (cf. 1:25–27). It is striking that Paul wants God to "open a door" for this proclamation, even though he is "in chains" at the time of writing (4:3). He does not ask the Colossians to pray for his prison door to be opened but asks only that the message would have an open door.

While Paul has a special responsibility to proclaim the mystery of Christ, all believers have a duty to make the most of their time with outsiders, paying attention to their speech and being ready to answer their questions or objections about the faith (4:5–6).

Final Greetings

■ READ COLOSSIANS 4:7–18 ■

While Colossians' household code is minimal compared to its parallel in Ephesians, the reverse is the case for the final greetings. Ephesians mentions none of Paul's readers or coworkers by name except for Tychicus, who carried the letter, while Colossians is full of personal references.

Tychicus is once again the carrier of the letter (4:7), but this time he is accompanied by Onesimus (4:9), who is the subject of Paul's letter to Philemon. In fact, there are several people common to both Colossians and Philemon: Tychicus, Onesimus, Epaphras, Aristarchus, Demas, and Luke, which suggests that the letters were written at the same time and sent together (Philemon lived in Colossae).

We also see Paul's expectation that his letter to the Colossians will be shared with the church at Laodicea, which possibly met in the home of a woman named Nympha (4:15). And the letter he wrote to Laodicea (now lost) is to be shared with the Colossians (4:16).

Implementation—Reading Colossians as Christian Scripture Today

Colossians presents the highest Christology (along with John's Gospel) in the New Testament: not only is Christ head over all powers and authorities, but also everything was created through him and for him. Christ is the means of creation and its purpose. The fullness of God dwells in Christ, along with all the treasures of wisdom and knowledge.

Believers have died and risen with Christ, meaning that they are no longer bound to the standards of earthly life. They now belong to a higher reality, hidden with Christ until they are revealed with him in glory.

This means that the Colossian heresy is completely robbed of its appeal. Its powers and authorities are no match for Christ, and its offer of wisdom and spiritual fulfillment is misleading because such things are found only in Christ. While the heresy is occupied with the elements of the world, believers look to things above.

Instead of just saying that the Colossian heresy is wrong and should be avoided, Paul mounts an argument that is both positive and negative, demonstrating that Christ is supreme and sufficient, which is why the Colossian heresy is folly and ultimately unhelpful. This message has much to say to the church today, as we are surrounded by many forms of spirituality that offer fulfillment and wisdom. These may not look like the Colossian heresy, but they are based on similar ideals—spiritual practices and rules that claim to lead their practitioners into divine fullness. But as Paul reminded the Colossians, Christ is still supreme and sufficient. He is all we need, and any other path will turn out to be a false one.

KEY VERSES IN COLOSSIANS

- He is the image of the invisible God, the firstborn over all creation. 1:15
- Be careful that no one takes you captive through philosophy and empty deceit based on human tradition, based on the elements of the world, rather than Christ. 2:8
- So if you have been raised with Christ, seek the things above, where Christ is, seated at the right hand of God. 3:1
- Act wisely toward outsiders, making the most of the time. Let your speech always be gracious, seasoned with salt, so that you may know how you should answer each person. 4:5–6

Christian Reading Questions

1. Read Colossians 1:15–20 and reflect on the significance of this passage for your understanding and appreciation of who Christ is.
2. Articulate in your own words what Paul means by the "mystery of Christ."
3. Read Colossians 2:20–3:4 and think about how dying and rising with Christ might affect life today.
4. How can the whole Letter to the Colossians help to prepare someone to know how to answer each person (4:6)?

CHAPTER NINETEEN

The First Letter to the Thessalonians

Orientation

Regarded by many as Paul's earliest known letter, and therefore the earliest writing of the New Testament, 1 Thessalonians is famous for its emphasis on the return of Christ, which is the subject of half of chapters 4 and 5 but is mentioned also at the end of every chapter. The new church in Thessalonica is so new, and so interested in the coming of Christ, that they are not sure what will happen to believers who die before he comes.

But the letter should also be appreciated for its great insights into the methods, motivations, as well as emotions, that characterized Paul's ministry among the Thessalonians. It is a heartfelt letter that reveals a pastor who loves his people.

HISTORICAL MATTERS

The Historical Origins of 1 Thessalonians

Author: Paul

Date: AD 50

Location: Corinth

Setting: Paul is in Corinth after being chased out of Thessalonica.

HISTORICAL MATTERS

Thessalonica

Thessalonica was named after Alexander the Great's half sister and in the first century was a major port city in Macedonia (Thessaloniki is now part of northern Greece). Paul, Silas, and Timothy first visited Thessalonica on Paul's second missionary journey (AD 49 or 50). Their visit was met with severe opposition, causing them to leave prematurely (Acts 17:1–9). Paul sent Timothy back to Thessalonica to encourage the believers (1 Thess. 3:2–3), and when he rejoined Paul in Corinth, he reported on how the Thessalonians were doing, which prompted Paul to write this letter (1 Thess. 3:6; Acts 18:5).

Figure 19.1. Location of Thessalonica

Exploration—Reading 1 Thessalonians

From Idols to the True God

■ READ 1 THESSALONIANS 1:1–10 ■

After the initial greeting from Paul, Silvanus, and Timothy (1:1), the entire first chapter of 1 Thessalonians is given to their thanksgiving for the Thessalonians. This thanksgiving is exceptionally positive, recognizing their work, labor, and love, produced by the Thessalonians' faith, love, and hope (1:2–3). The gospel message has had powerful effect among the Thessalonians, who became imitators of Paul and his companions, despite severe persecution (1:4–6).

The Thessalonians have become an example to believers throughout Macedonia and Achaia (Greece), as the word of the Lord has radiated out from them (1:7–8). The key to their transformation is that the Thessalonians "turned to God from idols to serve the living and true God" (1:9). They are waiting for God's risen Son from heaven, "who rescues us from the coming wrath" (1:10). This key also flags two major themes of the letter: the return of Christ and his rescue of believers from judgment.

Caring for You as Our Own Children

■ READ 1 THESSALONIANS 2:1–12 ■

Paul reflects on their visit among the Thessalonians (cf. Acts 17:1–9), and their motivation and conduct when speaking the gospel to them—seeking to please God, not people, never using flattery or seeking human glory (2:1–6). Instead, they treated the Thessalonians as their own children (2:7, 11), sharing their lives with them, working hard, and living blamelessly among them (2:8–10). Their goal was to encourage the Thessalonians to live worthy of God (2:12).

You Welcome the Word of God

■ READ 1 THESSALONIANS 2:13–20 ■

When Paul visited them, the Thessalonians received the word of God as it truly is, not as a word from

LITERARY NOTES

The Structure of 1 Thessalonians

First Thessalonians has by far the longest thanksgiving section of all Paul's Letters, accounting for the first three chapters of the five-chapter letter. This thanksgiving reveals Paul's loving, pastoral heart: he was like "a nursing mother nurturing her own children" (2:7), and like "a father with his own children" (2:11), and he longed to see them again (2:17). Chapters 4 and 5 address living in light of the end—the kind of living that will be pleasing to God (4:1–12)—waiting for the return of Christ (4:13–5:11), and final instructions and greetings (5:12–28).

people (2:13). And like believers in Judea, who have suffered from the Jews who rejected Jesus, the Thessalonians have suffered persecution from their own people too (2:14–16). Paul and his companions were forced to leave the Thessalonians after a short time (cf. Acts 17:5–10) and longed to see them again—their glory and joy (2:17–20).

Longing for You

■ READ 1 THESSALONIANS 3:1–13 ■

Paul went by himself to Athens (cf. Acts 17:14–15), while Timothy was sent to encourage the Thessalonians and to report back to Paul as to how things were going with the faith (3:1–5). Timothy brought news of their faith and love, and their longing to see Paul, just as Paul longed to see them (3:6, 10). The Thessalonians' faith is a source of joy and thanksgiving for Paul and his companions (3:7–9). Paul prays to see them again, that they would overflow with love for one another, and that God would make them blameless at the coming of Christ (3:10–13).

Keep on Doing What You're Doing

■ READ 1 THESSALONIANS 4:1–12 ■

Paul wants to encourage the Thessalonians to live in a way that pleases God, according to their instructions. In fact, they are already living this way, but he wants them to do so even more (4:1–2). First, this will mean keeping away from sexual immorality. Believers should avoid lustful passions and not take advantage of one another. Sexual manipulation and exploitation will incur the anger of God, since "the Lord is an avenger of all these offenses" (4:3–6). Instead, God has called us to holiness. To reject this teaching is to reject God himself and God's presence among us—the Holy Spirit (4:7–8).

Second, the Thessalonians already know how to love one another and have demonstrated this throughout Macedonia. But they should do so all the more (4:9–10). They should live "a quiet life," which probably means a life without unnecessary drama, and they are to be diligent in their work to enable self-sufficiency (4:11–12).

Taught by God

Paul says that the Thessalonians have been "taught by God to love one another" (4:9). This is an allusion to Isaiah 54:13: "Then all your children will be taught by the LORD." Isaiah looked forward to the blessings of the messianic age, when God's Spirit would so indwell his people that they would learn directly from God.

THEOLOGICAL ISSUES

Return to Judge the Living and the Dead

The New Testament is thoroughly forward-looking. The message of the gospel is based on Jesus's *past* coming into the world—his life, death, and resurrection in the first century—but it is focused on living now in light of the *future* salvation that is going to be revealed to the world. Christians are people whose lives and loves are shaped by hope in the future that God is going to bring.

Central to this future hope is the idea of judgment, with Jesus as the king and judge who will separate the righteous and the unrighteous (Matt. 25:31–46). The Apostles' Creed says it this way: "He will come again to judge the living and the dead." This confession does not sound very positive, but it is! The only ones who have need to fear a good and fair and righteous judge are those who are evil, unjust, and unrighteous. Christians have been given Christ's righteousness (2 Cor. 5:21) and will be found blameless because of him (Eph. 5:27). But just judgment will come on all the evil and wickedness of the world.

The Lord's Coming from Heaven

In 1 Thessalonians 4:16 Paul describes the coming of the Lord as a descent from heaven with a shout, the archangel's voice, and the trumpet of God. In several Old Testament texts the **day of the Lord** is pictured as when God will come to judge the wicked and save the righteous (Isa. 2:10–12; Ezek. 7:19; Joel 1:15; Amos 5:18–20; Zeph. 1:7–8; Zech. 14:1; Mal. 3:2). In the Old Testament the trumpet is used as an instrument of announcement, marking appearances of God (Exod. 19:13, 16, 19; 20:18) and the future day of the Lord (Isa. 27:13; Joel 2:1; Zeph. 1:14–16; Zech. 9:14). Thus, Paul imagines the coming of Christ as the fulfillment of prophecy regarding the judgment and salvation of God.

Grieving with Hope

READ 1 THESSALONIANS 4:13–18

Paul turns his attention to a question that seems to have bothered the Thessalonians: What happens to people who die before Jesus returns? The question is raised because the Thessalonians are among the first generation of Christians and are wrestling with the fact of Christian death for the first time. Before he answers the question, Paul gives the pastoral conclusion up front: "You will not grieve like the rest, who have no hope" (4:13).

The short answer comes first: "If we believe that Jesus died and rose again, in the same way, through Jesus, God will bring with him those who have fallen asleep" (4:14). "Have fallen asleep" is a metaphor for death that implies impermanence—the dead will awaken to resurrected life. And those who have fallen asleep will be raised from the dead just as Jesus was. God will do this through Jesus, and the resurrected dead will accompany Jesus.

The longer answer follows. When Jesus comes again, some believers will already be dead, but others will still be alive. Those still alive will have no advantage over those who have already died (4:15). Apocalyptic imagery will accompany the coming of Christ: he will descend from heaven "with a shout, with the archangel's voice, and with the trumpet of God." At that point, those who have already died as believers will rise from the dead (4:16). Then believers who are alive at the coming of Christ "will be caught up together with them in the clouds to meet the Lord in the air" (4:17).

The Metropolitan Museum of Art, Frederick C. Hewitt Fund, 1910.

Figure 19.2. Pilaster of angels sounding trumpets from the parapet of a pulpit by Giovanni Pisano

Like a Thief in the Night

■ READ 1 THESSALONIANS 5:1–11 ■

Speaking of the coming of Christ, Paul turns to focus on the question of when that will happen. The short answer this time is that "the day of the Lord will come just like a thief in the night," which recalls Jesus's words in Matthew 24:42–44. Jesus's return cannot be predicted and so will surprise those not waiting for him (5:1–3).

Though no one knows when Jesus will come again, believers will not be caught off guard. Believers are children of the light and children of the day, and do not belong to the darkness or the night (5:4–5). The metaphors of night and day direct how people will live: those who belong to the night do the things that are covered by darkness, while believers are to be awake and self-controlled, wearing the armor of faith, hope, and love (5:6–8). This will be consistent with the salvation that God has appointed for believers, so that we may live with Christ (5:9–10).

Final Encouragements

■ READ 1 THESSALONIANS 5:12–28 ■

A few final encouragements round out the letter. Paul wants to make sure that the Thessalonians respect and love their spiritual leaders, who work hard for them (5:12–13). On the other hand, anyone who does not work hard enough should be prodded (5:14). Everyone should pursue what is good for everyone else (5:14–15). They are to be people who rejoice, pray, give thanks, hold on to what is good, and stay away from evil (5:16–21).

Paul concludes with a prayer that the God of peace will keep believers blameless in spirit, soul, and body, for the coming of Christ. He will do it because he is faithful (5:23–24).

Implementation—Reading 1 Thessalonians as Christian Scripture Today

Paul's First Letter to the Thessalonians makes an important contribution to the New Testament's teaching about the return of Christ. The resurrection of the dead

THEOLOGICAL ISSUES

The Rapture

Popular conceptions of the **rapture** imagine believers snatched from the world, inexplicably disappearing from life on earth, while everyone else is left behind. This "rapture" comes from *rapere*, the Latin translation of the Greek for "caught up" (1 Thess. 4:17). But the text gives no support to the "left behind" idea. Instead, it pictures the return of Christ and the coming together of the resurrected dead, believers who are still living, and Christ himself.

THEOLOGICAL ISSUES

Meeting the Lord in the Air

The language of the Lord's coming and believers meeting him (1 Thess. 4:15, 17) is borrowed from the image of a Roman emperor visiting a city with a welcome party coming out from the city to meet him as he approaches. The welcome party then accompanies the emperor as he enters the city. This image supports the idea that Christ's people will meet him on his way back to this world, and they will accompany him on his arrival. Because of the imagery involved, it's possible that Paul does not literally mean that believers will float up in the air as Jesus descends to earth—but then again, he might mean that!

What Is "Prophecy"?

First Thessalonians 5:19–22 gives instructions about not quenching the Spirit or disregarding prophecies. What is this prophesying that Paul is referring to? Today many assume that "prophecy" and "prophesying" refer to predictions about the future, usually given by some supernatural means. In the modern Pentecostal tradition prophesying is understood and practiced as spontaneous pronouncements that direct the church or individuals. Throughout most of the church's history, however, "prophesying" was understood very differently, as what today we would call "preaching." In his commentary on 1–2 Thessalonians John Calvin explains that "prophecy means the art of interpreting scripture" in a clear way. The same is said by countless others, such as John Wesley and Matthew Henry, who in commenting on 5:19–20 says that "prophecyings" are "the interpreting and applying of the scriptures." This is not just a Protestant and early modern idea, however. Augustine, in his expositions on the Psalms, likewise describes prophecy as the explanatory exposition of Scripture, and Aquinas interprets the prophecies in 5:20 as divine doctrine and all who teach this as prophets.[2]

at Christ's coming and the timing of these events are taught for the encouragement of these early believers. Believers today can be encouraged, as the Thessalonians were, to look ahead to the coming of Christ; the resurrection of the dead enables us to grieve with hope for those who have fallen asleep in Christ.

The believers in Thessalonica continue to set an example for the church today in their radical transformation from pagan idol worshipers to become servants of the true and living God. Though idolatry might not take the same form today, it is alive and well in our culture's obsession with wealth, success, fame, sex, and other things that compete with God for devotion. The church would do well to follow the Thessalonians in their thorough turnaround and in their hope in the coming of God's Son from heaven.

Paul's example too stands as an encouragement to all believers, but especially to those who seek to lead within the church. His loving and affectionate disposition toward the Thessalonians offers a better model for Christian ministry than the often professionalized, and sometimes impersonal, approaches that can be seen today in many churches.

KEY VERSES IN 1 THESSALONIANS

- You turned to God from idols to serve the living and true God and to wait for his Son from heaven, whom he raised from the dead—Jesus, who rescues us from the coming wrath. 1:10
- This is why we constantly thank God, because when you received the word of God that you heard from us, you welcomed it not as a human message, but as it truly is, the word of God, which also works effectively in you who believe. 2:13
- For if we believe that Jesus died and rose again, in the same way, through Jesus, God will bring with him those who have fallen asleep. 4:14
- For the Lord himself will descend from heaven with a shout, with the archangel's voice, and with the trumpet of God, and the dead in Christ will rise first. Then we who are still alive, who are left, will be caught up together with them in the clouds to meet the Lord in the air, and so we will always be with the Lord. 4:16–17
- For God did not appoint us to wrath, but to obtain salvation through our Lord Jesus Christ, who died for us, so that whether we are awake or asleep, we may live together with him. 5:9–10

Christian Reading Questions

1. Read Acts 16:6–18:5 and 1 Thessalonians 1:1–3:6. Note all the connections that you can find between the two passages.

2. List all the descriptions of the Thessalonian believers found in 1 Thessalonians 1–2.

3. Describe the characteristics of Paul's ministry among the Thessalonians as seen in 1 Thessalonians 2.

4. Read 1 Thessalonians 4:13–18 and 1 Corinthians 15. Compare and contrast the two passages.

CHAPTER TWENTY

The Second Letter to the Thessalonians

Orientation

There is hardly a letter more fully eschatological—that is, concerned with the "end"—than Paul's Second Letter to the Thessalonians. Though the letter is short, the entire first half of the letter deals exclusively with issues related to the end of the age, which will be heralded by the return of Christ.

The Thessalonians have been enduring persecution, and the return of Christ is the hope to which Paul points. When the Lord comes, he will bring peace for the afflicted and wrath for those who persecute God's people. The day of the Lord will see the terrible vengeance of God alongside the glory of Christ. It will bring salvation and judgment. In the meantime, believers must stand firm, holding on to what they have been taught, knowing that Christ himself will encourage their hearts.

HISTORICAL MATTERS

The Historical Origins of 2 Thessalonians

Author: Paul

Date: AD 50

Location: Corinth

Setting: Paul writes to the same church again a few months after his first letter to them, addressing similar issues.

Exploration—Reading 2 Thessalonians

Judgment and Glory

■ READ 2 THESSALONIANS 1:1–12 ■

The letter begins with a greeting from Paul, Silvanus, and Timothy (as does 1 Thessalonians), after which Paul expresses his thankfulness for the Thessalonians' flourishing faith and love, and for their perseverance through persecutions and afflictions (1:3–4).

Figure 20.1. Thessalonica ruins

The persecutions and afflictions that the Thessalonians have faced spark one of Paul's most fiery descriptions of God's righteous judgment. While their persecution is evidence that the Thessalonians will be counted worthy of God's kingdom, it will cause God to "repay with affliction those who afflict you" (1:5–6). God will bring relief for the afflicted at the revelation of the Lord Jesus from heaven, which will also bring "vengeance with flaming fire" on those who reject God (1:7–8).

God's vengeance on the disobedient will result in their eternal destruction. This is described as "from the Lord's presence," though is sometimes understood as "*away* from the Lord's presence" (1:9). Most likely the former option is correct, indicating that the Lord himself will enforce the destruction of those under his judgment through his glorious strength.

All of this will happen on the day of Jesus's return. Though it will be a day of judgment, it will also be a day of glory, as Christ is glorified by all who have believed in him (1:10). In this way, we see that glory and judgment go hand in hand. The final victory of Christ and his people can be fully consummated only when evil has been overthrown and abolished. Both are wrapped up in the return of Christ.

This reality inspires Paul's prayers for the Thessalonians, that they will remain worthy of Christ and that the Lord Jesus would be glorified in their lives according to the grace of God (1:11–12).

When the Day of the Lord Comes

■ READ 2 THESSALONIANS 2:1–12 ■

Since Paul has been talking about the return of Christ, he addresses the issue of when this will or will not happen. He doesn't want the Thessalonians to become distressed

LITERARY NOTES

The Structure of 2 Thessalonians

The three-chapter structure of the letter is fairly straightforward. In short, the first two chapters address the end, when Christ comes with glory and judgment, and include an excursus about the **man of lawlessness**. Chapter 3 addresses how to live now in light of that end.

CANONICAL CONNECTIONS

The Day of the Lord

An important concept in the Old Testament, the day of the Lord was an expectation of God's future intervention into human history for judgment and salvation: "For the day of the LORD is near, against all the nations. As you have done, it will be done to you; what you deserve will return on your own head" (Obad. 15; other examples include Isa. 2:1–4:6; Jer. 46:10; Ezek. 30:2–3). The New Testament views Jesus as the Lord concerning whom "the day of the LORD" spoke. At his return, these Old Testament expectations will finally be consummated.

The Man of Lawlessness

This mysterious figure is often equated with the "anti-christ" mentioned in 1 and 2 John, but in those contexts the term refers to people who have left the community of believers. Using familiar imagery borrowed from the Old Testament (e.g., Isa. 14:12–14; Ezek. 28:2; Dan. 6:7) and from the history of Israel, Paul depicts the man of lawlessness occupying God's temple and exalting himself above God. The Seleucid ruler Antiochus IV Epiphanes desecrated the Jerusalem temple in 167 BC, and the Roman emperor Caligula set up a statue of himself inside the temple in AD 40.

Wrath, Judgment, Hell, and Fire

Throughout Christian history most traditions within the faith have spoken plainly about God's wrath coming upon the sinful world in the form of judgment, hell, and fire. In the modern West these themes are not highlighted as much, even though there are many places in the Bible that speak in this way, such as in 1–2 Thessalonians (1 Thess. 2:16; 4:15–16; 5:3, 9; 2 Thess. 1:5–9; 2:10–11).

Even though it may make modern hearers uncomfortable to think and speak of God in this way—and it can certainly be overdone at the expense of God's love—the church fathers did not shy away from speaking about the rightness and certainty of God bringing justice to the world in the form of judgment and punishment.

Two of the motivations for preaching on this topic were (1) to encourage people's moral development and (2) to combat a wrong view of God. In the first instance, John Chrysostom warns his hearers not to be skeptical and unbelieving like people were in Noah's day and in Sodom and Gomorrah. But, he concludes, "I say not these things to frighten you" but as salutary medicine.[1] As he says in his *Homily* 2 on 2 Thessalonians 1, "If we always think of hell, we shall not soon fall into it. . . . It is not possible that a soul anxious about hell should readily sin."

In the second instance, both Irenaeus and Tertullian emphasize the importance of God's coming wrath as a reminder against the mistaken theology of the Gnostics and the Marcionites. These groups wrongly believed that the Creator God of the Old Testament is different than the God of the New Testament, that the God of the Old Testament is wrathful but the God of the New Testament is only loving and mild.[2] This breaks apart the Bible in a way that dishonors who the eternal and unchanging God is.

by people claiming that the day of the Lord has already come and they missed it somehow (2:1–2).

The Thessalonians should not be deceived by such false claims, since the day of the Lord will be preceded by certain things that have not yet come. First there will be "the apostasy," and the "man of lawlessness" will come. Whoever this man of lawlessness is, he will make himself an object of worship, proclaiming himself to be God. This man of lawlessness is currently being restrained, but he will be released and revealed (2:3–8).

But the lawless one will be destroyed by the Lord Jesus "with the breath of his mouth," and he will come to nothing. The lawless one works in conjunction with Satan to perform false miracles, signs, and deceptions. Sadly, he will drag people away with his deceptions. God even allows such people to be deceived because that will confirm their rejection of the truth (2:8–12). All in all, this is a tough passage that raises several unanswered questions. We can only assume that Paul's readers knew what he was talking about (2:5).

Chosen for Salvation

■ READ 2 THESSALONIANS 2:13–3:5 ■

Again thanking God for the Thessalonians, Paul reflects on the fact that they were chosen by God from the beginning. God called them to sanctification by the Spirit and to share in the glory of Christ through the gospel. Because of this work of God in their lives, the Thessalonians are to stand firm in what they have been taught (2:13–15). God gives eternal encouragement and good hope to strengthen the believers in every good work (2:16–17).

Just as Paul and his colleagues pray for them, he asks the Thessalonians to pray for their needs too. Paul asks for prayer concerning the word of the Lord, that it would spread and be honored. He also asks that he and his team would be delivered from wicked people. Paul trusts in the faithfulness of God, who will guard the Thessalonians from the evil one. They have done well so far, and the Lord gives Paul confidence that they will continue in the same way (3:1–5).

Against Idleness

■ READ 2 THESSALONIANS 3:6–15 ■

It seems that idleness is a bit of a problem in Thessalonica. After the gentler encouragement in 1 Thessalonians 4:10–12, now Paul steps it up to disciplining action. Believers are to disassociate from anyone who remains lazy (3:6, 14–15). Instead of being idle, believers should follow Paul's example: he and his colleagues worked hard day and night and were a burden on no one (3:7–8).

Though the servants of the gospel have a right to be supported financially, they set an example for the Thessalonians to follow, insisting that everyone should make a meaningful contribution of work. Instead of being busy with work, some are "busybodies," probably occupying themselves in gossip and idle chitchat. Paul again commands them to work and provide for themselves (3:9–13).

Final Greetings

■ READ 2 THESSALONIANS 3:16–18 ■

Paul concludes the letter with his own handwritten greeting, wishing peace for the believers in every way. The Lord of peace will grant them peace, will be with them, and will give them grace (3:16–18).

The Walters Art Museum. Acquired by Henry Walters with the Massarenti Collection, 1902.

Figure 20.2. *The Last Judgment* by Pieter Huys

CANONICAL CONNECTIONS

The Breath of His Mouth

This language comes from Isaiah 11:4, where a messianic figure "will strike the earth with the rod of his mouth; with the breath of his lips he will slay the wicked" (NIV). Paul draws on this imagery of a messianic warrior, asserting that the man of lawlessness will be no match for the Lord Jesus and his powerful word, which Paul elsewhere calls "the sword of the Spirit" (Eph. 6:17).

Implementation—Reading 2 Thessalonians as Christian Scripture Today

Persecution of believers still happens today. Though Western believers may experience it only verbally or socially, nevertheless these subtle forms of persecution challenge us to live out our faith in Christ. And the harsh reality for many non-Western believers around the world involves physical persecution and violence. Though often neglected, 2 Thessalonians continues to offer hope to persecuted believers.

The return of the Lord Jesus Christ is the event toward which all history is headed, and when he comes, his magnificent glory will be revealed for all to see. But alongside his glory will come his wrath, poured out upon those who are opposed to God and those who have so violently persecuted the faithful.

The call for believers today is the same as in Paul's day: stand firm. Believers have been called through the gospel to obtain the glory of Christ. The world as we know it is passing away, and glory is coming. Until then we must allow the Lord to direct our hearts to God's love and Christ's endurance.

KEY VERSES IN 2 THESSALONIANS

- They will pay the penalty of eternal destruction from the Lord's presence and from his glorious strength on that day when he comes to be glorified by his saints and to be marveled at by all those who have believed, because our testimony among you was believed. 1:9–10
- For that day will not come unless the apostasy comes first and the man of lawlessness is revealed, the man doomed to destruction. He opposes and exalts himself above every so-called god or object of worship, so that he sits in God's temple, proclaiming that he himself is God. 2:3–4
- But we ought to thank God always for you, brothers and sisters loved by the Lord, because from the beginning God has chosen you for salvation through sanctification by the Spirit and through belief in the truth. He called you to this through our gospel, so that you might obtain the glory of our Lord Jesus Christ. 2:13–14
- For you yourselves know how you should imitate us: We were not idle among you; we did not eat anyone's food free of charge; instead, we labored and toiled, working night and day, so that we would not be a burden to any of you. 3:7–8

Christian Reading Questions

1. Do you find the idea of Jesus's vengeance difficult to accept (2 Thess. 1:7–8)? Why or why not?

2. The phrase "they will pay the penalty of eternal destruction from the Lord's presence" (2 Thess. 1:9) could also be rendered "they will pay the penalty of eternal destruction away from the Lord's presence." Discuss which you think is most likely and why.

3. Interpretations of who "the man of lawlessness" might be (2 Thess. 2:3–4) abound throughout church history. Who do you think it might be? Does it refer to an actual person, or a "type" of person?

4. What exactly is wrong with idleness (2 Thess. 3:6–15)? Why should believers work, and what about those who can't work for reasons of health, age, or situation?

CHAPTER TWENTY-ONE

The Pastoral Letters

1–2 Timothy and Titus

Orientation

Four of Paul's Letters are addressed to individuals rather than churches, and in three of them he writes to his sons in the faith Timothy and Titus to instruct them in their roles as leaders within the churches of Ephesus and Crete. We call these the Pastoral Letters. While their purpose seems simple enough, the issues that swirl around the Pastoral Letters are far from simple. First, many scholars today doubt that they are genuine letters of Paul. Second, they contain some of the most controversial texts in the entire New Testament, concerning women and teaching in the congregation. While each of these issues must be considered, the Pastoral Letters are part of the Christian canon and have always played an important role in the church's understanding and practice.

The Pastoral Letters provide a fascinating sneak peak into one pastor's advice to another. Paul addresses a wide range of matters that are bound together by Timothy's and Titus's responsibilities to lead God's people. The one thread that runs through each letter is the warning about false teachers and the destruction they cause. Timothy and Titus are to present themselves as godly examples, in contrast to these false teachers, both in their conduct and in their teaching.

HISTORICAL MATTERS

The Historical Origins of the Pastoral Letters

Author: Paul, but this is heavily disputed (see below)

Date: Ca. AD 63–65 (1 Timothy, Titus, 2 Timothy is the likely order)

Location: Possibly Macedonia for 1 Timothy, Rome for Titus and 2 Timothy

Setting: After Paul's house arrest in Rome, he writes to Timothy and Titus, who lead the churches in Ephesus and Crete.

Exploration—Reading 1 Timothy

A Pure Heart, a Good Conscience, and a Sincere Faith

■ READ 1 TIMOTHY 1:1–11 ■

Paul's affection for Timothy is obvious as he refers to him as "my true son in the faith" (1:2). Paul launches immediately to address Timothy's ministry responsibilities in Ephesus. Timothy is to work against false teaching that promotes empty speculations instead of God's plan (1:3–4). Genuine ministry comes from a pure heart rather than impure motives. It is issued from a good conscience and sincere faith, unlike the "ministry" of false teachers (1:5).

These false teachers are driven by their ambition to be teachers without knowing what they are doing (1:6–7). A key element of their teaching is related to the law of Moses, but they do not understand its real function. Paul argues that the purpose of the law is to highlight a person's sinfulness and whatever is contrary to the true teaching of the gospel (1:8–11).

Fight the Good Fight

■ READ 1 TIMOTHY 1:12–20 ■

Paul reflects on the role that God gave him to be a minister of the gospel, even though he was once a blasphemer and a persecutor. But God showed Paul mercy; and if someone like Paul could be saved, anyone can receive eternal life (1:12–16). Now Timothy is to fight the good fight as Paul has done, with faith

The Authorship of the Pastoral Letters

For nearly two millennia, until the nineteenth century, the Pauline authorship of 1 Timothy, 2 Timothy, and Titus was not seriously doubted. Then it was claimed that these letters are pseudonymous—bearing Paul's name but written by someone else. While pseudonymous documents were common in the ancient world (though pseudonymous letters were not), the church vigorously rejected such writings from the canon of Scripture. So, if the Pastoral Letters really are pseudonymous, then the early church was deceived in thinking them genuine. But instead, the church accepted these as genuinely Pauline. Modern arguments swirl around the letters' language, historical setting, and instructions about church structure. While the language differs from Paul's other letters, the writing sample is too small to adjudicate. The historical setting does not easily fit into Paul's chronology from Acts, but Acts is selective and leaves things out (including what happened after Paul's Roman house arrest). Finally, claims that the Pastoral Letters reflect second-century church leadership structures are overstated. Paul appointed elders in churches when he revisited them. In short, arguments against Pauline authorship are not strong enough to overturn two thousand years of tradition and the unanimous conviction of the early church.

Who Was Timothy?

Paul met Timothy in Lystra on his second missionary journey (Acts 16:1–5). Timothy was already a disciple at this time, so probably he had become a Christian after Paul's first missionary visit to Lystra (Acts 14:8–20). We are told that Timothy's mother was Jewish but his father was Greek, and everyone spoke highly of him, which made him well suited to become Paul's missionary companion. He went with Paul through the rest of his second missionary journey into Macedonia and Greece and part of the third missionary journey too (Acts 20:4).

The Structure of 1 Timothy

Though scholars of an earlier era regarded the structure of 1 Timothy as incoherent, it must be remembered that it is a personal letter to a young pastor from his mentor. Paul simply addresses issues about which he thinks Timothy needs instruction. The first chapter reminds Timothy of God's mercy to Paul, and Timothy's responsibilities to protect his people from false teachers. Chapters 2–4 address worship and order within the church. Chapter 5 is about how to care for widows and how to treat elders, while chapter 6 consists of instructions concerning how to teach specific individuals, such as servants and masters.

Figure 21.1. Remains of Roman dwellings known as terrace houses, in the ancient city of Ephesus

RECEPTION HISTORY

The Condemnation of Slave Traders

Although various forms of slavery and servanthood existed in New Testament times, Christianity regularly emphasized the value and dignity of all people and that the family bond between brothers and sisters in Christ was more important than any other social structure (Gal. 3:28; see also Philemon).

Many Christians in the past have utilized 1 Timothy 1:10 to emphasize that slave trading is a kind of kidnapping that goes against Jesus's teachings. For example, John Wesley describes such "men-stealers" as "the worst of all thieves," and the abolitionist George Cheever notes that "a more tremendous passage against slavery does not exist than this."[1]

THEOLOGICAL ISSUES

God Wants All to Be Saved?

Theologians sometimes puzzle over the statement "God wants everyone to be saved and to come to the knowledge of the truth" (2:4), since, if he is God, why does this not come to pass? Is it God's will that everyone will be saved or not? Indeed, this statement, along with 2:6 and 4:10, is sometimes taken as an indication that 1 Timothy teaches the doctrine of **universalism**, which holds that all people will ultimately go to heaven, even if they don't repent and believe in Jesus. It is clear, however, that belief is required for eternal life (1:16; 2:15; 4:16; 6:12). It is also clear throughout the letter that there are dire consequences for those who turn away from the truth (e.g., 1:19; 3:6; 4:1–3; 5:6, 15, 24; 6:9–10, 20–21). So the statement in 2:4 is best understood as indicating God's love for all humanity, even though he wills only some to be saved in the end (Rom. 9:10–24; Eph. 1:2–4).

and a good conscience. Sadly, others have shipwrecked their faith, but there is hope even for them if they are corrected (1:18–20).

Corporate Prayer

■ READ 1 TIMOTHY 2:1–7 ■

Paul switches subject and addresses items related to the church in Ephesus. The first is prayer. Prayers should be offered for everyone, including kings and those in authority. It is worth noting that Paul is imprisoned under the corrupt emperor Nero at the time he writes this. But the goal of such prayer is that people would be free to live godly lives without trouble (2:1–2). Such prayer pleases God our Savior, and this God is one "who wants everyone to be saved and to come to the knowledge of the truth" (2:3–4). Though not all people will be saved, this statement reflects God's love for all.

Indeed, the one mediator between God and humanity, Jesus Christ, gave himself as a ransom for all people. The scope of his saving work does not exclude anyone except by their own choice. His work is sufficient to cover everyone (2:5–6). Paul's role in all of this is that he was appointed to proclaim this good news, especially to the gentiles, but to do so in faith and truth, unlike the false teachers, who are neither faithful nor true (2:7; cf. 1:6, 19).

Men and Women in the Church

■ READ 1 TIMOTHY 2:8–15 ■

As Paul continues to address items related to the gathered church in Ephesus, he embarks on one of the most controversial passages in his writings—indeed, in the whole New Testament. Men and women are addressed, with men receiving only one instruction—pray without anger or argument (2:8)—while women are addressed for several verses (2:9–15).

Women are to dress modestly, relying on their good works to commend them, rather than outward appearance. They are to learn quietly with full submission and are not permitted to teach or to have authority over men (2:9–12). Paul anchors this controversial instruction in the Genesis narrative of Adam and Eve. Adam was formed before Eve, and she was the one deceived in the garden by the serpent (see Gen. 2–3). However, women will be saved "through childbearing" by continuing in faith, love, and holiness (2:13–15). Needless to say, there is much here that requires further unpacking.

Several issues need to be addressed in trying to understand this passage. Is Paul a misogynist? Does he think that women are inferior to men? Why can't they teach men? Why must they be quiet in the congregation? And what does all this have to do with Adam and Eve?

First, it is unfair to label Paul a misogynist. While he does seem to believe that men and women have different roles within the church and within marriage (though this is heavily debated), this does not mean that he denies the equality of men and women. It is a modern Western understanding to link equality with identical roles. That is, today we tend to believe that anyone should be able to do anything they want, and that any kind of role

Figure 21.2. *The Fall of Man* by Giovanni Battista Foggini

The Walters Art Museum. Acquired by Henry Walters, 1903.

expectation is a form of oppression or inequality. That kind of thinking is completely alien to Paul and to anyone living in the first century.

Second, there is no indication that Paul believes that women are inferior to men. This is not what he means in 2:14 by mentioning Eve as the one deceived (see the fifth point below), and nothing else in his letters indicates anything of the sort. Indeed, he regularly upholds the dignity of women and freely acknowledges the essential work of women alongside him (e.g., Rom. 16:1–3, 6–7, 12).

Third, if we take Paul's statements at face value, yes, he does seem to inhibit women from teaching men. This is not a general statement—as though women can never teach men anything—but is relevant only for the gathered church, which is the context of this passage, and applies only to the role of authoritative teaching. Some scholars argue that Paul's instruction here is relevant only to the church in Ephesus—perhaps there was a problem with the women there in particular. This is possible, considering what Paul says about younger widows in 5:11–15. But this does not explain the blanket statement concerning all women (not just young widows).

Fourth, when Paul says that women must learn quietly in the congregation, this does not mean "be silent." It is clear from elsewhere that Paul does not intend women to be silent when the church gathers (cf. 1 Cor. 11:5, 13). Here he means for women to learn quietly with respect to the authoritative teaching when the church gathers.

Fifth, how does this all relate to Adam and Eve? First, Paul makes the point of the order between the two. Adam was formed first, then Eve. This seems to imply an order of relationship between them, as though Adam has some kind of leadership responsibility. But Eve was deceived and transgressed. This does not mean that women are somehow more easily deceived than men and for that reason Paul doesn't want them teaching men—that would be genuine misogyny. Rather, the point is more likely that although Adam had a role of responsibility, he did not live up to it and instead followed Eve's misdirected lead.

As for the woman being "saved through childbearing," this is probably the hardest element to understand in this passage (2:15). It could mean that if women just stick to their role as wife and mother, all will be okay (cf. 5:14). It could also mean that women will be physically protected during childbirth, since many women in the first century died during it. But it more likely refers to the promise that God made in Genesis 3:15, that through Eve would come the one who would overcome evil by crushing the serpent's head. This, then, is a reference to Jesus—the one who conquered sin and Satan—who enables all people to be saved. He was born of a woman and is the savior of women. 📜

A wide variety of interpretations can be found regarding this passage. But the important first step is to notice carefully what the text does and does not say. From that point, the reader must ask honestly what God is communicating to us today. It is difficult simply to dismiss the text for "cultural" reasons, since Paul so clearly grounds it in the narrative of Genesis 2–3, a text that applies not just to some cultures but to all. Whatever application seems appropriate, we must remember to read this biblical text, as all others, as Christian Scripture.

CANONICAL CONNECTIONS

Adam and Eve

Genesis 2–3 is a carefully crafted narrative with several symbolic nuances. The order between Adam and Eve is clear, as is Eve's role as helper and companion to Adam (2:18, 21–23). While Adam and Eve are regarded as equals, both made in the image of God and coregents over creation (1:26–28), nevertheless an ordering remains. Such ordering is not about worth or essence, but about the nature of their relationship together. In Genesis 3 the order is inverted, with the serpent—part of the animal kingdom that Adam and Eve were supposed to rule over (1:28)—telling Eve what to do, and then Eve telling Adam what to do (3:1–7). Genesis 3, then, is a commentary on how sin ruptures relationships.

Overseers and Deacons

■ READ 1 TIMOTHY 3:1–16 ■

In keeping with his concerns about the gathered church, Paul addresses two key roles within it: the overseer and the deacon. To be qualified to serve as an overseer, a man must live an exemplary Christian life, both within the Christian community and outside it. The only ability that is listed is the ability to teach (3:1–7). This likely means that Paul views overseers as having the responsibility to teach in the congregation. Deacons likewise are expected to live an exemplary Christian life, but the ability to teach is not listed (3:8–10). Hence it seems the primary difference between overseers and deacons is that the former have the authority to serve through teaching, while the latter serve in other ways.

In 3:11 Paul either refers to the wives of deacons or to female deacons. Since the wives of overseers were not mentioned in 3:1–7, it seems unlikely that Paul means deacons' wives. Thus we can see that Paul, addressing female deacons, certainly does imagine leadership and servant roles for women within the church. But, as with their male counterparts, teaching is not part of their job description (cf. 2:12).

Paul addresses these issues so that Timothy will know how the church ought to conduct itself. He describes the church as God's household, so its orderly conduct ought to honor God (3:14–15). Indeed, the church ought to be godly, and for the supreme example of godliness they should look to the incarnate Jesus (3:16).

Instructions for Ministry

■ READ 1 TIMOTHY 4:1–5:2 ■

Paul returns to the theme of false teaching (4:1–5), and Timothy's responsibility to point it out to fellow believers. This will make him a good servant of Christ, filled by good teaching. Timothy is to train himself in godliness, which has benefits for this life and the life to come. That is the point of Paul's and Timothy's ministry—to lead others to hope in God, the Savior of all people (4:6–10).

Timothy is to teach the truth and set an example for others to follow, despite his relative youth (4:11–12). He is to give attention to the public reading of Scripture, exhortation, and teaching, thus not neglecting his gift to do so, as confirmed by the ordination of elders (4:13–14). Timothy's progress in these things ought to be evident to all as he keeps a close eye on his life and teaching, which will keep him and his hearers on the right path (4:15–16). He is to treat the members of the church as his family, regarding older men as fathers, younger men as brothers, older women as mothers, and younger women as sisters (5:1–2).

How to Treat Elder Family Members

■ READ 1 TIMOTHY 5:3–6:2 ■

Speaking of treating church members like family members, Paul instructs Timothy to take care of widows in need. But if they have their own children or grandchildren, this is first their responsibility. Indeed, to neglect one's own family is a denial of the faith (5:3–8).

The widows eligible for support should be at least sixty years old and known for their faithfulness and good works (5:9–10). But younger widows are better off marrying again rather than receiving support from the church. This will enable the church to look after those widows in genuine need (5:11–16).

As for elders who lead well within the church, especially through preaching and teaching, they are worthy of double honor (5:17–18). Out of respect for such leaders, and out of respect for their position, accusations should not be brought against them without decent corroboration. But if they require public correction, they ought to be rebuked without prejudice. This means that elders should not be appointed lightly but rather with due consideration (5:19–22, 24–25).

False Teaching . . . Again!

■ READ 1 TIMOTHY 6:3–21 ■

Once again Timothy is warned of the dangers of false teachers and the ungodliness that comes from

---

THEOLOGICAL ISSUES

The Savior of All People, Especially of Those Who Believe?

The statement that God is "the Savior of all people, especially of those who believe" (4:10) sometimes is understood to support universalism (see the sidebar "God Wants All to Be Saved?"). But it is better understood as indicating the sufficiency of God's saving work in Christ: this work is sufficient to save all people but is effective only for those who believe. It is clear throughout the letter that belief is required for eternal life (1:16; 2:15; 4:16; 6:12).

their false doctrines. Teaching is not a ticket to riches, as the false teachers seem to think, and the desire for wealth is a trap that leads to destruction (6:3–10, 17–19). On the contrary, Timothy is a man of God who is to pursue righteousness and godliness, fighting the good fight of the faith, and taking hold of eternal life (6:11–12). Paul charges Timothy before God and Christ to keep this command without fault until Christ appears again (6:13–14). God will do this as the King of kings and Lord of lords, to whom belongs all honor and power (6:15–16).

Paul's final words to Timothy are a reminder to guard what has been entrusted to him: the true teaching of the gospel, as well as the people under his care. He is to avoid the traps that false teachers fall into and to lead his people in the right spiritual way (6:20–21).

Exploration—Reading 2 Timothy

Don't Be Ashamed of the Gospel

■ READ 2 TIMOTHY 1:1–18 ■

Paul writes his second letter to Timothy, his dearly loved son (1:2–4). Timothy has sincere faith, as did his mother and grandmother, and now is to "rekindle the gift of God that is in you through the laying on of my hands" (1:5–6). Probably Paul refers to Timothy's gift of teaching, which he was commissioned to do by Paul and the elders of the church in Ephesus (1 Tim. 4:13–14). This is to be done in the face of persecution and difficult circumstances. But God has not given him a spirit of fear; rather, Timothy has the Holy Spirit, who produces power, love, and sound judgment (1:7).

Armed with the Holy Spirit, Timothy should not be ashamed of the testimony about Christ (or ashamed of Paul). In an honor-shame culture it can be tempting to disown a message that might bring public disapproval to oneself—it is a powerful social force. But Timothy is not to succumb to such social force if it means denying the truth. Instead, he will be sustained by the power of God (1:8).

The gospel for which Timothy will suffer is the message that God has saved and called people according to his grace, not works—a fact that mysteriously defies the borders of time. God's plan has been revealed in Christ, "who has abolished death," and his life-giving work is revealed through the gospel

LITERARY NOTES

The Structure of 2 Timothy

As Paul's last testament, he encourages Timothy in the matters that he most wants to impress on the young pastor. Timothy is to fan into flame the gift of God, join in suffering for the gospel, and guard the gospel (1:1–18). He is to be a good soldier of Jesus Christ and remember that it is all about Christ (2:1–13). As a workman approved by God, he will oppose false teachers gently and in love (2:14–3:9). Timothy will continue in the way he has learned from the Scriptures and preach the word in season and out, just as Paul has done as he comes to the end of his life (3:10–4:8). The letter concludes with final instructions and greetings (4:9–22).

message that Paul and Timothy preach (1:9–11). Indeed, this is what Paul was appointed for and is why he suffers as he does. But he does not succumb to the pressure of social shame because he trusts God to enable him to do what he must do (1:12). Timothy, likewise, is to follow in Paul's footsteps and guard "the good deposit," the gospel message that has been entrusted to him (1:13–14).

Be Strong in the Grace of Christ

■ READ 2 TIMOTHY 2:1–13 ■

The strength required for Timothy's work, and for sharing in suffering for the gospel, will come not from him but from the grace that is in Christ Jesus (2:1). Part of Timothy's work will be to raise up other teachers to do what he already does (2:2). Here Paul shows his vision for ministry beyond his own time: he has taught Timothy, who will teach others, who will teach yet others. Timothy will share in suffering (cf. 1:8) "as a good soldier of Christ Jesus" (2:3). Paul draws on the images of a soldier, athlete, and farmer to emphasize the importance of hard work and dedication in his task (2:4–6).

Above all, Timothy must "remember Jesus Christ, risen from the dead and descended from David" (2:8). This may seem a strange thing to say to a preacher of Christ—is Timothy likely to forget about him? But the pastoral point is important: ironically, tragically, people who teach the gospel of Christ can lose sight of Christ himself. Paul is reminding Timothy that he needs Christ in his own life to be faithful in perseverance. Paul suffers for the gospel of Christ like a criminal, but he endures all for the elect and for their salvation and eternal glory (2:9–10).

Paul then launches into a "trustworthy saying" (2:11–13), which appears to be a poetic statement about endurance and faithfulness. Dying with Christ ensures life with him. Enduring for Christ will ensure reigning with him in the kingdom of heaven. But denying Christ will result in his denial of us at the judgment. While people may be faithless, he is faithful—unable to deny himself—which is why he must deny those who deny him. To do otherwise would make Christ reject himself. The poetic statement is an encouragement about the long-term value of suffering for Christ; in the end, Christ will vindicate those who suffer for his sake. But giving up on Christ amid persecution must be avoided.

Be an Approved Worker

■ READ 2 TIMOTHY 2:14–26 ■

Timothy is to present himself to God as an approved worker who correctly handles the word of truth. Despite those around him who continue to deny the truth, all who call on the name of the Lord will be saved, since the Lord knows who are his (2:14–19). Ultimately, the sovereignty of God is comforting in the face of false teaching because he will not lose those he has chosen. Nevertheless, Timothy is to prepare himself in order to become a special instrument, useful to God for every good work (2:20–21).

This preparation will primarily involve Timothy's character. He is to flee youthful passions and pursue the characteristics of godliness. Though Timothy is relatively young (cf. 1 Tim. 4:12), he is not to be defined by the trappings of youth, which, in this context, probably refer especially to youthful pride and arrogance. Instead of being quarrelsome, he should teach with gentleness and patience. Even his opponents must be treated with gentleness, entrusting their repentance to God (2:22–26).

The Contrast between False and True Teachers

■ READ 2 TIMOTHY 3:1–17 ■

In the **last days** false teachers will be plentiful and will be known by their lifestyle: they will be lovers of self and money, proud and unholy, lovers of pleasure and not God—among other damning characteristics (3:1–5). They prey on the vulnerable with their deceptions and resist the truth. Like Jannes and Jambres, who opposed Moses, they will make their foolishness evident to all (3:6–9).

In direct contrast to them, Timothy has followed Paul's example of teaching, conduct, purpose, faith, patience, love, and endurance (3:10). And these have been accompanied by Paul's sufferings, all from which the Lord has so far delivered him. But Paul is not to be regarded as unique in this respect, since "all who want to live a godly life in Christ Jesus will be persecuted" (3:12). Knowledge of the Scriptures prepares Timothy and all people for salvation (in contrast to the deceptions of false teachers) by producing faith in Christ Jesus (3:13–15).

THEOLOGICAL ISSUES

The Last Days

Throughout the New Testament "the last days" refers to the period between Jesus's ascension and his eventual return. That is, the last two thousand years have been the last days. So, Paul's statement about the hard times that will come in the last days (3:1) simply refers to difficulties that will take place as we await Jesus's return. One of these difficulties is the presence of false teachers.

CANONICAL CONNECTIONS

Jannes and Jambres vs. Moses

Paul refers to the story of the magicians of Egypt opposing Moses in Exodus 7–9, drawing a parallel to those who oppose Paul's teaching of the gospel. While Jannes and Jambres are not named in Exodus, Paul learned their names from Jewish traditions about those events. The Egyptian magicians showed impressive feats of power, but they were opposed to God's will. So false teachers in Paul's day may commend themselves with the appearance of godliness (3:5), but they are opposed to God.

Figure 21.3. Saint Paul fresco in Saint Peter's Church (Mansfield, Ohio)

This claim for Scripture leads to one of the New Testament's most significant statements about its nature: "All Scripture is inspired by God and is profitable for teaching, for rebuking, for correcting, for training in righteousness, so that the man of God may be complete, equipped for every good work" (3:16–17).

Whatever else might be said about the inspiration of Scripture, its function is very clear: it serves to teach, rebuke, correct, and train. God's inspired word accomplishes a purpose besides simply providing information: it shapes people for service. More than that, it is able to *fully* shape people for such service, making them complete for this task.

Preach the Word

■ READ 2 TIMOTHY 4:1–8 ■

Approaching his last recorded words, Paul has one final charge to issue to Timothy. The charge is issued before God and Jesus Christ, the judge of the living and the dead, and in view of his coming kingdom. Timothy must preach the word. He is to be ready to preach the word in all situations with the same purpose that the Scriptures have: to shape and to form people (4:1–2). This is Timothy's solemn task (cf. 1:6; 1 Tim. 4:13–14).

But this will not be an easy task because people will not want sound doctrine. They will prefer what the false teachers offer because of their own inclinations and will turn away from the truth (4:3–4). Timothy, however, is to keep his head amid all the chaos. He is to be self-controlled, endure the hard times, be an evangelist, and fulfill his ministry duty (4:5).

Again, Paul offers himself as the paradigm to follow. His life has been offered as a sacrifice to God, already poured out, and his time on earth is ending. He has fought the good fight, finished the race, and kept the faith. He now looks forward to the final completion of the race and its reward, the crown of righteousness reserved for him. This crown will be given to him by Jesus himself, the righteous judge. But such a crown does not await Paul alone; all who have loved Christ will share it with him (4:6–8).

THEOLOGICAL ISSUES

The Inspiration of Scripture

Paul literally says that all Scripture is "breathed out by God" (3:16). This imagines that the words of Scripture come directly from God's mouth. While we affirm the human authorship of each part of the Bible—complete with each author's distinct writing style, theological emphases, and personal character—at the same time the Scriptures consist of God's own words. The abiding authority of Holy Scripture is rooted in the teaching that Scripture faithfully records what God intended to say.

Paul's Final Words

■ READ 2 TIMOTHY 4:9–22 ■

Paul's very last words to Timothy, and to us all, record his request for Timothy to come visit him. Paul is most likely imprisoned in Rome and has been deserted by others, except for Luke, his longtime travel companion. Paul has sent Tychicus to Ephesus—presumably to take Timothy's place while he visits Paul—and asks Timothy to bring the scrolls and parchments. Though Paul's ministry has virtually come to an end, he still plans for further ministry of the word (4:9–13).

Figure 21.4. Ruins in Crete

Though deserted by others, Paul was strengthened by the Lord to preach the word to the gentiles. The Lord rescued him from the lion's mouth—possibly a reference to Emperor Nero. And the Lord will continue to rescue him—not from death, but from evil. He will deliver Paul safely into his heavenly kingdom (4:16–18). In the end, no one can harm Paul. The worst they can do is kill him. But for Paul, that is the ultimate deliverance into God's loving arms.

Exploration—Reading Titus

Ministry in Crete

■ READ TITUS 1:1–16 ■

In an unusually long greeting, Paul reflects on his purpose as an apostle of Christ: it is for the faith of the elect, their knowledge of the truth, in the hope of eternal life. Paul's responsibility to preach for this purpose was entrusted to him by God himself (1:1–3). He writes to Titus, whom he regards as his true son in the faith (1:4).

Paul says that he left Titus in Crete to appoint elders for the churches in each town. Elders are to possess exemplary character, and they ought to teach sound doctrine (1:5–9; cf. 1 Tim. 3:1–7). This is important because there are many who deviate from the truth, especially those who want to make gentiles into Jews (known as the circumcision party). Their teaching is destructive,

LITERARY NOTES

The Structure of Titus

Concerned entirely with the health of the church in Crete, Paul instructs Titus to appoint godly elders for leadership and to silence false teachers (1:1–16). Chapters 2 and 3 focus on the Christian behavior of older men and women, younger men and women, and slaves and masters (2:1–10), and on Christian teaching concerning the grace of God, godliness, and redemption (2:11–3:11). The letter closes with final instructions (3:12–15).

When Was Paul in Crete?

The only record of Paul being in Crete is during his journey to Rome as a prisoner (Acts 27:7–12). Though the ship's crew planned to spend the winter in Crete, it is unclear whether that's what they did—but it seems they did not (Acts 27:21). So on that particular voyage Paul spent either a winter in Crete or no time there at all. Even if they wintered there, it is unlikely that Paul was able to establish the churches in Crete (Titus 1:5), since he was a prisoner under centurion guard (Acts 27:1). There are two other possibilities. First, Paul may have visited Crete during one of his missionary journeys, though Luke did not record it—after all, Luke did not tell us everything he could have (since all history is selective). Second, Paul may have visited Crete after being released from his house arrest in Rome (AD 62) but before his second, more severe imprisonment that led to his death.

Our Great God and Savior

One of the most debated features of the letter is whom Paul identifies as God in 2:13: "the appearing of the glory of our great God and Savior, Jesus Christ." Does he directly call Jesus "God"? Either he refers to God the Father *and* the Savior Jesus Christ ("our great God, and our Savior Jesus Christ"), or he calls Jesus "God and Savior." While part of the answer depends on a complicated issue in Greek syntax (involving something known as Granville Sharp's Rule), there are a few other issues to consider. Paul normally calls Jesus "Savior," not the Father as "Savior," but in this letter he appears to do so in 1:3 and 3:4. There is no reason why he should not do so, since salvation depends on the grace of God (2:11). But he also calls Jesus "Savior" in 2:13 and 3:6. The real question is not whether Paul can call God "Savior" but whether these references to "God our Savior" (1:3; 3:4) might actually refer to Jesus too, apparently in keeping with 2:13. While debate continues to swirl around these expressions, it is more than likely that Paul does call Jesus "God" in 2:13, and it is possible that 1:3 and 3:4 also refer to Jesus (but this is less likely). (See also the sidebar "Does Peter Call Jesus 'God'?" in chap. 26.)

and, as Crete's own prophets have said, "Cretans are always liars, evil beasts, lazy gluttons." Paul agrees! So they should be rebuked and corrected (1:10–16).

Proclaim Sound Teaching

■ READ TITUS 2:1–15 ■

Given this backdrop, Titus is to engage in sound teaching that will help people to live godly lives as appropriate to who they are. Older men should be worthy of respect; older women, reverent; young women should love their husbands and children; young men should be self-controlled; slaves should submit to their masters (2:1–10).

After all, the grace of God has come, bringing salvation for all and instructing them to live in a godly way while waiting for the appearing of Christ. He gave himself to redeem people and to cleanse them to belong to him. In this way, Paul points out the goal of salvation and redemption: it is not simply so that people can be forgiven of their sins, but also that people will be transformed in order to belong to Christ. It is about Christ creating a people for himself, so believers must live in a way befitting the people of Christ. Titus is to proclaim these things with authority (2:11–15).

Living in the World

■ READ TITUS 3:1–11 ■

Believers are to live in a way that commends Christ to the world outside. This will involve submitting to the authorities, doing good deeds, and being kind to people. Though once foolish and disobedient people, the kindness and love of God led him to save us according to his mercy, not our deeds. And God has poured out his Spirit through Christ, making believers the heirs of eternal life (3:1–7).

Titus is to insist on these things in his leadership and teaching. This is so that those who believe in God will also be devoted to good works, not merely believing. They should avoid foolish debates and unnecessary division. All such things are unprofitable and lead to self-condemnation (3:8–11).

Final Greetings

■ READ TITUS 3:12–15 ■

Paul will send one of his coworkers, Artemas or Tychicus, to Crete, and then he hopes that Titus will come to visit him in Nicopolis (Greece). Before signing off, Paul once more stresses the importance of good deeds and fruitfulness (3:12–15).

Implementation—Reading The Pastoral Letters as Christian Scripture Today

Nearly all the issues addressed in the Pastoral Letters remain relevant to the life of the church today. While the care for widows may not be as pressing as it once was, still the principle of taking care of people as members of one's own family is the duty of the church. The threat of false teaching is as vibrant as ever, though taking different forms from those encountered by Timothy and Titus. The importance of Timothy and Titus, and all leaders of the church, to be faithful in their teaching and godly living remains central to the health of the churches.

KEY VERSES IN 1–2 TIMOTHY AND TITUS

- But if I should be delayed, I have written so that you will know how people ought to conduct themselves in God's household, which is the church of the living God, the pillar and foundation of the truth. 1 Timothy 3:15
- Pay close attention to your life and your teaching; persevere in these things, for in doing this you will save both yourself and your hearers. 1 Timothy 4:16
- Be diligent to present yourself to God as one approved, a worker who doesn't need to be ashamed, correctly teaching the word of truth. 2 Timothy 2:15
- For the grace of God has appeared, bringing salvation for all people, instructing us to deny godlessness and worldly lusts and to live in a sensible, righteous, and godly way in the present age, while we wait for the blessed hope, the appearing of the glory of our great God and Savior, Jesus Christ. Titus 2:11–13

Christian Reading Questions

1. Scan 1 Timothy for direct instructions to Timothy about his ministry. Summarize his responsibilities in your own words.

2. What does it mean for Timothy when Paul tells him, "Pay close attention to your life and your teaching . . . in doing this, you will save both yourself and your hearers" (1 Tim. 4:16)?

3. Find all the references in 2 Timothy to suffering. Why is suffering such a significant element in this letter?

4. Search Titus for all its references to good works and godly living. If God saves people because of his mercy, not because of our works (Titus 3:4–5), why does Paul stress the importance of good works so much in this letter?

CHAPTER TWENTY-TWO

The Letter to Philemon

Orientation

The shortest of Paul's Letters packs a punch. The Letter to Philemon is extraordinary for its subject matter, the situation
behind the letter, and for Paul's way of making
a big request from a brother in Christ. Paul is
imprisoned (probably in Rome, though possibly
in Ephesus), and writes to his friend Philemon,
who lives in Colossae.

The letter concerns a runaway slave, Onesimus. Apparently Onesimus had belonged
to Philemon, but after running away from
his master, he met Paul and came to faith in
Christ. Now Paul has sent Onesimus back to
Philemon (carrying this letter) and not-so-
subtly requests that Philemon grant Onesimus
his freedom.

The way that Paul makes this request is
intriguing. He never comes right out and says
what he wants. Instead, he gives a series of
strong hints that make his desire clear. The
reason for speaking this way seems to be out of
respect for Philemon. He does not command
Philemon to let Onesimus go, since he knows
that Philemon has no obligation to do so, and

HISTORICAL MATTERS

The Historical Origins of Philemon

Author: Paul

Date: AD 61–62

Location: Rome

Setting: Paul is imprisoned in Rome, under
imperial guard.

HISTORICAL MATTERS

Who Was Philemon?

Philemon was a Christian who lived in Colossae. It
seems that he came to faith through Paul's ministry (19), though we know no details of how that
happened. But it must have happened outside
Colossae, since Paul never visited that town (Col.
2:1). Probably Philemon heard Paul's preaching
in Ephesus, which was the major hub of Paul's
third missionary journey—around one hundred
miles west of Colossae. Philemon became a faithful believer, serving others (7) and hosting the
Colossian church in his home (2). That the church
met in his house, together with the fact that he
had been a slave owner, indicates that he was
relatively wealthy.

Figure 22.1. *Conversion of Onesimus* by Benjamin West

The Museum of Fine Arts, Houston, The Bayou Bend Collection, gift of Miss Ima Hogg

HISTORICAL MATTERS

Slavery in the Greco-Roman World

In the first-century Roman Empire approximately one-third or one-fourth of the population consisted of slaves. This slavery was not based on race, as it was in the history of the United States and Europe, but came about as the Romans conquered other people or as the result of great debt or as the punishment for crime. While some slaves experienced great suffering and experienced subsistence living (especially those on ships and in mines), many were educated and skilled and played important roles in households, businesses, and government.[1]

Because slaves made up so much of the population, it is common to find instructions from philosophers and moral teachers to masters about how to handle their slaves, often with encouragement to treat slaves well, at least for the practical reasons of caring for one's property.

The New Testament likewise often gives instructions to Christian masters to be examples of kindness and fairness to their servants and slaves, treating them as brothers (Eph. 6:9; Col. 4:1). The New Testament Letters also address slaves directly, exhorting them to be like Christ, indicating that they too were welcome in the Christian assemblies (Col. 3:22–24; 1 Tim. 6:1–2; 1 Pet. 2:18–21).

LITERARY NOTES

The Structure of Philemon

Because Philemon is such a short letter, the structure is straightforward. Paul begins by giving thanks for Philemon (1–7) and then pivots to make his appeal on behalf of Onesimus (8–22). The letter ends with brief greetings (23–25).

he does not want to pressure his friend to do something he is not willing to do. Yet at the same time, Paul leans on their friendship—and even the fact that he led Philemon to Christ—to encourage him to do the right thing.

At the heart of the letter is the conviction that master and slave have become brothers in Christ. While Philemon's love for Paul is to be a factor in considering Paul's request, so is his love for his new brother, Onesimus. The letter therefore testifies to the amazing power of Christ to transform relationships across cultural boundaries and the structures of society.

Exploration—Reading Philemon

Participation in the Faith

■ READ PHILEMON 1–7 ■

Paul, with his cosender Timothy, writes to Philemon, whom he describes as their dear friend and coworker, and to the church that meets in Philemon's house (1–3). Paul thanks God for Philemon's love and faith, and he prays that his partnership, or fellowship, in the faith might become effective. Paul takes joy and encouragement from the fact that Philemon has been loving toward the other believers in Colossae (4–7).

Paul's prayer about Philemon's partnership in the faith becoming effective is not for nothing. Rather, it sets things up for Paul to make his request of Philemon. He wants to see Philemon put his faith into action in a very specific way, as he will go on to reveal.

Figure 22.2. Engraving of the slave Onesimus coming back to Philemon his master with a letter from the apostle Paul

The Appeal

■ READ PHILEMON 8–16 ■

Paul pivots to address his main concern. Though he feels he has the authority to command Philemon to do what he wants, he makes a point of saying that he will not do that. Instead, he will appeal to Philemon based on love. It is the appeal of an elderly man in prison (8–9).

Paul's appeal is for the sake of Onesimus, whom he describes as his son. Paul became his father while in chains, meaning that Onesimus came to faith in Christ through Paul while Paul was imprisoned. Onesimus, it turns out, was a slave belonging to Philemon (16) who ran away from his master. He met Paul while running away from Philemon, and now he is a brother in Christ.

Paul is sending Onesimus back to his rightful owner, Philemon, but comments that before his conversion Onesimus was useless to him. Now, as a Christian, Onesimus is useful both to Philemon and to Paul. In other words, Onesimus is a new man, and not the man Philemon once knew him to be. Nevertheless, Paul sends Onesimus, whom he describes as "my very own heart," back to Philemon (11–12).

The closest Paul gets to saying explicitly what he wants is in the next phrase: "I wanted to keep him with me, so that in my imprisonment for the gospel he might serve me in your place" (13). Paul wants Onesimus to

Philemon and Slavery in the American South

The racially based enslavement of Africans in the eighteenth and nineteenth centuries in America was atrocious and has continued to mark American history with racial, social, and economic tensions. Many arguments against abolition were made by Southerners, including that the end of slavery would destroy the agricultural economy and result in massive unemployment and chaos in society. John C. Calhoun and others suggested that American slavery was actually a benefit to the uncivilized and uneducated pagans of Africa, who now had work and care from their owners. Sadly, Christianity and the Bible often were employed by slaveholders and preachers in support of the ownership and even unjust treatment of slaves. One favorite text was Philemon because, the argument goes, Paul did not abolish slavery but instead sent Philemon's runaway slave, Onesimus, back to him. The problems with this use of Philemon are many, including the very different system of slavery in the ancient world and, most importantly, Paul is far from supporting the status quo: he appeals to Philemon to reconceptualize his relationship with his former slave, seeing him now with more important categories, as a fellow brother worthy of love (9, 16).

A Brother in the Flesh and in the Lord?

It is difficult to know what Paul means when he describes Onesimus as a brother to Philemon both in the flesh and in the Lord. Clearly, in the Lord they are spiritual brothers. Brothers "in the flesh" does not refer to a blood relationship (or this letter would be entirely different). Most likely, it means that a new relationship will develop between the two men once Philemon grants Onesimus his freedom. They are already on equal footing spiritually as brothers in the Lord. Paul's reference to their brotherhood in the flesh may constitute another element of his appeal for Onesimus's freedom, so that they will no longer be master and slave but be "brothers"—on an equal footing in human terms, as they already are in spiritual terms.

stay with him. He is useful now that he is a believer. He can work alongside Paul while Paul is imprisoned.

But, says Paul, he has not acted on his wish and instead wants to do the right thing by Philemon, who, by law, is the rightful owner of Onesimus. This gives Philemon the freedom to decide what to do about Onesimus so that his "good deed" will come from his free will, not out of obligation (14). Paul does not come straight out and say it, but it is clear that Philemon's "good deed" should be to grant Onesimus his freedom.

Before going on, Paul speculates on the plan of God through these events. In the sovereign plan of God, perhaps Onesimus's running away was for the purpose of his conversion. After coming to Christ, Onesimus would be returned to Philemon permanently, meaning that they will enter an eternal relationship of brotherhood in Christ. He certainly is loved as a brother of Paul, and he will be even more so to Philemon—a brother in the flesh and in the Lord (16). Maybe that is the whole point of these events. It was God's will that Onesimus should run away. Now, will Philemon play along with God's plans?

Give a Warm Welcome to Your New Brother

■ READ PHILEMON 17–25 ■

Paul draws on Philemon's partnership to ask him to welcome Onesimus just as he would welcome Paul himself (17). Anything that Onesimus owes Philemon—perhaps by stealing from him before running away—will be repaid by Paul. He will pay it even though Philemon owes Paul his very self (18–19)!

Paul hopes to benefit from Philemon and for his heart to be refreshed (20), just as the Colossians have been refreshed by Philemon's love (7). No doubt Paul means that he hopes to be refreshed by Philemon's loving release of Onesimus. Paul is confident of Philemon's obedience (even though he has not commanded anything of him) and says, "I write to you, knowing that you will do even more than I ask" (21 NIV). This is a not-so-subtle way of nudging Philemon to go beyond the simple request to welcome Onesimus as a loved brother. Granting his freedom might be one way to do that—nudge, nudge. 📖

Now that Paul's request is complete, with both a surface application (welcoming Onesimus) and a deeper application (giving Onesimus his freedom), Paul comments that he hopes to visit Philemon (22). This reaffirms the love that Paul has for Philemon, in which his request concerning Onesimus is couched.

Finally, Paul sends greetings from his fellow prisoner, Epaphras, who founded the church in Colossae (Col. 1:7), and from Paul's coworkers Mark, Aristarchus, Demas, and Luke (23–24).

Implementation—Reading Philemon as Christian Scripture Today

The theological reality of the brotherhood in Christ of master and slave is truly mind-blowing. This is the enduring legacy of Paul's Letter to Philemon. It testifies to the way that Christ makes brothers and sisters of people who otherwise would be separated by cultural divisions and social structures. The poor and the rich, Jews and gentiles, masters and slaves are all one in Christ Jesus. Though Philemon is still technically Onesimus's slave master (until he grants Paul's request), they are also brothers in Christ. Paul requests Philemon to consider Onesimus in this light and to treat him as his equal.

Although master-slave structures may not exist legally in today's society, there are lots of structures that elevate some people and devalue others. The workplace, the mainstream media, politics, and social media all value people according to a hierarchy. Authority and leadership are necessary and good, but these should not determine the value of human beings. In Christ, people at opposite ends of the social spectrum are made one. While it may still be appropriate to respect certain social structures—say, if one Christian is the employer of another—nevertheless, it remains true that the social and cultural structures that divide us are overcome by faith and love.

LITERARY NOTES

The Relationship of Philemon to Colossians

Paul's Letter to Philemon traditionally has been associated with his Letter to the Colossians. Philemon was a prominent member of the church in Colossae; both letters were written during a Pauline imprisonment (Col. 4:18; Philem. 1, 23); Timothy is the coauthor of both letters (Col. 1:1; Philem. 1); and Paul's same coworkers are listed in both letters: Luke, Mark, Demas, Aristarchus, and Epaphras (Col. 4:10–14; Philem. 23–24). Significantly, the sending of Onesimus is mentioned in both letters (Col. 4:9; Philem. 10, 12, 17). It is likely that the letters were sent to Colossae together.

We do not know whether Philemon granted Paul's request. But we do know that a key leader later came to prominence in the major city of Ephesus—the bishop of Ephesus, in fact. His name was Onesimus.

KEY VERSES IN PHILEMON

- I pray that your participation in the faith may become effective through knowing every good thing that is in us for the glory of Christ. 6
- For this reason, although I have great boldness in Christ to command you to do what is right, I appeal to you, instead, on the basis of love. 8–9
- For perhaps this is why he was separated from you for a brief time, so that you might get him back permanently, no longer as a slave, but more than a slave—as a dearly loved brother. He is especially so to me, but how much more to you, both in the flesh and in the Lord. 15–16

Christian Reading Questions

1. Search this letter for all the references to Paul's relationship with Philemon. How would you characterize it?
2. Trace throughout this letter each "hint" that Paul makes to Philemon about what he should do with Onesimus.
3. What does this letter say about Paul's attitude toward slavery?
4. How would you respond to someone from the eighteenth or nineteenth century defending American slavery based on the Letter to Philemon?

CHAPTER TWENTY-THREE

The Letter to the Hebrews

Orientation

The Letter to the Hebrews is the most mysterious book of the New Testament. Its author and audience are unknown to us. It is also the book that most directly focuses on Israel's religion, how the old covenant points forward to Christ, and how Christ is its ultimate fulfillment.

The letter is remarkably Christocentric, with its main points looking to the supremacy of Christ over all other revelations of God, the angels, Moses, and Israel's priesthood, temple, and sacrificial system. Jesus is the great high priest who mediates between humanity and God, making all other mediators redundant. Jesus mediates the new covenant, which is far superior to the old, and offers himself as the ultimate and final sacrifice for sins.

Given the supremacy of Christ over all previous revelations of God, the old covenant, and Israelite religion, the author strongly urges his readers not to turn back from Christ in the face of pressure or persecution. Instead, they ought to endure to the end,

HISTORICAL MATTERS

The Historical Origins of Hebrews

Author: Unknown

Date: mid-60s?

Location: Unknown

Setting: The traditional understanding has been that the author writes to Jewish Christians who may have experienced persecution and feel pressure or temptation to return to Judaism. Recent scholarship, however, favors a gentile audience under pressure to observe Jewish customs.

LITERARY NOTES

The Structure of Hebrews

The structure of Hebrews revolves around the superiority of Jesus. Jesus is God's superior last word (1:1–4), superior over the angels (1:5–2:18), and superior over Moses (3:1–4:13). Jesus is the superior high priest (4:14–7:28) over the superior new covenant (8:1–13) and the superior new **tabernacle** (9:1–10:39). The final three chapters exhort readers with the examples of faith (11:1–12:3), discipline and worship (12:4–29), and general instructions (13:1–25).

311

LITERARY NOTES

Who Wrote Hebrews?

The authorship of Hebrews remains one the great puzzles of the New Testament. Though early copies of the New Testament included Hebrews along with Paul's Letters, the early church was divided as to whether Paul was the author. The book does not indicate authorship, Pauline or otherwise, and the language is very different from that of Paul's Letters. Some speculated that Paul was the original author of the letter in Hebrew and Luke translated it into Greek (its known form), since the language is much more similar to Luke's than Paul's. Alternatively, a modern suggestion is that Paul preached its contents in Aramaic and Luke transcribed the sermon into Greek. Other suggestions have included Apollos (Luther), Clement of Rome (Calvin), and Barnabas. But in short, there is not enough evidence to endorse any such suggestions. We admit ignorance as to who wrote Hebrews. Probably its original readers knew the author, a well-educated (Hellenistic?) Jewish believer versed in the Old Testament.

LITERARY NOTES

Is Hebrews Really a Letter?

Hebrews lacks most of the features of a normal letter. There is no greeting, no author is mentioned, and the recipients are not named. Though the author refers to the document as something he has written, he also calls it "a word of exhortation" (13:22), which was a common way to refer to a sermon. There are also many references to saying, speaking, hearing, and so forth scattered throughout. These facts have led some interpreters to regard Hebrews as a sermon that has been written down. Perhaps it was written down by the person who originally preached it, or perhaps it was transcribed by someone who heard it. Either way, this explanation goes a long way to account for the document's unusual features.

following the example of Israel, whose history demonstrated faith in the face of opposition.

Exploration—Reading Hebrews

The Superior Son

■ READ HEBREWS 1:1–14 ■

Hebrews begins by establishing the superiority of the Son of God over all others. He is superior to the heroes of Israel's history to whom God spoke (1:1–2), just as he is superior to the heavenly angels (1:3–14). The opening verses articulate the Son's superiority in revealing God, in his power in and over creation, in saving humanity from sin, and in his position over all things. Though God has revealed himself to Israel's patriarchs (the fathers) and to Israel's prophets, such as Samuel and Isaiah, in these final days he has spoken by his Son (1:1–2a). This Son is heir of all things, and all things were made through him (1:2b). The Son perfectly reveals God's glory and nature and is the sustaining force of the created universe (1:3a). He dealt with human sin and was exalted to the ultimate position of authority at the right hand of God (1:3b).

The Son is also superior to the angels (1:4). To prove this point, the author launches into a collection of Old Testament texts (known as a "catena") taken from Psalms, 2 Samuel, 1 Chronicles, and Deuteronomy (1:5–13). Together, this collection of texts definitively declares that the Son has a unique relationship with the Father and is enthroned as God's anointed king (Messiah), and all the heavens and earth owe their existence to him. Though they are temporary, he is eternal. The angels acknowledge the Son's superiority, and their job is to help and serve those who will receive salvation through the Son (1:14).

Hold On to Your Salvation

■ READ HEBREWS 2:1–18 ■

The author shifts to exhortation, drawing on all of what was set up in chapter 1: we must pay attention to what was heard so that we don't drift away (2:1). Now the comparison with angels in chapter 1 is applied: if their message was legally binding (referring to the law of Moses), with its punishments for failures, how much more serious is it to neglect the salvation that comes through the superior Son (2:2–3)? In other words, the old covenant was very serious; how much more serious is the covenant that overtakes it? God ratified it through signs and wonders—miracles and gifts from the Spirit (2:4).

Although Jesus is superior to the angels, he became a man in order to share in our humanity. Psalm 8 talks about humanity being made "lower than the angels" but crowned with glory and honor with everything under their feet (2:6–8). Though we do not yet see the reality of this, we *do* see Jesus, who was lowered below the angels so that he might die for humanity, and then was crowned with glory and honor (2:7–9). In other words, Jesus fulfilled God's intention for humanity.

Jesus shares in our humanity in order to save humanity, so that the one who sanctifies (Jesus) and those who are sanctified (believers in Jesus) "all have one Father," and Jesus calls them his brothers and sisters (2:11–13). Jesus shared in our flesh and blood in order to destroy the devil and free those in slavery to him and to death (2:14–15). Jesus did not become human in order to save angels, but Abraham's offspring (2:16), which meant that he had to become like us in every way in order to serve as a high priest for us, making atonement for us, and experiencing human temptation like us (2:17–18).

All this underscores the greatness of our salvation (cf. 2:3). Not only is Jesus superior to the angels (1:4–14), but also the salvation he brings is superior to anything prior to Jesus's ministry. Though superior, Jesus lowered himself to save humanity and to serve as mediator between God and humans.

Glory, Descension, Ascension, Glory

Theologians have long observed that the story of Jesus can be helpfully depicted as a huge U:

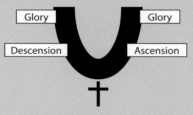

Figure 23.1.

This U shape comes from putting together the many statements about who Jesus is as the divine Son of God, what he accomplished on earth, and where he now is as the ascended Savior at the right hand of God. The eternal Son of God was glorious before the creation of the world (John 1:1–3). He descended to the earth by taking on flesh and becoming the man Jesus of Nazareth (Matt. 1:18–24; John 3:13; Eph. 4:9). He suffered, died, and was resurrected (Mark 15:1–47). Then he ascended bodily to reside in glory again in heaven with God the Father (Acts 1:9–11; Heb. 1:3), having received the name that is above every other name (Phil. 2:5–11).

Figure 23.2. *Moses and the Brazen Serpent and the Transfiguration of Jesus* by Cristóbal de Villalpando

Jesus Is Superior to Moses Too

■ READ HEBREWS 3:1–19 ■

Believers should consider Jesus, who is described as "the apostle and high priest of our confession" (3:1). He was sent by God (apostle), and he mediates between God and humanity (high priest). Like Moses, Jesus was faithful to the one who sent him, but he is worthy of more glory than Moses because "the builder has more honor than the house" (3:3). As the author explains, God built the house and Moses was a servant within it (3:4–5). But Christ was faithful as a *Son* over the household (3:6a). Because he is God's Son, Jesus rules over his Father's house, since it belongs to him as the Son who inherits from his Father. But Moses was simply a servant within the Son's house. The author adds that "we are that household" (3:6b), indicating that the house he's talking about is the collected people of God.

Given that Christ is over the household, believers should not turn away. The author offers a lengthy citation of Psalm 95:7–11, warning his readers not to harden their hearts like the Israelites did during their forty years in the desert (3:7–11). Instead, they should encourage one another daily so that they hold fast until the end (3:13–15) and enter God's rest, unlike the rebellious Israelites (3:16–19).

Receiving the Promised Rest

■ READ HEBREWS 4:1–13 ■

Though the rebellious Israelites failed to enter God's rest (the promised land of Israel), believers in Christ should make sure not to fall short of God's promise of heavenly rest (4:1–3). This rest is grounded in God's rest after the creation of the world (4:4). This Sabbath day of God's rest is available for his people to share in, but not if they persist in disobedience

(4:5–11). The word of God is his instrument for judging the thoughts and intentions of the heart so that no one is hidden from him (4:12–13). This means that disobedience cannot be ignored or overlooked.

Our Great High Priest

■ READ HEBREWS 4:14–5:10 ■

Believers are encouraged to hold on to the confession of their faith because Jesus is our great high priest, who has lived the human experience and understands our weaknesses (4:14–15). As priestly intercessor between God and us, Jesus enables believers to approach God's throne with boldness rather than fear (4:16).

This is similar to the high priest in Israelite religion, who too was human but, unlike Jesus, was sinful and had to offer a sacrifice for his own sins before sacrificing for the sins of the people (5:1–3). Just as that high priest had to be called to the role, so Jesus was called by God to be a priest in the order of Melchizedek (5:4–6, 10). Because of his obedience through suffering to the point of death, Christ now offers salvation to all who obey him (5:7–9).

Growing in Faith

■ READ HEBREWS 5:11–6:12 ■

The author turns to rebuke his readers for their laziness and the fact that they should be teachers by now rather than students again of the basics. Instead of being mature enough to eat "solid food," they are infants in the faith still requiring a diet of milk. So it is time to move them beyond the basics (5:11–14).

Moving forward in maturity of faith is the only direction to take, since going backward is spiritually very dangerous. To fall away and then try to come back would be to recrucify Christ and to show him contempt (6:1–8). But the author is confident of better things for his readers, who have demonstrated good deeds and love in the past. Now they must continue to the end in the same manner as those who inherit God's promises through faith (6:9–12).

Falling Away and Coming Back?

In Hebrews 6:4–8 the author says that someone who falls away from Christ cannot be brought back to repentance. The harshness of this warning seems to contradict the Protestant Reformation principle "once saved, always saved." How could a genuine Christian fall away? And if a believer rejects Christ and then turns back, how can there be no forgiveness for them? Some have argued that this refers not to a true believer, but to someone who appeared to be but was not. However, descriptions such as tasting the heavenly gift, sharing in the Holy Spirit, and tasting God's word and the powers of the age to come (6:4–5) seem to push against that reading. Additionally, even the apostle Peter denied knowing Christ and was restored. Since Hebrews addresses the problem of turning away from Christ because of persecution, the author warns his readers against public and final apostasy. Once a decisive rejection of Christ has occurred, there is no possibility for restoration.

CANONICAL CONNECTIONS

Melchizedek

Melchizedek appears twice in the Old Testament, in Genesis 14:18–20 and Psalm 110:4. In Genesis 14 Melchizedek appears out of nowhere and is introduced only as the king of Salem (Jerusalem) and a priest of God Most High. He brings Abraham (at this point still called Abram) bread and wine and blesses him. Abraham then gives him a tenth of his belongings. And as mysteriously as Melchizedek appeared, so he disappears and is never again mentioned in the book. Psalm 110 is the most quoted psalm in the New Testament, seen as fulfilled in Jesus as David's "Lord" who will sit at God's right hand (110:1), rule over his enemies (110:2), and be a priest forever in the order of Melchizedek (110:4). In the New Testament Melchizedek appears only in Hebrews (5:6, 10; 6:20–7:1; 7:10–11, 15, 17), where the author quotes Psalm 110:4 twice (5:6; 7:17).

God's Promises Can Be Trusted

■ READ HEBREWS 6:13–7:28 ■

Speaking of those who inherit God's promises through faith, the author turns to consider the example of Abraham. God promised to bless Abraham and to greatly multiply him, meaning that his descendants would be many. Abraham waited patiently and received the promise (6:13–15).

But God has sworn an oath to Abraham's heirs (believers in Jesus) too so that believers can hold on to hope even amid difficulty (6:17–18). This hope is an anchor for our souls and connects believers to the most holy place of God's dwelling, "the inner sanctuary behind the curtain" (6:19). This hope is secured by Jesus, who entered the inner sanctuary for us because he is a high priest in the order of Melchizedek (6:20).

The author explains the significance of Melchizedek, describing him as a priest who blessed Abraham and whose name means "king of righteousness." Strangely, he had no father, mother, or genealogy, and no beginning or end of life. In fact, he resembled the Son of God (7:1–3). In a complicated little piece of argumentation the author effectively asserts Melchizedek's superiority of both Abraham and the **Levitical priesthood** that would develop later from Abraham's descendants (7:4–10).

The author then leaves Abraham to focus on the Levitical priesthood and its contrast to Melchizedek. Since perfection did not come through the Levitical priesthood, there was need for another priest of a different order (7:11). The author argues how Jesus can be regarded a high priest though he comes not from the tribe of Levi—the source of all Levitical priests—but from the tribe of Judah (7:12–17). And through Jesus's priesthood a better hope is introduced as he enables believers to draw near to God (7:18–19).

God made Jesus a priest by an oath (unlike the Levitical priests), in connection with a better covenant than the old covenant (7:20–22). Under the old covenant, the Levitical priests could not remain in office because each one died, but the eternal Jesus is a permanent priest, enabling him to unceasingly intercede for his people (7:23–25). He is without fault or sin and offered only one sacrifice—himself—once and for all. Unlike the weak high priests of the past, God's perfected Son has been appointed to be the ultimate priest (7:26–28). 👥

Figure 23.3. Sixteenth-century Roman coin depicting Abraham and his captains met by Melchizedek

The High Priest of the New Covenant

■ READ HEBREWS 8:1–13 ■

Jesus the high priest sat down at God's right hand, serving his people in the presence of God (8:1–2). Just as the previous high priests offered gifts and sacrifices, so Jesus as high priest makes an offering (8:3). The earthly priests, however, were just a copy and shadow of the heavenly reality that is fulfilled in Jesus (8:4–5). His ministry is superior to theirs, and the covenant that he mediates is superior to the old covenant (8:6).

The author turns now to focus on the superiority of this new covenant. With a lengthy quotation from Jeremiah 31:31–34, the author reminds readers of God's promise that a new covenant would come that would be different from the covenant made with Israel through Moses. This new covenant will see God write his law on the people's minds and hearts, and each one will know God personally. He will forgive their sins forever (8:7–12). The author then interprets Jeremiah's mention of a new covenant to mean that the old covenant is now obsolete (8:13).

Old- and New-Covenant Ministry

■ READ HEBREWS 9:1–28 ■

The author describes the earthly sanctuary for the tabernacle (9:1–5).

CANONICAL CONNECTIONS

The Levitical Priesthood

Levi was one of Jacob's twelve sons (Gen. 35:23–26), and his descendants therefore became one of the twelve tribes of Israel. In Numbers 8 the members of the tribe of Levi (known as Levites) were commissioned to serve God in the tent of meeting (the tabernacle) as priests reserved for that task. This Levitical priesthood consisted of male members of the tribe of Levi between the ages of twenty-five and fifty (Num. 8:24–25).

RECEPTION HISTORY

Melchizedek in the Preaching of Jonathan Edwards

The reference in Hebrews 7:1–3 to Melchizedek, the mysterious priest from Abraham's day (Gen. 14:18–20), has fascinated and perplexed theologians and preachers throughout the church's history. One famous preacher who loved exploring and unpacking the wonders of Melchizedek was Jonathan Edwards, the great Puritan preacher and early American intellectual giant. Edwards saw in Melchizedek a very important *type*, or analogous picture, of Christ. Edwards explored the multiple ways in which Melchizedek is a prepicture of who Christ is, the shadow of whom Jesus is the substance. Melchizedek's name means "king of righteousness" or "king of peace," things that are ultimately true for Jesus more than any person in the world. Edwards also notes that Melchizedek brought out bread and wine to bless Abraham (Gen. 14:18), providing a powerful connection with the church's celebration of the Lord's Supper. Melchizedek also performed duties that combined the roles of king and priest, something not done in the Old Testament, but which Jesus incarnated in himself. In these ways and more, Edwards models a Christian reading of the whole Bible, drawing out intracanonical connections freely and joyfully.[1]

Figure 23.4. Drawing of the high priest offering a sacrifice, from
Treasures of the Bible by Henry Davenport Northrop

The priests entered the first room of the sanctuary regularly, but only the high priest would enter the second room, and only once a year (9:6–7). All of this served as a symbol pointing to the fact that access to the most holy place had not yet been achieved for humanity, and sacrifices for sin did not cleanse people's consciences (9:8–10).

But Christ is the ultimate high priest, who ministers in the true tabernacle, which is not a creation of human hands, entering the most holy place permanently through the sacrifice of his own blood (9:11–12). If the blood of animals served a purpose in sacrifice, how much more does the blood of Christ cleanse believers' consciences and enable them to serve God (9:13–14)?

Christ is the mediator of a new covenant, offering believers an eternal inheritance and dealing with sins under the old covenant (9:15). An inheritance can be received only once someone has died, so believers receive their eternal inheritance because of the death of Christ. Blood was required under the old covenant, since without the shedding of blood there is no forgiveness of sins (9:16–22). The same is true under the new covenant, but Christ's sacrifice of himself supersedes the old animal sacrifices (9:23). As ultimate high priest, Christ has entered heaven itself to intercede for us to God (9:24). This was done only once, having removed sin once and for all (unlike the old priests). And Christ will appear a second time to bring salvation to those who trust in him (9:25–28).

The Ultimate Sacrifice

■ READ HEBREWS 10:1–18 ■

The sacrificial system under the old covenant was unable to make worshipers perfect by the blood of bulls and goats, which was clear from the fact that the sacrifices had to be offered again and again each year (10:1–4). But the sacrifice of Jesus successfully cleanses believers in fulfillment of God's will (10:5–10; cf. Ps. 40:6–8). While earthly priests must stand and repeat their sacrifices, Jesus offered one sacrifice and *sat down* at God's right hand—symbolic of his completed work (10:11–13). His completed work has completely sanctified his people in fulfillment of Jeremiah's expectation of a new covenant and the final forgiveness of sins (10:14–18).

Godliness and Deliberate Sin

■ READ HEBREWS 10:19–39 ■

Since believers can confidently enter the sanctuary of God's presence through Jesus's blood and priesthood, we should draw near to God (10:19–22). We ought to hold on to hope, love one another, do good deeds, and continue to meet together (10:23–25).

But the author warns his readers that believers' **deliberate sin** falls outside Christ's sacrifice for sins and will lead to God's judgment and fury (10:26–27). Deliberately turning away from Christ and all that he has done is to trample on him and dishonor the new covenant and the Spirit (10:28–29). God will take vengeance on such rebellion and judge his people (10:30–31).

The author clarifies the sin he has in mind by reminding his readers of the persecution they once endured for their faith in Christ, including public taunts and confiscation of their possessions (10:32–34). Instead of giving up their faith in the face of persecution, believers should hold on to their confidence in Christ and run with endurance (10:35–38). But those who fall back to their pre-Christian lives will be destroyed by God's judgment (10:39).

The Great Examples of Faith

■ READ HEBREWS 11:1–39 ■

In order to encourage his readers not to fall back from their confession of Christ, the author offers an extended discussion about the robust faith of Israel's heroes. Faith is defined as the assurance of what is hoped for and the conviction of what is not seen (11:1). After all, faith understands that God created what is seen from what is unseen (11:2). The author works through the faithful examples of Abel, Enoch, and Noah before reaching Abraham (11:3–7). Abraham and Sarah trusted in God's promises of a land of inheritance and descendants to inherit it (11:8–12). They and their sons— indeed, all of Israel's heroes mentioned here—died before receiving all of God's promises and lived by faith as aliens and strangers in the world, as all believers should, in anticipation of a better, heavenly home (11:13–22).

THEOLOGICAL ISSUES

What Is Deliberate Sin?

Theologians debate what is meant by "deliberate sin," which, according to Hebrews, cannot be forgiven: "For if we deliberately go on sinning after receiving the knowledge of the truth, there no longer remains a sacrifice for sins" (10:26). In the context of Hebrews, the most likely understanding of "deliberate sin" is that it is the conscious, intentional, and permanent rejection of Christ. After all, there can be no salvation outside Christ. And it seems that the original readers of Hebrews were facing temptation to reject Christ in the face of persecution (10:32–36). To do so would be apostasy.

By faith Moses chose to identify with his suffering people instead of Pharaoh's family, and he led the Israelites out of captivity in Egypt (11:23–29). The Israelites took the promised land by faith, and several individuals demonstrated faith as they performed great feats and endured great persecutions and suffering (11:30–38). All of these faithful believers had to wait for what was promised so that later believers in Christ could share the inheritance with them (11:39–40).

William Perkins's *A Cloud of Faithful Witnesses*

William Perkins was a scholar and preacher in Cambridge, England, who lived in the second half of the sixteenth century (1558–1602). He was a highly influential and popular leader in the Reformed tradition in the Church of England, seeking to purify the church from within, in contrast to the Separatists, who broke away. Of the 210 books printed in Cambridge between 1585 and 1618, over 50 were written by Perkins, including many biblical commentaries.

In the 1590s he preached a series of sermons on Hebrews 11 that were published after his death under the title *A Cloud of Faithful Witnesses* (1609), and this book has been translated and reprinted countless times since.

For Perkins, following the Reformed tradition, the Christian doctrine of *vocation*, or calling, is central to his whole discussion of faith. Saving faith is an "effectual calling" that goes beyond having a general faith to good works from a purified heart. These works do not attain salvation, but their presence is a mark of saving faith. The long list of examples in Hebrews 11 tells of people whose lives evidenced the effectual calling and who then serve as examples for all later Christians. Christians are invited to "live under the Gospel" through following the scriptural examples of faithful people.[2]

Run the Race with Endurance

■ READ HEBREWS 12:1–29 ■

Like a crowd of runners who have already finished the race, these faithful ones cheer on those who are running it now. Encouraged by them, believers need to throw off whatever slows them down and run the race without giving up (12:1). As they run, they need to keep their eyes on the prize—Jesus, the one who began the race of faith and completed it (12:2). He is the model runner, and just as Jesus endured hostility, so believers need to resist opposition (12:3–4). God trains his runners with discipline, and such discipline reminds us that we are his children. The training of discipline is not always pleasant, but it pays off (12:5–11). Since the Christian life is like a marathon, runners need to strengthen their knees and make a clear path for their feet (12:12–13). This means they should pursue peace and holiness, avoiding bitterness and immorality (12:14–17).

Unlike those in Moses's day who were terrified by the presence of God at Mount Sinai—with its blazing fire, gloom, and storm—believers now come to the heavenly Mount Zion, the heavenly Jerusalem (12:18–22). By coming to the heavenly city, believers join myriads of angels, the gathering of believers to God himself and to Jesus (12:23–24). Unlike the Israelites in Moses's day who rejected God, believers today ought not reject God. Instead, we should hold on to his grace to us (12:25–29).

Final Exhortations

■ READ HEBREWS 13:1–25 ■

As the author concludes, he offers his readers some final exhortations. They should continue in brotherly love, show hospitality, remember prisoners, respect marriage, and resist greed (13:1–5). They should respect their leaders and not be led astray by false teachings (13:7–9).

Just as animal sacrifices were burned outside the camp, so Jesus suffered on the cross outside the city of Jerusalem in order to sanctify the people by his blood (13:10–12). Believers must also identify with him there, outside the metaphorical gate, sharing his disgrace (13:13). After all, this world is not our home, but we belong to the one to come (13:14). Believers are to offer up sacrifices of praise to God, to do good, and to obey their leaders (13:15–17). The author prays that the God of peace will equip his readers with all that is good for doing his will (13:20–21) and urges them to receive his written message (13:22). He informs them that Timothy has been released from prison and may accompany the author when he visits from Italy (13:23–24).

Implementation—Reading Hebrews as Christian Scripture Today

The Letter to the Hebrews is both scary and encouraging. It has some of the strongest warnings in the New Testament about the dangers of falling away from Christ. But it also presents an amazingly supreme Jesus, who towers above previous servants of God, above the old covenant, and above all previous revelations of God. He is their fulfillment and culmination. Thus, believers are to stick with him through thick and thin. Even in the face of severe persecution it is never worth abandoning Jesus, and believers must endure the race until the end. Jesus himself has already run the race, has faced temptation, and has endured to the end. He stands at the finish line beckoning all to finish well like him, encouraging us not to give up, and mediating for us with God in the meantime.

Individuals and churches alike will benefit richly by drinking from the deep well of Hebrews' Christology, encouragements, and warnings. But we also learn from Hebrews how to understand the whole Bible. The relationship between the old and new covenants is explained, as are the old and new priesthoods, mediators, and revelation of God. In every way the new is superior to the old, with Jesus as the key to it all. So when believers read the Old Testament, we are able to see how it fits in the framework of the whole Bible, and how it points to Jesus, its ultimate fulfillment.

KEY VERSES IN HEBREWS

- Long ago God spoke to the fathers by the prophets at different times and in different ways. In these last days, he has spoken to us by his Son. God has appointed him heir of all things and made the universe through him. 1:1–2
- Therefore, since we have a great high priest who has passed through the heavens—Jesus the Son of God—let us hold fast to our confession. For we do not have a high priest who is unable to sympathize with our weaknesses, but one who has been tempted in every way as we are, yet without sin. 4:14–15
- Therefore, brothers and sisters, since we have boldness to enter the sanctuary through the blood of Jesus—he has inaugurated for us a new and living way through the curtain (that is, through his flesh)—and since we have a great high priest over the house of God, let us draw near with a true heart in full assurance of faith, with our hearts sprinkled clean from an evil conscience and our bodies washed in pure water. 10:19–22
- Therefore, since we also have such a large cloud of witnesses surrounding us, let us lay aside every hindrance and the sin that so easily ensnares us. Let us run with endurance the race that lies before us, keeping our eyes on Jesus, the source and perfecter of our faith. For the joy that lay before him, he endured the cross, despising the shame, and sat down at the right hand of the throne of God. 12:1–2

Christian Reading Questions

1. Read Psalms 8 and 110. How do these two psalms inform the author's understanding of Jesus throughout Hebrews?
2. Trace the word "better" throughout Hebrews. How many times does it occur, and what is "better" than what in each instance?
3. Put into your own words why Christians no longer sacrifice animals, no longer need priests, and no longer need a temple. Support your conclusions with relevant texts from Hebrews.
4. What encouragements does Hebrews offer to help believers endure until the end? How do they apply to believers today?

CHAPTER TWENTY-FOUR

The Letter of James

Orientation

The Letter of James is so much shorter and so much less celebrated than many of its canonical siblings like the Gospels and Romans that it is easy to overlook. Yet no other New Testament book rivals James for its direct, no-nonsense approach to living out the Gospel of Jesus Christ.

The Letter of James is best described as a "wisdom paraenetic encyclical." This is a fancy way of saying that James is written as a letter to be copied and sent to various Christian communities (**encyclical**), and that the letter's content focuses on moral teaching (**paraenesis**) about how to live a good life in Christ (wisdom). The author of James is almost certainly the biological half brother of Jesus, who became the leader of the Jerusalem church in the decades after Pentecost. Before Paul was even on the scene James the Just (or Righteous) was an influential and well-respected leader, regarded as a prominent wisdom teacher in the tradition of many other Jewish sages, most notably Jesus himself.

The Letter of James is a compilation of sayings designed to teach us wisdom in a striking, challenging, and applicable way. Although the collection covers an array of topics, we can discern thematic patterns (trials and testing; our speech; wealth and poverty; faith and works) that together have one primary goal: *that readers would grow toward being whole, complete,*

Figure 24.1. Russian Orthodox icon of James the Just

and mature. The opposite of this is being "double-minded" and therefore unstable (1:8; 4:8). Five times James uses the important Greek word for wholeness or maturity (*teleios*). Modern English translations often render this as "perfect," which misconstrues the true meaning. James's exhortation to be *teleios* contains the expectation not that we will reach a sinless state ("perfect"), but that our lives will be marked by a developing wholeness and mature living based on the Wisdom of God, Jesus Christ. This whole-person wisdom promises true life now and in the life to come.

Exploration—Reading James

The Proper Perspective

■ READ JAMES 1:1–27 ■

Like Jesus before him, James gives instructions that teach his hearers how to think about the world and how to live in it rightly so that they may experience wholeness and fullness of life. We see this from the start: the stated goal is that hearers might become mature and complete (1:4). This can also be called wisdom (1:5). This wisdom produces stability, endurance, and character, culminating in the crown of life (1:2–3, 12). The alternative is the double-minded life of being tossed about, unstable, and disconnected from the Lord (1:6–8).

What makes the difference? It all depends on viewing one's life rightly, and this takes some readjustment of perspective. First, Christians must learn to embrace difficulties as meant for good because of how they shape character (1:2–4, 12). Yet Christians must not let difficulties tempt them to sin. People's temptation to sin is not God's fault but rather is the result of misplaced desires. God is only good and gracious (1:13–18). Also, people must not imagine that riches give security and status. This is foolish thinking because wealth and glory will fade away (1:9–11).

In addition to a changed perspective, Christians must move from passivity to activity. It is not enough for them to merely hear and understand God's instructions; they must also practice what God teaches. It is nothing more than self-deception if someone hears from God but their

HISTORICAL MATTERS

The Historical Origins of James

Author: Traditionally, this letter is considered to have been written by James the Just, the biological half brother of Jesus, who became the leader of the Jerusalem church after Peter departed.

Date: Possibly as early as the middle AD 40s. Tradition records James being martyred in 62.

Location: The letter was written from Jerusalem to be circulated to Christians outside Palestine, maybe especially Jewish Christians in the former area of Babylonia.

Sources: James shows knowledge of Jesus's teachings, sharing many themes especially with Matthew. James also shows familiarity with the genre of **wisdom literature**.

Setting: James reflects the Jewish wisdom tradition with its emphasis on wholeness. Also, James shows awareness of the conflicts in the early church concerning the relationship of faith and good works.

life is marked by anger, immorality, hurtful speech, and lack of care for others (1:19–27).

Wholeness as Loving Our Neighbor

■ READ JAMES 2:1–13 ■

Ancient wisdom teaching, including James, is often presented in a spiral pattern. Topics are introduced and explored briefly and then revisited in more detail, descending toward deeper understanding. The first chapter of James introduces the wisdom themes. In the following chapters they are revisited and deepened. The first topic is the issue of wealth and the temptation to treat the wealthy with favoritism while neglecting the poor. James is very pointed and straightforward. The tendency to favor the rich and powerful, offering them honor over the lower people in society, reflects a childish favoritism that is directly opposed to the maturity that should mark believers' lives. James gives two reasons why this practice is sin. First, "favoritism" (which translates a Greek idiom that means "receive the face"), or partiality, focuses on outward appearance and foolishly judges one person as more valuable than another (2:1–4). But despite outward appearances, it is the poor who are usually the richest in faith, James says, and the ones who will receive the greatest inheritance of all—the kingdom of God (2:5). The other reason why partiality is wrong is that it is disobedience to the second-greatest commandment in God's law: "Love your neighbor as yourself" (2:8). People who disobey even one part of the law are thereby breakers of the whole law (2:9–11). The wholeness that God wants from us is that we show mercy toward everyone (2:12–13).

Wholeness in Both Faith and Works

■ READ JAMES 2:14–26 ■

The Bible regularly exhorts readers to believe and trust in God, though he is unseen. This is faith (Heb. 11:1). Yet humans often distort this call to faith in self-serving and self-protecting ways. One distortion is to create a wall between belief and deeds, emphasizing the mind without mention of what we do with our bodies. We can understand God rightly yet be no better than the demons, who also comprehend the truth (1:19). The key, according to James, is wholeness between thinking and doing. Correct mental belief (**orthodox doctrine**)

LITERARY NOTES

The Structure of James

If one is used to reading the straightforward question-and-answer arguments found in Paul's Letters, James is confusing. In fact, scholars have long debated the structure of James. James is *wisdom literature* before it is a letter. This means that topics are raised in the introduction (1:1–27) and then revisited as a string of ethical teachings on various themes. James 1:26–27 is the macrolevel idea that holds together all the other topics. James exhorts his hearers to consider the marks of true faith as distinct from false and useless religion. This true faith is proved by words and works that accord with God's view of people and the world. Maturity in speech and service to those in need constitute the primary idea driving the book. The rest of James's letter is built on a spiraling exploration of this truth.

James and Paul on Justification and Works

The Letter of James is probably most famous because of an ongoing debate, triggered five hundred years ago, concerning Paul's meaning when he talks about justification by faith and not by works (Rom. 3:28; Gal. 2:16). For Protestant Christians, this idea has been central to the Reformation. As a result, Luther himself disliked this letter because he thought that James 2:14–26 was a dangerous expression that might undermine the message of justification through faith alone. Indeed, there is an apparent contradiction between Paul and James in these passages, with both using the same example of Abraham to argue the opposite point (James 2:23).

But this apparent contradiction is only that—apparent. For both Paul and James, both faith and works that evidence true faith are necessary (see 2 Cor. 5:10; Eph. 2:8–10). The seeming incongruity resolves when we realize that Paul and James are addressing two different senses of "justified" and of "works." Paul speaks about the impossibility of anyone (Jew or gentile) entering a covenantal relationship with God through obeying the Mosaic law rather than through following Jesus. One cannot be declared right (justified) through obedience to a set of stipulations (works). James speaks about an equally true reality: to be a follower of Jesus (having faith in him) never means only believing correct doctrine. In this, Paul and James are in complete agreement.

Do James and Paul Contradict Each Other? Unity in the Canon and the Problem of Biblical Language

In Genesis 15 God promises Abraham that he will become the father of countless descendants. Genesis 15:6 says that Abraham believed God's promise and "it was credited to him as righteousness." As discussed in the sidebar "James and Paul on Justification and Works," Paul and James use Abraham to make different points regarding the role of works in justification.

This raises an important question about biblical language. To read the Bible Christianly means that we assume a theological unity across the diversity of perspectives that make up the two-part canon. This is good but can become problematic if we seek unity in a way that flattens diversity, especially when it comes to biblical language. There is an ultimate theological unity between the language of "justified" in Genesis, Romans, and James, but it cannot be found by simply transporting the content of the idea from one text to another. We should let each author speak and utilize terms (such as "justification" and "works") in ways that may vary across the canon. Canonical unity exists within a tapestry of diversity, not a monochromatic use of technical terms.

without embodied good works (**orthopraxy**) is not biblical faith. Faith without works is not alive but dead and therefore not real faith. True faith—like true religion in 1:26–27—has functional feet and hands. True faith inevitably results in helping the impoverished and defenseless (1:27; 2:15–16), in being slow to speak and slow to anger (1:19), and in treating the poor with as much dignity as the wealthy (2:1–13). True faith can be seen in saints like Abraham (2:22–23) and Rahab (2:25), who *did* what God commanded *because* they believed him.

Wholeness with Our Tongues

■ READ JAMES 3:1–12 ■

James 3:1–12 unpacks a theme that was raised in chapter 1: the power of speech. According to James, people who consider themselves religious and yet don't control their tongues are self-deceived and their religion is worthless (1:26). Just like fire, which can be useful or destructive, so is the tongue. Using the analogies of the rudder of a ship, the bit in a horse's mouth, and a sweeping fire, James makes his point clear: though it is small, the tongue is shockingly powerful. Words can be used to bless others, to praise God (3:9), and teach the truth (3:1). But tongues can also boast and deceive (3:14) and curse people made in God's image (3:9). Such double-talking lacks the wholeness that God desires. The complete person is mature in speech, moving toward wholeness in one's life (3:2).

The Wholeness of Humility

■ READ JAMES 3:13–4:12 ■

The Scriptures continually give lists of virtues and vices, ways of being and character traits that are either life-giving and beautiful or destructive and deformed. In these verses James notes several of both. Some vices include selfish ambition, envy, boasting, slander, pride, and judging others. Virtues include peacemaking, mercy, sincerity, impartiality, and being considerate of others. James shows one quality that is the opposite of these vices and lies underneath these virtues. It is humility.

The good life comes from wisdom and looks like humility (3:13). Humility has long been considered the queen of the virtues. God opposes the proud person, but, precisely the opposite, he gives grace to those who are humble (4:6; see also Prov. 3:34; 1 Pet. 5:5).

The warnings are clear: the person whose life is marked by pride is no friend of God (4:4), but rather stands in opposition with God (4:6). Yet the promises are more wonderful than the warnings are dire. God promises that for those who draw near to him and joyfully submit to his ways—an act of humility—he will draw near and be with them (4:8). Those who humble themselves he promises to exalt (4:10).

Wholeness and Humility with Our Wealth

■ READ JAMES 4:13–5:6 ■

Building on his exhortation to humility, James applies this virtue to the matter of money. Again, he stops and urges the reader to listen, an approach meant to rivet the hearer's attention to what he is about to say (4:13; 5:1).

Humility's first application to wealth concerns self-reliance and the tendency to organize lives apart from God. People often live glibly, not considering that they are not in control, *God* is. People act foolishly, James says, when they make plans for this trip or that business transaction while not acknowledging God's sovereignty

Royal Library of Denmark

Figure 24.2. Sketch of Søren Kierkegaard by Niels Christian Kierkegaard

(4:13–14). Why? Because life is so uncertain. Everyone is but an evaporating breath. It is sheer arrogance to live ignorant of the living God (4:16). This does not mean it is wrong to make plans. It is wise to do so. But one's attitude must be rooted in humility. Christians can obey the exhortations to humble themselves (4:7, 10) by approaching everyday life under the banner of "If the Lord wills . . ." (4:15). This is not a magical incantation but rather the expression of a heart that humbly submits to God's control.

The second application of humility to wealth denounces those who use wealth corruptly and to oppress the poor. This injustice and arrogance stores up wrath for the time when God will bring justice to the world (5:3). Once again, the solution is humility before God.

A Proper and Patient Perspective . . . Again

■ READ JAMES 5:7–20 ■

The introduction to James's letter focuses on gaining the proper perspective to live wisely. James concludes his epistolary exhortation with the same point. As mortals in a broken world, people often face suffering and trials. The mature person must grip the hope that God will return to bring justice and vindicate his children. Like a good wisdom teacher, James piles up images and illustrations to drive home his point. A good farmer waits patiently for the rains and the sun to produce fruit (5:7). And godly people of the past, including the faithful Job, were blessed as they waited patiently for God's justice (5:10–11). Likewise, Christians can endure by being mindful of the Lord's future return.

Christians should also be patient and perseverant in prayer. Using the example of Elijah (5:17–18) and giving promises of the power of prayer (5:15–16), James redirects attention to God. Wise living must ultimately be connected upward in dependence on God.

This wisdom paraenetic encyclical that we call James concludes in what seems to be a rather anticlimactic way (5:19–20). Rather than a personal final greeting, James encourages readers to carefully instruct others in such a way that they might be saved from death and destruction. These verses reiterate James's consistent point, exhorting people to grow and persevere in godly wisdom, that they might become whole and mature. 👥

Implementation—Reading James as Christian Scripture Today

Because James is practical and pointed from beginning to end, it is not difficult to move from the reading of this letter to its implementation today. There is very little doctrine in James that needs to be translated and reexplained to today's readers. Rather, the task before readers of James today is in doing what James himself cared the most about: people must not just be hearers of the word and then walk away unchanged (1:22–25). The point of wisdom teaching is that hearers must be open to ponder what is being said, even if it is uncomfortable and challenging, and be willing to change their values, words, and actions.

The topics that James raises for his Christian readers are just as practical today as they were in the ancient world. Disciples of Christ must pursue a true and pure faith. This looks like controlling one's speech, not slandering others or being overly confident in one's own opinions. This looks like caring for those who are "lesser" in society, the orphans, widows, and anyone suffering in poverty, while rejecting the foolish temptation to praise and honor the wealthy. In all of this, beliefs and speech must match real-life actions. Anyone who thinks and speaks correctly but doesn't really live a life of love and service is self-deceived.

On a more positive note, when people do pursue the wholeness and completeness that James is inviting hearers into, the result is a flourishing life. When people embrace sufferings in faith and seek the good of others, they will be blessed, fulfilled, and in right relationship with God and other humans. This is wisdom straight from God.

KEY VERSES IN JAMES

- If anyone thinks he is religious without controlling his tongue, his religion is useless and he deceives himself. Pure and undefiled religion before God the Father is this: to look after orphans and widows in their distress and to keep oneself unstained from the world. 1:26–27
- For just as the body without the spirit is dead, so also faith without works is dead. 2:26
- Who among you is wise and understanding? By his good conduct he should show that his works are done in the gentleness that comes from wisdom. 3:13

Christian Reading Questions

1. Read the Sermon on the Mount in Matthew 5–7. Then trace the major themes of that sermon throughout James.

2. Read through James asking the question, "What does it mean to be whole?" and make a list of the answers that James gives. Then compose a prayer of hope, in the spirit of James 1:5–6, reflecting on areas of your life in which you are broken and incomplete and asking God to build wisdom and maturity.

3. Think of people in your immediate social context who are currently suffering or in the middle of a trial (illness, financial struggles, a death, a divorce, etc.). Make a plan to encourage them with words and actions.

4. Make a list of the places in James that deal with wealth and poverty. Then consider and write down situations in which you are tempted to honor the wealthy and dismiss the poor. How can you pursue wholeness in this area of your life?

CHAPTER TWENTY-FIVE

The First Letter of Peter

Orientation

The apostle Peter, the leader of the original twelve disciples, has two letters in the New Testament associated with him, the two being very different in style (see also chap. 26). Two letters is maybe less than we would expect from intrepid Peter, the first leader of the church. But though they often are overshadowed by the larger corpus from Paul, Peter's Letters are no less important, and they have a beauty and power all their own.

The First Letter of Peter is a general letter—that is, written not to one specific group of Christians but designed to be widely circulated. The letter would have been hand-delivered by a messenger, read aloud in the church, copied down, and then sent to the next location, where the process would begin again. First Peter 1:1 identifies this wide group of recipients (possibly

Figure 25.1. Woodcut of Peter preaching the gospel

in the order of the mail route) as Christians scattered throughout what today is eastern Turkey.

Such general letters in the ancient world were often paraenetic, meaning they were written for the purpose of exhorting hearers toward growth in virtue and character. Peter's paraenetic goal is clear: he is calling Christians to grow in holiness and humility, even amid suffering and pain. Holiness means imitating God himself while living in an ungodly world. Humility means relating to others with a posture of service and love, even when wronged, while also submitting to God's control of the world. In all of this, Peter continually reminds his hearers that Jesus is the ultimate model of holiness and humility.

This exhortation toward holiness and humility is based on the powerful vision that Peter paints of what it means to be a Christian—to be the chosen ones of God, who are valuable to God, and who will receive a great reward for being faithful to God.

HISTORICAL MATTERS

The Historical Origins of 1 Peter

Author: Traditionally, this letter has been understood as coming from Peter the apostle, possibly written through the help of a scribe, Silvanus (5:12).

Date: Based on traditions concerning persecution and Peter's death, this letter likely was written between AD 64 and 66.

Location: Peter says that he is writing from "Babylon" (5:13). This is almost certainly a metaphorical description for Rome, the capital of the great empire of Peter's day.

Sources: First Peter combines references to several Old Testament texts as well as teachings from Jesus, especially the Sermon on the Mount. There is considerable overlap with similar teachings in Paul and James, thus showing common traditions.

Setting: For the first several centuries Christians faced persecution to varying degrees and in various places, sometimes officially sanctioned and widespread, sometimes more localized. First Peter is written to Christians in Asia Minor (modern-day Turkey) who are experiencing some form of generalized persecution, maybe during Nero's reign.

Exploration—Reading 1 Peter

Praise Be to God, You Billionaire Refugees!

■ READ 1 PETER 1:1–12 ■

The opening of Peter's letter sets the tone as one of amazed praise for what God has done through Jesus Christ. God has chosen believers, sprinkled them with Jesus's blood, and is sanctifying them by his own Spirit (1:2). Because of God's merciful nature, he has caused spiritually dead humans to be born again into a spiritual inheritance that is extravagant and eternal, reserved in heaven, where Jesus now is (1:3–5). These truths are so amazing that even angels long to understand their depth, and though Christians may now suffer great hardships, they still can be filled with joy (1:6–12).

This combination of trials and glorious joy is the undergirding theme of the whole letter and is summed up in the paradoxical description of Christians that Peter gives in the first words of 1:1: "elect exiles." Christians are simultaneously God's elect ones and exiles. "Elect" means chosen and set apart for a special covenantal relationship with God like Israel was under the Mosaic covenant. Peter (along with the rest of the New Testament) says that this special relationship is now available for all people who are united with Christ, Jews and gentiles. "Exiles" means that Christians are currently homeless and landless, suffering the hardships of not being in their native land; Christians are heaven's refugees on the earth. This combination of election and exile is deeply ironic and paradoxical. It well describes the Christian experience that was also Jesus's own experience—elect exiles, billionaire refugees.

God's Holy People

■ READ 1 PETER 1:13–2:10 ■

The cause for joy in 1:1–12 leads naturally into a call to holiness in 1:13–2:3. With a series of powerful images Peter exhorts Christians, who have been born again by God, to now live a new life that is based on who God is. This is natural and good; God made every believer alive again through Jesus's own resurrection, and therefore the Christian's identity and allegiance and behavior should be rooted in the reality of God's nature. What is God like? He is holy, meaning that he is consistent in his character and is good, not evil in any way (1:14–16). He is loving, meaning that Christians must also be people of sincere love for one another (1:22). He is good, meaning that the Christian life should be increasingly free of malice, deceit, hypocrisy, envy, and slander (2:1–3).

Peter is strong on encouragement, and in 2:4–10 he gives one of the most beautiful and powerful descriptions of Christians anywhere in the New Testament. This series of images is meant to hearten and strengthen the Christian life amid difficulties. The paradox of being chosen by God while rejected by humans (see the discussion

The Structure of 1 Peter

First Peter follows the typical pattern of ancient letters, with a grand opening that identifies both the sender and the recipients—in this case, a wide range of scattered people (1:1–2).

The body of the letter breaks into three main parts:

- 1:3–2:10—The first part focuses on the privileges and responsibilities of being God's people in Christ Jesus. This section ends with a reiteration of 1:1–2, highlighting the idea of being chosen by God for a purpose.
- 2:11–4:11—The second part is dominated by the urgent exhortation for Christians to live differently than their sinful desires and the society around them would dictate. The key idea of submission ties together the main part (2:13–3:12), exhorting Christians to humility in a variety of relationships.
- 4:12–5:11—The third part gives final exhortations regarding how to respond to suffering and reiterates the foundational virtue of humility in relating to God and to one another.

First Peter ends with traditional closing words and a blessing (5:12–14).

The Roles of the Trinity

The orthodox understanding of God as Trinity was articulated with increasing clarity over the first four centuries of the church, but the ideas are present in many texts in the New Testament. First Peter 1:2 provides a good example of the way the New Testament authors speak seamlessly about the one God, who is three distinct persons, each with roles and activities.

In 1:2 God the Father's sovereign knowledge and control are emphasized. Jesus the Son is described as worthy of obedience, and his incarnation and priesthood are noted with reference to his sprinkled blood. The Spirit's role is highlighted in the ongoing sanctification—making holy—of God's people. This one God in three persons acts in unity through distinct activities.

of "elect exiles" above) was true of Jesus himself and therefore will be true of all followers of Jesus. In these verses Peter especially unpacks what "chosen by God" looks like. Peter piles up a series of images based on descriptions of God's people in the Old Testament. Christians are like stones that are alive and are together being built into a temple. At the same time, Christians are like the priests in that temple offering praiseful sacrifices to God. Christians together are a holy nation, a gathered people who are the recipients of God's mercy and who now have a clear mission, which is to openly praise God, who has mercifully brought them from darkness into light.

The Christian Way of Humble Service

■ READ 1 PETER 2:11–3:7 ■

The troubled relationship of Christians to the outside world has been hinted at in the letter, but now it comes to the forefront of Peter's exhortation. Because Christians are foreigners and exiles (1:1; 2:11), there will inevitably be conflict and tension, with Christians being misrepresented, wrongly accused of evil, and insulted (2:12; 4:14; cf. Matt. 5:10–12). Peter knows that this can't be avoided but wants to make sure that Christians are only *falsely* being accused of wrongdoing; they must in fact truly be doing good, and when God does return, Christians' good works will bring glory and honor to God (2:12; 3:16; 4:16–19; based on Jesus's teaching in Matt. 5:16).

So what does doing good when being falsely accused look like? Peter describes the Christian way as the way of humble submission to authorities at every level (2:13–14). Christians are free but should show proper respect to earthly authorities, even the emperor, thus disproving the accusations against Christians (2:15–17).

Peter then gives two specific examples of what humble submission looks like: the relationship of servants to masters and of wives to husbands. Peter exhorts Christian servants/slaves to humbly perform their tasks regardless of whether their master is good or bad (2:18). If a servant is rebellious and brings trouble on himself, there is no credit there; but if suffering comes unjustly, then humble submission is in fact commendable and honorable in God's eyes (2:20). (See the sidebar "Slavery in the Greco-Roman World" in chap. 22.)

The second example, from the marriage relationship, has the same point—be humble—though with a couple of important qualifications. The first qualification is that Peter does not encourage women to endure ill treatment but does invite them to focus on their virtue and goodness in relationship to their husbands, whether the man is a believer in Christ or not (3:1–6). Second, Peter immediately turns to the husbands and gives them an important command: be considerate and treat your wives with respect (3:7).

These examples of servants and wives are not meant to be comprehensive but are representative of the Christian call on all people regardless of status or gender—the call to humble service and self-sacrifice.

The basis and the source for this vision come from none other than Jesus's own example. Peter gives believers one of the most profound reflections on Jesus's life as the model for every follower: "Christ also suffered for you, leaving you an example, that you should follow in his steps" (2:21). Jesus's righteous suffering meant that even though he was misrepresented and mistreated, he did not retaliate but instead "entrusted himself to the one [God the Father] who judges justly" (2:23). Jesus as the model of trusting God amid troubles is the engine that drives the entire exhortation of 1 Peter.

Christ Is Lord

■ READ 1 PETER 3:8–4:11 ■

This section continues and expands the argument from chapter 2. The application of Christian humility to the situation of servants and wives is now broadened out to include all Christians. Peter sums up his point by saying that every Christian should be sympathetic, loving, compassionate, and humble (3:8; 4:8–9). This way of being and doing good is once again supported through the promise that it honors God and therefore will result in goodness and life (3:9–12). And once again, Peter offers Jesus himself as

Peter, Paul, and James

Scholars have observed that the content of First Peter is remarkably similar to the writings of Paul and especially the Letter of James. For example, Peter's description of Jesus going into heaven and sitting at the right hand of God (3:22) is paralleled closely in Paul's Letters (Rom. 8:34; Phil. 2:9–11; Col. 3:1; Eph. 1:20–21). Such is also the case for Peter's phrases "die to sin but live to righteousness" (2:24; cf. Rom. 6:2, 11) and "put to death in the flesh but made alive by the Spirit" (3:18; cf. Rom. 8:6, 14; Gal. 6:8). The overlap between Peter and James is particularly apparent. Both 1 Peter and James begin by emphasizing the value of faith tested by trials (1 Pet. 1:6–8; James 1:2–4; see also Rom. 5:1–5), and 1 Peter 5:5–9 and James 4:6–10 both speak about embracing humility and submission and resisting the devil, and then both cite Proverbs 3:34.

While it certainly is possible that these authors were familiar with one another's writings and there is some literary dependence between them, what is more likely is that these parallels reveal the existence of a body of traditions that developed in earliest Christianity. These traditions consisted of sayings from Jesus and of early Christian readings of Old Testament texts in certain, christological ways. These traditions existed in oral form and then probably in written portions as well, thus explaining the parallels throughout many segments of the New Testament as seen in Peter, Paul, and James (and also these letters in comparison to the Gospels).

Christians' Civil Disobedience

In general the New Testament exhorts Christians to obey the laws and customs of whatever society they are living in (Rom. 13:1–7; 1 Tim. 2:1–3; 1 Pet. 2:13–17). This is because Christianity is not a political revolutionary movement. We are to give to Caesar what is his and to God what is his (Matt. 22:15–21). Jesus is the king, but his kingdom is not of this world (John 18:36), thus his followers must be people of peace and love.

Within the practice of these virtues, however, there are times when the church and individual Christians can and should stand up against unrighteousness and ungodliness. There are times when Christians must wisely be involved in civil disobedience.

Modern examples of Christian resistance include Martin Luther King Jr.'s stand against racial injustice in America, and the movement led by the Reformed Church pastor László Tőkés that eventually led to the overthrow of the Romanian tyrant Nicolae Ceaușescu. In both cases (and many others), Christian leaders suffered but did so with integrity and humility. The result was indeed social and political revolution, but this came about through submission to God's will and with the exercise of the kind of Christian virtues that Peter is talking about and that Jesus himself modeled.

The Imitation of Christ and of Christians

Throughout this letter Peter bases his exhortations on Jesus's own example: "Christ also suffered for you, leaving you an example, that you should follow in his steps" (2:21). Other New Testament texts speak the same way, such as the Christ hymn in Philippians 2:5–11, where Jesus's model of humble service even to the point of death forms the basis for Paul's exhortations regarding how Christians should relate to one another. Christ's two natures (divine and human) in one person make the imitation of Jesus powerful and primary. Because he is fully human (contrary to unorthodox views such as **Monophysitism** and Docetism), the model of Jesus's earthly life is crucial to Christianity. His human example is not mere illustration; it is the foundation of the ethical teachings of the Bible. Jesus fully and faithfully imitated God the Father, and therefore Christians are those who likewise follow his example.

This pattern of imitation then continues—albeit with many flaws and imperfections—within the church. Many times Paul exhorts believers to imitate him and other leaders, even as they imitate Christ (1 Cor. 4:16; 11:1; Phil. 3:17; 4:9; 1 Thess. 1:6). God has designed the world so that people can grow in godliness by following the example of other godly people, who are in turn imitating Christ, who is perfectly imitating God.

the ultimate example for what he is calling all Christians to do. Christ suffered unjustly, even to the point of death (3:17–18). This can give the Christian the courage to do the same, by making Christ the focus of one's heart and life—"in your hearts revere Christ as Lord" (3:15 NIV).

Mention of Jesus's death and resurrection leads Peter down a side trail that contains a great theological treasure. First Peter 3:19–22 is not easy to understand and has been debated throughout the church's history. Peter references Jesus proclaiming to imprisoned spirits, though what he proclaimed and to whom is not clear—to imprisoned spirits, to disobedient ones (spirits? humans?) during Noah's day. Then Peter moves from Noah to a discussion of water baptism being a means of salvation, by analogy with Noah's ark. However, this baptism is not really about water but about the cleansing of the inner person through Jesus's resurrection (3:20–21). What all these quick exegetical steps mean is not entirely clear. In 4:5–6 we get a little bit more information: Jesus is the judge of both the living and the dead, and everyone will have to give an account to God, resulting in either judgment or life. What *is* clear about this whole section is that Jesus is now seated in the place of authority with God the Father in heaven (3:22). This is why Christians can have sure hope for the future, even if they suffer now.

Christus the Shepherd

Christ the Shepherd

■ READ 1 PETER 4:12–5:14 ■

Typical of a paraenetic letter (a letter that exhorts people to live virtuously), before the final section, the main body of the letter ends with a reiteration of the main point. This is what we see in 4:12–19, which provides a good summary of what Peter wants his hearers to understand and to act on. In short, suffering as a Christian is inevitable, so it should not be surprising. Rather than being a cause for sadness and shame, suffering and persecution can in fact be a source of great joy, because it means that one is united with Christ himself. What should the Christian do, then? "Those who suffer according to God's will should commit themselves to their faithful Creator and continue to do good" (4:19 NIV). It's hard to find a better summary of Peter's vision than this.

Figure 25.2. Stained glass depicting the harrowing of hell

RECEPTION HISTORY

Preaching to the Spirits in Prison

First Peter 3:19–22 has been read in a couple of very different ways in the church's history. First, already in the second century many people interpreted these verses to mean that Jesus went into hell and proclaimed the gospel there, bringing many people out with him at his resurrection. This interpretation is found in the apocryphal Gospel of Peter and in many pieces of sacred art in the following centuries.

A second interpretation, which may have been clearer to Peter's recipients than to later Christian readers, understands these verses to be referring to the story of the Watchers that comes to us from Genesis and is expanded in the book called 1 Enoch (chaps. 6–36). In Genesis 6, right before God speaks to Noah and sends the flood, there were angels who rebelled against God and bore children with women on the earth, creating giants. In 1 Enoch we are told that these disobedient spirits are imprisoned until God judges them. In this interpretation Peter is referring to these stories and these disobedient spirits and reinterpreting what happened in light of Jesus coming into the world and triumphing over all evil.

THEOLOGICAL ISSUES

Christ's Descent into Hell and Ascent into Heaven

One of the most important early Christian statements of faith, the Apostles' Creed, includes the confession "He descended into hell; on the third day he rose again from the dead." The biblical support for this confession comes from Romans 10:7; Ephesians 4:8–9; and 1 Peter 3:19–22.

Various branches of Christianity have interpreted the idea of Christ's descent into hell or the place of the dead in different ways. Some Protestants have downplayed this idea, while the Roman Catholic tradition has emphasized this is how Jesus saved virtuous Jews and gentiles from before the time of Christ. Eastern Orthodox Christianity has underscored how Jesus's descent and ascent defeats death itself, starting with Adam and Eve.

Central to all Christian understanding is that death has lost its power and sting because of Christ's death, burial, resurrection, and ascension. Christians, united with Jesus through their confession and baptism, have spiritually experienced the same journey that Jesus did physically—life to death to life (1 Cor. 15:12–58). Christ's descent to the place of the dead and victorious ascension out of death is at the core of Christian theology.

God as Shepherd

God reveals himself throughout Scripture via many images or metaphors, each of which contributes to our understanding of who he is and how he relates to his creation in particular ways. The idea of God as a shepherd comes from the agricultural world of the ancient Near East and is found in numerous places in the Old Testament (e.g., Ps. 23; Isa. 40:11; Ezek. 34:11–22). A shepherd leads, defends, and provides for his flock. This image is then connected with the role of a king, especially appropriate in Israel's history because their great king, David, was a shepherd first (2 Sam. 5:2; Ps. 78:70–72). The Old Testament looks forward to a time when a new descendant of David would come as a shepherd-king (Mic. 5:2–4).

The New Testament understands Jesus to be this Davidic shepherd-king (Matt. 2:1–6), and Jesus described himself as "the good shepherd" (John 10:11–16).

In 1 Peter 5:2–4, Peter continues these traditions by describing the church as God's flock, the leaders of the church as shepherds, and Jesus as the Chief Shepherd, who will return from heaven to reward his faithful people.

The Historical Peter

In the providence of God some surprising individuals play a significant role in world-changing events. Simon Peter, a lowly fisherman from the backwaters of Palestine, was one such person. He is mentioned over 150 times in the New Testament and was the leader of the twelve disciples and then the church in its earliest days after Jesus's ascension. Along with his brother Andrew and his fellow fishermen James and John, Peter was one of the first people Jesus called to be a disciple. He became one of the most intimate friends and followers of Jesus, stepping into the leading role. Originally his name was Simon, but like God's renaming of Abram to Abraham, Jesus renamed Simon "Peter" because he would be the "rock" (Greek, *petros*) of the church's witness in the world, with Jesus as the cornerstone of this new temple (Matt. 16:18; Eph. 2:20; 1 Pet. 2:6–7). After preaching the first Christian sermon at Pentecost (Acts 2:14–41), Peter traveled and helped establish and spread the young Christian movement. He eventually ended up in Rome and died as a Christian martyr around AD 64–66 by being crucified like his Lord (some traditions say that he was crucified upside down). Because of Peter's dominant role in the New Testament, by the second century several apocryphal stories about him arose and were written in documents such as the Acts of Peter and the Apocalypse of Peter.

Also typical of an ancient letter like this, the closing section contains final greetings and instructions to specific people. First, Peter speaks to the elders among his readers (5:1–4). "Elders" here does not mean older and more mature people (as compared to the younger people in 5:5); it is more than a designation of chronological age. Peter is addressing Christians who help lead the Christian community, like shepherds over a flock—humble, caring, providing, serving, being a role model. In all of this, Jesus is once again the great example, the Chief Shepherd, who will reward his faithful under-shepherds (5:4). Second, Peter addresses those who are not elders and, consistent with the whole letter, exhorts everyone once again to humility. This time the call to humility is based on the fact that God sets himself in opposition to those who are proud and, quite the opposite, shows favor and kindness toward those who are humble (5:5).

Peter then concludes his short letter with a final reminder that God's people do have an active enemy in the world, the devil, so Christians must not be lackadaisical. The sure hope is that Christ is more powerful and is going to return in glory and restore the honor of his people (5:8–11). A benediction of "peace" concludes Peter's communication (5:14).

Implementation—Reading 1 Peter as Christian Scripture Today

When modern Christians in Western Europe and North America read in the New Testament about suffering for being a Christian, it is difficult to connect emotionally and experientially. The kind of faith-based persecution that Peter is writing about is mostly foreign to Christians in the modern West—though it is not foreign to many Christians in Africa and Asia today.

Nonetheless, Peter's message is still deeply relevant and personal today, regardless of whether one has experienced persecution for being a Christian. This is because Peter's exhortations are rooted in the universal reality of God's own nature and character. The First Letter of Peter is calling all Christians to adopt a new, self-aware identity as people who are different from the world around them: Christians have been born again, reborn into a new inheritance and hope, a new story! This new story is one of amazing glory, benefits, riches, and joy.

Figure 25.3. *Crucifixion of St. Peter* by Caravaggio

This new narrative identity means that sooner or later, at various times and places in history, Christians will have a strained relationship with their surrounding society. Peter makes clear that this relationship should look like God's own relationship to the world: loving, winsome, distinct, and respectful. This new Christian identity is related to the present world while it is rooted in the hope for the future, when Jesus will return from heaven to earth and bring the world into submission to God, thus God's household in the church will become the kingdom of God in all the earth.

KEY VERSES IN 1 PETER

- Therefore, with your minds ready for action, be sober-minded and set your hope completely on the grace to be brought to you at the revelation of Jesus Christ. As obedient children, do not be conformed to the desires of your former ignorance. But as the one who called you is holy, you also are to be holy in all your conduct; for it is written, "Be holy, because I am holy." 1:13–16
- As you come to him, a living stone—rejected by people but chosen and honored by God— you yourselves, as living stones, a spiritual house, are being built to be a holy priesthood to offer spiritual sacrifices acceptable to God through Jesus Christ. 2:4–5
- Dear friends, don't be surprised when the fiery ordeal comes among you to test you as if something unusual were happening to you. Instead, rejoice as you share in the sufferings of Christ, so that you may also rejoice with great joy when his glory is revealed. 4:12–13

Christian Reading Questions

1. First Peter focuses intently on the identity of God's people. How does he describe their identity throughout his letter, and how does this understanding change the way you think about yourself as a Christian?

2. How would you explain being an "elect exile" to an unbeliever?

3. In what circumstances might you find yourself at some point needing to practice some level of civil disobedience toward your government? What virtues do you think Peter would want you to maintain in your life in the way you pursue civil disobedience?

4. What type of persecution do you think the Christians whom Peter was writing to were experiencing? How do you think his exhortations concerning persecution apply to your life?

CHAPTER TWENTY-SIX

The Second Letter of Peter

Orientation

It has been called the ugly stepchild of the New Testament. Whole books have been written about why it should not even be in the New Testament. And yet, Peter's fiery second letter contains a message that, if properly absorbed, could radically transform the church.

Its message is grounded in Peter's eyewitness testimony of the glory of Jesus, and it projects forward to Christ's certain return on the day of the Lord. In between these two events,

HISTORICAL MATTERS

The Historical Origins of 2 Peter

Author: Simon Peter, but this is heavily disputed

Date: Ca. AD 65

Location: Rome

Setting: Peter writes to counter false teachers who have rejected authority and engage in various sinful practices.

LITERARY NOTES

The Authorship of 2 Peter

Second Peter has the dubious honor of being the letter in the New Testament whose authorship is most doubted by scholars. Though the letter claims to be written by "Simon Peter, a servant and an apostle of Jesus Christ" (1:1), and includes personal remembrances (1:13–14, 15–16), scholars doubt that Peter is the author for several reasons. First, the language seems to be that of someone formally educated rather than a fisherman from Galilee. Second, the early church struggled to accept 2 Peter, noting its disputed authenticity. Third, Peter mentions Paul's letters in 3:15–16, which some scholars think refers to a collection of his letters, which would have developed only after Peter's death. Fourth, the false teaching that Peter opposes is regarded by some to be the Gnosticism of the second century.

Nevertheless, each of these criticisms is overstated, and reasonable responses are available. As with other disputed letters in the New Testament, we should not be quick to dismiss the opinion of the early church, which struggled with such considerations carefully and was much closer to the time of writing than we are. Sometimes modern scholarship suffers from "chronological snobbery" (as C. S. Lewis called it), thinking that our forebears were less intelligent or more gullible than we are. But should there be any chronological snobbery with respect to the authorship of 2 Peter, it should favor the ancients, not us.

THEOLOGICAL ISSUES

Does Peter Call Jesus "God"?

The short answer is yes. The longer answer is more complicated. When Peter refers to "our God and Savior Jesus Christ" (1:1), he may mean "our God, and our Savior Jesus Christ," keeping God and Jesus distinct. But because of a rule of Greek syntax (known as Granville Sharp's Rule), both the phrases "our God" and "Savior Jesus Christ" refer to the same person. In other words, Peter does in fact directly refer to Jesus as God. (See also the sidebar "Our Great God and Savior" in the section on Titus in chap. 21.)

THEOLOGICAL ISSUES

What Does It Mean to "Share in the Divine Nature"?

Peter says that God, through his great and precious promises, has enabled believers to "share in the divine nature" (1:4). The Eastern Orthodox Church has always regarded this phrase as pointing to the **deification** of believers, meaning that we somehow become *like God*. This is sometimes misunderstood to mean that we become divine ourselves, but that is not correct. "Deification" means that believers share in fellowship with God in a profound sense, which is also Peter's most likely meaning. He says that we become *partners* or *companions* with the divine. This means that believers share in a deep life of fellowship with God.

LITERARY NOTES

The Structure of 2 Peter

The letter begins by articulating both the faithfulness of God in delivering his promises and the requirement of believers to live out their faith in godliness (1:1–11). Peter himself was an eyewitness of God's fulfillment of prophecy (1:12–21). Peter warns about false teachers and the certainty of their judgment (2:1–3:7), and about the imminence of the devastating day of the Lord (3:8–13). Believers are to wait patiently for these things (3:14–18).

believers must live with confidence in both, rejecting false teaching and avoiding the sinful excesses of this world, which is soon to be purified through the fire of judgment.

Exploration—Reading 2 Peter

Confirm Your Calling and Election

■ READ 2 PETER 1:1–15 ■

Peter introduces himself as "Simon Peter" (some manuscripts have "Simeon Peter"), a servant and apostle of Christ, and writes to those who share in the same faith through "our God and Savior Jesus Christ" (1:1). Peter begins by claiming that Christ has given believers everything they need for a godly life (1:3), including great and precious promises that allow believers to "share in the divine nature" and escape the corruption of this world (1:4).

As such, believers ought to live according to goodness, knowledge, self-control, endurance, godliness, brotherly affection, and love (1:6–7). These things will make believers fruitful rather than shortsighted and blind (1:8–9). In this way, they will confirm their calling and election and will avoid stumbling, entering with confidence into the eternal kingdom of Christ (1:10–11). Peter's job is to remind his readers of these things for as long as he lives, knowing that his time to die is coming soon (1:12–15).

Eyewitness Testimony, Not Invented Myths

■ READ 2 PETER 1:16–21 ■

Peter reminds his readers that what they learned about the coming of Christ was not cleverly created myth, but rather he and the apostles were eyewitnesses of Jesus's majesty (1:16). Then Peter recounts his experience of Jesus's transfiguration, when he, James, and John saw Jesus appear in radiant glory alongside Moses and Elijah, and they heard a voice from heaven say about Jesus, "This is my beloved Son,

Figure 26.1. *The Transfiguration of Christ* by Titian

with whom I am well-pleased!" (1:17–18; cf. Matt. 17:1–9).

Peter also appeals to the prophetic nature of Scripture, referring to what we call the Old Testament. He has seen its prophecy strongly confirmed in Christ (see, e.g., 1 Pet. 2:21–25), and believers ought to pay attention to it. Prophecy comes from God, as the prophets were led by the Holy Spirit (2 Pet. 1:19–21).

Warnings about False Teachers

■ READ 2 PETER 2:1–22 ■

The main body of the letter consists of Peter's warning about false prophets and teachers who spread destructive heresies, denying the Lord, living crooked lives, and who will be condemned (2:1–3). Peter then launches a long account of God's acts of judgment in the past, not sparing fallen angels, or, at one point, the whole world (except for Noah and his family), or the cities of Sodom and Gomorrah

CANONICAL CONNECTIONS

The Transfiguration

Three Gospels record the story of Jesus's transfiguration (Matt. 17:1–9; Mark 9:2–10; Luke 9:28–36). Jesus took his closest disciples, Peter, James, and John, up on a high mountain where Jesus was "transfigured" in front of them, with his face shining like the sun and his clothes dazzling white. Then Moses and Elijah appeared with Jesus. These are two of the most significant figures from Israel's history, as the giver of the law (Moses) and possibly Israel's greatest prophet (Elijah). The effect of this gathering was to present Jesus in esteemed company, thus revealing his greatness. But when a voice from heaven is heard, Jesus alone is singled out as God's Son, pleasing to him, and as the one to whom others must listen (Matt. 17:1–5). This is quite something, considering who else was standing there—Jesus's authority surpasses even Moses and Elijah. One famous figure notably absent was King David. The implicit point might be that Jesus *is* the new David, God's anointed king.

Figure 26.2. *The Burning of Sodom* (formerly *The Destruction of Sodom*) by Camille Corot

2 Peter and Jude

There is an incredibly strong connection between 2 Peter and the Letter of Jude (the penultimate book of the New Testament). In fact, most of Jude—nineteen out of twenty-five verses—is used in 2 Peter. Most scholars agree that 2 Peter has used Jude as a source, since the shorter document (Jude) is more likely the source for the longer (2 Peter), rather than the other way around. However, while the thoughts of Jude are used in 2 Peter, the wording is different, so that Peter has shaped the content for his own purposes. The following table shows where Peter has used Jude as a source:

2 Peter	Jude
2:1	4
2:2	4
2:3	4
2:4	6
2:6	7
2:9	6
2:10	7b, 8
2:11	9
2:12	10
2:13	12a
2:15	11
2:17	12b, 13
2:18	16
3:1–2	17
3:3	18
3:14	24
3:18	25

(2:4–8). But amid these acts of judgment God rescued the righteous, such as Noah and his family (2:5) and Lot (2:7–8), and therefore he knows how to rescue the godly while bringing judgment on evil (2:9–10a).

False teachers are not afraid to slander God's glorious ones and, as "creatures of instinct," will be destroyed and paid back for the harm they have done (2:10b–13). They are full of adultery, seduction, and greed and are under a curse (2:14). They walk in the footsteps of Balaam, the mad and wicked prophet who required rebuke by a donkey (2:15–16; cf. Num. 22:22–35).

Such false teachers make empty promises, like springs without water, promising freedom but are themselves slaves of their own desires (2:17–19). Though they came to some sort of freedom through Christ, they got themselves tangled up again in the slavery of the world, which puts them in a worse situation than they began with (2:20–21). They are best described by the proverb "A dog returns to its own vomit" (2:22; cf. Prov. 26:11).

Remember the Day of the Lord

■ READ 2 PETER 3:1–13 ■

Peter turns from warning about false teachers to encouragement regarding the day of the Lord. He wants his readers to remember the words of the holy prophets (in the Old Testament) as well as what Jesus has commanded them through his apostles (3:1–2). In particular, they need to know that people will doubt that Jesus will return, scoffing at the idea because he hasn't come back yet (3:3–4). But just as God judged the earth through the flood (Gen. 6–9), so he has reserved a day of judgment in the future, in which the heavens and earth will face fire and the destruction of evil (3:5–7).

Instead of doubting God's promise that this day is coming, believers should realize that for the Lord, a day is like a thousand years, and a thousand years are like a day (3:8). He is not delaying, but is showing patience so that more people will come to repentance before it is too late (3:9). That day will come suddenly, unexpectedly, and the heavens and earth will be radically cleansed of all evil (3:10). Thus, believers ought to live according to holiness and godliness as they wait for that day, which will see the dawn of a new heavens and new earth, filled with righteousness (3:11–13).

Wrapping Up

■ READ 2 PETER 3:14–18 ■

Having reassured his readers of the trustworthiness of the apostolic witness, warned them about false teachers, and reminded them about the coming of the day of the Lord, Peter concludes his fiery second letter with some final exhortations. While believers wait for that day, they should make every effort to live without blemish and in peace (3:14). The patience of the Lord results in the salvation of others, as the apostle Paul has written. Peter acknowledges that some of Paul's writings are difficult to understand (!), but he also affirms their status as sacred Scripture (3:15–16). He wants his readers to be on their guard so that they are not led astray and so that they grow in the grace and knowledge of the Lord and Savior Jesus Christ (3:17–18). Amen!

Implementation—Reading 2 Peter as Christian Scripture Today

Peter's second letter sometimes gets a bad rap. Most think that it was not written by the apostle Peter, it borrows heavily from Jude, and it is obsessed with warnings about judgment and false teachers. But this is unfair.

THEOLOGICAL ISSUES

Will the Universe Be Destroyed?

Peter uses very strong wording to depict what will happen on the day of the Lord: the heavens will pass away and the elements will burn and be dissolved (3:10). This seems to parallel Revelation 21:1 (cf. Isa. 66:22), but it contradicts Paul, who says that the creation will be *renewed* rather than *replaced* (Rom. 8:18–22). Elsewhere Peter uses the image of the flood to depict the destruction of the world (1 Pet. 3:18–22), but even there the world is actually *cleansed* of its sin rather than destroyed and replaced. Since God promised never to flood the whole world again (Gen. 9:11), here Peter uses the image of fire (2 Pet. 3:10). But it should be understood in the same way: sin will be judged and the world will be cleansed through this "fire." Peter's language is rhetorically strong to make a point about the radical cleansing that will take place, but it should not be pressed literally. God will renew his creation.

This letter calls believers to escape the ungodly world through faith in Christ and by looking forward to the final judgment of evil. The coming day of the Lord helps believers to fix their eyes on the endgame and not get caught up in the desires and sin that so easily entangle us. The letter reminds believers of the eyewitness testimony that grounds their faith in Christ, and it allays their doubts about the apparent delay of his return. It is a deeply eschatological letter that ultimately is about Christian hope.

The church today certainly can benefit from 2 Peter's eschatological outlook. Too often the (Western, especially) church forgets that Christ will one day return. The day of the Lord, if considered at all, is regarded as a far-off event that bears little relevance to life here and now. Peter challenges this shortsightedness and reminds us that the day *is* coming, and the fact of its coming ought to affect our lives dramatically.

KEY VERSES IN 2 PETER

- By these he has given us very great and precious promises, so that through them you may share in the divine nature, escaping the corruption that is in the world because of evil desire. 1:4
- For we did not follow cleverly contrived myths when we made known to you the power and coming of our Lord Jesus Christ; instead, we were eyewitnesses of his majesty. 1:16
- There were indeed false prophets among the people, just as there will be false teachers among you. They will bring in destructive heresies, even denying the Master who bought them, and will bring swift destruction on themselves. 2:1
- Dear friends, don't overlook this one fact: With the Lord one day is like a thousand years, and a thousand years like one day. The Lord does not delay his promise, as some understand delay, but is patient with you, not wanting any to perish but all to come to repentance. 3:8–9

Christian Reading Questions

1. Read all of 2 Peter. Write up a list of the characteristics of false teachers and compare them to the characteristics that Peter expects believers to exhibit.
2. Read Matthew 17:1–9 and 2 Peter 1:16–18. What role does Jesus's transfiguration play in Peter's argument?
3. Read 2 Peter 2 and the Letter of Jude. Are you convinced of their relationship? Why or why not?
4. How does the day of the Lord affect your own life? Is it something that you think much about? Why or why not?

CHAPTER TWENTY-SEVEN

The Letters of John

1–3 John

Orientation

The Letters of John are among the most neglected parts of the New Testament, especially 2 John and 3 John, which are the two shortest books in the Bible. They tend to be neglected because of their brevity, and because on the surface they don't appear to offer much instruction for today. First John tends to be neglected because it is difficult to navigate and even more difficult to preach. And yet together the three letters offer very rich theology, practical application, and some of the most profound statements about the love of God in Christ.

The twin themes shared across the three letters are love and truth. A believer cannot claim to know the truth about God and Christ and at the same time not show love to others. A lack of love is incompatible with truth. By the same token, the person who truly loves demonstrates truly knowing God, since God is love. God's love is most profoundly demonstrated in the sacrificial gift of his Son as an atoning sacrifice, and believers likewise must demonstrate love in practice—not in word alone. 🏺

HISTORICAL MATTERS

The Historical Origins of the Letters of John

Author: John, though 1 John technically is anonymous; 2 John and 3 John are written by "the elder." The early church was unanimous in believing the author of 1 John to be John the apostle, while some doubts initially lingered regarding 2 and 3 John. Today's scholars are skeptical about the apostolic authorship of all three letters.

Date: Early 90s

Location: Ephesus and surrounding regions in Asia Minor

Setting: John writes to protect the churches (and Gaius in 3 John) from false teachers who have departed from the truth and from fellowship with other believers.

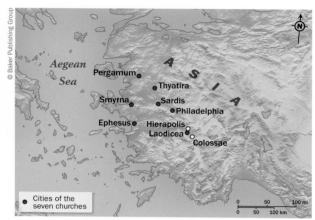

Figure 27.1. The seven churches of Asia Minor

One way that love and truth come together in these letters is through the theme of fellowship. Especially in 1 John, believers share in fellowship with God and with one another. In 2 John and 3 John, fellowship is expressed in practical ways through hospitality. Hospitality is an expression of love toward those who hold to the truth. In the same way, withholding hospitality is a way to prevent false teachers from spreading their deceptions. In this case, the withholding of hospitality is ultimately a loving act because it serves to protect others from falsehood.

LITERARY NOTES

The Structure of 1 John

The structure of 1 John is a notorious problem, unless we think differently about it. Unlike Paul's Letters, it is not ordered with a step-by-step logic. Instead, it has a recursive structure in which themes are returned to again and again, so that they wash over the reader. The best approach is simply to list the contents:

1:1–4	Prologue
1:5–10	Walking in the light versus walking in the darkness
2:1–6	Avoiding sin and keeping God's commands
2:7–11	Love versus hate
2:12–17	Love of the Father versus love of the world
2:18–27	Remaining in the Son versus being led astray
2:28–3:10	Being and acting as the children of God
3:11–18	Love expressed in action
3:19–24	Reassurance and confidence before God
4:1–6	Recognizing the Spirit of truth versus the spirit of falsehood
4:7–21	Loving one another because love is from God
5:1–12	Theological conclusion
5:13–21	Pastoral conclusion

Exploration—Reading 1 John

This We Declare to You

■ READ 1 JOHN 1:1–4 ■

First John begins unlike a normal letter, without any kind of greeting, diving straight into the deep end. It opens obscurely so that the first-time reader does not know exactly what the author is talking about. Something "was from the beginning" (1:1a); it was heard, seen, observed, and touched by the author and whomever else the "we" refers to (1:1b). And this *something* concerns the word of life (1:1c).

The second verse reveals a little more of the subject matter, so that the *something* of the first verse is now called the "life" (1:2a). This life was revealed, has been seen, and "was with the Father and was revealed to us" (1:2b). At this point, the reader probably realizes that the author is talking about Jesus, though he is still spoken of in an abstract, impersonal way. In this way, the first two verses are similar to the opening of John's Gospel in the way that it refers to Jesus as the "word" (John 1:1). This impersonal title is slowly unpacked as the reader eventually discovers that it refers to Jesus (John 1:14). In 1 John, the "life" refers to Jesus, and this is whom the author has heard, seen, observed, and touched. 📖

John's eyewitness account of Jesus is declared to his readers for a specific purpose: that they may have fellowship with John and other believers (1:3a). And this fellowship is not just for those who believe in Jesus, but is *with* Jesus and his Father (1:3b). Indeed, one of the major themes of the letter is the idea that believers can have fellowship—a deep, intimate relationship—with God himself through faith in Jesus Christ. Perhaps more than any other letter in the New Testament, 1 John depicts the Christian life as one of deep relationship with God. 📖

Finally, John says that he writes these things "so that our joy may be complete" (1:4). In other words, John and his fellow witnesses are ultimately interested in bringing about this fellowship mentioned in 1:3. This is what will bring them joy. They do not testify to the reality of Jesus's incarnation and resurrection just for the sake of theological information or historical credibility. The whole goal of their testimony is to draw others into the fellowship that believers have with God. Doing so brings them complete joy.

What Fellowship with God Looks Like

■ READ 1 JOHN 1:5–10 ■

John passes on a message from Jesus, that God is pure light without any darkness within him (1:5). Light is a common metaphor used throughout the Bible to indicate God's glory and holiness as well as the revelation of truth. Because God is pure light, it is not possible to have fellowship with him if we walk in darkness (1:6). Though the light/darkness metaphor refers in part to truth versus falsehood, it also refers to holiness versus sin, as 1:7 makes clear: walking in the light enables fellowship with one another, and all sin has been cleansed by the blood of

LITERARY NOTES

1 John, a Strange "Letter"

Like Hebrews, 1 John lacks most of the features of a normal letter. There is no greeting, no author is mentioned, and the recipients are not named. Nor does the document become more like a letter as it progresses, with its recurring themes that twist and turn on one another. While clearly it was originally written (rather than spoken, as Hebrews may have been; see 1 John 2:1, 7, 8, 12–14, 26), it is not a letter in any normal sense. It is better to regard 1 John as a theological treatise or encyclical. Without specific addressees, it is possible that 1 John was intended to be circulated to several churches in the region of Asia Minor, where John spent the last decades of his life.

LITERARY NOTES

Who Are the "We"?

"We" refers to at least two different groups in 1 John. In the first four verses "we" refers to the eyewitnesses of the resurrected Jesus, of which John is the last surviving witness. Though the other witnesses have died, John represents their testimony, which continues to speak to the followers of Jesus. The other use of "we" refers to all believers in an inclusive sense, and can be seen beginning in 1:6–10.

THEOLOGICAL ISSUES

What Exactly Was Witnessed?

Given that John later talks about the error of denying the human nature of Christ, that he came "in the flesh" (4:2–3), the opening of the letter (1:1–4) has been understood as a testimony to Jesus's humanity. He was heard, seen, and touched. While this testimony certainly does affirm the physical humanity of Jesus (he is no ghost or spirit), 1:1–4 could also refer to the post-resurrection appearances of Christ. The seeing, hearing, and touching fit very well with, for example, John 20:24–29, in which the resurrected Jesus invites Thomas to touch his hands and his side in order to believe.

Figure 27.2. *The Incredulity of Saint Thomas* by Caravaggio

CANONICAL CONNECTIONS

God Is Light

The Old Testament is full of connections between God and light. He brought light into the world (Gen. 1:3), and believers walk in his light (Ps. 89:15). God wears light like clothing (Ps. 104:2), and it is connected to his glory (Isa. 60:1). While light is described only as an *attribute* of God in the Old Testament, in John's Gospel Jesus refers to himself *as* the light of the world (John 8:12; 9:5). He came to dispel the darkness and make people into children of the light (John 12:35–36, 46). In this sense, Jesus is the personification of God's divine light.

THEOLOGICAL ISSUES

The Forgiveness of Sins

Included in many of the Christian creeds is the statement that we believe in "the forgiveness of sins." This is rooted in the whole Bible's witness that even though humanity has dishonored and disobeyed God, beginning with Adam and Eve, God is gracious, kind, and willing to forgive sins. In the Mosaic covenant there were many sacrifices that could be made so that one's sins could be forgiven, and the priesthood was established to oversee and perform these sacrifices (see especially Leviticus). In the New Testament Jesus is understood to come into the world, to suffer and die, as the final and perfect sacrifice that secures eternal forgiveness (Heb. 10:14). Jesus describes the ritual meal of bread and wine as a picture of his broken body and spilled blood "for the forgiveness of sins" (Matt. 26:28). One can err on either side of this truth, either denying that one is sinful or that it matters to God (1 John 1:8), or despairing such that one's sins are too great to be forgiven (Ps. 103:12). Central to the Christian understanding of the Bible is that Jesus's life, death, and resurrection are sufficient to forgive all sin (1 John 1:9).

Jesus. Jesus's blood enables sinners to walk in the light and to have fellowship with God, because it removes our sin. If sin remained, we would still be in darkness.

Walking in the light demands that we be honest about ourselves, and this means admitting that sin is in our lives. So John says that if we claim to be without sin, we deceive ourselves and the truth is not in us (1:8). But if we recognize and admit the sin in our lives, we are able to confess it. And if we confess our sins, God will forgive us and cleanse us (1:9). But, again, if we claim to be without sin, we not only deceive ourselves but also call God a liar (1:10). God has judged us sinful, so to claim otherwise would be to regard his word as false. Perhaps this comes as a surprise for some readers: the person who really knows God and who walks in his light is the person who freely acknowledges being a sinner! God doesn't want us to pretend otherwise. Only by acknowledging the truth can we be cleansed and restored.

The Good Advocate

■ READ 1 JOHN 2:1–6 ■

It is good to acknowledge our sinfulness, but that does not mean it is good to go on sinning! John writes so that his readers would not sin. But if we do sin—and John has already established that we will—he comforts his readers with the reassurance that Jesus Christ serves as our "advocate with the Father" (2:1). Christ is like a defense lawyer who pleads your case in a court of law. He is on your side. Furthermore, he is a *righteous* advocate (2:1c). He is not like a corrupt defense lawyer who seems just as shady as the crooks he represents. Christ himself is in good standing before his Father, so his representation is effective.

But Christ is not just our advocate before the Father. He is also our "atoning sacrifice" (2:2). His death by crucifixion paid the penalty for our sins, and indeed for the sins of the whole world. This means that Jesus not only represents us before the Father as our advocate but also makes amends for our failures and sins. He has done all that is necessary to secure our status with God. 📜 🧑‍🤝‍🧑

Jesus is on our side. He is our advocate and atonement. But the question is, Are we on his side? This is one of the key questions that 1 John addresses: How do believers know whether they really know Jesus? John says that we know that we know Jesus if we keep his commands (2:3). Of course, this raises the question of what these commands are, but John will address that later. His point here is that a believer cannot claim to know Jesus and at the same time not do what Jesus has commanded. Such a person is a liar (2:4). There is a connection between knowing and doing. In the same way, someone who keeps his word has the love of God completed within. And so, believers can know that they are in Jesus: the one who remains in him will walk as he walked (2:5–6).

The Old and New Command

■ READ 1 JOHN 2:7–11 ■

John has just referred to the importance of keeping Jesus's commands. Now John begins a discussion about a command that is old, but also new. He first states that he is *not* writing a new command but an old one that his readers already know about (2:7). Then he states that he *is* writing a new command (2:8a). This apparent contradiction can be

CANONICAL CONNECTIONS

Our Atoning Sacrifice

Debate has swirled over the nature of Christ's sacrifice, especially as to whether it is one of expiation or of propitiation. *Expiation* is the type of sacrifice that removes guilt from the sinner, such as the scapegoat on the Day of Atonement (Lev. 16:20–22). The sins of the people were laid on the head of the goat, which was then sent away into the wilderness carrying Israel's sins with it. *Propitiation* refers to the redirection of God's wrath away from the sinner toward the sacrificial animal. This kind of sacrifice was exercised daily in Israel as bulls and goats were killed for sins. The animals took the penalty of sin in place of the people, thus redirecting God's wrath away from them. While propitiation has been criticized because of association with pagan religious practices, it is most likely in view in 1 John 2:2. Jesus's advocacy with the Father (2:1) implies a context of judgment and averted punishment for sin. In such a context, propitiation is the best way to understand the sacrifice of Christ.

RECEPTION HISTORY

The Sins of the Whole World?

The great French Reformer John Calvin famously claimed that Jesus's sacrifice for the sins of the whole world (1 John 2:2) meant not that Jesus died for everyone, but only for the elect of the whole world. This view became known as **limited atonement**, or **definite atonement**, and is a key characteristic of the movement known as Calvinism. The main argument for limited atonement is that God intended Jesus's death to save the people he predestined. If Jesus died for everyone, and yet not everyone will be saved, then God's purposes are not fulfilled. This is an unacceptable conclusion for adherents of limited atonement, since all of God's purposes are fulfilled in Christ. First John 2:2 became a "difficult" text for Calvinism, since it seems to say that Jesus's death *was* for the whole world, and Calvin's own explanation is still the most popular. However, in its context, there is no evidence to suggest that John intended to limit the reference of Jesus's sacrifice.

resolved only once we know what command(s) John is talking about. Given that he goes on to address love and hate (2:9–11), it is clear that the old/new command is concerned with love. This then makes sense of the old/new contradiction. Jesus said, "I give you a new command: Love one another. Just as I have loved you, you are also to love one another" (John 13:34). He called this a "new command." But this command is also "old" because Israel was instructed to love God (Deut. 6:5) and neighbor (Lev. 19:18). In other words, Jesus's "new" command is a reissuing of an old command. That's why John can call the instruction to love one another both old and new. The one who loves lives in the light, but the one who hates is in the darkness (2:9–11).

John's Readers Have Been Changed Already

■ READ 1 JOHN 2:12–14 ■

This poetically structured section in the middle of chapter 2 is arguably the centerpiece of the letter. John speaks to three groups within his audience: little children, fathers, and young men. The "little children" probably refers to all of John's readers (the whole group), just as he addresses them elsewhere (e.g., 2:1). The fathers and young men are subgroups that may represent leadership within the churches. Each group (little children, fathers, young men) is addressed twice. John addresses each group first with "I am writing to you . . ." (2:12–13) and then with "I have written to you . . ." (2:14). This structure enhances its poetic shape and provides a multifaceted rationale for John's letter.

In each case, John writes to these groups because of what God has already done in their lives. The little children have had their sins forgiven (2:12) and have come to know the Father (2:14a). The fathers have come to know the one who is from the beginning (2:13a, 14b). The young men have conquered the evil one (2:13b), and God's word remains in them (2:14c). In other words, John writes to these believers because God's work is already evident among them. One of John's main goals in writing this letter is to reassure believers that they are in the truth and in fellowship with God. He assures them of these things because the evidence is already there. 🛐

RECEPTION HISTORY

Johann Bengel and the Tradition of Annotations

Rooted in ancient traditions of education, Christians have always written commentaries based on Scripture, explaining what the texts are saying to clarify and emphasize for later readers. Similar to but somewhat distinct from a full commentary is the tradition of writing **annotations**—a list of short notes that explain phrases or verses in an isolated manner. Annotations can be more devotional or more scholarly, depending on their purpose. One such scholarly version is the five volumes of notes on the New Testament written by the important Christian teacher Johann Albrecht Bengel (1687–1752) that are still in print today, called the *Gnomon* ("index" or "arrow pointer"). Bengel's notes show his breadth and depth of knowledge of Greek and Latin, textual criticism, and literary and rhetorical devices. These have long served to teach more academically oriented Christians how to read Scripture in a very close and detailed way.

So Stay in the Truth

■ READ 1 JOHN 2:15–29 ■

Since God is already at work in the lives of his readers, John now encourages them to remain in the truth. First, they should not love the world or anything in the world (2:15a). John means the world in rebellion against God, not literally everything in the world, which would also include fellow believers—whom John insists they ought to love! If someone loves the world, including lust and pride, then the Father's love is not in them (2:15b–16).

Second, believers must beware that **antichrists** have gone out from among the churches (2:18–19). These are people who have turned away from the truth about Christ and thus are now anti-Christ. This reality is evidence that it is "the last hour," which is a way of referring to the last period of salvation history.

But unlike these antichrists, genuine believers have an anointing from God and know the truth (2:20). This anointing probably refers to the gift of the Spirit, who leads believers in the truth (cf. John 14:16–17). While the antichrists deny that Jesus is the Christ, genuine believers accept Christ and therefore have fellowship with the Father too (2:22–25). Believers' anointing of the Spirit teaches them to reject the deceptions of deceivers (2:26–27) and enables them to remain in Christ with confidence (2:28). When Christ comes, believers will have no reason for shame, since all who do right have been born of God (2:29).

Who's Your Father?

■ READ 1 JOHN 3:1–10 ■

Throughout this section John contrasts the children of God with the children of the devil. God's love has made believers his children (3:1), and this means that they will become like him (3:2–3). But those who continue in their sinful ways do not know God (3:4–6). Such people actually belong to the devil, who is the original sinner and the one whose works the Son of God came to destroy (3:7–8). The true children of God, however, are not able to live according to sin because they have been born of God (3:9), and they reveal themselves as God's children by their love for one another (3:10).

Love, Not Hate

■ READ 1 JOHN 3:11–18 ■

John has already shown that love reveals the children of God, and this is illustrated by Cain and Abel. Cain was the world's first murderer, killing his righteous brother, Abel (3:11–12; cf. Gen. 4:1–16). In the same way, the

Figure 27.3. *Cain Leadeth Abel to Death* by James Joseph Tissot

world opposed to God will hate the children of God, and all haters are murderers, like Cain (3:13–15). On the contrary, those who love do not murder but rather lay down their own lives for others, as Jesus did (3:16–17). Such love is expressed in practical ways, not only in word (3:17–18).

Having Confidence before God

■ READ 1 JOHN 3:19–24 ■

One of John's concerns in this letter is to reassure believers of their standing with God, and here he does so directly. If our hearts condemn us—meaning that we know we have failed and feel guilty about it—God's forgiveness is bigger than that (3:19–20). And if our hearts don't condemn us—meaning that we don't feel guilty—we can have confidence before God too (3:21–22). The basis for such confidence, whether we feel guilty or not, is belief in Jesus Christ, which leads to love for one another (3:23). By trusting in the Son and by loving one another, believers fulfill God's commands and have confidence before him by the Spirit he has given (3:24).

Test the Spirits

■ READ 1 JOHN 4:1–6 ■

Speaking of the Spirit given by God, John warns about false spirits. Believers should "test" the spirits to determine their origin, because there are many false prophets in the world (4:1). The existence of false prophets indicates false spirits because the false spirits empower the false prophets. The Spirit from God empowers believers to confess that Jesus Christ came in the flesh, while false spirits do not empower such a confession (4:2–3). These are the spirits of the antichrists—those who deny the truth about Jesus (2:18–22). God's children, however, overpower false spirits because the Spirit in them is greater than those under the devil's charge (4:4). Whereas they are from the world and listen to

---

CANONICAL CONNECTIONS

Cain and Abel

It is striking that the only direct reference to the Old Testament in 1 John is his discussion of Cain and Abel (3:12; cf. Gen. 4:1–16). Why does John mention the infamous fratricidal Cain but make no mention of foundational figures such as Abraham, Moses, David, or Elijah? Why recount a story of murder but neglect to mention God's promises to Abraham, the redemption of Israel out of Egypt, or the establishment of the promised land? First, the story about Cain and Abel perfectly illustrates John's point that hate is effectively a type of murder (3:15); murder is the physical expression of true hatred. Second, although 1 John does not demonstrate other direct connections to the Old Testament, it demonstrates several to John's Gospel. Since the Gospel is heavily indebted to the Old Testament, 1 John in effect leans on the Gospel's connection to the overarching story of God. First John assumes the unfolding story of the Old Testament by adopting the framework of John's Gospel.

the world, believers are from God and listen to John's message by the power of the Spirit of truth (4:5–6).

Ultimate Love

■ READ 1 JOHN 4:7–21 ■

John reissues the call to love one another, which is evidence that we have been born of God and know God, since God is love (4:7–8). But calling God "love" is not an empty description. He has revealed his love by sending his Son into the world to be an atoning sacrifice for our sins (4:9–10, 14, 16a). God's love is expressed in self-sacrificial action, and we must love others in the same way (4:11). When we love like God loves, his presence is made complete within us by his Spirit (4:12–13, 16b).

Love made complete in us is a further reason for confidence on judgment day, because those who love will resemble God's character (4:17). Love drives out fear, and there is comfort in the fact that God first loved us (4:18–19). Anyone who does not love fellow believers does not truly love God, since the one who really loves God will love others too (4:20–21).

Bringing It All Together

■ READ 1 JOHN 5:1–21 ■

In the final chapter John draws together all the various threads that he has woven throughout the letter. He reminds his readers that everyone who believes that Jesus is the Christ has been born of God, and everyone who loves the Father will love his children too. They will overcome the rebellious world by their true faith in the Son of God (5:1–5).

In the most confusing little section of the letter, John speaks of Jesus Christ coming by water and by blood, which together with the Spirit testify about him (5:6–8). While the details of these verses require further explanation (see the sidebar "Water, Blood, and the Spirit"), the overall point is clear: God's testimony (represented by water, blood, and Spirit) is greater than human testimony about Jesus (5:9). Believers accept God's testimony about Jesus, while those who reject it make God a liar (5:10). And God's testimony is that he has given us eternal life in his Son (5:11–13).

As his children, believers can ask God for anything according to his will and have confidence that they will receive it (5:14–15). An example of such

> **THEOLOGICAL ISSUES**
>
> #### Water, Blood, and the Spirit
>
> First John 5:6–8 are confusing verses with three main interpretations. Jesus "came by water and blood" could refer to (1) his baptism and death, (2) his crucifixion (remembering John's account of water pouring out from Jesus's side [John 19:34]), or (3) his birth and death. The first option is most likely, meaning that Jesus enters his ministry through baptism (note also the testimony of the Spirit at that moment [John 1:32–33]) and enters his role of Savior through his death. The water and the blood testify that Jesus came to serve and die for humanity, while the Spirit testifies that he is God's divine Son.

a request is to pray for a believer caught in sin, and God will restore that person, provided that the offense is "sin that doesn't lead to death" (5:16). According to John, all sin is unrighteousness but not all leads to spiritual death (5:17). Most likely the only sin that leads to spiritual death is a refusal to repent of sin and to believe in Jesus Christ. With repentance and faith, all sins can be forgiven and therefore do not ultimately lead to spiritual death.

No one born of God continues a life of sin but is kept safe by Jesus, the original Son of God, who protects his brothers and sisters from the evil one, under whose influence the rebellious world remains (5:18–19). The Son of God keeps believers safe by giving them true knowledge of the true God (5:20). Even so, believers must beware of false gods (5:21).

Exploration—Reading 2 John

To the Elect Lady

■ READ 2 JOHN 1–3 ■

Unlike its big brother, the letter of 2 John is in fact shaped like a letter, though its greeting is still strange. It comes from "the elder," whom tradition regards as the apostle John, and it is addressed to "the elect lady and her children" (v. 1). This elect lady may be an actual person but is more likely a metaphorical person who represents the church. Her children are the believers who constitute the church.

John immediately launches into the intertwined themes that characterize this short letter: love and truth. He loves his readers in the truth, as do all who know the truth (v. 1). This truth lives in believers eternally (v. 2). Even the standard wish for grace, mercy, and peace from the Father and the Son is characterized by truth and love (v. 3).

LITERARY NOTES

The Structure of 2 John

As the second-shortest book in the New Testament, the structure of 2 John is very simple. After a brief greeting (vv. 1–3), the elder commends his readers for walking in the truth and encourages them to live in love (vv. 4–6). He warns of deceivers out in the world and stresses the importance of not supporting them (vv. 7–11). The elder's desire to see his readers completes the letter (vv. 12–13).

Walking in Truth and Love

■ READ 2 JOHN 4–11 ■

The elder's readers are already walking in the truth, as instructed (v. 4), but now he wants them to love one another too (v. 5). The command to love is not new, but rather is one that they have had from the beginning (see 1 John 2:7–11). To love is to keep God's commands, and his command is to love—showing that obedience to God is ultimately expressed through love (v. 6).

Opposed to the truth are the deceivers who deny that Jesus Christ came in the flesh. Such a person is opposed to the true Christ, and is therefore an *anti*christ (v. 7; see 1 John 2:18–22). The elder's readers need to watch out that they too don't lose the truth, since only those who remain in the truth will have a relationship with the Father and the Son (vv. 8–9). In striking fashion, the elder even forbids his readers to show hospitality to the deceiving antichrists (v. 10). To do so would be to participate in their evil work (v. 11).

Farewell

■ READ 2 JOHN 12–13 ■

The end of 2 John shows the elder's love for his readers as he anticipates visiting them in order to talk face-to-face. Doing so will make both his and their joy complete, since they love one another as brothers and sisters in the Lord (v. 12). The elder concludes by sending the greetings of "the children" of his readers' "elect sister" (v. 13). This is further evidence that the elect lady of verse 1 is, in fact, a congregation rather than an actual individual. The church that the elder writes to is the "sister" of the church at which the elder is currently based. The congregations are like sisters, just as individual believers are brothers and sisters of one another.

Exploration—Reading 3 John

Walking in Truth and Love

■ READ 3 JOHN 1–8 ■

The Third Letter of John is the shortest book of the Bible (2 John is the second shortest) and is also issued from "the elder." This time, however, it is addressed to an actual individual, Gaius. We don't know anything about this Gaius except what we find in this letter. As with 2 John, the intertwined themes of love and truth are immediately

Jesus in the Flesh

The deceivers in 2 John 7 denied "the coming of Jesus Christ in the flesh." This fits with Docetism, an early form of Gnosticism. Docetism was the belief that Jesus was divine but not human. He only appeared to be so, and did not actually take on human flesh. This error is strenuously denied in 1 John and 2 John, since the humanity of Christ is essential to his role as Savior of humanity. It is not possible to know God truly if one denies the humanity of Jesus. While the elder's instruction of antihospitality might seem ungracious, it is actually motivated by love for others, that they would not be led astray by a grave theological error that results in the loss of God's full reward (v. 8).

Hospitality in the Ancient World

The kind of hospitality that the elder addresses in 2 John 10–11 does not refer to sharing a meal or a coffee. It refers to taking someone in as a guest, accommodating them overnight and perhaps for several nights. The ancient world did not have hotels or hostels like we do today. Whatever public accommodation was available was often unsafe and/or morally dubious. Jews, for example, would never stay in such establishments because of their unholy reputation. This explains why denying hospitality is an important defense against false teachers. Without private accommodation, such people would be forced to move on, thus limiting the influence they are able to wield in any one location.

Figure 27.4. Byzantine medallion with Saint John the Evangelist from an icon frame

The Structure of 3 John

The shortest book of the New Testament also has a very simple structure. After the greeting (vv. 1–4), the elder commends Gaius for his love (vv. 5–8), warns about the wayward Diotrephes (vv. 9–10), and commends Demetrius as an example to follow (vv. 11–12). The letter concludes with the elder's desire to see Gaius (vv. 13–15).

Missionaries and Hospitality

Just as antihospitality was an important way to undermine the influence of false teachers (2 John 10–11), so hospitality was an essential aid to missionaries who preached the truth (see also Matt. 10:9–14). In the ancient world, Christians and Jews avoided hotels and hostels because of their reputation for being unsavory and unsafe. This meant that travelers relied on private accommodation offered through the hospitality of individuals. Such hospitality was therefore an important way to support and to participate in missionary activity. As the elder says, it is coworking with the truth (3 John 8).

introduced, as the elder loves Gaius in the truth (v. 1). The elder prays for Gaius's good health and praises him for walking in truth, which gives the elder great joy (vv. 2–4).

Not only does Gaius walk in truth, but also he demonstrates love to his brothers and sisters, especially those whom he does not know (v. 5). Apparently, these believing strangers were missionaries traveling for the sake of "the Name," that of Christ (vv. 6–7). Showing hospitality and caring for these missionaries makes Gaius a coworker with the truth (v. 8). Thus we see that Gaius demonstrates his commitment to the truth by showing love to those dedicated to the truth.

Diotrephes vs. Demetrius

■ READ 3 JOHN 9–15 ■

If Gaius is doing well in truth and love, there is a certain Diotrephes who is failing on both counts. He loves to have first place and rejects apostolic authority (v. 9). He is a slanderer and does not welcome believers and even rejects those who do want to welcome believers (v. 10). Although we don't know who this Diotrephes was, we do know that he is Gaius's counter-example when it comes to truth and love.

Though Gaius is already a model believer, the elder encourages him not to be influenced by evildoers like Diotrephes. Doing good is evidence of relationship with God, while those who do evil do not know God (v. 11). A positive example is Demetrius, whose character is praised by everyone—even, the elder says, truth itself (v. 12)! Such a person stands in stark contrast to Diotrephes and is a model to other believers, like Gaius. The elder concludes the letter by expressing his desire to say more to Gaius, but face-to-face—expressing his intentional relationship with him (vv. 13–14).

Implementation—Reading the Letters of John as Christian Scripture Today

Love and truth are serious issues. Without love, it is not possible to know God, since God is love. Believers today need to be reminded that knowledge of God is not simply about believing the right doctrines or preaching or evangelism. It is easy to think that if those things are in place, believers are doing well in their relationship with God. But the reality is that many of these things may be in place while love is absent. And that is a huge problem for believers and the wider church at large. Furthermore, love must be more than mere sentiment or nice words. It must be expressed by sacrificial action, just as God has loved us, giving his Son as a sacrifice for our sins. Without love, we deny God himself.

But the Letters of John show us that love must be matched with right belief. John does not endorse a fluffy kind of love that accepts everything and causes no conflict. No, just as love emanates from God, so does truth, and without the truth no one can have fellowship with God. It is therefore a tricky balance for the church to get the marriage of truth and love right. On the one hand, we desire to show love, acceptance, and mercy to all people regardless of their beliefs. But on the other hand, it is not possible to endorse or tolerate falsehoods that strike at the core of who God is. Relationship with God must be shaped by love and by truth. The challenge of the church is to hold both together as well as we can.

KEY VERSES IN 1–3 JOHN

- My little children, I am writing you these things so that you may not sin. But if anyone does sin, we have an advocate with the Father—Jesus Christ the righteous one. He himself is the atoning sacrifice for our sins, and not only for ours, but also for those of the whole world. 1 John 2:1–2
- Who is the liar, if not the one who denies that Jesus is the Christ? This one is the antichrist: the one who denies the Father and the Son. No one who denies the Son has the Father; he who confesses the Son has the Father as well. 1 John 2:22–23
- Love consists in this: not that we loved God, but that he loved us and sent his Son to be the atoning sacrifice for our sins. Dear friends, if God loved us in this way, we also must love one another. 1 John 4:10–11
- Anyone who does not remain in Christ's teaching but goes beyond it does not have God. The one who remains in that teaching, this one has both the Father and the Son. 2 John 9
- Dear friend, do not imitate what is evil, but what is good. The one who does good is of God; the one who does evil has not seen God. 3 John 11

Christian Reading Questions

1. What is the connection between love and truth according to 1 John?
2. Put into your own words what it means for Jesus to be our advocate (1 John 2:1).
3. Why is it bad to go beyond Jesus's teaching (2 John 9)?
4. Why was it important that missionaries accepted nothing from pagans (3 John 6–7)?

CHAPTER TWENTY-EIGHT

The Letter of Jude

Orientation

Given its brevity, the Letter of Jude contains several fascinating elements. It is written by a half brother of Jesus. It quotes one nonbiblical text and alludes to another. It is full of Old Testament references to people who sinned and faced judgment. It is nearly entirely plagiarized by 2 Peter. And the letter is overwhelmingly negative and harsh. 🏺

Despite these elements, Jude is written out of love. His compassion becomes evident at the end of the letter as he encourages believers to be built up in the faith and to care for others whose faith may be failing. This reveals the ultimate concern of the letter: to protect the true faith and to protect true believers. Jude's negativity and harshness are necessary to achieve this positive, loving end. 🏺 📖

Exploration—Reading Jude

Contend for the Faith

■ READ JUDE 1–4 ■

Jude identifies himself as a servant of Christ and a brother of James (v. 1a) (see the sidebar "Jude's Lord and Brother"). He writes to all who are called

HISTORICAL MATTERS

The Historical Origins of Jude

Author: Judas the brother of Jesus

Date: AD 50s?

Location: A Jewish community located somewhere in the gentile world

Setting: Jude opposes a group that rejects moral authority and indulges in immoral behavior.

HISTORICAL MATTERS

Who Was Jude?

Jude has traditionally been identified as Judas, one of the four half brothers of Jesus (Matt. 13:55; Mark 6:3), and there is little reason to doubt this. Like the other brothers, Jude probably was not a follower of Jesus during his earthly ministry but came to faith after his resurrection (Acts 1:14). Paul described the brothers of Jesus as missionaries (1 Cor. 9:5), most likely among Jewish people though not necessarily limited to Palestine.

and loved by the Father and kept for the Son (v. 1b). This presents the Father as the initiator of salvation, calling his people because of love, while Jesus is presented as the one for whom they are called and kept. Belonging to Jesus is the ultimate goal and purpose of our calling.

After a standard greeting (v. 2), Jude indicates that though he intended to write a more positive letter about their common salvation, it was necessary to write something more defensive. He calls his readers to contend for the faith: they must battle and wrestle for the true body of beliefs that have been handed down to the church (v. 3). The reason for this defensive stance is that some people have been perverting the grace of God. He describes these people as ungodly, as having infiltrated the church, and—most disturbing of all—they have already been designated for the judgment of God (v. 4a). Their crime is to take the grace of God as an excuse for "sensuality," no doubt meaning that they give themselves over to sexual immorality and other things, while excusing their behavior on account of God's grace. They reason that if God will forgive it, they might as well do it. According to Jude, this is totally unacceptable.

The Problem

■ READ JUDE 5–16 ■

Jude then appeals to the history of Israel, looking back to God's saving work when he delivered his people out of

Jude and 2 Peter

As noted in chapter 26 on 2 Peter, there is a remarkably strong connection between Jude and 2 Peter. In fact, most of Jude—nineteen out of twenty-five verses—is used in 2 Peter. Most scholars agree that 2 Peter has used Jude as a source, since the shorter document (Jude) is more likely the source for the longer (2 Peter), rather than the other way around. The following table shows where Peter has used Jude as a source:

Jude	2 Peter
4	2:1
4	2:2
4	2:3
6	2:4
6	2:9
7	2:6
7b, 8	2:10
9	2:11
10	2:12
11	2:15
12a	2:13
12b, 13	2:17
16	2:18
17	3:1–2
18	3:3
24	3:14
25	3:18

Jude's Lord and Brother

Jude begins by identifying himself as "a servant of Jesus Christ and a brother of James" (v. 1). Both of these descriptions are interesting if the traditional belief about this letter is accepted. According to tradition, Jude is a younger half brother of Jesus, and therefore also of James. So it is striking that he calls himself a servant of Jesus—his brother! He does not draw attention to the fact of their brotherhood, perhaps out of a sense of humility, or not expecting special treatment because of his familial closeness to his Lord. Though he does not mention that he is Jesus's brother, he does reveal his brotherly relationship to James. Again, perhaps this is done out of humility: being the brother of James identifies him as *that* Jude but avoids directly drawing attention to the fact that Jesus is his brother.

The Structure of Jude

Jude appeals to his readers to contend for the faith (vv. 1–4), reminding them of wayward people of the past who parallel wayward people of the present (vv. 5–16). His readers are to remember what the apostles told them (vv. 17–19) and live out their faith (vv. 20–23). The letter concludes with a glorious doxology (vv. 24–25).

The Metropolitan Museum of Art. Gift of George Blumenthal, 1941.

Figure 28.1. Plaque of St. Jude (twelfth century)

slavery in Egypt (Exod. 12). The pertinent point here is that although God is in the business of saving people, he also destroys those who reject him—as was the case with Israel (v. 5). Even angels who rebelled were subjected to God's judgment (v. 6). And the story of Sodom and Gomorrah stands as a chilling warning of what God is willing to do to destroy evil (v. 7; cf. Gen. 18:16–19:29).

Jude draws a parallel between these examples and the false teachers he is currently combating. They rely on their dreams instead of God's word, and they defile, reject, and slander (v. 8). To show how wrong it is to slander, Jude uses an example about the **archangel** Michael and the devil, who apparently had an argument about Moses's body (v. 9a). Such a story is not found in the Old Testament and there is much speculation about it, but the main point becomes clear: even in that context, Michael did not slander the devil, but instead rebuked him in the Lord's name (v. 9b). Unlike Michael's self-control, these false teachers act according to instinct like animals (v. 10) and have chosen the wrong path like Cain, Balaam, and Korah (v. 11).

The Walters Art Museum. Gift of Mr. Daniel M. Friedenberg, 1993.

Figure 28.2. *St. Michael Standing on the Devil* (artist unknown) copied by Wändemmu Gashaw in *Anaphora of Mary*

In verses 12–13 Jude employs a series of metaphors to convey how dangerous and futile these people are. They are like dangerous reefs that cause shipwreck; shepherds who don't care about the sheep but only about themselves; waterless clouds, which do not offer the nourishment of rain that clouds are designed for; trees that are not only fruitless but also uprooted (v. 12). Their wildness is like the waves of the sea, with their deeds coming up to the surface like the surf; they are like stars in the night sky whose home is permanent darkness (v. 13).

Then Jude appeals to a nonbiblical Jewish text known as 1 Enoch. According to that book, Enoch prophesied about the coming of God's judgment, alongside tens of thousands of angels, to condemn ungodly people for their ungodly deeds and ungodly words (vv. 14–15). Instead of being grateful to God, such people grumble and complain. Instead of living according to godliness, they follow their own desires. Instead of speaking out of humility and love, they speak arrogantly and seek their own interests (v. 16).

But Not You, Friends

■ READ JUDE 17–25 ■

Jude reminds his readers that the apostles pointed forward to this time, when ungodly scoffers would show themselves as worldly, divisive, without the Spirit (vv. 17–19). Their existence should come as no surprise. This means that believers ought not be discouraged, as though God is not in control. The reality of such people was anticipated ahead of God's judgment; there is no reason to doubt his authority or control.

Finally, Jude returns to something more positive, as he sees his readers building their

CANONICAL CONNECTIONS

Cain, Balaam, and Korah

Jude draws on three Old Testament "villains" as illustrations of taking the wrong path. Cain is the first recorded murderer, who took his brother's life because of jealousy (Gen. 4:1–16). Balaam was a diviner who sabotaged the Israelites as they entered the promised land (Num. 22–24) by enticing them with sin (Rev. 2:14), which led to God's judgment on the Israelites (Num. 31:16). Korah (not to be confused with the Korah of Psalms) was a Levite leader who led a rebellion against Moses and Aaron, motivated by lust for authority (Num. 16). In judgment, Korah and all the rebels were swallowed by the earth, taking them straight to Sheol (Num. 16:31–33). All three took the wrong path, leading to their judgment.

THEOLOGICAL ISSUES

Why Does Jude Quote 1 Enoch?

The longest actual quotation in Jude is not from the Old Testament but from 1 Enoch, a Jewish text whose parts date from the third century through to the first century BC. Jude seems to cite 1 Enoch authoritatively, which raises questions about whether Jude regarded it as Scripture or as inspired by God. While the issues are complex, it is best to recognize that one may cite a source authoritatively without regarding it as Scripture, as we do today all the time. The confusion comes in when we expect quotations to come from the Old Testament—from Scripture—and not from other sources. But there is no need to restrict the biblical authors' frame of reference. There is, in principle, no reason why Jude could not quote from a nonscriptural source. He does not call it Scripture, so we should not assume that he regards it as such.

RECEPTION HISTORY

The Influence of Jude on the Canon

Because Jude quotes 1 Enoch, some Christians regarded the latter as Scripture and included it in the canon. This is true of the Epistle of Barnabas and several early church fathers, such Clement of Alexandria, Irenaeus, and Tertullian. While the church at large later rejected the canonicity of 1 Enoch, it remained part of the canon for the Ethiopic Orthodox Church and the Eritrean Orthodox Church. Regardless, most church denominations today accept 1 Enoch as holding some historical and theological interest, even though it is not regarded as Scripture.

faith, praying by the Spirit, keeping inside the love of God, and waiting for their promised eternal life in Christ (vv. 20–21). But even as their faith strengthens, some among them may experience doubt or stumble in their walk with Christ. Believers ought to show mercy to such people and seek to save them from a worse fate. But as they show mercy, they need to watch themselves too so that they are not also defiled (vv. 22–23).

The letter concludes with a doxology that praises God, who can protect believers and cause them to stand in his glory without defect and with joy—to him is glory, majesty, power, and authority for all time (vv. 24–25).

Implementation—Reading Jude as Christian Scripture Today

Without question, Jude is a dominantly negative letter. This fact no doubt contributes to its lack of popularity compared to other parts of the New Testament. There does not seem to be much about the letter that is uplifting, nor would we feel comfortable today saying such harsh things about our opponents.

Nevertheless, Jude serves an important role in the canon. It is not the only text that warns about false teaching and false believers. Several letters do that. The key difference, however, is that those other letters generally address other things too and are not focused solely on combating error. One of Jude's contributions is to show us that sometimes it is necessary to focus on combating error—and urgently so. Some distortions of the truth are so significant that opposing them must take top priority. We can benefit from Jude, with all its negativity and harshness, by taking seriously the importance of safeguarding the truth and protecting believers from falsehood. Our churches need occasionally to do the uncomfortable work of pointing out serious error and encouraging believers to fight for the faith once and for all delivered to the saints.

Though Jude is harsh toward his opponents, he is gentle toward genuine believers who are wavering in the faith. On a personal, one-to-one level, believers ought to take care with one another, showing one another mercy and watching out for the safety of each. In this way, we see that strong opposition to error is not to be our only mode of operation. No one likes combative Christians. Guarding the faith must be tempered by mercy and love.

Christian Reading Questions

1. Put into your own words the error of Jude's opponents.
2. Make a list of all the references to Old Testament characters and stories in Jude's letter. Then read all the relevant Old Testament texts. How do you think these stories support Jude's argument?
3. If you were to preach the Letter of Jude, how would you avoid sounding overly negative?
4. How would you explain Jude's use of noncanonical texts to someone disturbed by the fact that he uses texts not found in the Bible?

CHAPTER TWENTY-NINE

The Book of Revelation

Orientation

No New Testament book is as infamous as Revelation as a springboard for wacky theology, end-of-the-world predictions, and crazy speculations about world events and world leaders. It is a happy hunting ground for eschatological weirdos and cult leaders. On top of that comes the understandable fear that the book is enormously difficult to interpret, with its bizarre imagery, impenetrable symbols, and just plain freakiness. Because of these factors and others, Revelation either is ignored and unpreached or is the object of crazy-eyed obsession.

Although Revelation has more than its share of interpretive difficulties, it is not as impenetrable as many think. In fact, its central message is very simple: *God wins in the end*. The whole book is concerned with the victory of God in Christ over the destructive forces of evil. It is a testimony to the fact that God is bringing about a renewal of his creation in which evil will no longer be allowed to distort, disfigure, or destroy. And at the very center of the story is Jesus Christ, a victorious lion who is also a humble, slaughtered lamb. It is his blood and his conquering of death that seal the fate of evil spiritual beings, evil people, and evil itself.

It is no accident that Revelation contains some frightening images, and even Christ himself is

HISTORICAL MATTERS

The Historical Origins of Revelation

Author: John the apostle. There is also an ancient view that the author is a figure known as "John the elder" (perhaps also the author of 2 and 3 John), rather than John the apostle. Modern views tend to be skeptical about apostolic authorship.

Date: Ca. AD 95

Location: Patmos

Setting: John writes to encourage the seven churches of western Asia Minor (western Turkey today) so that they would have confidence that Christ is and will be victorious over evil.

depicted as truly terrifying. Revelation is no joke, and neither is the impression it seeks to make. The vanquishing of evil is a very serious matter, and the warrior warlord Jesus Christ is not to be trifled with. He is powerful, he is righteous, and he is coming to obliterate the enemies of God.

The real purpose of Revelation is not to fill our minds with speculative timelines about the end of the world, or to identify the latest tyrannical leader as the antichrist (a term that never occurs in Revelation, by the way). Revelation exists to encourage believers everywhere and at all times that God is in control. Evil will not dominate forever. God will deliver his people. God will restore his whole creation. Its message is one of profound hope and speaks especially to those enduring persecution and suffering. It is a great gift to the church, and we would be impoverished without it.

Exploration—Reading Revelation

To the Seven Churches

■ READ REVELATION 1:1–8 ■

The book is named for its first word in Greek, *apokalypsis*, which is translated as "revelation." It refers to the revelation of a vision about Jesus Christ given to John by God (1:1–2). John describes his written account of this revelation as a prophecy that will bless its readers (1:3).

John addresses the prophecy to the seven churches in Asia, which are named later (1:11) and were located in the region that is now western Turkey. John's greeting is actually from Father, Spirit, and Son, described respectively as the one who is, who was, and who is to come; the seven spirits; and Jesus Christ, the firstborn from the dead and ruler of all kings (1:4–5a).

Apocalyptic Literature

A Jewish style of literature, apocalyptic conveys a vision mediated by an otherworldly being. Using picture language, symbols, and highly dramatic scenes, apocalyptic can be difficult to read if we are not used to the genre. Such images and symbols must be interpreted rather than understood literally. The main purpose of apocalyptic literature is to convey the reality "behind the curtain" of what can be seen and experienced in this world. It *reveals* (the Greek word *apokalyptō* means "reveal") the spiritual reality that God will defeat evil and deliver his people. Apocalyptic developed in the Second Temple period of Judaism as Jews were oppressed by foreign powers. It offered an alternative vision of reality when evil seemed triumphant and God was silent. The book of Revelation is a classic example of apocalyptic literature (indeed, the genre is named after it, since revelation is apocalyptic), and it is full of picture language, symbols, and dramatic scenes. It is a vision given to John, mediated by angelic beings, and offers hope to the Christian community as they experienced persecution under the Roman emperor Domitian.

What Time Frame Does Revelation Address?

A key issue in interpreting Revelation is the matter of when its events will take place or have already taken place. There are four main positions. The **idealist view** regards Revelation as addressing timeless spiritual truths about the nature and purposes of God. The **futurist view** sees Revelation predicting the imminent end of time and the inauguration of a **millennium** age. The **church-historical view** understands Revelation to address events throughout history up to and including the present day. The **preterist view** regards Revelation as primarily addressing its own day, with almost no future reference at all. There are strengths and weakness to each view. The best interpretive stance for reading Revelation, however, is to accept certain elements of each. Revelation does convey timeless truths about God, but it also depicts final judgment and the end of all things as we know them. It addresses the first-century situation of its original audience, while also being relevant for interpreting the trends of world history.

Figure 29.1. *Vision of St. John the Evangelist on the Patmos Island* by Tommaso Sandrini, fresco in La Chiesa di San Giovanni Evangelista, Reggio Emilia, Italy (1613)

LITERARY NOTES

The Structure of Revelation

While the book is quite confusing, the structure of Revelation is at least a little more straightforward. The number to remember is *seven*. After the prologue (1:1–20), we see letters to the seven churches (2:1–3:22) and John's heavenly vision (4:1–5:14). Then we see the seven seals (6:1–8:5), the seven trumpets (8:6–11:19), the seven signs (12:1–14:20), and the seven bowls (15:1–16:21). The climax of the book is the triumph of Almighty God with the fall of Babylon, the wedding supper of the Lamb, the final battle and judgment, and the inauguration of the new heaven and new earth (17:1–22:5). The book ends with its epilogue (22:6–21).

CANONICAL CONNECTIONS

Revelation and the Old Testament

Revelation has more allusions to the Old Testament than does any book in the New Testament. Though there are few quotations, nearly every verse contains an Old Testament echo. The references include the Pentateuch, Judges, 1–2 Samuel, 1–2 Kings, Psalms, Proverbs, Song of Solomon, major prophets, and minor prophets, but half the allusions come from Psalms, Isaiah, Ezekiel, and Daniel—with Isaiah taking top spot. The creation account of Genesis, along with humanity's fall into sin, is foundational because Revelation looks to the restoration of creation and the destruction of evil. The plagues recorded in Exodus are key, and Isaiah provides background for the new heaven and new earth. The final battle, judgment, and new Jerusalem come from Ezekiel 37–38, while Zechariah provides imagery such as the four horsemen and the lampstands. John's concern for faithful witnesses amid persecution draws especially on Daniel. Given its extensive reliance on the Old Testament, Revelation cannot be understood without knowledge of major Old Testament themes.

God is eternal, existing then, now, and later. The Spirit is described as seven spirits, since seven represents the completion of God.

A brief doxology is offered to Christ, the one who has brought freedom from sin through his blood and made us into a kingdom of priests forever (1:5b–6). And this is supported by a pastiche of Old Testament quotations that sound like they had always belonged together, talking about Jesus (1:7). Finally, God identifies himself as the Alpha and the Omega—the first and last letters of the Greek alphabet (1:8).

Seeing the Son of Man

■ READ REVELATION 1:9–18 ■

John is on the island of Patmos (now part of Greece) when the revelation is given (1:9–10). He is instructed to write down what he sees and send it to seven churches, in Ephesus, Smyrna, Pergamum, Thyatira, Sardis, Philadelphia, and Laodicea. All of these locations are within John's sphere of influence while he is based in Ephesus for the last several decades of his life. In other words, Revelation is addressed to churches known to John and as part of the pastoral relationship he shares with them.

John tries to see who had spoken to him but instead sees seven golden lampstands and the Son of Man standing among them (1:12–13a). He is an awesome figure with eyes like fire and his face shining like the sun (1:13b–16). So awesome is he, in fact, that John falls at his feet in dread, but the Son of Man comforts him (1:17–18a). Jesus is "the First and the Last" (= the Alpha and the Omega), the one who died but is now alive forever. He holds the keys to death and Hades (1:18b). He again instructs John to write what he sees in his vision and explains that the seven lampstands represent the seven churches to which he is to write (1:19–20).

Letters to the Seven Churches

■ READ REVELATION 2:1–3:22 ■

Chapters 2–3 consist of letters to the seven churches in which Jesus directly addresses each one in turn. The letters follow a similar pattern in which Jesus praises each church (except two) and then challenges and warns each. For example, to the church in Ephesus, Jesus praises their work, endurance, rejection of false teaching, and perseverance (2:1–3), but he also draws attention to the fact that this church has lost the love it first had and must repent (2:4–5).

The church in Sardis is the first of two that receives no praise from Jesus. They appear to be spiritually alive but are in fact dead, with the exception of a few individuals (3:1–4). The church in Laodicea is neither hot nor cold, and if they stay lukewarm they will be spit out of Jesus's mouth (3:14–16). But

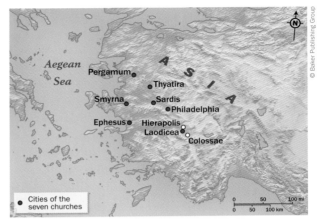

Figure 29.2. The seven churches of Revelation

© Baker Publishing Group

HISTORICAL MATTERS

Why Was John on Patmos?

The apostle John left Jerusalem around AD 70 and relocated to Ephesus, which today is on the western coast of Turkey. Ephesus was a major hub in the Roman Empire for religion, economy, and spirituality and was home of Artemis, the popular goddess of fertility. After the deaths of Paul and Peter in the mid-60s, John was the apostle in residence in that part of the world for nearly two decades, serving the churches throughout the region. But in the 90s he apparently upset the Roman emperor Domitian (different stories about what took place have been preserved in cultural traditions) and was exiled to the island of Patmos, off the coast of Ephesus. While on Patmos, John received the vision that became the book of Revelation. After two years on Patmos, John returned to Ephesus and continued his ministry throughout the region. He died at an old age and was buried in Ephesus, where his grave can still be visited.

LITERARY NOTES

Numbers in Revelation

One of the most perplexing elements in Revelation is the meaning of the various numbers. In short, the numbers should be understood symbolically rather than literally. A few general principles will help with interpretation. The number *four* indicates universal scope (e.g., four living creatures, four corners of the earth). *Seven* is the number of God and completion (e.g., seven churches, seven spirits, seven seals, seven bowls), which means that *six* falls short of God and is used of sin or the evil one (e.g., 666). The number *twelve* recalls the twelve tribes of Israel and is symbolic of the people of God. *Ten* represents completeness or power (e.g., ten horns, ten crowns), while a *thousand* indicates vastness (e.g., a thousand years). It is important to take note of multiples too. For example, 12 multiplied by 12 multiplied by 1,000 equals 144,000, which indicates a vast multitude of God's people.

even these two churches are loved by Jesus, since he rebukes and disciplines those he loves, but they must repent (3:19).

Each letter is followed by a refrain, "Let anyone who has ears to hear listen to what the Spirit says to the churches." This recalls Jesus's words during his earthly ministry (Mark 4:9, 23; Luke 8:8; 14:35). But it also draws a connection between the ministry of the Spirit and Jesus, since Jesus's message is described as what the Spirit says (2:7a, 11a, 17a, 29; 3:6, 13, 22).

Finally, each church is encouraged by the refrain "To the one who conquers . . ." followed by a different promise with each instance (2:7b, 11b, 17b, 26; 3:5, 12, 21). For example, to the church in Ephesus, Jesus says that the one who conquers will be given the right to eat from the tree of life in the paradise of God (2:7b).

The Heavenly Throne

■ READ REVELATION 4:1–11 ■

After the letters to the seven churches have been composed, John is escorted by the Spirit to a glorious throne in heaven on which someone is seated (4:1–3). This throne is surrounded by twenty-four other thrones, with elders, dressed in white and wearing golden crowns, seated on them, indicating that all other rulers are subjected to the one sitting on the central throne (4:4).

The scene is replete with thunder and lightning, fiery torches, and a sea of glass like crystal (4:5–6a). There are four living creatures covered with eyes: one like a lion, one like an ox, one like a man, and one like an eagle (4:6b–7). Each has six wings and never stops praising God (4:8). As the four living creatures praise God, the twenty-four elders fall before the central throne, worshiping God. They throw their crowns before the throne and give God all honor and glory because he is the creator of all things (4:9–11). Suffice to say, it was an awesome and frightening vision.

The Scroll with Seven Seals

■ READ REVELATION 5:1–14 ■

John sees that the one seated on the throne has a scroll in his hand, which is sealed with seven seals (5:1). John weeps because no one is worthy to open the scroll, until an elder points to the Lion of Judah, the Root of David, who is able to open the scroll (5:2–5).

Having been introduced as the Lion of Judah, the figure that John sees is a slaughtered Lamb standing amid those gathered around the throne. This Lamb has seven horns and eyes and takes the scroll from the one seated on the throne (5:6–7). The living creatures and the elders fall down before the Lamb and sing in his honor, declaring him to be worthy to open the scroll because he purchased people from every tribe and nation by his blood (5:8–10).

To this worship is added the voices of countless angels who also declare the worthiness of the Lamb (5:11–12). Finally, all creatures of the heavens and the earth ascribe blessing, honor, glory, and power to the one seated on the throne and to the Lamb for all eternity (5:13).

Figure 29.3. Yellow Lion of Judah painted on the old gravestone in the old Jewish cemetery in the Ukrainian Carpathians

Opening the Seals

■ READ REVELATION 6:1–17 ■

After all the buildup, the Lamb begins to open the seven seals. With the first four seals, a rider on horseback is revealed. Each rider is identified by a different color (white, red, black, green), and each brings devastating power on the earth. The white rider is a conqueror (6:2); the red rider removes peace from the earth (6:4); the black rider brings judgment (6:5); the green rider brings death (6:8). 📖

With the opening of the fifth seal, John sees under an altar the souls of those killed as martyrs. They cry out for justice for their murderers but must wait until the full number of martyrs has been completed (6:9–11). With the sixth seal comes a violent earthquake, the blackening of the sun, and a blood moon. The stars fall to earth, the sky splits apart, and mountains and islands are rearranged (6:12–14). The seventh seal is not opened for now.

CANONICAL CONNECTIONS

Lion of Judah, Root of David, Slaughtered Lamb

These are images used to depict Jesus in light of important Old Testament motifs. The "lion from the tribe of Judah" connects to Genesis 49:8–12 (esp. v. 9), where it is prophesied that the lion of Judah will rule over all people. The "Root of David" comes from Isaiah 11:1–10, where "the root of Jesse" (= King David, Jesse's son) points forward to the coming messianic king of Israel in the lineage of David. The "Lamb who was slaughtered" is a common image in Revelation referring to Jesus as the fulfillment of the Passover lamb, whose blood was shed in order to deliver God's people from bondage in Egypt. When we put these three images together, we see a picture of Christ as a ruling Davidic king who died to rescue his people. The imagery of lion and lamb are obviously juxtaposed to show that Christ's power and authority are mediated through humility and sacrifice.

LITERARY NOTES

What Is the Significance of the Scroll and Its Seals?

This imagery comes from Ezekiel 2:9b–10; Daniel 12; Isaiah 29:11. It conveys the idea of a sealed book or scroll that conceals divine revelation about divine judgment. In order for the judgment of God to be unleashed, the seven seals must be opened, and this can be done only by the Lamb who was slain. As each seal is opened, various disasters befall the earth, leading up to the climactic seventh seal. When that seal is opened, seven trumpets announce further doom for the earth and the final victory of the Lamb over evil.

After the opening of the first six seals, every class of people—whether kings or slaves—hide themselves in caves, trying to escape the devastation that has been unleashed (6:15). They would rather be killed by falling rocks than face the wrath of God and Christ (6:16–17).

The Vast Multitude

■ READ REVELATION 7:1–17 ■

John sees four angels restraining the winds of the earth from four corners of the earth. Another angel arises from the east with the remaining seal, calling out to the first four angels not to harm the earth or the sea until the servants of God receive their own seals on their foreheads (7:1–3). The symbolic number of those sealed is 144,000, with 12,000 from each of the twelve tribes of Israel (12,000 × 12 = 144,000) (7:4–8). The number twelve symbolizes fullness, so 12 × 12 represents the complete fullness of the multitude of people who will be sealed for salvation.

Sure enough, this multitude is not limited to the twelve tribes of Israel but includes people from every nation, tribe, people, and language. And rather than taking symbolic numbers literally (i.e., 144,000), the multitude cannot be counted as they stand before the throne and the Lamb, bearing white robes and palm branches (7:9). They cry out, ascribing salvation to God and to the Lamb (7:10) as the angels, elders, and four living creatures again fall down before the throne in worship (7:11–12).

The multitude wears white robes that have been washed in the blood of the Lamb (7:14). While it may seem counterintuitive that blood has turned clothes white, the point is that these people have been cleansed from sin by Jesus's death. As a result, they serve God day and night and find their shelter in him, no longer needing for anything, and being shepherded by the Lamb (it is also counterintuitive that a lamb is the shepherd) to the water of life as God wipes away their every tear (7:15–17).

The Seventh Seal and the Seven Trumpets

■ READ REVELATION 8:1–9:21 ■

The seventh seal has been set apart from the first six so that by the time we reach it, some anticipation has been built. So it is striking that after the seventh seal is opened, heaven remains in silence for half an hour (8:1). In a scene full of action, the silence is deafening. Then seven angels take up seven trumpets and an eighth angel offers up the prayers of all believers like burning incense (8:2–4). But then the action really begins, as this angel fills the incense burner with fire and throws it to the earth, creating a great disturbance with thunder, lightning, and an earthquake (8:5).

In contrast to the great silence comes the sound of the seven trumpets. With the sounding of each comes a great disaster on the earth: a third of the earth burns up (8:7); a third of the sea becomes blood (8:8); a third of rivers and springs become **wormwood** (8:11); a third of the heavenly lights are darkened (8:12). 📖

In an ominous warning, a flying eagle declares woes to those living on the earth because of the remaining three trumpets (8:13). With the sounding of the fifth trumpet, the abyss is opened and an army of locusts is released on the earth. Their only task is to torment all people who lack God's seal on their foreheads—a torment worse than death (9:1–6). The locusts look like warhorses, wearing golden crowns and having human faces, women's hair, lion's teeth, and tails like scorpion stingers (9:7–10). They are under the control of the angel of the abyss, whose name is Apollyon, meaning Destroyer (9:11).

With the sounding of the sixth trumpet, four angels are released to kill a third of the human race. A huge, terrifying army is amassed, and it slaughters a third of humankind through fire, smoke, and sulfur coming from the mouths of warhorses (9:13–19). But even after this horrifying act of judgment, the remaining two-thirds of humanity does not repent of their evil and idolatry (9:20–21).

The Seventh Trumpet

■ READ REVELATION 10:1–11:19 ■

Just as there was a delay leading up to the opening of the climactic seventh seal, so there is with the sounding of the seventh trumpet. It begins with a mighty and terrifying angel with a face like the sun and legs like fire. He holds a little scroll while his feet straddle land and sea (10:1–2). He swears an oath to God, saying that when the seventh trumpet sounds, the mystery of God will be completed, as the prophets have said (10:5–7).

John is then instructed to take the little scroll from the angel's hand (cf. 10:2) and to eat it, which he does. It is sweet to eat but becomes bitter (10:8–10). John is told to prophesy and is given a measuring rod in order to measure the temple of God and to count those worshiping there (11:1). The rebellious nations will attack Jerusalem for forty-two months, and God's two witnesses, described as two olive trees and two lampstands (cf. Zech. 4), will be protected while

LITERARY NOTES 📖

What Is Wormwood?

Wormwood is a bitter herb that can poison water and is associated with the exodus plagues. It recalls Jeremiah 9:15 and 23:15, where the Lord says that he will feed the rebellious people wormwood—poisoned water—because of their ongoing unrepentant sin. Just as Babylon has poisoned the world with its idolatry, so the judgment will fit the crime by making people drink poisoned water that will bring about their suffering.

prophesying and demonstrating the powers that Moses and Elijah exercised (11:2–6; cf. Exod. 7–11; 1 Kings 17:1).

When they have completed their testimony, the two prophets will be killed by the beast from the abyss in the great city, figuratively known as Sodom and Egypt—where Christ was also crucified—and their bodies will be openly mocked by the rebellious nations (11:7–10). But the two prophets return to life after three and a half days and go up to heaven in full view of all, many of whom are killed by a violent earthquake (11:11–13). Now, finally, the seventh trumpet sounds, and heavenly voices sound praise for Christ, and the twenty-four elders worship God for the impending destruction of those who destroy. The heavenly temple opens with its ark of the covenant on display (11:16–19).

CANONICAL CONNECTIONS

The Two Witnesses

The two witnesses resemble Moses and Elijah in their abilities and signs, but most likely they represent the whole community of faith that witnesses to Christ. Their witness is prophetic, since the entire community has received the Spirit's gift of prophecy (Joel 2:28–32). Through this prophetic gift the church witnesses to the whole world (Acts 1:8).

CANONICAL CONNECTIONS

Who Are the Woman and Her Son?

The pregnant woman represents the covenant community, from which the Messiah will come. She wears a crown of twelve stars that point to the twelve tribes of Israel (Gen. 37:9–10), and she gives birth to a Son, who will rule the nations with an iron rod (Ps. 2:7–9). The woman represents Israel, not Mary, and her son is clearly a messianic, kingly figure whom history reveals to be the person of Jesus Christ. That the Son is snatched up to God means that he is delivered from the threat of the red dragon, most likely pointing to the resurrection of Christ, which delivers him from the dominion and threat of death.

The Cosmic Pregnant Woman

■ READ REVELATION 12:1–18 ■

A pregnant woman clothed with the sun and a crown of twelve stars is ready to give birth (12:1–2). Immediately there appears a fiery red dragon that has seven heads and seven crowns. Its tail wipes out a third of the stars, and it stands ready to eat the woman's baby (12:3–4). She bears "a Son," who is snatched up to God while she flees into the wilderness (12:5–6).

A war breaks out between the dragon's army and the archangel Michael's angels. The dragon—Satan—and his angels are cast out of heaven to the earth (12:7–9). A heavenly voice celebrates God's victory over Satan and believers' victory over him by the blood of Christ (12:10–12). The earthbound dragon persecutes the woman, who is given the means of escape. The frustrated dragon then goes after the rest of her offspring—believers in Christ (12:13–17).

The Dragon's Beasts

■ READ REVELATION 13:1–18 ■

A beast arises out of the sea, and it has ten crowned horns, seven heads bearing blasphemous names, and animal-like features. Satan gives it power and authority as the world becomes its worshipers (13:1–4). The beast has power to blaspheme against God to wage war against his people, while everyone else worships it (13:5–8).

A second beast arises from the earth, looking like a lamb but sounding like a dragon. It compels people to worship the first beast, performing signs and deceiving people (13:11–14). It gives the beast's worshipers a mark that indicates participation in their community. The mark of the beast is the number 666 (13:15–18).

Figure 29.4. Illustration of Revelation 13:11–13 in "Four Miniatures from an Apocalypse" (thirteenth century)

The 144,000

■ READ REVELATION 14:1–20 ■

The Lamb appears on Mount Zion with 144,000 people bearing the seal of the Father's name on their foreheads. They sing a new song and as followers of the Lamb have been redeemed from humanity (14:1–5). Three angels announce the gospel to all people on earth as judgment approaches(14:6–7), the fall of Babylon the Great (14:8), and a warning for those who worship the beast (14:9–12). The Son of Man then appears on a cloud and harvests the earth with a sickle, while an angel throws the earth's "grapes" into the winepress of God's wrath (14:14–20).

The Seven Bowls

■ READ REVELATION 15:1–16:21 ■

Seven angels appear with seven plagues of God's wrath. There is also a sea of glass and fire with God's people standing on it singing to the Lamb (15:1–4). The seven angels are given seven bowls of God's wrath and are instructed to pour them out on the earth, unleashing severe sores, seas and rivers of blood, the sun's scorching heat, darkness, drought, and a severe earthquake (15:5–16:18). As a result, cities fall, Babylon the Great drinks the cup of God's wrath, islands and mountains disappear, and huge hailstones fall on the rebels against God (16:19–21).

The Mother of Prostitutes

■ READ REVELATION 17:1–18 ■

After the pouring out of the seven bowls of God's wrath, John is shown the judgment of the notorious prostitute who has seduced the world with her sexual immorality. She sits on a scarlet beast and is dressed in scarlet, carrying a golden cup full of her impurities. She is named Babylon the Great, the Mother of Prostitutes, and she is drunk on the blood of the saints (17:1–6).

The beast she sits on is the same that came up from the abyss and is going to destruction, taking with it the kings of the earth. These rulers will make war with the Lamb but will be conquered and destroyed (17:8–14). But before that, they will also turn against the prostitute and destroy her, according to God's plan (17:15–18).

The Fall of Babylon and the Celestial Celebration

■ READ REVELATION 18:1–19:10 ■

A great angel comes down from heaven to announce the fall of Babylon the Great, who has led the world and its leaders astray. Her people are called to leave her to avoid her fate (18:1–8). Instead the kings, merchants, and seafarers of the earth mourn her destruction (18:9–20). The final step in the destruction of Babylon the Great will be to be thrown into the sea like a large millstone (18:21–24).

After the fall of Babylon the Great, a vast heavenly multitude erupts into praise of God's judgment and justice (19:1–5). They also celebrate the coming of the marriage of the Lamb and his bride, who is prepared in pure white linen for her bridegroom (19:6–8).

Who Is the Rider?

Just when readers expect to witness the marriage of the Lamb and his bride, instead of meeting the bridegroom they meet a mighty warrior. Clearly this rider on a white horse represents Jesus, with his name "Faithful and True," his multiple crowns, and his title "the Word of God" (cf. John 1:1–14). His mouth unleashes a sharp sword, in keeping with messianic expectation (Isa. 11:4), that he uses to strike the nations, and he rules them with an iron rod (Ps. 2:9). He is the King of kings and Lord of lords. We encounter this final battle scene here in Revelation because evil must finally be conquered in order for the marriage of the Lamb to take place. The consummation of all of God's plans and promises will ensue only once his enemies have been judged and all evil has been destroyed.

The Rider on a White Horse

■ READ REVELATION 19:11–21 ■

Preparations for the marriage feast give way to the appearance of a white horse and its rider, who is called Faithful and True. He is a frightening figure with eyes of fire, multiple crowns, a robe dipped in blood, and a sharp sword coming from his mouth (19:11–15a). He will rule with an iron scepter and execute God's wrath on the nations. His name is written, "KING OF KINGS AND LORD OF LORDS" (19:15b–16). 📖

In anticipation of the fall of kings, commanders, their armies, and all who are opposed to the rider on the white horse, an angel calls the birds of the air to be ready to eat their flesh once they have been defeated (19:17–18). Then the beast, the kings, and their armies gather to wage war against the rider, but the beast and its false prophet are thrown into the lake of burning sulfur, and everyone else is killed by the sword coming from the mouth of the rider. The birds eat their flesh (19:19–21).

The First Resurrection

■ READ REVELATION 20:1–15 ■

An angel binds Satan with a chain and throws him into the abyss for a thousand years, so that he can no longer deceive the nations (20:1–3). Those belonging to Christ are resurrected and reign with him for a thousand years (20:4–5).

Those raised to be with Christ at the first resurrection will not be subject to the second death, but will reign with Christ as his priests (20:6). After a thousand years Satan will be released to deceive the nations again, but he and his followers will be consumed by fire and thrown into the lake of fire for eternal torment (20:7–10).

Then John sees someone sitting on a great white throne with all the dead standing before him. The book of life is opened and the dead are judged, with the sea, death, and Hades giving up all their dead. Then death, Hades, and everyone whose name is not found in the book of life are thrown into the lake of fire (20:11–15).

The Millennium

The period of a thousand years is best understood figuratively rather than literally (Ps. 90:4; 2 Pet. 3:8), but different opinions about this have shaped Christian **eschatology** throughout the centuries. **Amillennialism** (Augustine) views the thousand-year reign as a symbol for the current period of the church. **Premillennialism** understands the thousand years as a period beginning with the return of Christ, but the period can be taken as a literal thousand years or as an undefined era. **Postmillennialism** takes the thousand years either literally or figuratively to refer to a period before the return of Christ in which all the nations will be converted. Many early church fathers understood the millennium to be a literal thousand-year period (Justin, Irenaeus, Tertullian), while others took it in a spiritual sense (Clement of Alexandria, Origen, Augustine). Thus there are two interpretive issues at stake: (1) whether the millennium is a literal thousand-year period, and (2) when the millennium will occur with reference to the return of Christ—now, after, or just before.

Figure 29.5. Lithography of the Holy Trinity (God's throne) in Missale Romanum by an unknown artist with the initials FMS from the end of the nineteenth century and printed by Typis Friderici Pustet

Will There Be a New Creation?

Revelation depicts a new heaven and a new earth, with the passing of the first heaven and earth (cf. Isa. 66:22), but it contradicts Paul, who says that the creation will be renewed rather than replaced (Rom. 8:18–22). In this way, Revelation parallels the imagery of 2 Peter 3:13, which holds the clues for interpreting it. Peter had already used the image of the flood to depict the destruction of the world (1 Pet. 3:18–22), but the world is cleansed of its sin rather than destroyed and replaced. Since God promised never to flood the world again (Gen. 9:11), Peter uses the image of fire (2 Pet. 3:10). But it should be understood the same way: sin will be judged and the world will be cleansed through this "fire." Peter's language is rhetorically strong to convey the radical cleansing to come, but it should not be pressed literally. The same conclusion can be drawn about Revelation 21:1–2.

The New Heaven and New Earth

■ READ REVELATION 21:1–27 ■

The ultimate climax of the book is when the new heaven and the new earth appear, with the first heaven and earth passing away (21:1). The new Jerusalem comes down out of heaven, and a voice declares that the dwelling place of God is now with humanity. He will wipe every tear from their eyes, and death, grief, and pain will no longer exist (21:2–4). The one on the throne is making everything new and will give the water of life to his people, while evildoers will experience the second death in the lake of fire (21:5–8). 📖

An angel shows John the bride of the Lamb, which is the holy city of Jerusalem, radiant like jewels, with a high wall and twelve gates bearing the names of the twelve tribes of Israel. On the twelve foundations of the city are written the names of the twelve apostles of Christ (21:9–14). The angel measures the city, which stands as a giant cube made of jasper, glass, pearls, and every kind of jewel (21:15–21).

There is no temple in the new Jerusalem because God and the Lamb dwell directly with their people. There is neither sun nor moon because the

Figure 29.6. "The New Jerusalem" from Tapestry of the Apocalypse

glory of God illuminates the city. The nations walk by its light, bringing their glory to the city, while nothing unclean can ever enter it (21:22–27).

Life in the New Jerusalem

■ READ REVELATION 22:1–21 ■

Flowing through the city is the river of the water of life, with the tree of life on each side of the river, offering life and healing. The throne of God and of the Lamb is there, with their servants worshiping God. They see his face and bear his name, enjoying his presence in his light forever (22:1–5).

The words that John writes are declared by God to be faithful and true and a prophecy of what will happen soon (22:6–7). Jesus, the Alpha and Omega, declares that he is coming soon to judge all people. Those who are washed will have access to the tree of life, but evildoers will be kept outside the city (22:10–16). John concludes his book with the warning that it must not be altered and with the prayer "Amen! Come, Lord Jesus!" (22:18–20).

Implementation—Reading Revelation as Christian Scripture Today

Revelation is a majestic, awe-inspiring, and deeply hopeful book that offers to enrich our lives and our churches. The time it takes to carefully work through it is a well-made investment that will continue to pay dividends until Jesus comes again. While Revelation needs to be wrestled with by individuals as we puzzle over some of its symbols and details, it really is a book best handled in community. We need one another's help to interpret it, and to absorb its life-changing, mind-altering message.

Apart from simply offering hope, Revelation expands our vision of Jesus Christ and of what God is doing in the cosmos. Christ is bigger and more glorious than we ever imagined, and God's plans for renewal are vaster than the universe itself. Perhaps more than any other book, Revelation helps us to grasp the big picture. It gives us perspective so that we can live according to reality. It blows open our little lives in our little worlds and shows us that we are part of a cosmic drama that will revolutionize the entire creation. And it encourages us to pray, along with John, "Come, Lord Jesus!"

CANONICAL CONNECTIONS

The Garden and the City

The new Jerusalem bears obvious parallels with the garden of Eden (Gen. 2), demonstrating that ultimately God is working to restore and renew his broken creation. There is a river in it (Rev. 22:1; cf. Gen. 2:10), and the tree of life is there (Rev. 22:2; cf. Gen. 2:9). It will be the place in which humanity dwells with God in direct relationship (Rev. 22:3–4; cf. Gen. 3:8). But perhaps most important is what is *not* in the new Jerusalem: the tree of the knowledge of good and evil is conspicuously absent (Gen. 2:9; 3:1–24). This means that in the renewed creation there will be no possibility of sin; no possibility that the creation will be ruined again through human rebellion; no possibility that God and humanity will once again break their fellowship together.

- When I saw him, I fell at his feet like a dead man. He laid his right hand on me and said, "Don't be afraid. I am the First and the Last, and the Living One. I was dead, but look—I am alive forever and ever, and I hold the keys of death and Hades." 1:17–18
- I wept and wept because no one was found worthy to open the scroll or even to look in it. Then one of the elders said to me, "Do not weep. Look, the Lion from the tribe of Judah, the Root of David, has conquered so that he is able to open the scroll and its seven seals." 5:4–5
- A great sign appeared in heaven: a woman clothed with the sun, with the moon under her feet and a crown of twelve stars on her head. She was pregnant and cried out in labor and agony as she was about to give birth. 12:1–2
- Let us be glad, rejoice, and give him glory, because the marriage of the Lamb has come, and his bride has prepared herself. She was given fine linen to wear, bright and pure. 19:7–8
- Then I saw a new heaven and a new earth; for the first heaven and the first earth had passed away, and the sea was no more. I also saw the holy city, the new Jerusalem, coming down out of heaven from God, prepared like a bride adorned for her husband. 21:1–2

Christian Reading Questions

1. Summarize the message of Revelation in one sentence.
2. Outline the structure of Revelation.
3. If you were to explain the genre of Revelation to someone, what would you say?
4. Read Revelation 21–22. Compile a list of references to the Old Testament you can detect in these chapters. Why do you think John relied so heavily on the Old Testament throughout Revelation?

Reading the New Testament as Christian Scripture in the Twenty-First Century

An Altitudinal Review

When you live in a place for a while, it is an enlightening experience to get up in the air and see your world from the window of a plane. Whether the altitude is a few thousand feet in a friend's single-engine Cessna or many miles above the earth in a jet, the abnormal height allows a perspective that normal driving and walking about cannot offer. Connections between places, relationships of buildings, roads, and neighborhoods to one another, and the overall shape of your city or town are revealed in surprising and thought-provoking ways.

If you're reading this chapter you've probably spent quite a few hours reading about the New Testament (and hopefully reading the New Testament itself!). Now that we have walked around the pages of the New Testament

Figure 30.1. Plaque with Christ in majesty

at the ground level, what can we observe by taking a brief, higher-altitude look? Particularly, from the perspective of reading the New Testament as Christian Scripture, what do we see?

An altitudinal view of the New Testament highlights several major highways and how they connect the various features of its topography:

- **Jesus the Son, Jesus the Christ**

  Undoubtedly, the New Testament's vision is centered on the belief that God has finally and ultimately revealed himself to the world through the incarnation, life, death, and resurrection of the God-man, Jesus of Nazareth, who is in fact the promised Messiah. As the first verse of the New Testament says, Jesus is the Son of Abraham and the Son of David (Matt. 1:1) who is then revealed also as the Son of God (Matt. 3:17). Whatever else one sees in the New Testament, the person of Jesus is the central feature of the biblical landscape.

- **The Good News**

  The New Testament is continually proclaiming that the message of Jesus's coming into the world is good news, a happy announcement, or "gospel." The gospel is good news because now there is a way to have an honest, trustworthy, accessible, gracious relationship with the one true God, who is the creator of the world and the Father of Jesus. This good news / gospel is that humanity's sins can be forgiven and our sinfulness can be replaced with a growing righteousness and wholeness. This good news / gospel is that God has begun his return to the earth to restore it and his highest creation, humanity. This forgiven, restored humanity will live together under God's perfect rule, his kingdom that will cover the earth.

- **The Abiding Holy Spirit**

  The New Testament is written after Pentecost, after the great outpouring of the Holy Spirit at the inception of the church and the beginning of a new covenant between God and humanity. The New Testament repeatedly emphasizes that now, after Jesus's physical ascension, God's presence still exists in the world through the power of the Holy Spirit. The Spirit of God works in the world and also empowers individual believers in Jesus and the gathered church to witness and to be transformed over time into the image of God himself.

- **Hope for the Future**

  The New Testament leans heavily forward. That is, the vision of the New Testament includes a backward look at history, but it especially casts our vision forward to the future that God will bring. This future will be a renewed and restored creation under the perfect, just, and peaceful reign of God. This future vision of hope is the basis for the Christian life now amid suffering, pain, and brokenness.

- **Faith and Faithfulness**

Figure 30.2. Fresco depicting the descent of the Holy Spirit (ca. 1000)

This overall New Testament vision of Jesus, the Holy Spirit, the gospel, and future hope is ultimately focused on the present, in the invitation for the New Testament's readers to respond in faith and faithfulness. Faith is trust in the truth of what God has revealed through Holy Scripture. Faithfulness is a continual (though imperfect) orientation of one's life toward following Jesus's teaching and model. The New Testament sees itself not merely as a historical or theological book, but as a guide for how one should live now as we await the return of Jesus to establish the reign of God fully on the earth.

Holy Scripture's Role in Forming Wise People

So if it is true that Christianity is a forward-looking faith that requires something of us—faith and faithfulness—what does it mean to read the New Testament as Christian Scripture in the twenty-first century? The short answer is that God has given Holy Scripture (Old Testament and New Testament together) to develop the faith and faithfulness of his people. To read the New Testament as Scripture is to read it as a disciple who is ever growing in the knowledge of God and of oneself. We can summarize all of this with one word: wisdom.

Whether in the twenty-first century BC or the twenty-first century AD (or anywhere in between), humanity needs wisdom. Wisdom is the combination of knowledge, skills, insight, experience, and character that produces in us the highest and most beautiful form of humanity. Wisdom is not an object to be collected; rather, it is practical knowledge in which one can grow over time. Wisdom alone can create and sustain true human flourishing. All other ways of being in the world—materialism, isolation, arrogance, hate, pleasure seeking, power grabbing, and warmongering—may give short-term pleasure and benefit, but ultimately they are self-destructive. Only wisdom brings life.

Every society, religion, and philosophy offers some form of wisdom that promises human flourishing. Christianity claims that the Holy Scriptures have the most comprehensive and trustworthy wisdom because the words come from the Creator God himself and most fully reveal who he is. It is no accident that the ultimate revelation of God both in Jesus Christ and in the Scriptures is described with the weighty term "the Word." The two-Testament canon provides the world with the Word that promises wisdom, consummately pointing to Jesus as the Word incarnate.

Thus, Christians see Holy Scripture as playing a unique role in shaping the thinking, sensibilities, desires, loves, habits, and behaviors of God's people. God's words, when believed and acted on, reshape us into wiser people. There are other aspects of creation and human knowledge that can help people live and die well. But Holy Scripture is central to this activity, and the New Testament in particular gives a framework to rightly perceive the world's history and nature.

As a result, the ethical or moral thread of the New Testament is more than one aspect of the New Testament's teaching; it is the woven structure of the whole. We may say that Scripture is engaged in a project of resocialization, of re-formation of humanity, with Jesus as the model and the Holy Spirit as the enabling power. Thus, to read the New Testament well is to read it as guiding the continual reshaping of our lives.

Two important ideas must be woven into this vision. First, this reshaping is not only about the individual, nor does it end only with the individual's character development and happiness. God's restorative work is also about the individual as a member of the being-restored creation, for life together in the kingdom of God. Second, this group of transformed people lives and is being reshaped during an overlap of two ages: between the inauguration of the new age through Jesus and his church (now) and the consummation of this work, when God fully brings his reign from heaven to earth (the future). This means that inevitably there will be conflict. The existing world, living in a broken relationship with its Creator, is like a tectonic plate that is now being pushed up against a new landmass that is forming, the church. The result is that both parts feel the pressure, pinch, and pull of the other. Sometimes this is calm, sometimes there are subterranean rumblings, and sometimes there are earthquakes and volcanoes. The New Testament teaches that Christians should not be surprised when the tension between the world and Christian believers erupts in conflict. Because the central nature of God is love and therefore the ultimate vision for humanity is love, this means that when the tectonic plates collide, Christians must be willing to be wronged, to suffer, to be misunderstood and maligned, to be humble peacemakers.

In sum, to read the New Testament today is to read it to be transformed into a new way of being in the world, relating to others as people of love and life, inviting others to come and see, to taste the Lord's goodness, even if this means rejection, suffering, and persecution.

An Ending and a Beginning

Most books aren't still widely read two thousand years after their composition, and there is no book being read as broadly or deeply or in as many languages as the New Testament. Because the New Testament is God's canonical revelation and the faithful witness to the Son Jesus, who is himself the exact representation of God himself (Heb. 1:3), this is good.

What if you are not sure? What if all your questions have not been answered? What if you still have doubts about the truthfulness and value of Christianity? Come and see. When Nathanael heard about Jesus but wasn't sure, his friend Philip responded simply, "Come and see" (John 1:46). Read. Ponder. Pray. Ask for wisdom. This is wisdom.

The end of this introduction to the New Testament is at hand, but it can and should be only a beginning of a life of reading the New Testament as Scripture. It is all too easy for readers of a textbook like this to spend more time reading *about* the New Testament than actually reading it. But this introduction—as helpful as we hope it is—is *not* Holy Scripture; this book is not God-breathed (2 Tim. 3:16), or a lamp for our feet (Ps. 119:105), or pure spiritual milk (1 Pet. 2:2), or alive and active, dividing soul and spirit (Heb. 4:12); unlike Scripture, this book will fade and pass away (Isa. 40:8; Matt. 24:35). The implication is clear: prayerfully studying and obeying Holy Scripture is the ultimate sense of what it means to read the New Testament as Christian Scripture.

Christian Reading Questions

1. How would you explain "the gospel" in three sentences?
2. Has your view of Jesus changed or been affected at all as you have learned more about the New Testament? How so?
3. In what ways has learning how to read the Bible as Christian Scripture brought more wisdom into your life?
4. How do you plan to continue prayerfully studying and obeying Holy Scripture throughout your life?

Glossary

Abba   Aramaic word for "father" used by Jesus (Mark 14:36), Paul (Rom. 8:15; Gal. 4:6), and other early Christians to refer to God the Father.

allegory, allegorical   A literary device by which one understands certain aspects of a story symbolically.

amanuensis   A trained scribe who would write dictated letters at the direction of others.

Am ha-Eretz   "The people of the land," the poor, rural, less-educated Jewish people during Jesus's day.

amillennialism   The eschatological view that the thousand-year reign (Rev. 20:1–8) is a symbol for the current period of the church.

amphibology   Communication that is double in meaning, whereby a phrase simultaneously means more than one thing.

annotations   A list of short notes that explain phrases or verses in an isolated manner.

antichrists   Those who have turned away from the truth of the gospel and now oppose Christ and his people (1 John 2:18; 2 John 7).

apocalypse   A literary genre in which poetic and allegorical images and metaphors are used not for the purpose of straightforward teaching but rather to describe the paradox of God's work in the world, separating hearers into two groups: those who understand and those who do not.

Apocrypha   Fourteen or fifteen books (depending on how portions are calculated) in Greek that were produced during the Second Temple period. The Apocrypha consists of additions to some of the Hebrew books (additional parts of Esther and Daniel); some prayers and psalms; instructions in wise living; enjoyable novellas like Susanna, Tobit, and Judith; and the four large histories of the Maccabean period (1–4 Maccabees).

apocryphal Gospels   Noncanonical stories or collections of sayings about Jesus that often differ qualitatively from the four canonical Gospels.

apophatic theology   Theology focusing on the unknowability of God.

apostasy   The rejection or abandonment of one's faith.

apostle   A word meaning "messenger" or "one who is sent," normally used as a title for certain early church leaders, especially Jesus's twelve disciples and Paul.

Apostles' Creed   A statement of faith, used by many churches of the Western tradition, first introduced in the eighth century.

Apostolic Fathers   The Christian leaders of the generation after the original apostles. Their writings include letters from Clement of Rome, Ignatius of Antioch, and Polycarp, as well as the Didache, which gives instructions about early Christian practice, and the popular Shepherd of Hermas, which includes visions, instructions, and allegorical parables.

archangel   An angel with some level of authority over other angels.

Areopagus   A rock outcrop that sits just below the Acropolis in Athens, where the council of the Areopagus met in order to govern the city and to discuss philosophical ideas (education, morality, foreign cults, etc.) and where Paul preached to philosophers (Acts 17:16–34).

Arianism   An early heresy, beginning with Arius in the fourth century, that denies the divinity of Christ by understanding him to be the highest created being. Arianism was condemned by the Council of Nicaea in AD 325 but continued to thrive until the Council of Constantinople in 381.

armor of God   Paul's image, based on the Roman soldier's armor, to express the gifts given to Christians to combat the spiritual forces of darkness: the belt of truth, the breastplate of righteousness, the sandals of peace, the shield of faith, the helmet of salvation, and the sword of the Spirit, which is the word of God (Eph. 6:13–17).

ascension   The story of Jesus ascending into the clouds in front of his disciples as his last time physically on earth (Luke 24:50–53; John 20:17; Acts 1:6–11; Rom. 8:34; Col. 3:1; 1 Pet. 3:22).

asceticism   The practice of strict religious devotion, often self-renunciation of worldly pleasures.

atonement   A sacrifice made for sin that restores the at-one-ness between the holy God and sinner.

Beloved Disciple   The referent for the author of John's Gospel (John 13:23; 18:15–16; 20:4, 8), likely either John's own self-abasing, even somewhat humorous, self-reference or an affectionate name given to him by his own disciples.

bios   A Greek and Latin genre of literature centering on one person and his or her actions, with everyone and everything in the story relating back to that one person. The genre of the Gospels grew out of *bios* into its own genre, setting Jesus's teachings and actions into a broader, comprehensive story of the whole world, both human and divine, a story that points forward to its completion.

body of Christ   A Pauline metaphor used to express the unity and diversity of the different parts of the church that make up one unified whole (1 Cor. 12:12–26).

canon   A word meaning "rule" or "standard" that delineates authoritative texts. In Christianity, "canon" refers to the sixty-six books of the Bible as separate, distinct books worthy of heeding closely as uniquely authoritative.

canon tables   Beginning at least with Eusebius, a cross-reference system for reading the Gospel stories in dialogue with one another as part of the Fourfold Gospel Book.

Captivity (or Prison) Letters   Pauline Letters written while Paul was in prison: Ephesians, Philippians, Colossians, and Philemon (2 Timothy, one of the Pastoral Epistles, could be part of the list as well, as it was clearly written from prison).

cataphatic theology   Theology focusing on affirmations about God.

catechism   A summary of Christian doctrine used to instruct Christians, often made up of questions and answers.

centurion   A class designation for an important captain of one hundred soldiers (Luke 7:1–10; Acts 10:1; 27:1).

cessationism   The belief that miraculous signs, like those experienced in Acts, were reserved for the apostolic age, a period in salvation history in which God worked amazing feats that served as signposts for the inauguration of the age of the Spirit.

Christ   From the Greek word for "anointed" (*christos*), the title used to describe Jesus as set apart by God to be his good king over his people.

Christology   The study of the person and work of Jesus Christ.

church fathers   Prominent theologians and preachers of the first few centuries of the church.

church-historical view   The view of Revelation that understands it to address events throughout history, up to and including the present day.

circumcision   In Judaism, the removing of the foreskin of the penis, symbolizing the covenant between Yahweh and Israel (Gen. 17:9–14).

circumcision party   Some of Paul's opponents in Galatia who insisted that all believers become circumcised, whether Jewish or gentile, and refused to have fellowship with uncircumcised gentiles, even though they all believed in Christ.

codex   Any number of sliced manuscripts sewn or glued together in a stack. This is the earliest form of what now would be called a "book," and Christians were some of its earliest adopters.

Colossian heresy   A range of spiritual and religious practices that seem to combine Jewish and pagan elements, either a religion or philosophy unique to Colossae or simply a mishmash of religious and spiritual practices that existed in Colossae at the time.

continuationism   The belief that miraculous signs, like those experienced in Acts, continue into the present age without compromising the salvation-historical importance of the signs recorded in Acts.

conversion narrative   An autobiographical story of how someone came to see the world differently.

covenant   A relationship between two parties that has spelled-out expectations.

critical edition   A reconstructed text that scholars put together based on ancient manuscripts, providing a text that a committee has decided is most likely original. These editions also often include textual variants, as well as notes indicating how confident the scholars are on variants and their reasoning for textual decisions.

cruciformity   A way of living, thinking, and relating that is shaped by Christ's cross (1 Cor. 1:18).

curse of the law   The condemnation that falls on all who rely on the works of the law, because everyone fails to keep the law (Gal. 3:10–11).

Cynicism   A Greek philosophy that rejected conventional desires but found virtue in a simple, independent lifestyle.

day of the Lord   The Old Testament expectation of God's future intervention into human history for judgment and salvation (e.g., Isa. 2:1–4:6; Jer. 46:10; Ezek. 30:2–3), understood by Christians to anticipate future fulfillment in Jesus's judgment of the world.

deacons/deaconesses   Those responsible for helping with the practical service needs of the church.

Dead Sea Scrolls   A wide collection of writings that came from a community of Jews who had separated themselves from the rest of Judaism. This diverse library of some eight hundred writings includes copies of the biblical texts, commentaries and paraphrases on the Bible, pseudepigraphal writings, devotional material, and instructions about the community's life together.

definite atonement   *See* limited atonement.

deification   The state in which believers somehow become like God, though not divine themselves, in sharing fellowship with him in a profound sense.

deliberate sin   The conscious, intentional, and permanent rejection of Christ (Heb. 10:26).

disciple   A person who follows and learns from Jesus, or more specifically, one of Jesus's original twelve disciples.

discipleship   The path of life on which one follows Jesus's own ultimate example of humility, righteous suffering, and love.

discourse   A block of teaching, of which Matthew uses five in conjunction with narrative sections to structure his Gospel.

dissimulatio   A pretend argument being used to teach a lesson.

Docetism   An early heresy in which it was claimed that Jesus only appeared to be a human.

Donatists   Followers of an early heresy, similar to Novatianism, beginning in the fourth century that held a rigorous, purist view of the church, denying the validity of the sacraments as administered by those who had denied Christ by giving in to persecution.

doxology   A written or spoken expression of praise to God.

ecclesiology   The study of the church itself along with its structure.

elders   Those who are responsible for overseeing the church in general, including the preaching of the Word. *See also* pastors; shepherds.

elect   Chosen and set apart for a special covenantal relationship with God, like Israel under the Mosaic covenant.

elements of the world   In Greek, *stoicheia*, referring to weak and worthless cultural forces or entities that exist in any culture. God has sent Christ to redeem his people from out of their bondage (Gal. 4:3–9).

encyclical   A letter written to be copied and sent to various audiences.

Epicureanism   A Greek philosophy that rejected determinism in favor of free will, finding virtue in living in the present and pursuing pleasure in the form of mental peace and freedom from anxiety.

eschatology   The study of the end times.

Essenes A priestly Jewish group who focused on asceticism (typically including celibacy) and the rejection of the current priesthood as fraudulent.

exegesis The study of a biblical text with the intent to understand its meaning.

expiation The removal of guilt from the sinner through a sacrifice, such as the scapegoat on the Day of Atonement (Lev. 16:20–22).

faith More than simply a belief in a certain propositional truth, for Christians it is a relational disposition of trust and confidence in God, Jesus Christ, and the Holy Spirit.

Feast of Booths The Jewish festival in which Jews celebrated the harvest and remembered the booths/tents they lived in after their escape from Egypt.

Feast of Dedication/Lights The Jewish festival (today called Hanukkah) in which Jews celebrated their recapturing of the temple during the Maccabean period.

Feast of Pentecost The Jewish harvest Feast of Weeks (Exod. 34:22; Num. 28:26; Deut. 16:10), held on the fiftieth day of Passover, during which the Holy Spirit came upon the apostles, causing them to preach in the languages of those gathered for the festival (Acts 2:1–41).

***filioque* clause** The clause meaning "and the Son" (Latin, *filioque*), added to the Nicene-Constantinopolitan Creed referring to the Spirit's being sent by both the Father *and the Son*. The clause was affirmed by the Western church but rejected by the Eastern church, serving as a key part of the major split between the Roman Catholic and Eastern Orthodox churches in the eleventh century.

flat characters Literary characters who do not develop but rather serve as types or stock figures who play a set role.

form criticism Beginning in Old Testament studies in the early twentieth century, form criticism seeks to identify the different types of literature within the Gospels (parables, wisdom sayings, miracle stories, etc.) and speculate on what must have been happening in the church that would lead people to value and retell these stories.

four letters to the Corinthians If Paul's four letters to the Corinthians are labeled A, B, C, D, then B = 1 Corinthians and D = 2 Corinthians, while A and C are lost.

fruit of the Spirit The characteristics of a believer's life when walking by the Spirit: love, joy, peace, patience, kindness, goodness, faithfulness, gentleness, self-control (Gal. 5:22–23).

futurist view   The view of Revelation that understands it to predict the imminent end of time and inauguration of a millennial age.

Gemara   Later expansions and sayings of the Mishnah.

gematria   An ancient practice of finding connections between numbers and names, where the numeric value of words is calculated, seeing symbolic significance in the connection.

General Letters   The seven letters of the New Testament, sometimes called Catholic (i.e., universal), that are addressed to Christians in general rather than to a specific church: James; 1–2 Peter; 1–3 John; Jude.

genre   The category of a certain piece of literature. In the New Testament, books often fall into the genres of Gospel, historical narrative, letter, and apocalypse.

gentile   A person who is not Jewish.

Gnosticism   An early and varying heresy normally centering on a stark duality between the evil physical world and the good spiritual world, as well as presenting salvation as being found only through special "knowledge" (*gnōsis*).

God-fearers   Gentiles who were attracted to Judaism, perhaps participating in some aspects of Judaism without fully converting.

Golgotha   An Aramaic word meaning "skull." The hill where Jesus was crucified outside Jerusalem.

gospel   A word meaning "good news," referring to the good news of the message of Jesus Christ's life, death, and resurrection. It also refers to each of the four first books of the New Testament (the Gospels) and their genre. The genre of the Gospels grew out of the Greek and Latin genre of *bios* into its own genre, setting Jesus's teachings and actions into a broader, comprehensive story of the whole world, both human and divine, a story that points forward to its completion.

Great Commission   The story told in Matthew 28:18–20 of Jesus authorizing his disciples to make disciples of all the nations of the world, baptize them, and teach them to obey him.

Hades   In Greek thought, the name for the realm of the dead. In the New Testament, Hades often is synonymous with hell.

haggadah   A Hebrew term meaning "story" or "telling." One of the two forms of Midrash, it also appears in the Passover Haggadah, the liturgy meant to set forth the order and meaning of the Passover meal.

halakah   A Hebrew term meaning "the way." One of the two forms of Midrash. It is the collection of traditions about how to apply the Pentateuch to religious life and daily conduct.

Hasmonean dynasty   The dynasty of the Maccabee family following the Jewish revolt against the Syrians in 167 BC.

head coverings   In the Mediterranean region, women's hair often was an object of lust, so married women were expected to cover their hair. This was especially the case for Jewish women, while wealthy Roman women sometimes would want to show off their expensive hairstyles. In 1 Corinthians 11:1–16, Paul encourages women to cover their hair in worship, a cultural application symbolizing godly attitudes and relationships.

Hebrew Scriptures   *See* Jewish Scriptures.

Hellenization   Alexander the Great's campaign to spread throughout the world the superiority of Greek language, culture, and philosophy.

heresy   False teaching that deviates from official doctrine.

Herodian dynasty   The dynasty of Herod the Great and his family from 37 BC until the destruction of the temple in AD 70.

Herodians   Jewish people who supported the Herodian dynasty and were therefore part of the Roman imperial establishment.

high priest   The highest-ranking priest of Israel, from the line of Aaron.

High Priestly Prayer   Jesus's prayer in John 17:1–26, at the end of the Upper Room Discourse, in which he asks his Father to protect his disciples and to create among them a unity mirroring the unity of the Father and Son.

historical-critical method   An academic discipline that focuses on the historical setting of documents (author, date, location, audience, etc.).

honor-shame culture   The dominant relational culture in Jesus's day. Honor is like a currency that gives people status in society (much like money does in modern Western societies). Honor is granted according to what the society values and often promotes a more group-oriented society. Conversely, one receives shame by not conforming to the established standards of good and bad. Jesus's teaching often pushed against aspects of the honor-shame culture. The first become last (Matt. 19:30), the persecuted and ridiculed are honored (Matt. 5:10–12), the lame and blind and poor are welcomed and lifted up (Luke 14:15–24).

hypocrisy   External behavioral righteousness lacking a heart connected to God. It is the opposite of Jesus's "greater righteousness" (Matt. 5:17–20, 48)—the call to inward purity and wholeness between outer behavior and the heart.

idealist view   The view of Revelation that understands it to address time-less spiritual truths about the nature and purposes of God.

imperial guard   An elite group of Roman soldiers (also called praetorian guard).

incarnation   The doctrine that God became human, assuming a human nature, in the person of Jesus Christ, upon his conception.

inspiration   The doctrine that Scripture, while authored by humans, con-sists of God's own words given to teach, rebuke, correct, and train (2 Tim. 3:16).

Jerusalem Council   An early church meeting between messengers from the church in Antioch (Paul, Barnabas) and Jerusalem (James), as well as the apostles (Peter), in which they decided what should be required of gentile converts, concluding that gentiles should not be burdened with the law of Moses but should abstain from certain things that might cause Jewish believers to stumble (Acts 15:1–35).

Jesus traditions   Oral traditions about Jesus, widespread before they were utilized in the writing of the Gospels.

Jewish Scriptures   A term used today by Jewish people and many scholars to describe their canonical sacred writings.

Josephus (AD 37–100)   A Jewish general who surrendered to the Romans in AD 70 and ended up living in Rome, where he wrote several impor-tant works, including the lengthy *History of the Jewish War*, and from whom much of our information about Second Temple Judaism comes.

justification   God's declaration of a person to be righteous and thus in right relationship with him, achieved by the sacrifice of Jesus, which is received by faith (Rom. 3:21–26; 4:1–8).

kenosis   From a Greek word translated as "emptied," this term refers to Jesus's self-emptying in his incarnation (Phil. 2:7). Some have un-derstood it to mean that Jesus gave up his divinity when he became human, but the early church rejected this understanding, asserting that Jesus gave up his *divine privileges* in order to become human but never stopped being fully God.

kingdom of God   The space and time of God's absolute, just, and good rule over the whole world, where he is present as King, where justice and peace rule, and where evil, pain, and death are vanquished.

kingdom of heaven   Matthew's unique phrase that means the same thing as "the kingdom of God" in terms of its referent—God's now and fu-ture reign—but is different in terms of connotations. Matthew likes to describe God's reign as "of heaven," because this evokes the idea of the strong contrast between the kingdoms of this world and God's heavenly kingdom yet to come.

Koine Greek   A simplified hybrid of several dialects of Greek in which the New Testament was written. During Jesus's day Koine was the common (Greek, *koinē*) form of Greek spoken throughout the whole Mediterranean world and into the Middle East, because it allowed governance and trade to occur throughout the Roman Empire.

last days   The period between Jesus's ascension and his eventual return (2 Tim. 3:1).

Last (or Lord's) Supper   The Passover meal that Jesus ate with his disciples before he was betrayed. During the meal, Jesus established a ceremony to remember his body and blood through bread and wine. The church would continue this observation as the Lord's Supper after his death and resurrection (Matt. 26:27–28; 1 Cor. 11:17–32).

law of Christ   Paul's play on the term "law" that refers to love in action (Gal. 6:2), as Jesus sums up the entire law of Moses in loving God and loving one's neighbor (Matt. 22:34–40).

lawyers   A Jewish professional class of experts in the law, closely associated with the scribes.

lectionaries   Books of biblical readings to be used in worship services, written in many different styles and languages, mostly from the eleventh to the thirteenth century.

Levitical priesthood   The commission of male members of the tribe of Levi between the ages of twenty-five and fifty to serve God in the tent of meeting (the tabernacle) as priests reserved for that task (Num. 8:24–25).

limited atonement   The view that Jesus died sacrificially not for everyone but only for the elect.

literary criticism   Beginning in the late twentieth century, literary criticism focuses on the Gospels as pieces of literature rather than on how they were written (form, source, and redaction criticisms), including methods of interpreting Gospel stories, character analysis, and plot/structure analysis.

liturgy   A form, structure, or script by which Christian worship may be performed.

Lord's Prayer   The two-part prayer that Jesus uses as an anchoring model, orienting the believer in how to relate to God our Father and others in the daily life of faith (Matt. 6:9–13; Luke 11:2–4).

Lord's Supper   *See* Last (or Lord's) Supper.

Maccabees   The nickname, meaning "hammers," given to Judas and his rebel followers who revolted successfully against the Syrians in 167 BC. His family, the Hasmonean dynasty, continued to rule until Roman occupation in 63 BC.

magi   Astrologers or wise men from the East who came to worship Jesus as the king of the Jews (Matt. 2:1–12).

Magnificat   Mary's lyrical response in Luke 1:46–55 to Elizabeth's prophetic blessing, a song of praise rich with theological tones and foreshadowing. The Magnificat developed as a very important part of Christian worship, used in many parts of the church's various liturgies.

majuscules   Manuscripts written entirely in capital letters, especially from the fourth to the eighth century.

Manichaeism   An ancient religion beginning in the third century that required a strict asceticism based on dualistic cosmology and interpreted the resurrection as only a freedom from sin, not as bodily in nature.

man of lawlessness   A mysterious figure in 2 Thessalonians 2 whom Paul depicts as occupying God's temple and exalting himself above God (cf. Isa. 14:12–14; Ezek. 28:2; Dan. 6:7). He often is equated with the "antichrist" mentioned in 1 and 2 John, but in those contexts that term refers to people who have left the community of believers.

manuscripts   Ancient documents of the Bible or part of the Bible handwritten on some type of paper or leather.

Marcionism   An early heresy, beginning in the second century with Marcion, that creates a duality between the evil physical world and the good spiritual world (similar to Gnosticism) and also differentiates between the God of the Old Testament and the God of the New Testament. Marcion created his own canon, denying the entire Old Testament, using his own Gospel (similar to Luke's Gospel), and using only Pauline Epistles.

martyrs   Christians who are put to death because of their witness to the truth of Jesus Christ as God's Messiah, through whom salvation comes.

Messiah   From the Hebrew word for "anointed" (*meshiah*), the title used to describe Jesus as set apart by God to be his good king over his people.

Midrash   From a Hebrew word meaning "to seek answers." Midrash seeks to answer contemporary theological and practical questions by investigating the Scriptures. It consists of two categories: *halakah*, which inquires about laws and religious practices, and *haggadah*, which interprets biblical narratives.

millennium   The thousand-year reign of Christ (Rev. 20:1–8), variously interpreted and represented by the views amillennialism, premillennialism, and postmillennialism.

mimesis   A term referring to a literary work or an aspect of a literary work imitating another (e.g., Luke's presentation of Jesus imitating the Old Testament presentation of Israel).

minuscules   Manuscripts, usually on parchment, written in a small cursive style of Greek letters. We have thousands of minuscules, most dating from the eleventh to thirteenth century.

Mishnah   From a Hebrew word meaning "to study by repetition/review." The Mishnah is a written collection of oral teachings of various rabbis.

Modalism   An early heresy in which the three persons of the Trinity are not three distinct persons but rather are three modes by which God reveals himself.

monasticism   An ascetic way of life beginning as early as the late third century that centers on renouncing worldly and external pleasures for whole-life devotion to the spiritual life.

Monophysitism   An early Christian heresy that understood Christ to have only one nature—divine—rejecting the Council of Chalcedon.

monotheism   A religious belief that there is only one true and superior god.

New Perspective on Paul   A view popularized by scholars such as E. P. Sanders, J. D. G. Dunn, and N. T. Wright that critiques the typical Protestant approach to Paul's view of Judaism. For these scholars, Judaism was not a "salvation by works" religion but rather relied on God's grace. The problem with law-keeping Jews in Paul's day was that the law identified them as God's people, which was a source of pride and boasting. Therefore, Paul's critique of such Jews is more about how to identify the people of God: they are identified by faith in Christ and by having the Spirit, not by keeping the law of Moses.

New Testament   The term used by Christians starting in the early third century to refer to the writings of the apostles, deriving from the promise of the new covenant that Christians understand to be fulfilled in Jesus.

Nicene-Constantinopolitan Creed   The AD 381 revision of the original AD 325 Nicene Creed, affirming orthodox, trinitarian theology.

Nicene Creed An early Christian statement of belief written at the Council of Nicaea in AD 325, laying out the orthodox understanding of the relationship between God the Father and God the Son.

Novatianists Followers of an early heresy, similar to Donatism, taught by Novatian beginning in the third century that held a rigorous, purist view of the church, denying communion for anyone who had denied Christ or offered a pagan ritual sacrifice.

Old Testament The term used by Christians starting in the early third century to refer to the sacred Jewish writings in comparison with the writings of the apostles.

Old Testament Pseudepigrapha A collection of stories and prophecies that are ascribed to famous people from biblical times, such as Enoch, Solomon, and Abraham.

orthodox doctrine Correct and right teaching or belief.

orthopraxy Correct and right living.

overseers Men who live exemplary Christian lives, both within the Christian community and outside it, and hold the responsibility of teaching the congregation.

Palestine Also known as Roman Judea, the region roughly between the Mediterranean and the Jordan River where most of Jesus's ministry took place.

papyrus An early form of paper made from a reed plant. Some of the earliest portions of the New Testament are written on papyri, some as early as the second century AD.

parables Stories—often allegories, proverbs, short pithy sayings, similes, and metaphors—used by Jesus (and other teachers) to convey truth and, in the Gospels, to separate hearers into those who understand and those who do not.

paraenesis Writing meant to exhort hearers toward growth in virtue and character.

participation with Christ The doctrine that Christians are connected to Christ through faith and share not only in his righteousness and resurrection but also in his sufferings and death.

Passover The annual Jewish festival celebrating the sparing of Israel's children on the night before the exodus of Israel from Egypt. Passover also begins the Feast of Unleavened Bread.

Pastoral Letters Paul's letters to individual church leaders rather than churches themselves: 1 Timothy, 2 Timothy, and Titus.

pastors   Those who are responsible for overseeing the church in general, including the preaching of the Word. *See also* elders; shepherds.

patriarchs   The three main ancestors of Israel: Abraham, Isaac, and Jacob.

patron-client relationships   An institution vital to the culture and community of the Roman Empire. Patrons often were wealthier members of society who might provide money, grain, employment, land, or social advancement for their clients. In exchange, the socially and financially lesser client was obligated to express gratitude and to publicize the favor of the patron and thereby contribute to his reputation.

Pentateuch   The five books of Moses: Genesis, Exodus, Leviticus, Numbers, and Deuteronomy.

pericope   A self-contained literary unit, normally a story from one of the four Gospels.

pesher   An ancient Jewish commentary on parts of the Old Testament, many of which were discovered in the Dead Sea Scrolls.

Pharisees   The Jewish conservatives of Jesus's day who focused on the strict study and practice of God's commandments in the Torah and the rabbinic traditions that developed along those lines. Their name derives from the idea of being "separate" from others, and their focus was on purity or ritual cleanness. Their roots are from the Maccabean period, with its fervor for rediscovering and defending traditional Judaism.

Philo (20 BC–AD 50)   A highly educated Jewish philosopher in Alexandria, Egypt, which was the intellectual capital of the world at that time. Philo integrated the Greek philosophical system and methods of interpreting texts with Jewish thought and study of the Old Testament. His extensive writings were influential not only for Jews but also for many early Christian theologians.

physiognomy   The Greco-Roman cultural practice of judging someone's character based on their physical features.

postmillennialism   The eschatological view that the thousand years (Rev. 20:1–8) either literally or figuratively refers to a period before the return of Christ in which all the nations will be converted.

predestination   The doctrine that events are predetermined by God.

premillennialism   The eschatological view that the thousand years (Rev. 20:1–8) is a period beginning with the return of Christ, but the period can be taken either as a literal thousand years or as an undefined era.

preterist view   The view of Revelation that understands it to primarily address its own day, with almost no future reference at all.

proconsul The governor of a Roman province.

prophets People filled with the Spirit who spoke words of direction and encouragement (Judg. 3:10; 1 Sam. 10:10; Acts 15:32; 21:10; 1 Cor. 14:29–32; Eph. 3:5).

propitiation The redirection of God's wrath away from the sinner toward a sacrificial animal.

pseudonymous The term used to describe literary works written under a false name, often taking the name of a famous historical figure.

Q From the German word *Quelle*, meaning "source," this is the name given to a hypothetical collection of Jesus's sayings that supposedly circulated before the writing of the Synoptic Gospels and explains the shared material between Matthew and Luke that does not also occur in Mark.

rabbi A teacher of Jewish law. These teachers became a fixture within Judaism during the Second Temple period as their sayings and interpretations were memorized and written down.

ransom theory of atonement The theory that understands Jesus's death as a payment that satisfies the debt that humanity owes due to sin, and that Jesus's death frees and breaks the bonds of humanity's enslavement.

rapture The term used for the event described 1 Thessalonians 4:16–17 that some understand as believers being taken from the world, leaving unbelievers behind, in the end times. However, the text gives no support to the "left behind" idea, and instead pictures the return of Christ and the coming together of the resurrected dead, believers who are still living, and Christ himself.

reception history Rooted in a greater awareness of each interpreter's situatedness in his or her own culture, reception history seeks to understand how the New Testament was read in the past, especially before the modern era.

redaction criticism Beginning in the mid-twentieth century, redaction criticism seeks to understand the editorial activity of the Gospel writers, from which one may understand their theology more clearly.

redemption The purchase or buying back of something. In the New Testament, it often is associated with God's salvation, or purchase, of his people through the death and resurrection of Jesus Christ.

resurrection The act of being brought from death to life. In the New Testament, Jesus's resurrection from the dead assures Christians that they too will be resurrected from the dead into eternal life upon Jesus's return (1 Cor. 15).

righteousness Holistic moral uprightness, marked by right relationships of faithfulness and love. Christians become righteous through faith in Jesus Christ.

Roman citizenship A status of political and legal privilege, available only to free people (not slaves). Citizenship was given if both parents were Roman citizens, but also could be granted by generals and emperors. Male Roman citizens were given several privileges and protections that were defined by the Roman state, while Roman women experienced a more limited range of privileges.

Roman emperor The supreme ruler of the Roman Empire.

round characters Literary characters who are multifaceted and develop throughout the course of a story.

sacrifice The offering of a crop or an animal to express worship toward a god.

Sadducees Jewish people usually from the families that controlled the priesthood and political power going back to the later generations of the Hasmonean dynasty. This group typically was wealthy, controlled taxes and temple activities, and was in political relationship with the Roman government. They were followers of Moses and honored the Torah as binding, but not other writings such as the Prophets or other beliefs that had developed in the Second Temple period, such as the bodily resurrection and angels. As those in control of wealth and power, they had little interest in the hope for a messiah to come and overthrow the government to establish a new kingdom.

sage A teacher of wisdom.

salvation The act of God by which he saves humans from their sin through the death and resurrection of Jesus Christ.

Samaritans Samaria was the area north of Judea and south of Galilee in ancient Israel but was destroyed by the Assyrians in 722 BC. There were centuries of conflict and hatred between the Samaritans, who considered themselves Jews, and the other Jewish people of the surrounding areas. The Samaritans had their own version of the Pentateuch, along with their own temple on Mount Gerizim. By Jesus's time the Jews avoided the Samaritans completely (John 4:9), even traveling long distances to avoid going through their region.

Sanhedrin   The top Jewish council that decided matters of Jewish law. In Jesus's day it was made up of seventy-one members from the high priests, elders, and scribes.

scribes   A Jewish professional class who taught, copied, and interpreted the law.

Scripture(s)   A term used by Jewish people in both pre-Christian times and early Christianity to describe the Jewish sacred writings, before the New Testament was finalized. Now it is used by many Christians to refer to the Christian Bible as a whole.

scrolls   Rolled pieces of parchment containing writing.

Second Temple period   The period from 515 BC to AD 70 (or AD 135), from the Jews' return from exile to the destruction of the temple, which provides the complex background to Jesus and early Christianity.

Septuagint   The Greek version of the Old Testament produced in the last three centuries BC. Based on the tradition that it was translated from Hebrew to Greek by seventy (or seventy-two) scholars, the title is abbreviated as "LXX" (the Roman numeral for seventy).

seven signs in John   The seven miraculous signs of Jesus pointing to his being sent by God with divine power on earth, as recorded in John's Gospel: changing water into wine (2:1–11), healing of the nobleman's son (4:46b–54), healing of the lame man (5:2–47), feeding of the five thousand (6:1–15), walking on water (6:16–21), healing of the man born blind (9:1–41), and raising of Lazarus (11:1–44).

Shema   The confession from Deuteronomy 6:4 that "the Lord our God is one," which Jesus reiterates as the greatest biblical command (Matt. 22:35–40; Mark 12:28–31; Luke 10:25–28).

shepherds   Those who are responsible for overseeing the church in general, including the preaching of the Word. *See also* elders; pastors.

sin   Failure to follow God's moral law or will. Because of sin, humans are separated from God and condemned to eternal punishment, unless they receive his salvation through Jesus Christ.

Son of David   The descendant of the great king of Israel, David; Jesus took on this title to indicate that he was the final fulfillment of God's promise to David to restore his kingdom.

Son of God   A messianic title used for Jesus throughout the New Testament. He is the unique, beloved Son of God, who is not created but who shares the divine identity; who is the final and true arbiter of God's knowledge and wisdom in the world; who is the Messiah, the fulfillment of all the promises, hopes, and images of God's saving work in the world; and who exists in a unique father-son relationship with the God of Israel.

Son of Man   Jesus's self-designation that alludes to Daniel 7, portraying himself as God's anointed king sent to reign forever.

source criticism   Source criticism seeks to understand the order in which the Gospels were written and how they relate to one another literarily.

spiritual gifts   Gifts or abilities given by the Holy Spirit for the benefit of the whole church and not necessarily miraculous in nature (though some are).

spiritual warfare   The Christian battle against the spiritual forces of darkness (Eph. 6:10–12).

Stoicism   A Greek philosophy that found virtue in accepting fate and mastering one's passions so that one might live in accordance with the logical ordering of the universe.

substitutionary atonement   The doctrine that Christ takes on himself through his death the legal penalty that has been rightly declared over sinful humanity.

super-apostles   Outwardly impressive and skilled teachers (2 Cor. 11:5; 12:11) who taught a different Jesus and gospel from what Paul taught (2 Cor. 11:4).

symbolic world   The system of values, habits, and beliefs that operates at a conscious and subconscious level.

synagogue   The local place where Jews gather to worship, pray, and study the Hebrew Bible.

Synoptic Gospels   The Gospels of Matthew, Mark, and Luke. These are the three canonical Gospels that have a clear literary relationship, often containing stories and sayings that overlap significantly, and likely depending on one another's writing at some level.

systematic theology   The study of biblical teaching on a range of different topics that seeks a coherent account of them.

tabernacle   A portable tent that acted as the most important place of worship for Israel before the temple in Jerusalem because it housed the ark of the covenant, where God's presence rested among the Israelites.

Talmuds   Written collections of various rabbinical teachings and sayings, called the Mishnah, with later expansions and sayings, called the Gemara.

Targums   Translations of the Hebrew Scriptures into Aramaic, the language commonly used in Palestine and probably what Jesus spoke.

teachers   In the church, those who are skilled in explaining the Scriptures, like Apollos (Acts 18:24–28).

tetramorph   A combination into one image of the Four Symbols of the Evangelists: Matthew (human), Mark (lion), Luke (ox), and John (eagle).

textual criticism   The study of ancient texts that seeks to establish the most reliable version of their content and wording.

third heaven   The highest segment of the heavenly realms, according to Paul's cosmology, which he references in recounting his out-of-body experience (2 Cor. 12:1–5).

thorn in the flesh   A personal physical ailment, moral weakness, or spiritual problem that Paul understands to be a "messenger of Satan" that torments him. He asks God to remove it from him. When God does not, Paul learns that his own weaknesses and sufferings allow Christ's power to shine (2 Cor. 12:7b–10).

Torah   A Hebrew term meaning "covenantal instructions," referring to the law of Moses. It is also often used as a synonym for "Pentateuch."

transfiguration   The event in which Jesus takes Peter, James, and John onto a mountain, becomes radiant, speaks with Moses and Elijah, and is declared the Son of God (Matt. 17:1–8; Mark 9:2–8; Luke 9:28–36).

Trinity   The term used of God in the doctrine that God is both one and three, existing as one God in three persons: Father, Son, Holy Spirit.

triumphal procession   For Romans, a victory march led by a conquering general or emperor with the defeated leaders brought behind, bound and sometimes naked, to be mocked and abused by the crowd and often executed at the end. Paul applied this image to Christ, using it to depict true apostleship: the triumph of Christ over the formerly unbelieving Paul will lead to his mockery, abuse, and ultimately to his execution.

union with Christ   Paul's theology of being joined to Christ ("in Christ," "with Christ," "through Christ," etc.), best understood through four images: (1) *union* refers to a profound spiritual connection to Christ through mutual indwelling by the Spirit; (2) *participation* refers to sharing in the key events of Christ's narrative, such as his suffering, death, burial, resurrection, ascension, and glorification; (3) *identification* refers to shifting our allegiance from Adam and the realm of sin and death to Christ and his realm of righteousness and peace; (4) *incorporation* refers to being members together in a corporate entity shaped by Christ.

universalism   The belief that all people will ultimately go to heaven even if they don't repent and believe in Jesus.

Upper Room Discourse   Jesus's teaching of his disciples the core truths of the Christian faith during the Passover meal (John 13–17), centering on sacrificial love and relational unity.

vellum   A lambskin or calfskin that has been treated so that it can be used as a fine writing surface.

Vulgate   The late fourth-century Latin translation of the Bible made by Jerome, which became the official Bible used by the Roman Catholic Church.

wisdom literature   Ancient or biblical literature generally focused on moral living, virtue, and the meaning of life, like Proverbs and Ecclesiastes.

works of the law   Works, like circumcision, done by Jews both to obey the law and to serve as identity markers showing covenant membership in Israel. Paul emphasizes in Galatians that only by faith in Christ, not by works of the law (whether human performance or identity), can someone be made right with God.

wormwood   A bitter herb that can poison water and is associated with the exodus plagues.

Zealots   A Jewish group that focused on Jewish political independence from their Roman oppressors, often engineering assassinations, kidnappings, and Robin Hood–like attacks and thefts on Roman caravans.

Notes

Chapter 1 The New Testament as Christian Scripture

1. Joel B. Green, *Seized by Truth: Reading the Bible as Scripture* (Nashville: Abingdon, 2007), 56.

2. Adapted from Markus Bockmuehl, *Seeing the Word: Refocusing New Testament Study*, Studies in Theological Interpretation (Grand Rapids: Baker Academic, 2006), 68–74.

3. This metaphor of front-wheel drive versus rear-wheel drive comes from Neil B. Mac-Donald, *Metaphysics and the God of Israel: Systematic Theology of the Old and New Testaments* (Grand Rapids: Baker Academic, 2006).

4. Erich Auerbach, *Mimesis: The Representation of Reality in Western Literature*, trans. Willard R. Trask (Princeton: Princeton University Press, 1953), 12.

Chapter 2 The New Testament as a Book

1. For more information, see Edmon L. Gallagher and John D. Meade, *The Biblical Canon Lists from Early Christianity: Texts and Analysis* (Oxford: Oxford University Press, 2017).

Chapter 3 The World around the New Testament

1. Adapted from Luke Timothy Johnson, *The Writings of the New Testament: An Interpretation*, 3rd ed. (Minneapolis: Fortress, 2010); quotation from Luke Timothy Johnson, "Imagining the World Scripture Imagines," *Modern Theology* 14, no. 2 (April 1998): 165.

2. David Wenham and Steve Walton, *Exploring the New Testament: A Guide to the Gospels and Acts* (Downers Grove, IL: InterVarsity, 2001), 25–36.

3. David A. deSilva, "Honor and Shame," in *Dictionary of New Testament Background*, ed. Craig A. Evans and Stanley E. Porter (Downers Grove, IL: InterVarsity, 2000), 518.

Chapter 4 Jesus's Life and Teaching

1. John Calvin, *Commentary on a Harmony of the Gospels*, vol. 3, trans. William Pringle, on Matthew 26:37, https://ccel.org/ccel/calvin/calcom33/calcom33.i.html.

2. For further study, see Joan E. Taylor, *What Did Jesus Look Like?* (London: Bloomsbury T&T Clark, 2018).

Chapter 5 The Fourfold Gospel Book

1. Richard A. Burridge, *What Are the Gospels? A Comparison with Graeco-Roman Biography*, 25th anniversary ed. (Waco: Baylor University Press, 2018).

2. For more reading along these lines see Jonathan T. Pennington, *Reading the Gospels Wisely: A Narrative and Theological Introduction* (Grand Rapids: Baker Academic, 2012); N. T. Wright, *How God Became King: The Forgotten Story of the Gospels* (New York: HarperOne, 2016).

3. Augustine, *Harmony of the Gospels* 2.4.

4. See John Navone, *Seeking God in Story* (Collegeville, MN: Liturgical Press, 1990), chap. 3.

5. Frederick Dale Bruner, *Matthew: A Commentary*, rev. ed. (Grand Rapids: Eerdmans, 2004), 1:xxix–xxx

6. Francis Watson, *The Fourfold Gospel: A Theological Reading of the New Testament Portraits of Jesus* (Grand Rapids: Baker Academic, 2016).

7. Mark L. Strauss, *Introducing Jesus: A Short Guide to the Gospels' History and Message* (Grand Rapids: Zondervan, 2018), 9.

8. Justin Martyr, *Apology* 1.67.

9. The whole translation can be found in Scott McGill, *Juvencus' Four Books of the Gospels: Evangeliorum libri quattuor* (London: Routledge, 2016).

10. Origen, *Contra Celsus* [*sic*], Documenta Catholica Omnia, http://www.documenta-catholica.eu/d_0185-0254-%20Origene%20-%20Contra%20Celsus%20-%20EN.pdf.

11. For more information, see Watson, *The Fourfold Gospel*, chap. 5; Matthew R. Crawford, *The Eusebian Canon Tables: Ordering Textual Knowledge in Late Antiquity* (Oxford: Oxford University Press, 2019).

Chapter 6 The Gospel according to Matthew

1. R. T. France, *Matthew: Evangelist and Teacher* (Exeter, UK: Paternoster, 1989), 20.

Chapter 7 The Gospel according to Mark

1. These examples can be found collected in Thomas C. Oden and Christopher A. Hall, eds., *Mark*, Ancient Christian Commentary on Scripture (Downers Grove, IL: InterVarsity, 1998), 157.

Chapter 8 The Gospel according to Luke

1. Ben Myers, *The Apostles' Creed: A Guide to the Ancient Catechism* (Bellingham, WA: Lexham, 2018), 33.

2. For more on the idea of physiognomy and how it functions in Luke and Acts, see Mikeal Parsons, *Body and Character in Luke and Acts: The Subversion of Physiognomy in Early Christianity* (Waco: Baylor University Press, 2011).

Chapter 9 The Gospel according to John

1. A recent translation of this commentary is available in two volumes, Cyril of Alexandria, *Commentary on John*, trans. David Maxwell, ed. Joel C. Elowsky, Ancient Christian Texts (Downers Grove, IL: IVP Academic, 2013–15).

2. See Cyril of Alexandria, *Commentary on John*, 1:165.

3. Ben Myers, *The Apostles' Creed: A Guide to the Ancient Catechism* (Bellingham, WA: Lexham, 2018), 103–6.

4. Jerome, *Commentary on Galatians*, trans. Andrew Cain, Fathers of the Church 121 (Washington, DC: Catholic University of America Press, 2010), on Gal. 6:10.

Chapter 10 The Acts of the Apostles

1. Heidi J. Hornick and Mikeal C. Parsons, *The Acts of the Apostles through the Centuries* (Chichester, UK: Wiley-Blackwell, 2017), 2–11.

Chapter 11 The Apostle Paul's Life and Teaching

1. Translation is from Michael W. Holmes, ed. and trans., *The Apostolic Fathers: Greek Texts and English Translations*, 3rd ed. (Grand Rapids: Baker Academic, 2007).

Chapter 12 The Letter to the Romans

1. Based on Ambrosiaster, *Commentaries on Romans and 1–2 Corinthians*, trans. and ed. Gerald L. Bray, Ancient Christian Texts (Downers Grove, IL: InterVarsity, 2009), 1.

2. These observations come from the introduction in William of St. Thierry, *Exposition on the Epistle to the Romans*, ed. John D. Anderson, trans. John Baptist Hasbrouck, Cistercian Fathers (Kalamazoo, MI: Cistercian Publications, 1980).

3. *The Journals of John Wesley*, May 24, 1738, Christian Classics Ethereal Library, https://www.ccel.org/ccel/wesley/journal.vi.ii.xvi.html.

Chapter 13 The First Letter to the Corinthians

1. Quoted in Ambrosiaster, *Commentaries on Romans and 1–2 Corinthians*, trans. and ed. Gerald L. Bray, Ancient Christian Texts (Downers Grove, IL: InterVarsity, 2009), 119–20.

2. Ambrosiaster, *Commentaries on Romans and 1–2 Corinthians*, 182.

3. These insights come from Chris L. de Wet, "John Chrysostom's Exegesis on the Resurrection in 1 Corinthians 15," *Neotestamentica* 45, no. 1 (2011): 92–114.

Chapter 14 The Second Letter to the Corinthians

1. Quoted in Gerald Bray, ed., *1–2 Corinthians*, Ancient Christian Commentary on Scripture (Downers Grove, IL: InterVarsity, 1999), 197–98.

2. These notes come from Jacob Cherian, "2 Corinthians," in *South Asia Bible Commentary*, ed. Brian C. Wintle (Grand Rapids: Zondervan, 2015), 1585–614.

Chapter 15 The Letter to the Galatians

1. This paragraph is dependent on the work of Stephen J. Chester, *Reading Paul with the Reformers: Reconciling Old and New Perspectives* (Grand Rapids: Eerdmans, 2017), 13–20.

2. This paragraph is largely influenced by two essays: David A. deSilva, "Neither Tamil nor Sinhalese: Reading Galatians with Sri Lankan Christians," and Nijay Gupta, "Response: What Does Sri Lanka Have to Do with Galatia? The Hermeneutical Challenges, Benefits, and Potential of Global Readings of Scripture," in *Global Voices: Reading the Bible in the Majority World*, ed. Craig S. Keener and M. Daniel Carrol R. (Peabody, MA: Hendrickson, 2013), 39–55, 57–63, respectively.

3. See Richard Bauckham, *God Crucified: Monotheism and Christology in the New Testament* (Carlisle, UK: Paternoster, 1998).

4. See Larry Hurtado, *Lord Jesus Christ: Devotion to Jesus in Earliest Christianity* (Grand Rapids: Eerdmans, 2003).

5. See Chris Tilling, *Paul's Divine Christology* (Tübingen: Mohr Siebeck, 2012).

Chapter 16 The Letter to the Ephesians

1. These reflections come from Claire M. Powell, "Ephesians," in *The IVP Women's Bible Commentary*, ed. Catherine Clark Kroeger and Mary J. Evans (Downers Grove, IL: InterVarsity, 2002), 694–706.

Chapter 17 The Letter to the Philippians

1. These thoughts come from Markus Bockmuehl, "A Commentator's Approach to the 'Effective History' of Philippians," *Journal for the Study of the New Testament* 60 (1995): 57–88.

Chapter 19 The First Letter to the Thessalonians

1. From Luther's treatise *On the Jews and Their Lies* (1543), as discussed in Anthony Thiselton, *1 & 2 Thessalonians through the Centuries* (Chichester, UK: Wiley-Blackwell, 2011), 72.

2. Quotations from and references to Calvin, Henry, Augustine, and Aquinas are from Thiselton, *1 & 2 Thessalonians through the Centuries*, 5.

Chapter 20 The Second Letter to the Thessalonians

1. *Homily* 8.539. Quotations from Chrysostom are from Anthony Thiselton, *1 & 2 Thessalonians through the Centuries* (Chichester, UK: Wiley-Blackwell, 2011), 4.

2. Irenaeus, *Against Heresies* 4.28.1–2; Tertullian, *Against Marcion* 5.16. References to Irenaeus and Tertullian are from Thiselton, *1 & 2 Thessalonians through the Centuries*, 4, 193.

Chapter 21 The Pastoral Epistles: 1–2 Timothy and Titus

1. Quotations from Wesley and Cheever are from Jay Twomey, *The Pastoral Epistles through the Centuries* (Chichester, UK: Wiley-Blackwell, 2009), 25.

Chapter 22 The Letter to Philemon

1. David A. deSilva, *An Introduction to the New Testament: Contexts, Methods, and Ministry Formation* (Downers Grove, IL: InterVarsity, 2004), 141–42.

Chapter 23 The Letter to the Hebrews

1. This analysis is informed by Douglas Sweeney, *Edwards the Exegete: Biblical Interpretation and Anglo-Protestant Culture on the Edge of the Enlightenment* (Oxford: Oxford University Press, 2015).

2. These comments come from the introductory essays in John H. Augustine, ed., *A Commentary on Hebrews 11 (1609 Edition) by William Perkins* (New York: Pilgrim, 1991).

Chapter 24 The Letter of James

1. See Richard Bauckham, *James: Wisdom of James, Disciple of Jesus the Sage* (London: Routledge, 1999), 158–74.

2. Dale C. Allison Jr., *A Critical and Exegetical Commentary on the Epistle of James* (London: Bloomsbury T&T Clark, 2013), 109.

Index